WITHOUT INDENTURES:

Index to White Slave Children in Colonial Court Records

[Maryland and Virginia]

D1562900

Virginia, Marylandia et Carolina. Joh. Bapt. Homann, S.C.M. Geog.,
Norimberge. Close-up of Chesapeake Bay. The map shows Cecil County,
created in 1674, and Old Rappahannock County, abolished in 1692.

WITHOUT INDENTURES:

Index to White Slave Children in Colonial Court Records

[Maryland and Virginia]

Richard Hayes Phillips, Ph.D.

"This country was built on the backs of the broken-hearted."
– Judson Witham

"Cryeing and Mourneing for Redemption from their Slavery"
– Privy Council of King Charles II

For hardcover copies of this book, contact the author:
Richard Hayes Phillips, 4 Fisher Street, Canton, New York, 13617

Paperback edition published by
Genealogical Publishing Company
Baltimore, Maryland, 2013

LIBRARY OF CONGRESS CATALOGING-IN-PUBLICATION DATA
Phillips, Richard Hayes, 1951-
Without Indentures: Index to White Slave Children in Colonial Court Records
ISBN paperback edition: 978-0-8063-1979-7
1. History – 17th century   2. Slavery – Maryland – Virginia
3. Kidnapping – Ireland – Scotland – England – New England   I. Title
2013947101
CIP

Made in the United States of America

TABLE OF CONTENTS

PREFACE

"Your poor petitioner was spirited out of his native country, unknown to any of his friends, and shipped aboard for this country as a servant." So begins the petition of John Lyme, presented to the County Court in Somerset County, Maryland on 15 January 1690.

John Lyme was one of thousands of white children spirited out of their native countries, unknown to their families and friends, transported to America, and sold into slavery. The history books like to call them "indentured servants." But this is not true. They had no indentures.

An indenture is, by definition, a written contract. We were taught in school about indentured servants, impoverished young workers from England or Germany who wanted to come to America. They contracted, in writing, by indenture, to work without wages for a number of years to pay off the cost of their passage and lodging, after which time they were free.

John Lyme swore that, on board the ship, he was given indentures "for four years," and that some of his "ship mates are alive which can prove the same," but that his indenture "was by some deceitful means or other taken" from him. And so, "five months after landing," in 1686, he was brought before the court in Somerset County, adjudged to be fifteen years of age, and ordered to serve seven years.

A systematic search of the surviving Court Order Books from the county courts of Maryland and Virginia has turned up more than five thousand white children, all without indentures, who were brought before the courts to have their ages adjudged and to be sentenced to slavery. It is likely that nearly all of these children were kidnapped, according to law.

What is different about John Lyme is that he is the only one of the five thousand children who managed to get a petition on the record in the County Court stating that he was "spirited out of his native country." That is to say, he came here involuntarily. He was kidnapped.

According to *The First Dictionary of English Slang*, (B. E. Gent, c. 1699, reprinted by Bodleian Library, University of Oxford, 2010), "Kidnapper" was defined as "one that Decoys or Spirits Children away, and Sells them for the Plantations." Kids who were captured by constables were "Nab'd," being defined as "Apprehended, Taken or Arrested."

John Lyme's petition was presented to the court by Capt. David Brown (Browne), probably his master. Capt. Browne brought children without indentures to court in Somerset County on at least eight other occasions between 1675 and 1699. And he sat on the court. He was one of the "Worshippfull Commissioners," as the judges were called in Maryland. He knew that the court was unlikely to favor the petition of a kidnapped child, especially if presented by one of their brethren on the bench. "No indentures appearing," the court reaffirmed the seven year sentence.

Phillip Lynes (Lines, Linos), a "Worshippfull Commissioner" in Charles County, Maryland, owned twenty-five white children without indentures. Not all were well treated. Consider this passage from the Charles County Court Record, 11 August 1691: "Whereas James Thornbrough, Edward Darnall and Catherine Jones servants to Mr. Phillip Lynes came here into Court naked and made complaint that for want of clothes they were allmost starved, and ye said Phillip Lynes being absent. Itt is ordered that Major James Smallwood lett them have necessary clothes to preserve them from perishing with cold, and that Coll. Humphrey Warren sherife pay ye said Smallwood for what clothing they shall have of him out of what tobaccoe shall be allowed to ye said Lynes in ye County Levy this yeare."

Thrust into the same system was James Hambleton, my direct ancestor. Born and raised near Dover, New Hampshire, his Last Will and Testament, and that of Grace Hambleton, his wife, were recorded in Westmoreland County, Virginia. And so I hitchhiked to Montross, Virginia to photograph the wills, and to see what else I could find in the county records. It was there that I discovered that James had been a slave for fifteen years.

James Hambleton appears in the court records of Westmoreland County six times. His first appearance, on 26 April 1699, reads in its entirety:

> "James Hamelton, servant to James Bourn, is adjudged to be twelve years of age and is ordered to serve according to law." *

In this book, in the index, the above entry is abstracted as follows:

Hamelton (Hambleton), James, 26 April 1699, age 12, James Bourn

--- ---

* In all subsequent entries in the Court Order Books his name is spelled with a "B"

viii

If all the names in this index were thoroughly searched backward and forward in time, more stories like this one could be told:

Hambleton, James, 26 April 1699, age 12, James Bourn. Born 1682, Dover, New Hampshire, son of David Hambleton and Annah Jaxson. Sentenced to five months for running away, one year for violently assaulting his master, and twenty lashes for his "arrogant and saucy words and behavior" before the court, 26 March 1707. Sold to John Garner. Petition for freedom denied, 24 September 1712. Freed by court, 24 February 1714. Purchased 100 acres from Henry Asbury Jr., 21 July 1725. Married Grace. His will dated 17 November 1726. Her will dated 11 February 1727. Children: James, John, Ann.

This index, this book of names, can be the starting point for thousands of genealogical searches by the descendants of these unindentured children. In almost every case we have the name of the child, the name of the owner, the date they appeared in court, and the age assigned by the judges. * In some cases, where the family has traced their ancestry back to a name that appears in this index, they will know for the first time how their progenitor got to Maryland or Virginia. In other cases, the kidnapped child will be the sibling in the family chart for whom there is nothing but a birth record.

Never once, in Maryland or Virginia, do the court records reveal what law is referred to when these children are sentenced to slavery. I had to search the statutes of colonial Virginia to figure it out.

The court orders were pursuant to a Virginia law establishing terms of servitude for servants "brought into the collony without indentures." The law, as originally enacted in 1643, was intended to resolve differences between masters and servants whose agreements were not in writing:

"if they be above twenty year old to serve fowre year, if they shall be above twelve and under twenty to serve five years, and if under twelve to serve seaven years." [1]

In March 1655 the Virginia law was amended to require that the Irish serve longer than the English, and the law was retroactive:

-- --

* The adjudged ages were not always correct. It will be noted that James Hambleton was "adjudged to be twelve years of age" when he was actually seventeen. This resulted in a sentence of twelve years instead of five years.

"all Irish servants that from the first of September, 1653, have bin brought into this collony without indenture ... shall serve as followeth, all above sixteen yeares old to serve six years, and all under to serve till they be twenty-four years old, and in case of dispute in that behalfe the court shall be judge of their age." [2]

This was the first law in Virginia to differentiate between races or nationalities of servants, with or without indentures. In March 1662 the terms of the English were extended to equal those of the Irish:

"all servants hereafter comeing in without indentures shall serve five years if above sixteen yeares of age and all under that age shall serve untill they be fower and twenty yeares old, that being the time lymitted by the laws of England," and the "courts at the request of the master make inspection and judge of their ages." [3]

The Maryland Assembly passed a similar act in October 1654:

"all Servants Coming into this province without an Indenture or Covenant if they be above the age of twenty yeares shall serve four yeares, from Sixteene years of age unto twenty (shall serve) six years, from twelve to Sixteene, shall serve seven yeares, if they be under twelve, they shall serve untill they come to the age of one & twenty years. All masters and owners shall bring or Cause to be brought Such as aforesaid Servants at or before the third Court in their respective Counties, To the End that the said Court may Judge of their age which shall be Entred in a Book of Record to be kept for that purpose" [4]

The terms of servitude in Maryland for children without indentures were amended in May 1661 and affirmed in April 1662:

"every Servant transported into this Province ... being of the full age of twenty and two yeares or upwards not haveing Indenture or other sufficient testimony..., such servant shall serve ... after their first Arrivall into this Province the full tyme of foure yeares, if Betweene the age of Eighteene and two and twenty yeares such Servant shall Serve five yeares, if Betwixt the age of fifteene and Eighteene such Servant shall serve six yeares, and any Servant of what age soever under fifteene yeares and coming in as aforesaid shall serve till he or she Arrive to the age of one and twenty yeares." [5]

In October 1671 these terms were extended by one year:

"whosoever shall Transport any Servant into this Province without Indenture and such Servant being above the Age of Twenty Two yeares shall be obleiged to serve the full Space and Tearme of Five yeares if between eighteen and twenty two without indenture six yeares if betweene fivetene and eightene without Indenture Seaven years if under fiftene and coming in without Indenture as aforesaid Such Servant shall serve till he or she arrive to the full age of Two and Twenty Yeares" [6]

These laws of Virginia and Maryland were coincident with an English law dated 1659, a general authorization of kidnapping:

it "may be lawful for ... two or more justices of the peace within any county, citty or towne corporate belonging to this commonwealth to from tyme to tyme by warrant ... cause to be apprehended, seized on and detained all and every person or persons that shall be found begging and vagrant ... in any towne, parish or place to be conveyed into the port of London, or unto any other port ... from where such person or persons may be shipped ... into any forraign collonie or plantation ..." [7]

State sponsored kidnapping was nothing new in England. What was different about this law was that "justices of the peace" were now authorized to act on their own. Previously, the government itself had organized mass kidnappings. In January 1607, "three great caracks" departed "for the East Indies," carrying "150 youths to do labor" [8] In April 1608, fourteen ships departed "for the East Indies, taking 5000 soldiers, two thirds being children from 12 to 16 years of age" [9]

Kidnapping of children bound for America can be traced to a letter dated 13 January 1618, from James I, King of England, to Sir Thomas Smythe, Governor of the East India Company, quoted below, in its entirety:

"Whereas our Court hath of late been troubled by idle young people having no employment, we have thought fit to have you send them away to Virginia, that they may be set to work there, wherein you shall do a deed of charity by employing them who otherwise will never be reclaimed from the idle life of vagabonds." [10]

On 10 August 1618, the Common Council of London agreed that one hundred "vagrant boys and girls that lie and beg in the streets of the city" should be "taken up and transported to Virginia." [11] The Lord Mayor of London instructed his constables to "walk the streets ... and forthwith apprehend all such vagrant children, both boys and girls, as they shall find in the streets and in the markets or wandering in the night." [12] Seventy-five boys and twenty-four "wenches" were sent to Virginia, reportedly aboard three ships: the *Jonathan*, the *George*, and the *Neptune*. [13]

On 29 April 1619, the Virginia Company reported that the ship *Diana*, having "left England with the one hundred children from London, hath arrived with about eighty." [14] Or, as they informed the City of London, all one hundred "safely arrived, save such as died on the way." [15] They asked for "one hundred more" children "to be sent into Virginia the next spring." [16] The Common Council agreed. [17] But some of the children were "ill disposed," and "declare their unwillingness to go to Virginia" where "under severe Masters they may be brought to goodness." [18] And so, in January 1620, the Privy Council authorized the City of London and the Virginia Company "to deliver, receive and transporte into Virginia" one hundred children "against their wills." [19] In February 1620 the second batch of one hundred children was shipped from London, a number of them aboard the *Duty*, which arrived in Virginia in May. [20] Shortly after the massacre of 22 March 1622, in which 347 men, women and children at Jamestown were slain by Indians, [21] another one hundred boys were collected and shipped to Virginia as replacements [22] in two groups, fifty departing England in September aboard the *Southampton*, [23] and fifty in October [24] aboard the *Abigail*. An epidemic brought by the ship killed twice as many people as had died in the massacre. [25] When a census was taken in 1624, as few as eighteen of the three hundred vagrant children from London were still alive. [26] For the others, transportation to Virginia was a death sentence.

During the English Civil Wars, Scottish prisoners captured by Cromwell were sold into slavery in America. Five thousand captured at the Battle of Dunbar on 3 September 1650 were force marched to Durham Cathedral. Two thousand died during the march, and another sixteen hundred died in captivity at Durham. [27] Among the survivors, those who were deemed to be "well and sound and free of wounds" were shipped to America and sold into slavery. [28] One hundred and fifty were transported to New England. Nine hundred were transported to Virginia. [29] At the Battle of Worcester, on 3 September 1651, another ten thousand Scottish soldiers were taken prisoner. Of these, eight thousand were transported to New England,

Bermuda, and Barbados and sold into slavery, [30] "a thing not known amongst the cruel Turks, to sell and enslave those of their own country and religion" [31] The passenger list has survived for 271 Scottish prisoners of war brought to America in chains aboard the "John and Sara," [32] which departed from Gravesend, England on 8 November 1651. Among them was David Hambleton, (father of James Hambleton), who was "sold into slavery" [33] at a sawmill at Quamphegan Falls, South Berwick, Maine. [34]

Children displaced by Cromwell's invasion of Ireland were kidnapped, transported to America, and sold into slavery. By orders of the Council of State, four hundred Irish children were shipped to New England and Virginia in September 1653, [35] to which exact month Virginia law was retroactive, and one thousand Irish girls "and the like number of youths, of fourteen years or under" were shipped to Jamaica in October 1655. [36] This set the stage for the general authorization of kidnapping dated 1659.

Before 1660, seven white children without indentures have been found in the surviving Court Order Books of Maryland and Virginia (one in Kent County, three in Lancaster County, and three in York County). Beginning in 1660, child trafficking became an industry. The records, although incomplete, are illuminating. The peak year was 1699, when 677 white children without indentures appear in the surviving Court Order Books. All but 62 of them appear in eight counties (Somerset, Talbot, Charles, Westmoreland, Northumberland, Lancaster, Richmond, and Essex).

WHITE CHILDREN WITHOUT INDENTURES

1657	0	1673	105	1689	41	1705	25
1658	2	1674	161	1690	20	1706	41
1659	5	1675	194	1691	24	1707	14
1660	33	1676	226	1692	53	1708	34
1661	44	1677	146	1693	53	1709	7
1662	61	1678	175	1694	65	1710	34
1663	76	1679	215	1695	36	1711	8
1664	102	1680	140	1696	61	1712	17
1665	82	1681	76	1697	67	1713	8
1666	9	1682	106	1698	235	1714	18
1667	84	1683	63	1699	677	1715	10
1668	138	1684	52	1700	204	1716	5
1669	158	1685	150	1701	105	1717	8
1670	128	1686	145	1702	49	1718	25
1671	68	1687	74	1703	38	1719	45
1672	95	1688	58	1704	21	1720	16

By comparison, far fewer Negro and Indian children were imported to Maryland and Virginia during the seventeenth century. Not until 1702 were more Negro children than white children imported as slaves.

NEGRO AND INDIAN CHILDREN BROUGHT TO COURT

	Negro	Indian		Negro	Indian		Negro	Indian
1663	0	1	1679	0	0	1695	5	3
1664	0	0	1680	3	4	1696	7	3
1665	0	1	1681	1	0	1697	20	4
1666	0	0	1682	2	3	1698	20	5
1667	0	13	1683	19	33	1699	13	8
1668	0	1	1684	9	15	1700	2	3
1669	0	3	1685	18	3	1701	32	0
1670	2	7	1686	7	7	1702	50	0
1671	0	0	1687	15	2	1703	8	1
1672	0	1	1688	14	4	1704	58	2
1673	0	0	1689	9	1	1705	48	4
1674	0	0	1690	5	3	1706	52	2
1675	0	1	1691	23	8	1707	74	4
1676	0	0	1692	2	10	1708	56	2
1677	2	0	1693	9	6	1709	17	2
1678	0	3	1694	24	11	1710	31	1

White children had their advantages in the slave market. They were easier to train, because they already knew the language. Their cultural and religious backgrounds were compatible with those of their owners. And, if uncomfortable with what the neighbors would think of their having purchased a human soul, the owners could always pretend that their slave was the orphan child of some distant relative from the old country. But white children were harder to identify if they ran away, which happened frequently. The Court Order Books are replete with appearances of recaptured runaway servants, with and without indentures.

For each day of "runaway time," the penalty was two extra days of servitude in Virginia.

"all runaways that shall absent themselves from their said masters service shall be lyable to make satisfaction by service at the end of their tymes by indenture double the tyme of service soe neglected" [37]

xiv

In Maryland, the penalty was ten extra days of servitude.

> "any Servant or Servants whatsoever unlawfully absenting him
> her or themselves from his her or their said Master, Mistress,
> dame, or overseer shall serve <u>tenn dayes for every one dayes</u>
> absince" (emphasis in original) [38]

This penalty, although harsh, was not always effective. Many children ran
away multiple times. The owners were forced to recapture them time and
time again, while the runaways only had to succeed one time to be free. But
it was not easy. These children were tucked away on peninsulas of the
Chesapeake Bay, in completely unfamiliar territory. Traveling far enough
inland to bypass the inlets exposed them to untamed wilderness. Escaping
by water required that they steal a boat, sleep by day, and travel by night.

With or without indentures, those who outlived their servitude faced the
world with next to nothing. In 1663, Maryland repealed "that Clause
Injoyning fifty Acres of Land to be allowed to Servants att the end of his or
their Service," and "for the future there shall be nothing allowed to any
Servant att the end or Expiracon of his or their Service more then their
Clothes, Howes, Axe & Corne" [39] In Virginia, it was merely a "laudable
custom of allowing servants corn and cloaths" until 1705, when it became
mandatory for the master to pay

> "To every male servant, ten bushels of indian corn, thirty shillings
> in money, or the value thereof, in goods, and one well fixed
> musket or fuzee, of the value of twenty shillings, at least: and to
> every woman servant, fifteen bushels of indian corn, and forty
> shillings in money, or the value thereof, in goods" [40]

Those who transported settlers to the colonies, including traffickers who
imported kidnapped children, were rewarded. In Maryland, the law "allowed
to any Adventurer or Planter" fifty acres of land "within our said Province"
for any person "which shall be transported thether" [41] The law was the
same in Virginia. For example, in Northumberland County, on 5 September
1660, Major George Colclough (one of the "Gentleman Justices," as the
judges were called in Virginia), claimed 1050 acres of land for transportation
of 21 persons, including the five white children without indentures, aged ten
to fourteen, he had brought to court on 3 May 1660: Samuell Webb,
William Farlowe, John Hitchcock, Thomas Warwick, and William Hood.
These land grants, called "head rights," were one way to transplant the
landed aristocracy of England to America.

The "wicked custom" of seducing, or, as it was popularly called, "spiriting" away young people, "by fraud or violence," to go as servants to the Plantations, "was much resorted to and loudly complained of." "Petitions were presented to Charles II and his Council from merchants and planters as well as masters of ships against this custom." The Attorney General reported "there being scarce any voyage to the Plantations but some were carried away against their wills." [42] On 26 July 1660, the Privy Council, at Whitehall, issued the following order, presented here in its entirety: [43]

> Kidnapping. To the Cheife Officers of his Majestys Customes in the Port of London, and to all Searchers and other Officers and Ministers in the said Porte or at Graves-End or elswhere whom it may concerne. Whereas an Information hath been this day given at this Board, That diverse Children from their Parents, and Servants from their Masters, are daylie inticed away, taken upp, and kept from their said Parents and Masters against their Wills, by Merchants, Planters, Commanders of Shipps, and Seamen trading to Virginia, Barbado's, Charibee Islands and other parts of the West Indies, and their Factors and Agents, and shipped away to make Sale and Merchandize of, And if it happen any such bee found and discovered on board of any Shipp or Vessell outward bound, and the said Parents, Masters or other freinds of such Children or Servants demaund or require them of the said Merchants, Planters, Commanders of Shipps or Seamen, Yet they will not lett them goe, or sett them free, unless they have such Compensation for releasing them, as they shall rest satisfyed with; A thinge so barbarous and inhumane, that Nature itself, much more Christians, cannot but abhorre. And whereas this Board was Informed, That, at this tyme, there is a Shipp, called the Seven Brothers, lately fallen downe towards Graves-End, and two other Shipps in the River of Thames in good forwardnesse to follow after in which there are sundry such Children and Servants of severall Parents and Masters, so deceived and inticed away Cryinge and Mourninge for Redemption from their Slavery. [The searchers and other officers at Gravesend and in the Thames are to board these vessels and examine the truth of the complaint, discharging any persons found forcibly detained and in case of resistance placing the ship under arrest and bringing the Masters before the Council. If the Seven Brothers have left Gravesend, it is to be stopped in the Downs and similar measures taken there.]

This order would never effectually be executed without an Act of Parliament. [44] The kidnappings continued for another eighty years.

If I were not descended from two generations of Scottish slaves, I might never have come upon the story of white slavery in America. One thing led to another. After discovering that James Hambleton had been a slave for fifteen years, I returned to Westmoreland County to search the Court Order Books for other white children without indentures. I found more than three hundred. Then I traveled to the Virginia State Library in Richmond to find out if there were any other counties in which most or all of the seventeenth century Court Order Books had survived. I found that there were ten such counties. Now I knew there would be thousands of names. Then I found that nearly all of the seventeenth century Court Order Books had survived in four counties in Maryland, which would allow me to search most of the Chesapeake Bay. And so, at my own expense, I traveled four times to Maryland and Virginia to collect the evidence.

In Virginia, most of the seventeenth century Court Order Books have been transcribed and typewritten, and appear in bound volumes on the shelves of the Virginia State Library. These can be compared with microfilms, which exist for all the surviving books, whether or not transcribed, and are available in person or through interlibrary loan. Most of the original books still reside in the county court houses. I have relied upon the transcriptions when possible, and the microfilms when necessary. Anyone who wishes to check the accuracy of the published transcriptions may do so.

In Maryland, some of the seventeenth century court records have been transcribed and digitized, and these are available online. Others, notably those of Charles County, have been microfilmed and scanned, and these are available online. This was possible because the original books were written quite legibly, and in dark ink. Still others, notably those of Talbot County, have never been transcribed, and cannot be microfilmed successfully because the ink has faded. These records are only available by examining the original handwritten books, all of which are available at the Hall of Records in Annapolis. Sometimes, tucked between the pages, were notes and receipts which had yellowed the pages in precisely the same positions as I found them, thus proving that nobody had looked at those books for centuries. My hands tingled as I touched them.

The names of these children have been hidden in plain sight for three hundred years. No one has cared to look for them until now.

Not so very long ago, Robert Louis Stevenson wrote about kidnapped children "sold into slavery on the plantations." [45] How soon we forget.

Consider the wording of the Thirteenth Amendment:

"Neither slavery nor involuntary servitude, except as a punishment for crime whereof the party shall have been duly convicted, shall exist within the United States, or any place subject to their jurisdiction." (Ratified 6 December 1865)

The words "involuntary servitude" did not refer to indentured servants, for they were contract laborers who voluntarily signed an indenture. Nor did these words refer to prisoners duly convicted of a crime. These words were intended to prohibit the enslavement of persons without indentures, who did not agree, who did not consent, who never contracted in writing.

Kidnapping children and selling them into slavery is wrong, at any time, in any place, by any name, for any reason. The children who suffered this ordeal deserve to be singled out, by name, and enshrined in a reference book devoted exclusively to them. If the real names of the Negro and Indian children were on the record, I would include them too.

I regret that so many Court Order Books have been lost. The names of the children recorded in those books will never be known here on earth.

-- --

Not all of the servants without indentures were children, but most of them were. While the ages adjudged by the court are not always trustworthy, they are informative. Specific ages were found in the court records in 4419 individual cases. Of these, only 122 (2.8%) were adjudged to be twenty-one or older. A greater number, 187 (4.2%), were adjudged to be under ten. The median age was between fourteen and fifteen years old.

ADJUDGED AGES OF SERVANTS WITHOUT INDENTURES

age 1	1	age 10	198	age 19	125
age 2	0	age 11	253	age 20	141
age 3	3	age 12	439	age 21	73
age 4	4	age 13	528	age 22	38
age 5	4	age 14	623	age 23	3
age 6	13	age 15	546	age 24	6
age 7	23	age 16	506	age 25	2
age 8	41	age 17	416	age 26	0
age 9	98	age 18	335	age 27	0

NOTES

[1]   "Statutes at Large; Being a collection of All the Laws of Virginia from the First Session of the Legislature in the Year 1619," William Waller Hening, editor, March 1642-3, Act XXVI. Transcribed for the internet by Freddie L. Spradlin, Torrance, California.
URL: http://vagenweb.org/hening/vol01-10.htm

[2]   "Statutes at Large; Virginia," March 1654-5, Act VI.
URL: http://vagenweb.org/hening/vol01-17.htm

[3]   "Statutes at Large; Virginia," March 1661-2, Act XCVIII.
URL: http://vagenweb.org/hening/vol02-06.htm

The Gentleman Justices of Lancaster County, Virginia had their own formula, contrary to law. Nearly all persons without indentures, of any age, were ordered to serve until the age of twenty-four. The record shows: 22 persons adjudged to be 18 and ordered to serve six years; 15 persons adjudged to be 17 and ordered to serve seven years; 25 persons adjudged to be 16 and ordered to serve eight years; and 146 others, whose ages were not adjudged, ordered to serve six, seven, or eight years, none of which were lawful sentences.

[4]   "Proceedings and Acts of the General Assembly, January 1637/8-September 1664," Volume 1, Page 352, October 1654. Published in 1883, with William Hand Browne as the editor, under the direction of the Maryland Historical Society.
URL: http://aomol.net/000001/000001/html/am1--352.html

[5]   "Proceedings and Acts of the General Assembly, January 1637/8-September 1664," Volume 1, Pages 409, 453, April-May 1661, April 1662.
URLs: http://aomol.net/000001/000001/html/am1--409.html
        http://aomol.net/000001/000001/html/am1--453.html

[6]   "Proceedings and Acts of the General Assembly, April 1666-June 1676," Volume 2, Page 335, October 1671.
URL: http://aomol.net/000001/000002/html/am2--335.html

[7]   This passage was abstracted by Hilary McD. Beckles in his book, "White Servitude and Black Slavery in Barbados, 1627-1715," University of Tennessee Press, Knoxville, 1989, p. 47, citing Egerton Mss. 2395, folios 228-229, BL. Dr. Justin Clegg at the British Museum has confirmed its authenticity: "I have taken a look at the passage and can confirm that the ellipses do not obscure important words. They typically cover the presence of repetitious and qualifying phrases, so the gist of the text is pretty much as given in

Beckles' quote, which would otherwise have been about five times longer than its current length." Dr. Clegg states that the quoted text actually begins on folio 227 and ends on folio 229, and he dates it to 1659.

[8] "Calendar of State Papers Colonial, East Indies, China and Japan, Volume 2: 1513-1616," W. Noel Sainsbury (editor), published 1864, pages 145-148. 1607. Jan. 26./Feb. 5. Lisbon. 360. Hugh Lee to Salisbury.
URL: http://www.british-history.ac.uk/report.aspx?compid=68683

[9] "Calendar of State Papers Colonial, East Indies, China and Japan, Volume 2: 1513-1616," W. Noel Sainsbury (editor), published 1864, pages 171-173. 1608. April 10/20. Lisbon. 408. Hugh Lee to Thos. Wilson.
URL: http://www.british-history.ac.uk/report.aspx?compid=68698

[10] Image and transcript of Letter from King James I to Sir Thomas Smyth relating to the transportation of children to Virginia. URLs:
http://www.britainschildmigrants.com/timeline/thumbnails/01_073_web.jpg
http://www.britainschildmigrants.com/timeline/thumbnails/01_073a_web.jpg

[11] "The first republic in America: an account of the origin of this nation, written from records then (1624) concealed by the council, rather than from the histories then licensed by the crown," by Alexander Brown, D.C.L., Houghton, Mifflin & Company, Boston and New York, 1898, pages 273-275, citing City Records, Journal 30, fol. 374 b.
URL: http://www.archive.org/stream/firstrepublicina00browuoft/
firstrepublicina00browuoft_djvu.txt

[12] "The Transportation of Vagrant Children from London to Virginia, 1618-1622," by Robert C. Johnson, pages 139-140, in "Early Stuart Studies: Essays in Honor of David Harris Willson," Howard S. Reinmuth, Jr., editor, University of Minnesota, Minneapolis, 1970, citing City of London, Corporation of London Records Office, Journal of the Common Council, XXX, folio 382.

[13] "The Transportation of Vagrant Children," page 140.

[14] "The first republic in America," pages 307-308.
URL: http://www.archive.org/stream/firstrepublicina00browuoft/
firstrepublicina00browuoft_djvu.txt

These eighty vagrant children from London were the first slaves in the colony of Virginia, arriving at Jamestown no later than 29 April 1619, which was four months prior to the arrival at Point Comfort of "20 and odd Negroes" on "a Dutch man of Warr" commanded by Captain Jope in "the latter end of August."

Ref. Letter from John Rolfe to Sir Edwin Sandys, January 1620, Ferrar Papers. Document in Magdalene College, Cambridge. List of Records No. 154 URL: http://xtf.lib.virginia.edu/xtf/view?docId=2005_Q3_2/uvaGenText/tei/ b002245360.xml;chunk.id=d103;toc.depth=1;toc.id=;brand=default

[15]   "The Transportation of Vagrant Children," page 140, citing "The Records of the Virginia Company of London," The Court Book, Volume I, page 270, from the Manuscript in the Library of Congress, Washington, D.C., 1906. Edited by Susan M. Kingsbury, A.M., Ph.D.

[16]   "The first republic in America," page 351. URL: http://www.archive.org/stream/firstrepublicina00browuoft/ firstrepublicina00browuoft_djvu.txt

[17]   "Acts of the Privy Council of England, Colonial Series, Vol. I, 1613-1680," W. L. Grant, M.A., editor, published 1908, pages 28-29. URL: http://archive.org/texts/flipbook/flippy.php?id=cu31924026356299

[18]   Letter from Sir Edwin Sandys to Sir Robert Naunton, 28 January 1620, State Papers, Domestic, James I, Vol. 112, No. 26, Folio 49. Included in "Calendar of State Papers Colonial, America and West Indies, Volume 1: 1574-1660," W. Noel Sainsbury (editor), published 1860, page 23. Jan. 28. London. URL: http://www.british-history.ac.uk/report.aspx?compid=68969

[19]   "Acts of the Privy Council of England, Colonial Series, Vol. I, 1613-1680," W. L. Grant, M.A., Editor, published 1908, pages 28-29. URL: http://archive.org/texts/flipbook/flippy.php?id=cu31924026356299

[20]   "The Transportation of Vagrant Children," page 144, citing "The Records of the Virginia Company of London," The Court Book, Volume I, page 270, from the Manuscript in the Library of Congress, Washington, D.C., 1906. Edited by Susan M. Kingsbury, A.M., Ph.D.

Also: "The first republic in America," page 375. URL: http://www.archive.org/stream/firstrepublicina00browuoft/ firstrepublicina00browuoft_djvu.txt

[21]   "The Generall Historie of Virginia, New-England, and the Summer Isles: with the names of the Adventurers, Planters, and Governours from their first beginning Ano: 1584. to this present 1624," by Captaine John Smith sometytmes Governour in those Countryes & Admirall of New England, published 1624, London, pages 144-149. Transcribed for the internet by Apex Data Services, Inc. Images scanned by Bill Richards. URL: http://docsouth.unc.edu/southlit/smith/smith.html

Also: "The List of the Dead of Jamestown," According to "The Records of the Virginia Company of London," Volume III, United States Government Printing Office, 1933, pages 565-571. Abstracted and compiled by Linda Chandler © 1999
URL: http://www.cynthiaswope.com/withinthevines/jamestown/dead1622.html

[22] "The Transportation of Vagrant Children," page 144, citing City of London, Corporation of London Records Office, Repertories, XXXVI, folios 170, 196v.

Also: "The Records of the Virginia Company of London," The Court Book, Volume II, from the Manuscript in the Library of Congress, Washington, D.C., 1906. Edited by Susan M. Kingsbury, A.M., Ph.D. Pages 75, 90.
URL: http://www.archive.org/stream/recordsofvirgini02virguoft/recordsofvirgini02virguoft_djvu.txt

[23] "The Transportation of Vagrant Children from London to Virginia, 1618-1622," by Robert C. Johnson, page 146, citing City of London, Corporation of London Records Office, Repertories, XXXVI, folio 236v.

[24] "The Transportation of Vagrant Children from London to Virginia, 1618-1622," by Robert C. Johnson, page 146, citing City of London, Corporation of London Records Office, Repertories, XXXVI, folio 275.

[25] "Calendar of State Papers Colonial, America and West Indies, Volume 1: 1574-1660," W. Noel Sainsbury (editor), published 1860, pages 35-37. 1623. Jan. 24. James City, Virginia. 17. Geo. Harrison to John Harrison.
URL: http://www.british-history.ac.uk/report.aspx?compid=68993

Also: "Virginia Records Timeline, 1553-1743." URL:
http://memory.loc.gov/ammem/collections/jefferson_papers/mtjvatm4.html

[26] "Jamestown City, Virginia Census, 1624."
URL: http://familytreemaker.genealogy.com/users/s/e/a/Carey-Patrice-Seagraves-AK/FILE/0002text.txt

"1624 Census Elizabeth Cittie, Hog Island, Mulburie Island."
URL: http://www.rootsweb.ancestry.com/~vamip/vamip/1624_census_elizabeth_cittie.htm

Also: "Calendar of State Papers Colonial, America and West Indies, Volume 1: 1574-1660," W. Noel Sainsbury (editor), published 1860, pages 57-58. 1624. Feb. 16. List of names of the living in Virginia.
URL: http://www.british-history.ac.uk/report.aspx?compid=69005

For eighteen persons identified as "servants" in the 1624 census, their age, ship of entry, and date of arrival all match the records cited above: Christopher Bankus, Susan Blackwood, John Canon, Aaron Conaway, Samuell Davies, Joane Fairchild, John Freame, Gany (?) Ganey, Nicholas Granger, William Hatfield, Richard Johnson, Michael Lapworth, William Parnell, Read (?) Reade, John Thomas, John Trussell, Roger Williams, Joane Winscomb

[27]   "British Convicts Shipped to American Colonies," by James Davie Butler, in *American Historical Review*, October 1896, pages 12-33.
URL: http://www.jstor.org/stable/1833611

[28]   "Scots Prisoners and their Relocation to the Colonies, 1650-1654."
URL: http://www.geni.com/projects/Scots-Prisoners-and-their-relocation-to-the-colonies-1650-1654/3465

[29]   "The Aftermath of Dunbar," in "Scottish Regiments at the Battle of Worcester," by William Cone.
URL: http://www.electricscotland.com/history/articles/worcester.htm

[30]   "The British Civil War: The Wars of Three Kingdoms, 1638-1660," by Trevor Royle. Published by Palgrave Macmillan, 2004.
URL: http://en.wikipedia.org/wiki/Battle_of_Worcester

[31]   Petition of Marcellus Rivers and Oxenbridge Foyle, submitted to the House of Commons 25 March 1659 on behalf of "freeborn people of this nation now in slavery in the Barbadoes," found in "The Diary of Thomas Burton, Esq.," Volume 4: March-April 1659 (1828), pages 254-273. John Towill Rutt, editor.
URL: http://www.british-history.ac.uk/report.aspx?compid=36939

[32]   "Ship Passenger Lists: National and New England (1600-1825)," edited and indexed by Carl Boyer III, published by the compiler, Newhall, California, 1977, pages 154-161. URL: http://web.northnet.org/minstrel/scottish.slaves.htm

[33]   "New England Families: Genealogical and Memorial," Volume IV, Clearfield Company, 1913, pages 1683-1684. William Richard Cutter, editor.
URL: http://web.northnet.org/minstrel/hambleton.00.htm

[34]   "Scots Prisoners and their Relocation to the Colonies, 1650-1654."
URL: http://www.geni.com/projects/Scots-Prisoners-and-their-relocation-to-the-colonies-1650-1654/3465

[35]   "Calendar of State Papers Colonial, America and West Indies, Volume 1: 1574-1660," W. Noel Sainsbury (editor), published 1860, pages 407-409. 1653. Sept. 6. Order of the Council of State.
URL: http://www.british-history.ac.uk/report.aspx?compid=69274

[36]   "Calendar of State Papers Colonial, America and West Indies, Volume
1: 1574-1660," W. Noel Sainsbury (editor), published 1860, pages 431-432.
1655. Oct. 3. Order of the Council of State.
URL: http://www.british-history.ac.uk/report.aspx?compid=69297

[37]   "Statutes at Large; Virginia," March 1642-3, Act XXII.
URL: http://vagenweb.org/hening/vol01-10.htm

[38]   "An Act Relating to Servants and Slaves," Charles County Court
Record, 1684-1685, microfilm reel CR 35691-3, MSA CM376-12, images 169,
170, Hall of Records, Maryland State Archives, Annapolis, Maryland.
URL: http://guide.mdsa.net/series.cfm?action=viewSeries&ID=CM376

[39]   "Proceedings and Acts of the General Assembly, January 1637/8-
September 1664," Volume 1, Page 496, Sept.-Oct. 1663.
URL: http://aomol.net/000001/000001/html/am1--496.html

[40]   "Statutes at Large; Virginia," October 1705, Act XIII. Freedom dues.
URL: http://vagenweb.org/hening/vol03-25.htm

[41]   "Proceedings and Acts of the General Assembly, January 1637/8-
September 1664," Volume 1, page 331, August 1651.
URL: http://aomol.net/000001/000001/html/am1--331.html

[42]   "Calendar of State Papers Colonial, America and West Indies, Volume
5: 1661-1668," W. Noel Sainsbury (editor), published 1880, Preface, pages
xxviii-xxix. Spiriting away people to the Plantations.
URL: http://www.british-history.ac.uk/report.aspx?compid=76434

[43]   "Acts of the Privy Council of England, Colonial Series, Vol. I,
1613-1680," W. L. Grant, M.A., editor, published 1908, pages 296-297.
URL: http://archive.org/texts/flipbook/flippy.php?id=cu31924026356299

This order to stop the kidnapping and enslavement of children must have been
a high priority for the King and his Privy Council, as it is dated 26 July 1660,
a mere fifty-eight days after the Restoration of Charles II to the throne.

[44]   "Calendar of State Papers Colonial, America and West Indies, Volume
5: 1661-1668," W. Noel Sainsbury (editor), published 1880, Preface, pages
xxviii-xxix. Spiriting away people to the Plantations.
URL: http://www.british-history.ac.uk/report.aspx?compid=76434

[45]   "Kidnapped," by Robert Louis Stevenson, first published by Scribner's
Sons, New York, 1886. Chapter 7.

ACKNOWLEDGMENTS

Virginia:

Most of the Court Order Books from colonial Virginia have been transcribed and published, which spared me the task of traveling to many county court houses to examine the original handwritten books. The following is a complete list of the published transcriptions relied upon for the compilation of this index. The dates are consolidated.

Northampton County Virginia Record Book, 1674-1678, Edited by Dr. Howard Mackey and Marlene A. Groves, CG, Picton Press, Rockford, Maine

Northampton County Virginia Orders & Wills, 1678-1710, Transcribed by Frank W. Walczyk, Peter's Row, Coram, New York

Accomack County Virginia Court Order Abstracts, 1663-1710, JoAnn Riley McKey, Heritage Books, Inc.

Order Book Abstracts of Stafford County, Virginia, 1664-1668, 1689-1693, Compiled and Published by Ruth and Sam Sparacio, The Antient Press, McLean, Virginia

Westmoreland County Virginia Records, 1661-1664, Abstracted and Compiled by John Frederick Dorman

Westmoreland County Virginia Order Books, 1676-1721, Abstracted and Compiled by John Frederick Dorman

Order Book Abstracts of Northumberland County, Virginia, 1652-1679, Abstracted and Published by Ruth and Sam Sparacio, The Antient Press, McLean, Virginia

Northumberland County Virginia Court Order Books, 1678-1713, Transcribed and Edited by Charles and Virginia Hamrick, Iberian Publishing Company, Athens, Georgia

Lancaster County Virginia Orders, 1656-1706, Edited and Transcribed by Ruth and Sam Sparacio, The Antient Press, McLean, Virginia

Order Book Abstracts of Old Rappahannock County, Virginia, 1683-1692, Edited and Published by Ruth and Sam Sparacio, The Antient Press, McLean, Virginia

Order Book Abstracts of Richmond County, Virginia, 1692-1722, Edited and Published by Ruth and Sam Sparacio, The Antient Press, McLean, Virginia

Order Book Abstracts of Essex County, Virginia, 1692-1702, 1716-1718, Edited and Published by Ruth and Sam Sparacio, The Antient Press, McLean, Virginia

Order Book Abstracts of Middlesex County, Virginia, 1673-1710, Edited and Published by Ruth and Sam Sparacio, The Antient Press, McLean, Virginia

York County Deeds, Orders and Wills, 1657-1662, Transcribed by Vincent Watkins

York County Virginia Records, 1665-1676, Abstracted and Compiled by Benjamin B. Weisiger III

York County, Virginia Deeds, Orders, Wills, Etc., 1687-1697, Abstracted and Compiled by John Frederick Dorman

York County, Virginia Deeds, Orders, Wills, Etc., 1698-1706, Mary Marshall Brewer, Colonial Roots, Lewes, Delaware

York County, Virginia Deeds, Orders, Wills, Etc., 1706-1711, Sherry Raleigh-Adams, Colonial Roots, Lewes, Delaware

Charles City County Court Orders, 1658-1665, Fragments 1650-1696, Beverley Fleet, Richmond, Virginia

Charles City County, Virginia, Order Book, 1676-1679, Abstracted and Compiled by Margaret Mitchell Ayres

Charles City County, Virginia, Court Orders, 1687-1695, Fragment 1680, Abstracted and Compiled by Benjamin B. Weisiger III

Surry County Virginia Court Records, 1672-1711, Wynette Parks Haun, Durham, North Carolina

The Court Orders of Isle of Wight County, Virginia, 1693-1695, compiled by John Anderson Brayton, Memphis, Tennessee

Transcription of Lower Norfolk County, Virginia Records, Volume One, Wills and Deeds, Book D, 1656-1666, Compiled by John Anderson Brayton, Memphis, Tennessee

Ten Court Order Books were examined on microfilm at the Virginia State Library. All are listed at http://www.lva.virginia.gov/public/local

Essex County -- Orders, No. 3, 1703-1708, and No. 4, 1708-1714
York County -- Deeds, Orders, Wills, No. 6, 1677-1684, and No. 7, 1684-1687
Henrico County -- Order Book & Wills, 1683-1693, Order Book, 1694-1701, and Court Orders, 1707-1709
Norfolk County -- Orders, 1666-1675, and Order Book 1675-1686
Princess Anne County -- Order Book No. 1, 1691-1710.

Maryland:

Some of the Court Order Books from colonial Maryland have been transcribed, digitized, and published online. The following is a complete list of the published transcriptions relied upon for the compilation of this index. The dates are consolidated.

All are listed at http://www.aomol.net/html/countycourts.html

Kent County Court, Proceedings, 1658-1718, Archives of Maryland Volumes 54, 557, 730, 740, 765, 766, 767. Volumes 557, 730, 740 made possible by the generous support of the C. Ashley and Beverly B. Ellefson Endowment Fund.

Prince George's County, Court Record, 1696-1699, Archives of Maryland Volume 202. Published in 1964, with Joseph H. Smith and Philip A. Crowl as editors, under the direction of the American Historical Association and the Hall of Records Commission of the State of Maryland.

Somerset County, Judicial Record, 1665-1668, 1670-1677, 1683, 1687-1698, 1723-1735, Archives of Maryland Volumes 54, 86-91, 106, 191, 405-407, 687, 688, 839-842, 846. Volumes 86-91, 106, 191 and 405-407 published 1999-2004, transcribed by Atwood S. Barwick from the microfilm copies.

Talbot County, Judgment Record, 1662-1674, Archives of Maryland Volume 54. Published in 1937, J. Hall Pleasants, editor, under the direction of the Maryland Historical Society. Includes Kent 1658-1676 and Somerset 1665-1668.

Some of the Court Order Books from colonial Maryland have been microfilmed, scanned, and published online. The following is a complete list of the microfilms relied upon for the compilation of this index. The dates are consolidated. All are listed at
http://guide.mdsa.net/series.cfm?action=viewSeries&ID=CM376 and
http://guide.mdsa.net/series.cfm?action=viewSeries&ID=CE450

Charles County Court, Court Record, 1658-1694, 1696-1734, Maryland State Archives Volumes MSA CM376-1 to MSA CM376-32.

Queen Anne's County Court, Judgment Record, 1709-1716, 1718-1719, 1728-1742, 1744-1769, 1771-1777. Maryland State Archives Volumes MSA CE450-1 to MSA CE450-45.

Some of the Court Order Books from colonial Maryland have been neither transcribed nor microfilmed. The original books are at the Maryland State Archives. The following is a complete list of the original books relied upon for the compilation of this index. The dates are consolidated.

Anne Arundel County Court, Judgment Record, 1703-1720, Maryland State Archives Volumes MSA C91-1 to MSA C91-8.

Baltimore County Court, Proceedings, 1682-1686, 1691-1696, 1708-1715, Maryland State Archives Volumes MSA C400-1 to MSA C400-6.

Cecil County Court, Judgment Record, 1683-1701, Maryland State Archives Volumes MSA C623-1 to MSA C623-4.

Dorchester County Court, Judgment Record, 1690-1692, Maryland State Archives Volume MSA C704-1.

Prince George's County Court, Court Record, 1699-1720, Maryland State Archives Volumes MSA C1191-2 to MSA C1191-6.

Somerset County Court, Judicial Record, 1698-1722, Maryland State Archives Volumes MSA C1774-14 to MSA C1774-26.

Talbot County Court, Judgment Record, 1674-1689, 1692-1702, 1704-1708, 1715-1720, 1722-1734. Maryland State Archives Volumes MSA C1875-2 to MSA C1875-16, MSA C1875-18 to MSA C1875-23, MSA C1875-25 to MSA C1875-35.

For the compilation of this index, one hundred and fifty-six original books were examined, sixty-nine on paper, eighty-seven on microfilm.

My thanks to all the staff at the Hall of Records in Annapolis, Maryland for retrieving these sixty-nine original books, some of which do not ordinarily circulate, and making them available for scholarly research.

GUIDE TO THE RECORDS

In seventeen counties, most or all of the Court Order Books from the seventeenth century have been lost.

In Virginia: Charles City, Elizabeth City, Gloucester, Henrico, Isle of Wight, James City, King and Queen, Nansemond, New Kent, Old Rappahannock, Stafford, Warwick

In Maryland: Anne Arundel, Baltimore, Calvert, Dorchester, St. Mary's

Inventories of surviving Court Order Books can be searched online.

In Virginia: http://www.lva.virginia.gov/public/local
Click: name of county
Scroll down to County Court Order Books

In Maryland: http://guide.mdsa.net
Click: "View by Agency"
Enter – Jurisdiction: name of county
          Agency: court
Click: Filter
Scroll down to County Court

In Maryland, the County Court Order Books were called, by county:

Judgment Record: Anne Arundel, Cecil, Dorchester, Queen Anne's, Talbot
Judicial Record: Somerset
Court Record: Charles, Prince George's
Proceedings: Baltimore, Kent

GUIDE TO THE INDEXES

All information in the following indexes and tables is taken directly from the Court Order Books of colonial Maryland and Virginia. These were county courts, with panels of appointed judges, generally known as "Worshippfull Commissioners" in Maryland, and "Gentleman Justices" in Virginia. For each county, there is an alphabetized index to children without indentures, an alphabetized index to the judges who sentenced these children to slavery, and a table tallying, year by year, the racial breakdown of children imported against their will. There is also an alphabetized index to the ships upon which these children were transported, and the captains who commanded those ships.

The records are incomplete. In some counties, many, most, or all of the Court Order Books from the colonial era are lost. In one notorious example, at Calvert County, Maryland, the British burned the County Court House during the War of 1812. Among the surviving books, some of the pages are torn, rotted, worm eaten, or otherwise damaged. As with all historical records, one should be grateful for what we still have.

The counties are arranged in geographic sequence, beginning at the tip of the Delmarva Peninsula and ending at the James River, following the shores of the Chesapeake Bay in a counter-clockwise direction.

In the indexes to children without indentures, in almost every case, the entry lists the name of the child, the date the child appeared in court, the age assigned by the judges, and the name of the owner, always in that sequence. If additional information of genealogical value appears in the Court Order Book, it is abstracted and included in the index.

Examples of additional information are explained as follows:

The term of servitude was dependent upon the adjudged age of the child. Therefore, one can be derived from the other. Sometimes both the age and the sentence are specified, which confirms the formula. In such cases the sentence, in years, is included in the index. Sometimes the term of servitude is stated, but not the adjudged age of the child. In these cases the age of the child is derived and included, in parentheses, in the index.

Sometimes the child claimed to be older than the age assigned by the judges. Not once was any child able to prove it to the court. In these cases, the relevant proceedings are abstracted and included in the index.

Sometimes the master agreed to a shorter term of servitude than the law allowed. Sometimes the child agreed to a certain number of years, in exchange for being taught a trade, or not being required to labor in the field, or to avoid the likelihood of a longer sentence imposed by the court. All such arrangements are abstracted and included in the index.

Sometimes the child claimed to have indentures but could not produce them, or presented them in court only to have them rejected by the judges. In these cases, the relevant proceedings are abstracted and included in the index. If the indentures were approved by the court, the child, being an indentured servant, does not appear in the index at all.

Sometimes the child was presented to the court by someone other than the owner, in which cases the third party is identified in the index.

Sometimes the name of the ship upon which the child was transported, and/or the name of the ship's captain, or the port of departure, or the date of arrival, are stated in the Court Order Books, and this information is quoted in the index. Identified ports of departure are: Belfast, Biddeford, Bridgwater, Bristol, Derry, Dublin, London, New Haven, Plymouth, Topsham, Whitehaven, York, and somewhere in Scotland.

It should be noted that I have sometimes broken with standard practice regarding quotations. This is an index, not a transcription. All words included in quotes actually appear in the Court Order Books, but, to keep the index concise, superfluous legal wording is omitted.

This index includes only: white persons without indentures brought before the county court and sentenced to servitude. Almost all were children. With the possible exceptions of those who claimed to have indentures, they were imported against their will. They never agreed to come to America, not in writing, anyway. There was no contract, no indenture.

No others are included in this index. It is important to limit the scope and purpose of one's research in order that the goal be attainable.

Examples of children not included are explained as follows:

Indentured servants are not included. Some were brought to court to have their ages adjudged, but only to determine when they would be old enough to become tithable, or taxable, and this purpose is so stated lest the court records be misinterpreted to extend the terms of the indenture. They are not to be confused with children imported without indentures, whose ages were adjudged in order to determine the length of their servitude.

Negro and Indian children are not included. They were slaves for life. If imported from elsewhere, they, too, were brought to court to have their ages adjudged, but only to determine when they would become taxable. In the court records, Negro and Indian children are identified by race, and by a first name only, chosen by their master. Their real names are not known. That is why they are not included in this index. There would be little or no genealogical value in entries such as these from Somerset County:

"Samboe black negroe," 10 January 1677, age 12, David Browne
"Sambo a negro boy," 21 August 1733, age 14, John Gales

Orphan children, native born, are not included. They were brought to court to choose a legal guardian, or to have one assigned by the judges. Their fathers are named in the court records. Guardians were required, by court order, to properly feed and clothe the orphans, to teach them to read and write, and to teach them a trade. They are not to be confused with children imported without indentures, whose masters had no such obligations.

Children given up for adoption are not included. They were brought to court by their parents, who are named in the court records, and who affirm that this is their voluntary decision. They are not to be confused with children imported without indentures, whose parents are never identified.

Thus there is a wealth of genealogical information in the Court Order Books that is beyond the scope and purpose of this index.

(The affidavits and depositions are another example. The witnesses give their names and ages on a specific date in a certain county).

In the indexes to Gentleman Justices and Worshippfull Commissioners, the judges are paired with the surnames of the unindentured white children they owned. Sometimes the judge "comes off ye bench at ye judging of his servant," and sometimes not. Either way, the judges were not always disinterested parties. In nine counties (Northampton, Accomack, Talbot, Charles, Westmoreland, Northumberland, Lancaster, Middlesex, York), accounting for 4190 of the children in this index, a majority of the judges were among the owners. Twenty-eight judges, including twelve in Charles County, Maryland, owned ten or more of these children. One Gentleman Justice, in Lancaster County, Virginia, owned thirty-nine.

Altogether, 1543 of 5290 (29.2%) of the children in this index were owned by "Gentleman Justices" or "Worshippfull Commissioners."

In the tables of data, Negro and Indian children are included for statistical purposes. For each county, the years for which the Court Order Books were examined can be seen in the table. These include every surviving Court Order Book from 1657 to 1700 in Maryland and Virginia.

Altogether, during the seventeenth century, from 1657 through 1700, 4707 (92.1%) of the children without indentures were white, 231 (4.5%) were Negro, 167 (3.3%) were Indian, and four (0.1%) were Mulatto.

In Virginia, 2825 (87.9%) were white, 218 (6.8%) were Negro, 167 (5.2%) were Indian, and four (0.1%) were Mulatto.

In Maryland, 1882 (99.3%) were white, and 13 (0.7%) were Negro.

Around the turn of the century the racial breakdown changed abruptly. During the first decade of the eighteenth century, from 1701 through 1710, for which I have examined all of the surviving Court Order Books in Maryland and Virginia, 368 (45.2%) were white, 426 (52.3%) were Negro, 18 (2.2%) were Indian, and two were Mulatto. Partial data indicate that during the second decade, from 1711 through 1720, about two-thirds of the children imported without indentures were Negro.

When the trafficking in white children came to an end is not certain. Microfilms of the Court Order Books for Queen Anne's County, Maryland are online, including 1728 to 1777 almost continuously. During this period there were 17 white children and 54 Negro children. The last white children without indentures were found in 1742, the last Negro child in 1757.

What is certain is that, in the surviving Court Order Books of Maryland and Virginia, 92.1% of the children imported without indentures, that is, without their consent, and sentenced to slavery, during the seventeenth century, were white. The data do not include adults imported against their will, or children born into slavery in Maryland and Virginia. But the story of white slavery can no longer be ignored. We have five thousand names.

--- --

Scottish soldiers captured at the Battle of Preston during the Jacobite rebellion of 1715 were likewise shipped to America and sold into slavery. Of these, 281 were destined for Maryland or Virginia (see Appendix).

(534)

Charles County, Maryland, Court Record, 10 June 1679

Charles County, Maryland, Court Record, 19 April 1698

Charles County

(44)

At a County Court of our Soveraigne Lord William
the third by the grace of God of England Scotland
France and Ireland King &c at Port Tobacco in
Charles County on fourth day of Aprill in y[e] Eleventh
yeare of his Majesties Reigne Annoq[ue] Domini
1699: Before

Capt William Barton

Maj[r] James Smallwood — m[r] Richard Harrison
m[r] Joseph Manning — Capt Henry Hardy
m[r] Robert — Yates — m[r] Thomas Fancy
m[r] Philip Briscoe — Capt John Wilder

Justices thereunto appointed & authorized —

Thomas Smoot presents a man servant to y[e] Court knowne to be adjudged of his age named Thomas Hollis who is adjudged to be
fifteene yeares of age &c

James Petticott presents a man servant to y[e] Court knowne to be
adjudged of his age named James Lawrence who is adjudged to
be seaven teene yeares of age &c —

Anthony Neale presents a man servant to y[e] Court knowne to be adjudged of his age named Robert Browne who is adjudged to bee —
fifteene yeares of age &c

Thomas Hussey presents a man servant to y[e] Court knowne to be adjudged of his age named Owen Swilaught who is adjudged
to be fourteene yeares of age &c

James Smallwood jun[r] presents a man servant to y[e] Court knowne to be
adjudged of his age named John fitz Gerald who is adjudged to
be fourteene yeares of age &c

Francis Harrison presents a man servant to y[e] Court knowne to be adjudged of his age named James Mitchell who is adjudged to bee
thirteene yeares of age &c

James fforley presents a man servant to y[e] Court knowne to be adjudged
of his age named John Shott who is adjudged to be seaventeene
yeares of age &c

Benjamin Tovey presents a man servant to y[e] Court knowne to be
adjudged of his age named John Williams who is adjudged to be
twelve yeares of age &c

Samuel Luckett presents a man servant to y[e] Court knowne to be adjudged of his age named Nicholas Kennyday who is adjudged to bee
twenty two yeares of age &c

Test.

Charles County, Maryland, Court Record, 4 April 1699

(45)

Thomas Hussey presently a man servant to ye Court here to be adjudged of his age named Allen Dallison who is adjudged to be ... borne ... yeares of age.

Thomas Hussey presently a man servant to ye Court here to be adjudged of his age named Daniell MacDonald who is adjudged to be ... yeares of age.

John Sendall presently a man servant to ye Court here to be adjudged of his age named William Welch who is adjudged to be fifteene yeares of age.

John Sendall presently a man servant to ye Court here to be adjudged of his age named Daniell Ryley, and ye sd Daniell Ryley produc-ing his Indenture signed by one Robert Brownings ... which ye Indenture ... is only to serve foure yeares ... it is ... Indenture ... ye Court here was adjudged to be void ... and that ye sd Daniell Ryley ought only to serve foure yeares according to ye tenure of ye sd Indenture.

Mr George Tubman presently a man servant to ye Court here to be adjudged of his age named Alexander Killpatrick who is adjudged to be foureteene yeares of age.

Elizabeth Hawkins presently a man servant to ye Court here to be adjudged of his age named Robert Gillfroy who is adjudged to be thirteene yeares of age.

Edward Philpott presently a man servant named John Moore to ye Court here to be adjudged of his age who is adjudged to be sixteene yeares of age.

Mr William Hunter presently a man servant to ye Court here to be adjudged of his age named Oliver Burke who is adjudged to be thirteene yeares of age.

Robert Hagar presently a man servant named John Brancks ye Court here to be adjudged of his age who is adjudged to be fifteene yeares of age.

Alexander Wilson presently a man servant to ye Court here to be adjudged of his age named Markham Markpearson who is ad-judged to be sixteene yeares of age.

Thomas Simpson presently a man servant to ye Court here to be adjud-ged of his age named Robert Fletcher who is adjudged to be sixteene yeares of age.

Mr Richard Martin presently a man servant to ye Court here to be adjudged of his age named David Wilkison who is adjudged to be sixteene yeares of age.

William Herbert presently a man servant to ye Court here to be adjud-ged of his age named Alexander Stoubeck who is adjudged to be ... yeares of age.

Hugh

Charles County, Maryland, Court Record, 4 April 1699

NORTHAMPTON COUNTY

Ammon, William, 31 May 1667, age 13 "the tenth of Februarie Last past,"
  Thomas Dimer
Armitage, Francis, 28 May 1678, age 14, John Custis Junr., sworn as
  Sub Sheriff to Capt. John Custis (Senr.), 28 May 1688
Bird, Joseph, 28 November 1680, age 16, Col. John Custis
Bolingham, John, 28 December 1664, age 15, Richard Patrick
Boswell, Peter, 28 April 1671, age 13, Argoll Yardley
Brevitt, Samuel, 27 March 1679, age 15, Thomas Browne
Broadway, Jane, 31 January 1681, age 16, Capt. John Robins
Bryan, Darby, 30 December 1685, age 13 "from the time of the arrival of
  the ship he came into the country in, being the 9th of December
  instant," Henry Pike
Burr, Sarah, 30 November 1674, age 17, "by her owne acknowledgment
  beinge eighteene yeares of age next Aprill," Mrs. Dorothy
  Andrews
Bush, John, 3 March 1680, age 12, Col. John Stringer
Butler, Anne, 30 May 1681, age 14, Edmund Kelly
Callihan, Darby, 28 February 1700, age 13 "at the time of the arrival
  of the ship he came into the country in being the tenth of
  December last," Henry Stott
Carnell, Angus, 28 January 1692, age 8, Jonathan Shott
Carpenter, Charles, 29 December 1680, age 12, Capt. Isaac Foxcroft
Carpenter, James, 28 August 1673, age 13, "the time ye shipp arrived
  hee came into ye Country it beinge ye 11th of April last,"
  John Culpeper
Cartee, Timothy, 28 October 1680, age not stated, Nathaniel Wilkins
Caryl, James, 1 March 1683, age 17, Capt. Isaac Foxcroft
Cheese, Marmaduke, 30 May 1681, age 11, Capt. John Robins
Collins, Abraham, 29 February 1664, age 15, John Forsith
Combes, Jarbaco, 22 November 1677, age 12, Capt. John Savage
Corbett, Edward, 31 January 1665, age 12, Alice Wood
Cowen, Benjamin, 30 July 1677, age 12 "the first day of Aprill last,"
  John Waterson
Cox, William, 29 June 1668, age 14 "by his Confession," Abraham Vansalt
Crauford, William, 28 May 1700, age 13, Robert Andrews, "but his
  master declared that he bought the said Servant for ten years
  and no longer"
Cursell, Joane, 28 May 1679, age 16, Thomas Hunt
Daton, Sarah, 26 November 1677, age 16, John Eyres

1

NORTHAMPTON COUNTY

Davis, Joseph, 4 June 1703, age 17, Sary Edmunds

Davis, Richard, 30 May 1681, age 10 "at the time of the arrival of the ship, Sarratt Merchant he came into the country in," Lt. Col. William Waters

Davis, Thomas, 28 February 1665, age 15, Elizabeth Whitmarsh

Dennis, Bryan, 4 January 1683, age 15, Morgan Dowell

Donevan, Darby, 28 January 1686, age 16, "from the time of the arrival of the ship he came into the country in and being the ninth of December last," Col. John Custis

Donough, John, 9 January 1683, age 14, James Dermott, "there was no indenture passed between (the Servant) and Terrence Dermott who shipped him"

Douglas, John, 28 March 1692, age 9, Capt. Obedience Johnson

Dowell, John, 28 May 1688, age 5, John Burt

Dunn, Alexander, 2 May 1667, age 14, John Waterson

Ellett, Jasper, 30 August 1668, age 12, Thomas Hunte

Eyre, John, 28 March 1692, age 14, William Sterling

Gallaway, James, 28 May 1694, age 15, Mrs. Lydia Jackson

George, Samuel, 27 March 1679, age 13, Thomas Rydinge

Glassey, Alexander, 28 January 1692, age 12, Henry Harmanson

Goodson, Elizabeth, 28 February 1681, age 13, Major William Spencer

Grady, Bryan, 28 January 1686, age 11, "from the time of the arrival of the ship he came into the country in being the ninth of December last," Charles Holden

Grevine, George, 27 February 1679, age 13, John Custis Junr.

Gridley, Thomas, 28 February 1672, age 17, Mrs. Anne Melling

Hanson, John, 5 November 1674, age 16, Edmund Bibby

Harper, Alexander, 28 January 1692, age 12, Edmond Bebbee

Hart, Henry, 4 January 1683, age 12, Andrew Andrews

Hempson, William, 28 June 1672, age 15, William Sterlinge

Higgin, Daniel, 4 January 1683, age 14, Col. John Stringer

Hill, Mary, 6 May 1675, age 10, John Kendall

Holland, William, 28 February 1672, age 15, Lt. Coll. William Waters

Howard, William, 5 November 1674, age 16, Matthew Patrick

Joanes, John, 31 May 1667, age 14 "the tenth of Februarie Last past," John Parramore, by his wife Mary

Jones, Humphry, 28 May 1696, age 12, Henry Scott

Jones, Isaac, 27 March 1679, age 13, Phillip Fisher

2

NORTHAMPTON COUNTY

Jones, William, 30 May 1693, age 14 "by his own acknowledgement,"
    Elizabeth Smith, widow of John Smith
Kidder, John, 30 May 1681, age 14, John Michael
Laine, Darby, 28 January 1686, age 11, "from the time of the arrival of the
    ship he came into the country in being the ninth of December
    last," Col. John Custis
Lehay, Mathew, 28 February 1700, age 12 "at the time of the arrival
    of the ship he came into the country in being the tenth of
    December last," Hugh Floyd
Leonard, Faith, 28 May 1678, age 14, Walter Mathews
Lockey, John, 28 May 1679, age 13, John Luke
Lyes, Robert, 2 May 1667, age 10 "the tenth of Februarie last past,"
    John Michaell
MacDonough, John, 31 January 1683, age 13, Col. John Custis
MacTeigue, John, 30 December 1699, age 9, Robert Tompson, Taylor
Mason, John, 29 November 1686, age 14, Robert Bell
Mehire, A _____ , 10 January 1683, age 15, Lt. Col. William Waters
Michaell, John, 31 December 1677, age 15, Edmund Killy
Million, Edward, 28 March 1692, age 9, Capt. Arthur Robins
Moghull, Ellenor Dowill, 28 January 1686, age 16, "from the time of the
    arrival of the ship she came into the country in being the ninth
    of December last," Col. John Custis
Moore, John, 10 April 1665, age 13, John Waterson
Moore, Thomas, 30 May 1681, age 11 "and eight months," Capt.
    John Robins
Morgan, William, 22 November 1677, age 12, Capt. John Savage
Morton, Richard, 30 May 1676, age 15, Lt. Coll. William Waters
Mosely, William, 27 February 1679, age 13, John Bellamy
Murphey, Garrett, 28 October 1698, age 11, Capt. Phillip Fisher
Murray, John, 28 January 1692, age 12, Phillip Fisher
Nasely, Mary, 30 May 1681, age 11, Capt. John Robins
Neale, John, 4 January 1686, age 15 "from the time of the arrival of the
    ship he came into the country in being the 9th day of December
    last," Michael Purefey
Newton, Elizabeth, 28 May 1700, age 15, William Nicholson
Noble, Alexander, 28 March 1692, age 10, Capt. Arthur Robins
Packer, Edward, 28 February 1679, age 16, John Michaell
Paine, Mary, 30 November 1674, age 17, "by her owne confession shee is
    eighteene yeares of age next May," Thomas Jacob

Parrott, Richard, 30 December 1679, age 14 "and two months,"
    John Bellamy
Reade, Elizabeth, 28 January 1692, age 15, John Bradhurst
Ree, John, 3 March 1680, age 14, Col. John Stringer
Rose, Thomas, 28 October 1680, age 18, Col. John Custis
Sadler, James, 30 July 1694, age 13, Capt. Isaac Foxcroft
Saunders, Prisiser, female, 31 March 1685, age 14, Capt. Isaac Foxcroft
Scott, Anthony, 28 January 1692, age 12, John Harmanson
Scott, Mary, 2 February 1692, age 18, Daniel Neech
Settwell, Henry, 21 November 1677, age 18 "the Second of this Instant
    November," John Wilkins
Shore, William, 10 April 1665, age 13, Thomas Hunt
Simkin, William, 28 February 1678, age 16, Thomas Maddox
Simkins, John, 29 August 1673, age 12 "att ye time ye shippe arrived
    hee came into ye Country it being some time in Aprill last,"
    Capt. William Spencer
Smith, John, 3 March 1680, age 11, Col. John Stringer
Smith, Robert, 28 March 1671, age 16, Benjamin Cowdry
Spadinge, James, 28 January 1673, age 15, Mrs. Anne Dalby
Stilly, John, 28 March 1694, age 10, Henry Stott
Styles, William, 4 March 1679, age 17, Hancock Lee
Sullenhone, Donell, 28 July 1679, age 16, Col. John Custis, by
    Charles Holden
Sulley, Mary, 3 March 1680, age 16, Col. John Stringer
Swindall, Daniell, 28 April 1664, age 14, John Custis
Swithin, William, 31 December 1677, age 15, Benoni Ward
Taylor, Thomas, 28 January 1673, age 16 "the first day of December last,"
    Thomas Harmason
Taylor, William, 28 July 1681, age 17, Benjamin Robinson
Tompson, Thomas, 22 November 1677, age 12, Capt. John Savage
Twineman, Steven, 28 January 1686, age 14, "from the time of the arrival
    of the ship he came into the country in being the ninth of
    December last," Col. John Custis
Vert, Elizabeth, 28 May 1702, age 12 "at the time of the arrival of the ship
    she came into the country in being the first day of April last,"
    Hamond Firkettle
Walker, George, 30 May 1698, age 12, William Bell
Walker, Thomas, 28 February 1678, age 11, Edmund Bibbee
Walker, Thomas, 31 March 1684, age 13, Richard Robinson

NORTHAMPTON COUNTY

Walter, George, 28 November 1701, age 12 "the first day of February preceding being the time the ship arrived he came into the country in," William Bell

Watt, William, 28 January 1692, age 16, Edmond Custis

Wheeler, John, 27 March 1679, age 14, John Tompson

Whitty, Bridgett, 29 June 1668, age 13 "accordinge to her Confession," Abraham Vansalt

Wilkinson, Mary, 7 December 1674, age 18 "by her owne confession," Paule Trendall, six and a half years.

Williams, Mary, 24 November 1664, age 16, John Bagwell

Williams, Rowland, 28 April 1664, age 21, John Michaell

Wilson, James, 30 December 1672, age 9, Coll. William Kendall

Wilson, Mathew, 28 August 1673, age 17 "the time ye shipp arrived hee came into ye Country it beinge ye 11th of April last," Teige Harman

Woodgate, Daniell, 28 April 1663, age 15, Frances Renier, "widow"

Woodman, Robert, 28 January 1686, age 10, "from the time of the arrival of the ship he came into the country in being the ninth of December last," Col. John Custis

Wotton, Thomas, 30 November 1674, age 15 "at ye time of his arrivall in the Country beinge the 20th of October last," Capt. Isaac Foxcroft

Wyse, John, 28 May 1666, age 15, William Mellinge

Younge, Gowen, 28 July 1702, age 7, Hillary Stringer

_____ , Peter, 28 February 1672, age 13, Capt. William Spencer

NORTHAMPTON COUNTY

Gentleman Justices	Servants
Andrews, Andrew	Hart
Andrews, William, Capt., Major *	
Custis, John, Capt., Col., Esqr. *	Bird, Donevan, Laine, MacDonough, Moghull, Rose, Sullenhone, Swindall, Twineman, Woodman
Custis, John, Junr.	Armitage, Grevine
Eyre, John	Daton
Fisher, Phillip, Capt.	Jones, Murphey, Murray
Foxcroft, Isaac, Capt., Lieut. *	Carpenter, Caryl, Sadler, Saunders, Wotton
Harmanson, George	
Harmanson, John	Scott
Harmanson, Thomas	Taylor
Harmanson, William, Capt.	
Hunt, Thomas	Cursell, Ellett, Shore
Johnson, Jacob	
Johnson, Obedience, Capt. *	Douglas
Jones, William, Capt.	
Kendall, William, Col. *	Wilson
Lee, Hancock	Styles
Littleton, Nathaniel, Capt.	
Littleton, Southy *	

NORTHAMPTON COUNTY

Gentleman Justices	Servants
Luke, John	Lockey
Michael, Adam	
Michaell, John *	Kidder, Lyes, Packer, Williams
Pettitt, Francis	
Pigot, Francis, Capt.	
Pigot, Ralph	
Powell, John	
Robins, John, Capt., Major *	Broadway, Cheese, Moore, Nasely
Robins, Littleton	
Rydinge, Thomas *	George
Savage, John, Capt.	Combes, Morgan, Tompson
Savage, Thomas	
Spencer, William, Capt., Major	Goodson, Simkins, _____
Stringer, Hillary, Capt.	Younge
Stringer, John, Col. *	Bush, Higgin, Ree, Smith, Sulley
Waters, William, Lieut. Col. *	Davis, Holland, Mehire, Morton
Whittington, William, Capt.	
Willett, John	
Yardley, Argoll	Boswell

* see Accomack County

7

NORTHAMPTON COUNTY

Year	White	Negro	Indian	Year	White	Negro	Indian
1657	0	0	0	1684	1	0	1
1658	0	0	0	1685	2	0	0
1659	0	0	0	1686	8	0	2
1660	0	0	0	1687	0	0	0
1661	0	0	0	1688	1	1	1
1662	0	0	0	1689	0	0	0
1663	1	0	1	1690	0	0	0
1664	5	0	0	1691	0	0	0
1665	4	0	0	1692	12	1	0
1666	1	0	0	1693	1	0	0
1667	4	0	0	1694	3	2	0
1668	3	0	0	1695	0	0	1
1669	0	0	0	1696	1	1	0
1670	0	0	0	1697	0	3	0
1671	2	0	0	1698	2	2	0
1672	5	0	0	1699	1	5	0
1673	5	0	0	1700	4	0	0
1674	6	0	0	1701	1	12	0
1675	1	0	0	1702	2	12	0
1676	1	0	0	1703	1	0	0
1677	8	0	0	1704	0	4	0
1678	4	0	0	1705	0	4	0
1679	12	0	0	1706	0	1	0
1680	8	0	0	1707	0	6	0
1681	9	1	0	1708	0	4	0
1682	0	0	0	1709	0	0	0
1683	7	5	0	1710	0	5	0
				Total	126	69	6

ACCOMACK COUNTY

Ach, John, 17 April 1678, age 13, James Gray

Adams, Margret, 26 May 1679, age 17, William Chace

Adams, William, 6 February 1673, age 14, Peter Walker

Aily, Joseph, 19 April 1676, age 12, Mrs. Rhody Fauset

Allinson, Francis, 3 August 1697, age 17, John Stainton

Allisan, Jon., 17 March 1675, age 12, Allexander Addison

Allison, Edward, 16 February 1677, age 18, John Wise

Allum, Thomas, 16 January 1665, age 13, George Brickhouse

Anzer, William, 18 May 1674, age 18, Capt. Daniell Jenifer

Archer, John, 19 April 1676, age 18, Owen Collonel

Arkfeild, Robert, 16 March 1670, age 18, Capt. George Parker

Atkinson, Alice, 2 August 1680, age 18, John Drumond

Bacy, Thomas, 18 April 1676, age 15, John Mikell, Jr.

Badger, Reynold, 6 February 1673, age 11, Richard Bayly

Ballard, Elenor, 17 August 1682, age 13, Samuel Tayler

Bancks, Ann, 2 August 1680, age 15, Capt. Richard Hill

Barcum, Roger, 16 December 1667, age 18, Henry Smith. "Since he
claimed to be older, the court gave him liberty to produce
authentic records."

Barnes, Thomas, 16 March 1670, age 18, Capt. George Parker

Barton, Nathaniel, 18 May 1674, age 17, Capt. Daniell Jenifer, "agreed
to serve an extra three years in return for being taught the trade
of shoemaker"

Bates, Susan, 18 March 1679, age 14, Griffin Savage

Bell, John, 19 June 1694, age 10, Maj. Richard Bally

Bensten, Samuel, 12 April 1683, age 12 "and a half," Arthur Robins,
who "voluntarily conceded that Samuel should serve for only
seven and a half years"

Bern, Janet, 17 April 1677, age 15, William Anderson

Bickers, William, 12 May 1686, age 9, Joseph Robinson

Bodin, Thomas, 7 April 1685, age 11, Charles Leatherbury

Boolin, Peter, 19 December 1671, age 18, Edward Brotherton

Bourne, John, 27 May 1667, age 17 "on the first of August," Col. Edm.
Scarburgh. "The servants acknowledged these ages."

Bradshaw, Francis, 16 February 1676, age 11, John Sturges

Branduck, Issac, 17 May 1669, age 12, Capt. John West

Brickhill, Joseph, 18 April 1676, age 17, Capt. Richard Hill

Britain, Thomas, 22 May 1663, age 13, Capt. Geo. Parker

Broadway, William, 26 January 1670, age not judged, Col. Edm.
Scarburgh, who "said he had an indenture for Broadway,
but it couldn't be found," ordered to serve one more year
Bromely, Thomas, 17 July 1676, age 15, Mrs. Tabitha Browne
Brook, Thomas, 22 May 1663, age 12, John Williams
Brookes, William, 13 March 1665, "over 16," James Hinderson
Brown, Eliza, 26 January 1675, age 18, William Burton
Browne, Edward, 26 October 1668, age 23, Thomas Fowke, "claimed his
freedom, but could not produce an Indenture, ordered that he
serve one more year"
Bryan, Daniel, 6 February 1700, age 12, William Lingo
Burrell, James, 16 June 1682, age 16, Capt. Henry Curtis
Cammell, John, 4 October 1698, age 14, Francis Mackemie
Canady, Margret, 20 February 1678, age 14, Bartholomew Meares
Canady, Thomas, 10 February 1685, age 14, Thomas Fooks
Canny, Grace, 17 November 1671, age 16, William Taylor
Canny, Uriah, 17 November 1671, age 12, William Taylor
Carnell, Rebecca, 7 February 1673, age 18, John Brookes
Carter, Edward, 16 April 1675, age 13, Joseph Newton
Carty, Elinor, 2 February 1686, age 17, John Baily
Chandeler, William, 6 March 1672, age 18, John Brook
Chester, William, 6 December 1698, age 14, Jonathan Owen
Clark, Thomas, 16 February 1665, age 12, Robert Huitt
Clerck, Faith, 18 May 1674, age 17, Teag Anderson
Cleverly, Christopher, 17 May 1669, age 11, Capt. John West
Coarde, Elizabeth, 12 July 1681, age 18, John Cole
Coffey, James, 19 February 1683, age 11, William Nock
Collonon, James, 4 April 1699, age 10, Simon Foscue
Colly, Salvanus, 8 December 1685, age 16, Edward Kallam
Cooke, John, 17 February 1681, age 16, Capt. Obedience Johnson
Cossens, Stephen, 16 March 1669, age 11, Capt. Edm. Bowman
Cotton, John, 18 March 1679, age 14, Obedience Johnson
Coupes, Thomas, 7 March 1672, age 12, Christopher Thompson
Coward, Samuel, 9 March 1686, age 16, Robert Watson of Occahannock
Cox, Richard, 23 November 1669, age 10, Mrs. Ann Toft
Crabtree, John, 16 February 1677, age 15, Arthur Robins
Crawford, William, 19 June 1694, age 17, Richard Garretson
Croft, William, 16 March 1681, age 12, George Nicholas Hack
Crosin, Francis, 16 April 1675, age 14, Mr. Revill

Crotoff, Court, 9 November 1674, age 10, Maj. John West
Cutler, Elizabeth, 24 October 1667, age 14, Col. Edm. Scarburgh
Cutts, Sarah, 18 May 1674, age 18, Capt. Daniell Jenifer
Davinson, David, 17 April 1678, age 17, Richard Jones, Jr.
Davis, George, 19 December 1677, age 17, Edward Revell
Davis, James, 16 June 1673, age 16, Mrs. Tabitha Browne
Davis, Jeffry, 13 January 1675, age 12, Francis Robins
Davis, Thomas, 14 February 1676, age 13, Capt. Southy Littleton
Davis, William, 16 February 1665, age 15, Col. Edm. Scarburgh
Denison, Elinor, 6 June 1699, age 16, John Parker
Devenish, John, 16 February 1665, age 13, Col. Edm. Scarburgh
Dickison, Richard, 18 September 1688, age 11, Tully Robinson
Dixson, Francis, 16 June 1682, age 12, Joseph Robinson
Dixson, William, 2 August 1680, age 16, John Wallop
Dobins, Mary, 18 December 1676, age 15, John Thomson
Dowman, John, 2 February 1677, age 18, Phillip Fisher
Duell, Thomas, 16 April 1678, age 12, John Barnes
Duffee, Charles, 19 June 1694, age 15, John Parker, Jr.
Dunn, Nicholas, 16 March 1670, age 14, Robert Hutchinson, ten years
Dutch, Susannah, 16 June 1673, age 15, Mrs. Tabitha Browne
Dyer, John, 16 April 1675, age 15, William White
Ease, Peter, 17 November 1685, age 11, George Middleton
Easton, Patrick, 27 May 1667, age 13, Mrs. Anne Toft. "The servants
    themselves acknowledged their ages."
Edwards, Mordica, 12 March 1664, age 15, John Tompson
Edwards, Nicholas, 18 April 1676, age 14, John Smith
Elliot, John, 18 April 1676, age 14, William Tayler
Ellis, Henry, 1 June 1703, age 13, Capt. Richard Drumond
English, Anthony, 20 January 1672, age 12, Robert Hewett
Fairfax, James, 16 April 1678, age 11, Steaphen Warrington
Farsy, Munsly, 18 April 1676, age 10, John Wallop
Fearine, Thomas, 6 February 1673, age 14, George Johnson
Flaier, William, 16 March 1680, age 4, Samuel Sandford
Fordman, Anthony, 26 January 1675, age 18, John Drumond
Foster, Thomas, 17 May 1669, age 16, John Lewis
Gardner, William, 16 February 1665, age 9, Col. Edm. Scarburgh
Gary, Edward, 17 October 1670, age 8, "the court agreed with the boy's
    confession that he would be nine years old next 2 February,"
    Devorax Browne

ACCOMACK COUNTY

Gibson, John, 3 August 1680, age 16, Thomas Teakle
Gibson, Laurence, 18 April 1676, age 14, Edward Hamond
Gibson, Marck, 18 April 1676, age 12, Ambrose White
Gooding, Thomas, 16 June 1670, age 18, Roger Mikeel
Goulding, William, 18 July 1676, age 9, John Wise
Greene, Henry, 10 November 1674, age 15, John Culpeper
Greenold, Richard, 7 March 1672, age 13, John Drumond
Grey, John, 16 April 1675, age 18, William Brittingham
Hackitt, Mary, 20 June 1693, age 14 1/2, James Gray
Hadock, Alice, 25 March 1684, age 13, Richard Kellam, Sr.
Hainer, John, 12 May 1685, age 13, John Wise
Hall, Leonard, 17 September 1689, age 12, Alexander Notes
Hall, William, 18 December 1676, age 17, Capt. Southy Littleton
Hallock, John, 4 April 1699, age 13, Hill Drumond
Hampton, Henry, 16 April 1675, age 17, John Wallop
Hancock, John, 17 January 1678, age 17, Paul Carter, by James Tuck,
        "ordered to serve seven years from the time of his arrival"
Haning, John, 24 October 1667, age 18, Edm. Bowman
Hanson, John, 9 November 1674, age 13, Mary Parramour
Hardy, Anthony, 18 May 1674, age 16, Hugh Yoe
Hargis, Walter, 12 March 1664, age 11, Edm. Bowman
Harris, William, 3 August 1680, age 10, Owen Collonon
Harrison, William, 16 June 1673, age 10, Thomas Browne
Harwood, Godfry, 16 April 1675, age 18, Hugh Yeo
Hasleupp, George, 7 February 1673, age 16, William Major
Herring, Alexander, 19 September 1693, age 14, Capt. George Parker
Hill, George, 17 March 1679, age 10, Francis Robins
Holland, Hannah, 15 March 1692, age 8, William Brittingham
Holloway, Richard, 9 November 1674, age 14, Edmund Kelly
Holt, John, 27 May 1667, age 14, Mrs. Dorothy Jordan
Hopkin, John, 24 October 1667, age 10, Edm. Bowman
Hudson, Samuel, 3 August 1680, age 10, William Major
Hues, Edward, 18 January 1678, age 15, Richard Bally
Hutchinson, James, 7 April 1685, age 11, Col. John Custis, "declared
        that he had an indenture made in England for nine years, but
        it was clandestinely taken away from him"
Jackson, Ann, 17 March 1679, age 12, George Johnson
Jackson, Owen, 6 February 1673, age 18, John Fawsett
James, Robert, 16 April 1675, age 13, Daniel Derby

ACCOMACK COUNTY

Jeffries, Thomas, 16 February 1677, age 17, Francis Robins

Jenkins, Thomas, 20 April 1674, age 18, Mrs. Tabitha Browne

Jones, John, 16 December 1679, age 12, John Rowles

Jones, Morgan, 18 April 1676, age 17, Thomas Browne

Justice, Ralph, 23 November 1669, age 16, Mrs. Ann Toft

Kemp, William, 17 April 1672, age 17, Roger Mackeel

Knight, Henry, 16 February 1664, age 13, William Roberts

Knowles, Samuel, 7 April 1685, age 13, William Burton

Lahee, Ralph, 2 February 1686, age 11, Francis Roberts

Lamot, Charles, 18 March 1679, age 12, Isaac Dix

Landford, Francis, 19 February 1689, age 14, Richard Cutler

Langhorne, John, 16 January 1676, age 18, Thomas Riding

Lase, John, 17 December 1667, age 21, John Parker

Lattimore, John, 18 April 1676, age 15, John Shepard

Ledbury, William, 11 January 1687, age 10, Brian Pert

Linegar, Joseph, 27 May 1667, age 16, Col. Edm. Scarburgh.
"The servants acknowledged these ages."

Littleton, John, 17 May 1669, age 13, Capt. John West

Loe, Robert, 23 November 1669, age 17, Mrs. Ann Toft

Loikyer, Thomas, 16 July 1674, age 18, Mrs. Tabitha Browne

Lowry, John, 16 February 1692, age 8, Robert Watson

Loyd, Francis, 18 June 1695, age 12, John Abbot

Loyd, John, 16 February 1665, age 14, Henry Edwards

Mackdonnell, John, 16 February 1692, age 9, Robert Watson

Mackemy, Averick, 19 June 1694, age 13, John Wise

Mancklin, Richard, 4 August 1702, age 13, Arthur Upshor, Sr.

Marrinor, Richard, 17 October 1664, age not stated, Edm. Bowman,
"for five years, the custom of the country"

Marrott, Francis, 16 June 1673, age 12, Thomas Browne

Martin, Sara, 26 May 1679, age 15, Mrs. Tabitha Brown, by Capt.
Hillary Stringer

Martin, Susana, 18 May 1674, age 15, Capt. Daniell Jenifer

Marvill, Elizabeth, 26 May 1679, age 12, Tobias Selvy

Masker, John, 7 February 1673, age 17, Obedience Johnson

Mason, John, 26 May 1679, age 14, Mrs. Tabitha Brown, by Capt.
Hillary Stringer

Meeres, Ann, 19 April 1676, age 17, Edward Hammond

Merrea, John, 16 March 1669, age 18, Capt. Edm. Bowman

Millner, Robert, 30 November 1686, age 15, George Smith

13

Minnikin, Jane, 7 April 1685, age 13, Maxamillian Gore
Moore, Sara, 26 May 1679, age 17, Arthur Upshot
Moren, John, 5 March 1700, age 11, Samuel Fittiman
Mottly, Alexander, 22 December 1685, age 15, Thomas Bagwell
Moulton, Abraham, 17 March 1679, "should be entered as 17 years old,"
    Ony Macklauin, "willing to serve his master for seven years"
Mountfort, Robert, 16 February 1665, age 16, John Smith
Mukerell, Lancelot, 17 April 1677, age 13, William Willet
Murfee, John, 27 May 1667, age 15, Mrs. Anne Toft. "The servants
    themselves acknowledged their ages."
Murphy, Owen, 27 May 1667, age 15, Mrs. Anne Toft. "The servants
    themselves acknowledged their ages."
Nellson, John, 9 March 1686, age 12, Arthur Robins
Nicholes, Richard, 16 February 1677, age 14, William Nock
Nickolson, Thomas, 2 August 1680, age 17, Arthur Robins
Nickolson, William, 2 August 1680, age 16, Capt. Daniel Jenifer
Nightingale, Thomas, 18 November 1685, age 13, Isaac Metcalfe
Nodes, Edward, 17 March 1679, age 10, Richard Bally
North, John, 16 January 1676, age 17, Lt. Col. John Tilny
Nucomes, Thomas, 19 December 1676, age 16, Rowland Savage
Osburne, John, 17 June 1682, age 17, Robert Watson
Osburne, Mathew, 7 February 1673, age 11, Capt. Daniell Jenifer
Pattison, Daniel, 1 June 1703, age 9, Robert Bell
Penn, Crispian, male, 16 April 1664, age 12, William Roberts
Pennington, John, 19 July 1687, age 13, Joseph Robinson
Perrey, William, 7 June 1680, age 16, Mrs. Lydia Jackson
Phillipson, William, 17 March 1679, age 13, John Booth
Pillion, John, 12 February 1679, age 11, Roger Ternam
Pim, Richard, 12 March 1664, age 13, Luke Denwood
Pinfield, Thomas, 6 March 1672, age 17, Owen Collonel
Poole, Elizabeth, 16 April 1678, age 11, Thomas Welburne
Pope, Thomas, 2 February 1677, age 13, Isaack Dix
Pott, John, 16 February 1665, age 15, John Watts
Powell, John, 2 October 1693, age 15, Edmund Custis
Preston, Ellinor, 6 February 1684, age 18, William Nock
Price, Ellis, 18 June 1696, age 14, William Hudson
Price, William, 16 June 1696, age 16, Thomas Ryley
Prior, James, 23 November 1669, age 15, Mrs. Ann Toft
Pruitt, Benjamin, 11 May 1686, age 16, John Washbourne

ACCOMACK COUNTY

Pumroy, Samuell, 16 May 1672, age 16, Capt. Daniell Jennifer

Reynolds, Robert, 7 June 1680, age 11, George Hope

Richardson, John, 16 March 1670, age not judged, John Wise. "The servant claimed to have an indenture for less time, but was willing to serve five years," and "had voluntarily burned his indenture."

Rigg, Abraham, 11 January 1687, age 13, Edward Kellam

Rigg, Isaac, 11 January 1687, age 15, Simon Foscue, Jr.

Right, Thomas, 12 April 1683, age 9, William Sill

Roberts, Charles, 16 January 1676, age 16, Arthur Robins

Roberts, Cristopher, 25 January 1670, age 13, Ambross White

Robinson, Edith, 16 June 1673, age 18, Mrs. Tabitha Browne

Rooksby, John, 16 March 1683, age 16, William Burton, "but he alleged that he was older." The court gave "liberty to obtain a certificate from the register in the parish in England where he was born."

Rose (or Roe), Ester, 19 June 1694, age 13, John Lewis, Jr.

Rust, William, 16 March 1669, age 12, George Johnson

Sales, John, 4 April 1699, age 9, Mrs. Sarah Roberts

Salisbury, Elizabeth, 6 January 1674, age 10, Robert Hewett

Sanderson, Mary, 7 April 1685, age 14, William Anderson

Sands, John, 23 November 1669, age 14, Mrs. Ann Toft

Satterwhite, William, 7 April 1685, age 12, John Baily

Saunders, Richard, 19 April 1676, age 17, William Anderson

Scinons (?), Edward, 16 February 1664, age 13, Owen Collonel

Shars, Solomon, 18 April 1676, age 10, Capt. Richard Hill

Shepherd, Daniel, 20 June 1693, age 16, William Nock

Simpson, John, 17 April 1677, age 13, Richard Hinman

Sims, Thomas, 6 February 1673, age 14, Thomas Parramore

Slaughtery, Owen, 19 February 1683, age 12, Thomas Parramore

Smith, Henry, 30 November 1686, age 15, John Wise

Smith, John, 26 January 1675, age 14, John Core

Smith, Richard, 18 April 1676, age 12, George Brickhouse

Spicer, Mathew, 15 March 1687, age 17, William Anderson

Stanworth, Thomas, 17 March 1679, age 9, John Abbot

Starkey, Nathaniel, 6 February 1684, age 15, John Wise

Stenton, John, 16 January 1676, age 17, John Wise, "but Stenton claimed he was 19 years old; he requested and received permission to produce a certificate from the register to prove it"

Stevens, James, 16 December 1664, age 14, Robert Huitt

Stykes, Henry, 7 February 1673, age 12, Rowland Savage

Sumpter, Robert, 6 February 1673, age 19, Teige Andros
Supple, Garret, 27 May 1667, age 17, Mrs. Anne Toft. "The servants
    themselves acknowledged their ages."
Suters, Thomas, 17 May 1681, age 15, William Anderson
Talbot, Benedict, 16 April 1678, age 17, Capt. Hillary Stringer
Tatcham, Edmond, 16 January 1676, age 16, John Parker
Terricus, Marcus, 10 September 1674, age 15, George Brickhouse
Thomas, Rolph, 18 December 1676, age 14, Capt. Southy Littleton
Thomas, William, 19 December 1671, age 14, Edward Hammond
Thomson, Thomas, 2 February 1686, age 15, Mrs. Martha James
Thornbury, Thomas, 16 April 1675, age 14, William Chace
Tomkin, Ann, 16 June 1670, age 18, Mrs. Ann Toft
Trippy, William, 6 February 1673, age 19, Dorman Sellivant
Trueman, Bennett, female, 6 February 1673, age 15, Richard Bundick
Turlington, Peter, 16 February 1676, age 11, Thomas Jonson
Tyson, Robert, 15 June 1683, age 18, Owen Collonon
Waile, William, 19 April 1676, age 18, Robert Hutchinson
Warden, Michaell, 10 September 1674, age 14, John Wise
Warraloe, James, 10 February 1685, age 17, Arthur Robins
Washbourne, John, 18 June 1695, age 13, Richard Watkinson
Waters, John, 27 May 1667, age 13, Col. Edm. Scarburgh.
    "The servants acknowledged these ages."
Watkinson, Peter, 16 June 1668, age 15, Richard Bayley, nine years
Wattkins, Thomas, 20 April 1674, age 16, Mrs. Tabitha Browne
Webb, Richard, 8 April 1670, age 17, Edward Revell
Weilding, Edward, 17 April 1677, age 15, Mrs. Tabitha Browne
Welbeck, Eliz., 16 February 1675, age 18, Jon. Aires
Wheeler, Thomas, 18 April 1676, age 18, John Wallop
White, Elizabeth, 15 February 1676, age 18, Robert Huet
White, George, 10 September 1674, age 15, John Wallope
White, Thomas, 17 May 1675, age 14, Hugh Yeo
White, William, 17 October 1664, age not stated, Capt. Geo. Parker,
    "for the custom of the country, which is five years"
Wilde, Ann, 18 March 1679, age 14, John Fen
Williams, Leonard, 17 May 1681, age 11, William Anderson
Williamson, William, 17 April 1677, age 11, John Parker
Willson, John, 16 February 1692, age 10, Richard Kellam, Jr.
Willson, Thomas, 20 March 1694, age 16, John Bradhurst
Willson, William, 17 April 1677, age 13, Edmond Kelly

ACCOMACK COUNTY

Willson, William, 16 March 1683, age 16, George Hope, "but he alleged that he was older." The court gave "liberty to obtain a certificate from the register in the parish where he was born."

Windam, Anne, 16 May 1672, age 18, Mrs. Anne Charlton

Woodland, Joseph, 20 April 1674, age 14, Mrs. Tabitha Browne

Wright, Edward, 18 January 1678, age 16, Mrs. Amy Fowkes

_____ , _____ , 3 March 1673, age 15, Thomas Browne

_____ , _____ , 16 January 1676, age 18, John Sturges

ACCOMACK COUNTY

Gentleman Justices	Servants
Anderson, William	Bern, Sanderson, Saunders, Spicer, Suters, Williams
Andrews, William, Major *	
Bally, Richard, Capt., Major	Bell, Hues, Nodes
Bowman, Edmond, Capt., Major	Cossens, Haning, Hargis, Hopkin, Marrinor, Merrea
Bradhurst, John	Willson
Browne, Devorax	Gary
Browne, Thomas	Harrison, Jones, Marrott, _____
Burton, William	Brown, Knowles, Rooksby
Custis, Edmund	Powell
Custis, John, Capt., Maj. Gen. *	Hutchinson
Custis, William, Capt.	
Drummond, John	Atkinson, Fordman, Greenold
Foxcroft, Isaac, Capt. *	
Hack, George Nicholas, Capt.	Croft
Hill, Richard, Capt.	Bancks, Brickhill, Shars
Hodgkins, Antony	
Hutchinson, Robert	Dunn, Waile
Jenifer, Daniell, Capt., Lt. Col.	Anzer, Barton, Cutts, Martin, Nickolson, Osburne, Pumroy

18

ACCOMACK COUNTY

Gentleman Justices	Servants
Johnson, Obedience, Capt. *	Cooke, Cotton, Masker
Kendall, William, Col. *	
Littleton, Southy, Capt., Col. *	Davis, Hall, Thomas
Michaell, John *	Bacy (?)
Moore, Edward	
Parker, George, Capt.	Arkfeild, Barnes, Britain, Herring, White
Parker, William	
Pitt, Robert, Capt.	
Revell, Edward	Crosin, Davis, Webb
Robins, Arthur	Bensten, Crabtree, Nellson, Nickolson, Roberts, Warraloe
Robins, John *	
Robinson, Joseph	Bickers, Dixson, Pennington
Robinson, Tully, Lt. Col.	Dickison
Ryding, Thomas *	Langhorne
Scarburgh, Bennett, Capt., Major	
Scarburgh, Charles, Capt., Major, Col.	
Scarburgh, Edmond, Capt., Major, Lt. Col.	Bourne, Broadway, Cutler, Davis, Devenish, Gardner, Linegar, Waters
Stringer, John, Col. *	

ACCOMACK COUNTY

Gentleman Justices	Servants
Tilney, John, Major	North
Wallop, John, Capt.	Dixon, Farsy, Hampton, Wheeler, White
Waters, William, Lt. Col. *	
Watts, John	Pott
Welburne, Thomas, Capt.	Poole
West, John, Capt., Major, Lt. Col.	Branduck, Cleverly, Crotoff, Littleton
Wise, John	Allison, Goulding, Hainer, Mackemy, Richardson, Smith, Starkey, Stenton, Warden
Yeo, Hugh	Hardy, Harwood, White

* see Northampton County

Wives of Justices	Servants
Browne, Tabitha, Mrs.	Bromely, Davis, Dutch, Jenkins, Loikyer, Martin, Mason, Robinson, Wattkins, Weilding, Woodland

Tabitha Scarburgh, daughter of Col. Edmund Scarburgh, married
Devorax Browne before 1660, and Maj. Gen. John Custis after 1673

Toft, Ann, Mrs.	Cox, Easton, Justice, Loe, Murfee, Murphy, Prior, Sands, Supple, Tomkin

"Anne Toft married Daniel Jenifer," after 29 April 1671

20

ACCOMACK COUNTY

Year	White	Negro	Indian
1663	2	0	0
1664	9	0	0
1665	9	0	0
1666	0	0	0
1667	13	0	13
1668	2	0	1
1669	12	0	3
1670	10	2	7
1671	4	0	0
1672	8	0	0
1673	19	0	0
1674	18	0	0
1675	15	0	0
1676	33	0	0
1677	13	0	0
1678	10	0	0
1679	17	0	0
1680	11	0	0
1681	5	0	0
1682	4	0	0
1683	7	3	0
1684	3	0	3
1685	13	2	1
1686	9	0	2
1687	5	0	0
1688	1	2	0
1689	2	0	0
1690	0	0	0
1691	0	0	0
1692	4	0	0
1693	4	0 *	0
1694	6	0	0
1695	2	0	0
1696	2	0	0
1697	1	1	0
1698	2	2	0
1699	4	2	0
1700	2	0	0
1701	0	2	0
1702	1	2	0
1703	2	0	0
1704	0	4	0
1705	0	0	0
1706	0	1	0
1707	0	8	0
1708	0	3	0
1709	0	5	0
Total	284	39	30

* one Mulatto

Note: The Indian children brought before the Gentleman Justices of Accomack County in 1667 were from Kikotanck, Anancock, or Matomkin.

SOMERSET COUNTY

Adamson, John, 6 February 1677, age 13, George Betts

Aitchsunne, Thomas, 8 June 1708, age 12, Joseph Venables

Albourne, David, 13 June 1699, age 10, John Turpin

Anderson, Roger, 15 June 1725, age 12, Capt. James Lindow, "Imported into this Country in the Sloop Called John of Doublin"

Anderson, William, 13 June 1699, age 15, James Townsend

Archer, John, 8 August 1699, age 15, William Shankland

Ashley, William, 8 February 1676, age 15-18, Captn. William Colebourne

Atkins, Robert, 8 June 1686, age 13, Richard Ackworth, arrived 8 November 1685, freed by court 30 January 1695

Banes, George, 18 April 1676, age 14, Charles Ballard

Banes, William, 8 February 1676, age 18-22, Richard Davis

Barnett, James, 11 June 1700, age 14, James Weatherly

Barnett, Stephen, 8 June 1675, age 15-18, Lewin Denwood

Barry, Richard, 11 January 1699, age 12, James Curtis, "who was imported into this Province in the ship James and Mary of Bristoll where of Jeremiah Pearce is Commander"

Bayley, George, 8 June 1675, "who said he was" age 11, George Johnson

Bayley, Robert, 9 March 1675, age 17-18, Robert Houston

Beaten, Lydia, 9 January 1672, age 11, Christopher Nutter

Bemhannon, John, 11 June 1701, age 14, John Hendry

Benger, Richard, 11 January 1699, age 9, Samuell Handy, "who was Imported into this Province in the Ship James and Mary of Bristoll where of Jeremiah Pearce is Commander"

Bennett, John, 8 June 1675, age 18-22, Elleanor Keene

Bennett, Robert, 9 March 1675, age 17-18, Thomas Purnell

Benson, Thomas, 12 June 1694, age 16-17, Capt. Henry Smith, presented by Ephraim Wilson

Boardman, William, 13 June 1699, age 14, George Hoyle

Boone, William, 13 June 1699, age 14, Capt. John Woodside

Booth, John, 13 June 1699, age 11, William Massey

Bowden, Anne, 8 August 1692, age 16, William Round, "desired no more Service" than six years

Bowen, William, 14 September 1703, age 12, Robert Kene

Bradley, Rebecca, 9 March 1675, age 18-22, Ambrose London

Brandon, Charles, 21 August 1733, age 14, George Bozman Junr., "Imported into this Country in the Ship called the Tryall, Capt. Sinners, Commander"

Brellehand, John, 18 August 1720, age 12, Richard Knight

Britt, Thomas, 10 August 1708, age 14, Capt. Tunstall, "adjudged to be
    15 years of age Aprill Next Ensuing"

Brookes, Abraham, 9 January 1700, age 13, Major Captt. Nicholas Evans

Brown, James, 15 November 1706, age 10, Alexander Hall

Browne, James, 10 March 1675, age 18-22, Ambrose Dixon

Browne, John, 12 June 1694, age 14, Capt. Henry Smith, presented by
    Ephraim Wilson

Bryce, Samuel, 12 June 1694, age 14, George Betts, arrived "in the vessel
    calld the May floor, Rowland Jackson Comdr"

Buljer, Garrett, 13 June 1699, age 12, John Shirrett

Burke, John, 8 June 1708, age 9, Alexander Madux

Byford, Sarah, 10 March 1675, age 14, Charles Ballard

Callanane, John, 17 March 1724, age 15, Robert Martin Gentl., "who was
    Imported into this Country in the Sloop Called John of Doublin,
    John Videll, Master"

Camble, John, 7 June 1709, age 11, John Jones

Cameron, Hugh, 17 August 1715, age 10, Thomas Bell, Merchant

Campbell, William, 9 August 1699, age 12, James Round

Campison, Leonard, 11 August 1674, age 17-18, Thomas Dixon

Canniggin, Arthur, 7 June 1709, age 10, George Betts

Cannohand, Patrick, 12 March 1700, age 13, Isaac Covington

Card, William, 10 November 1674, age 14, Edward Southrin, presented
    by John Winder

Carle, Thomas, 10 June 1673, age not judged, Robert Houllston, "the
    servant pleades that he hath an Indenture but his witnesses not
    ready to prove the same"

Carr, Hugh, 10 June 1690, age 7, Thomas Dixon

Carrahan, Bryan, 13 June 1699, age 13, Thomas Wilson

Carrell, Patrick, 11 June 1700, age 12, Mr. Richard Ackworth

Cartee, Darby, 10 January 1699, age 12, George Dashield, "who saith he
    was Imported into this Province in the Ship Fisher of Beddeford
    where of Thomas Lashbrooke is Commander"

Catterton, Henry, 12 November 1700, age 10, Miles Gray

Cawdrey, John, 10 August 1675, age not judged, George Johnson

Cawin, Galines (?), 11 November 1708, age 19, Benjamin Aydolake,
    "Arived in ye ship Mary, Commander James Jeffreys"

Chapes, Thomas, 8 June 1708, age 14, George Phelbut

Chattwick, James, 8 August 1699, age 9, Major John Gray

Clark, Margery, c. 15 January 1685, age not judged, Capt. Winder, sold to
    Nicholas Tyler, "served five years" as of 15 January 1690

SOMERSET COUNTY

Clary, John, 13 June 1699, age 16, Francis Alexander

Cock, Anthony, 11 June 1672, age not judged, Richard Ackworth,
"the master and the servant agreed" to eight years

Cock, William, 8 August 1699, age 16, Thomas Davis

Conner, Margrett, 9 August 1698, age 14, John Hansett

Conner, Timothy, 13 June 1699, age 14, David Kennedy

Cooke, Mary, 8 June 1675, age 13-14, George Johnson

Cordewin, Richard, 9 June 1696, age 13, Nicholas Fountaine

Cowen, Mary, 13 June 1699, age 16, Edward Stockdell

Crabb, Alexander, 13 March 1701, age 16, Benjamin Idolett Senr.

Crary, Dennis, 11 June 1700, age 14, Capt. Arnold Elzey

Crawford, James, 8 August 1692, age 14, Isaac Horsey, arrived "in ye good
Shipp, Providence of London, William Mecoy Master thereof"

Cray, William, 13 June 1699, age 15, David Browne

Cross, Edmund, 10 January 1700, age 15, Samson Wheately

Crowder, Joseph, 12 March 1672, age not judged, James Nicholson,
"master and Servant jointly agree" to eight years

Custody, Owen, 7 February 1699, age 14, William Winwright,
"and was imported into this Province in the Ship Fisher of
Bedeford where of was Commander Thomas Lashbrooke"

Dagg, Andrew, 11 June 1689, age 14, James Weatherly

Dale, James, 13 June 1699, age 14, James McMurrie

Daley, James, 13 June 1699, age 9, John Woodside

Danilas, Alexander, 13 September 1699, age 16, Arthur Denwood

Dart, Nicholas, 8 August 1699, age 15, James Caldwell

Davis, James, 13 June 1699, age 6, Thomas Tull Junr.

Dawson, Joseph, 20 August 1718, age 10, Thomas Covington

Diamond, William, 22 June 1720, age 13 "ye 2nd day of last September,"
Edward Stockdell

Dillany, Dennis, 10 January 1699, age 16, Graves Jarrett, "who was
imported into this Province in the Ship Fisher of Beddeford
where of Thomas Lashbrooke Commander"

Doughell, Dennis, 14 June 1699, age 14, John Oulon

Drewe, Jane, 11 August 1691, age 15-18, James Sanster

Dunkin, John, 22 June 1720, age 15, Capt. William Skinner

English, John, 13 June 1671, age 14, Christopher Nutter

Erwin, Patrick, 8 August 1692, age 13, Thomas Davis, arrived "in ye
good shipp Providence of London, Wm. Mecoy Master"

Escreeke, Elizabeth, 8 August 1676, age 18-22, Charles Hall

Evans, David, 9 January 1700, age 14, Capt. Nicholas Evans

Fa(?)ure, John, 20 August 1718, age 15, John Evans Junr.
Farrell, James, 13 August 1700, age 13, Robert Hopkin
Farrinton, William, 11 June 1700, age 9, Jain Kemp
Fernsey, Francis, 13 June 1699, age 10, Gregory Murmurenough
Firney, Jeremiah, 10 September 1706, age 10, Mary Edger
Forrester, Michael, 11 June 1700, age 14, William Alexander
Foster, Thomas, 8 August 1699, age 14, Major John Strawbridge
Fraser, Allin, 14 March 1699, age 14, Thomas Newbald
Frazer, William, 13 June 1699, age 15, Thomas Beauchamp
Freney, Peter, 13 June 1699, age 14, James McMurrie
Furrell, John, 13 June 1699, age 13, James Wallis
Gibbons, Alexander, 8 August 1699, age 15, John White
Gibson, John, 13 March 1677, age 18-22, John Williams
Gibson, Joseph, 12 August 1702, age 12, Robert Givan
Godfrey, Charles, 12 June 1677, age 15-18, Edward Smith
Graden, Francis, 10 March 1697, age 16, Ephraim Wilson
Grant, Alexander, 14 March 1699, age 17, Thomas Newbald
Grant, William, 10 September 1701, age 13, George Phabus (?)
Greeneway, Elizabeth, 10 January 1677, age 18-22, Ambrose Dixon
Greenleafe, William, 14 June 1699, age 12, Thomas Cary
Greham, Thomas, 12 June 1688, age 12, Capt. David Browne
Greyly, John, 14 March 1699, age 12, William Bowen, "who was
    imported into this Province in the James and Mary of Bristoll
    where of was Commander Jeremiah Peirce"
Hall, Thomas, 10 August 1693, age 13, Nehemiah Covington
Harney, Phillip, 30 April 1689, age 14, Robert Collier
Hastings, Robert, 31 October 1699, age 14, Thomas Cox, "ordered
    tenn Lashes on his bare Back and was then by the Court
    adjudged fourteen years old"
Henly, John, 10 January 1677, age 15-18, Robert Wilson
Henson, Robert, 9 November 1698, age 12, Robert Henson,
    "adjudged to be twelve years of age next month"
Hewson, Elizabeth, 8 June 1675, age 21, Nehemiah Covington
Highway, Thomas, 10 August 1675, age not judged, William Stevens
Hopkins, Benjamin, 22 June 1720, age 12, John Williams
Hosso, Henry, 9 June 1674, age 13, John Lyon
Howard, Lidia, 9 March 1675, age 14, Edward Jones
Howe, Philip, 6 February 1677, age 18-22, George Mitchell
Hunter, Jeffry, 18 August 1720, age 12, William Wallis

SOMERSET COUNTY

Jackson, John, 20 June 1727, age 11, Patrick Mathews, "Imported into this Country in the Sloop Called the Manocan, James Lindow, Commander"

Johncock, Richard, 12 June 1677, age 14, Thomas Manlove

Johnson, Edward, 9 August 1699, age 16, James Round

Johnson, Henry, 8 August 1699, age 14, Benjamin Sawyer

Johnson, Margrett, 13 March 1677, age 15-18, William Stevens

Johnston, John, 11 June 1701, age 15, Edward Stockdale

Keiton, John, 12 March 1701, age 14, William Phillipson

Kelley, Richard, 10 January 1699, age 14, Robert Givans, "who was imported in to this Province in the Ship Fisher of Beddiford, Thomas Lashbrooke Commander"

Kelly, James, 13 June 1699, age 10, Isaac Boston

Kennedy, Anthony, 10 January 1699, age 15, Andrew Caldwell, "who saith he was Imported into this Province in the Ship Fisher of Beddeford where of Thomas Lashbrooke is Commander"

Knight, Richard, 14 June 1699, age 17, James Polke

Langford, John, 10 January 1677, age 15-18, James Dashiel

Langley, Henry, 9 January 1672, age 15-18, Owne Mackra

Lawrence, William, 16 June 1719, age 12, Henry Todvins

Linsey, James, 8 August 1692, age 12, Nathaniel Innis, arrived "in ye good shipp Providence of London, Mr. William Mecoy Master"

Lockman, Ann, 13 June 1671, age 8, John Apery

Lowden, John, 10 August 1693, age 14, Major Robert King, arrived "with one Capt. Harris, Wine Shipp"

Lyme, John, 15 January 1690, age not judged, arrived four years earlier, sentenced to seven years, "your poor petitioner was Spiritted out of his native Country unknown to any of his friends and Shipped aboard for this Country as a Servant"

Lyte, John, 9 January 1672, age 14, Charles Ballard

Macalding, John, 8 February 1676, age 13, Nehemiah Covington

Machanlas, John, 10 June 1690, age 15, Coll. David Browne

Mackarell, Archibald, 12 June 1688, age 14, Roger Phillips

Mackarell, Thomas, 12 June 1688, age 10, George Baily

Macklure, Andrew, 10 June 1690, age 14, James Curtiss

Macquid, Daniell, 12 June 1688, age 11, Edward Day

Magge, Richard, 12 April 1716, age 13 "from the arrivall of ye Shipp," William Richardson

Magguier, Thomas, 11 August 1708, age 13, Widdow Polke, "adjudged by ye Court heere to be 13 years of agge Last May 1708"

SOMERSET COUNTY

Mahanne, Teigue, 8 August 1699, age 17, Thomas Shaw
Makalegan, Hugh, 12 June 1688, age 12, Robert King
Manns, Samuell, 8 August 1699, age 13, William Round
Marcey, John, 14 September 1703, age 11, William Round
Marchment, Samuell, 12 June 1677, age 18-22, Capta. Thomas Jones
Marsh, George, 8 June 1675, age 15-18, Daniell Curtis
Martin, Edward, 23 June 1720, age 12, Lewis Jones
Mathewes, Mary, 8 November 1670, age 18-22 "in January last,"
    William Furnis
Matthason, John, 14 March 1699, age 12, Mrs. Sarah Luffe
Matthews, Richard, 8 August 1692, age not judged, Thomas Fenix,
    "came in a sloop from Jamaica Capt. Stephen Sargeant Master"
Matthews, William, 21 November 1721, age 12, Moses Fenton
McCloster, Alexander, 12 June 1700, age 13, William White
McCrealey, Alexander, 11 June 1700, age 13, Sampson Allin
McReyley, Andrew, 11 June 1700, age 11, Thomas Shaw
Meady, William, 12 March 1701, age 12, Natha. Hopkins
Meclaster, Patrick, 9 August 1692, age 17-18, Coll. David Browne
Mercer, Gabriell, 8 June 1675, age under 18, Abigall Kibble, "widowe"
Merretts, Benjamin, 10 August 1675, age 10, Benjamin Sumners
Metcap, Abraham, 6 February 1677, age 15-18, John Panther, master
    agreed to "noe longer than" six years
Mill, James, 11 June 1700, age 15, Samuell Collins Gent.
Moore, Edward, 8 August 1699, age 16, George Trewitt
Moore, Edward, 14 September 1703, age 14, Adam Spence
Morgan, John, 12 March 1672, age 14, Richard Ackworth
Mudford, Thomas, 10 January 1677, age 15-18, Peter Parsons
Mulhane, Andrew, 13 August 1700, age 13, Teague Riggan
Mullahanne, John, 7 February 1699, age 14, John Panter, "who was
    imported into this Province in the Ship Fisher of Bedeford
    where of was Commander Thomas Lashbrooke"
Murfee, Morris, 14 June 1699, age 11, William Bounds
Murrah, Timothy, 13 June 1699, age 14, Samuell Handy
Murrey, Daniel, 13 June 1699, age 15, Isaac Covington
Mybote, Ruth, 12 June 1677, age 18-22, Stephen Cannon
Nevill, Augustin, 12 June 1700, age 15, William Alexander Junr.
Nichollson, William, 13 March 1677, age 15-18, William Greene
Nichols, Robert, 9 June 1691, age 16, Major Robert King, "Came into this
    County with one Capt. John Jury Comander of the shipp Mary"
Norris, Hannah, 11 June 1689, age 7, Robert King

Obryan, Bryan, 13 August 1700, age 12, Isaac Horsey
Odougherty, James, 8 August 1692, age 16, Major Robert King, arrived
    "in the good Shipp Katherine of London Derry whereof was
    Master Captain Crookshanks"
Oliver, William, 11 June 1700, age 11, Ruth Heydon
ONeale, Patrick, 8 August 1699, age 16, Robert Collier
Parker, John, 6 February 1677, age 12, Francis Jenckins
Parker, Mary, 14 August 1677, age 15-18, William Stevens
Peirce, John, 12 August 1701, age 12, James Givan
Periman, Mary, 12 November 1672, age 16, Randall Revell, assigned to
    Katherinne Revell
Poe, John, 20 June 1727, age 13, John Evans Senr., "Imported into this
    Country in the Ship Called St. Turin, Edward Lows, Commander"
Power, George, 8 February 1676, age 18-22, Captn. William Colebourne
Price, Edward, 8 June 1697, age 10, Coll. David Browne
Prin, Richard, 12 March 1672, age 13, Lewin Denwood, ordered "to goe
    along with his master" and "serve according to order of Virginia"
Proofe, John, 14 June 1699, age 14, George Betts
Read, Calvin, 11 June 1672, age 21-22, Henry Boston, five years
Rennold, William, 17 August 1725, age 9, Coll. Arnold Elzey, "who was
    Imported into this County in the Ship Called the Mungummery"
Rigan, Thomas, 14 March 1699, age 10, Woney Mtt Clemy, "who was
    imported into this Province in the Ship James and Mary of Bristoll
    where of was Commander Jeremiah Peirce"
Roach, Morris, 13 June 1699, age 14, George Trewitt
Roberts, Anne, 8 June 1675, age 11-12, Samuell Long
Rosse, Walter, 8 June 1675, age 15-18, David Browne
Sawell, Thomas, 4 September 1666, age 17, Randall Revell, seven years
Screene, William, 8 June 1675, age 14-15, John Bossman
Shaw, Dennis, 14 March 1699, age 10, William Pearson, "who was
    imported into this Province in the James and Mary of Bristoll
    where of was Commander Jeremiah Peirce"
Sherwine, Thomas, 10 August 1697, age 10, Nehemiah Covington, "who
    was brought into this Province in the ship Ruby of White Haven"
Sherydine, Francis, 8 June 1697, age 15, Coll. David Browne
Short, Edward, 8 August 1699, age 14, Daniel Jones
Silverthorn, Sebasthan, 20 August 1720, age 13, Robert Mills
Smith, Adam, 13 June 1699, age 7, Affradozie Johnson
Smith, Elizabeth, 14 August 1677, age 15-18, John Williams
Smith, John, 8 August 1676, age 12, John Bound

Smith, Mary, 13 June 1699, age 19, Nehemiah Covington
Smith, Robert, 8 February 1676, age 13-14, Lazarus Madux
Spencer, Henry, 17 June 1719, age 9, John Gray
Spencer, John, 18 November 1718, age 11, Thomas La (?)
Steward, Alexander, 12 March 1701, age 13, Samuell Hopkins Junr.
Steward, Peter, 13 June 1699, age 15, Edward Stockdell
Stone, William, 8 June 1675, age 15-18, Nehemiah Coventon
Swillivan, John, 11 June 1700, age 12, Widdow Catlin
Tayler, Thomas, 9 August 1699, age 14, Thomas Ralph
Taylor, John, 8 June 1675, age 18-22, William Planner
Teage, Edward, 10 November 1674, age 14, Thomas Jones
Thomas, Edward, 13 June 1699, age 10, John Oulon
Thomson, George, 19 November 1718, age 8-9, Alexander Carlisle
Thomson, William, 8 June 1708, age 11, Christopher Nutter
Tomlinson, Mary, 9 August 1699, age 20, John Ellis
Troughten, Roger, 8 February 1676, age 14, David Browne
Tumblesonne, Henry, 8 February 1676, age 10, Ambrose London
Wall, Alice, 13 June 1699, age 15, Thomas Dashell
Ward, John, 12 March 1700, age 11, Richard Jefferson
Warner, John, 8 August 1671, arrived 12 November 1670, age not judged,
    Richard Ackworth, "he desires his service" for seven years
Warricke, William, 12 March 1672, age 18-22, Marke Cordin, presented
    by Nicholas Fountaine
Waters, Patrick, 18 June 1723, age 13, John Scott Gent., " being Imported
    into this County in the Ship Speedwell, Capt. Lanslott Speding,
    Commander"
Wheetly, Edward, 9 March 1698, age 14, Thomas Wilson, adjudged on
    same day "of his seven daies runaway time"
Williams, Elizabeth, 14 March 1671, age not judged, Christopher Nutter
Williams, William, 22 June 1720, age 14 "ye 28th day of last March,"
    James Curtiss
Wilson, Izabell, 11 June 1689, age 16, John Bounds
Wilson, Thomas, 11 June 1706, age 14, William Bavinster
Woollard, John, 14 August 1677, age 18-22, George Johnson
Young, John, 18 June 1718, age 11, Doctor Shervin, eleven years
_____ , _____ , 10 June 1702, age 13, George Betts Junr.

SOMERSET COUNTY

Worshippfull Commissioners	Servants
Ballard, Charles, Capt., Major	Banes, Byford, Lyte
Ballard, Henry, Capt., Coll.	
Boston, Henry	Read
Bozeman, John	Screene
Brereton, William	
Browne, David, Capt., Coll.	Cray, Greham, Machanlas, Meclaster, Price, Rosse, Sherydine, Troughten
Caldwell, John	Rathbone
Colebourne, William, Capt., Coll.	Ashley, Power
Cornish, John, Maj.	
Dashiell, George, Maj., Coll.	Cartee
Dashiell, James	Langford
Dashiell, Mitchell	
Dashiell, Thomas	Wall
Dixon, Thomas, Capt.	Campison, Carr
Edgar, John	
Elzey, Arnold, Capt.	Crary, Rennold
Fassitt / Fawcett, William, Capt.	
Franklin, John, Maj., Capt.	
Gale, George, Maj., Coll.	
Gillis, Thomas, Capt.	
Gray, Joseph	
Handy, Isaac	
Handy, John, Capt.	
Handy, Samuell	Benger, Murrah

30

SOMERSET COUNTY

Worshippfull Commissioners	Servants
Hatfield, James	
Hopkins, Samuell	Steward
Horsey, Isaac, Capt.	Bryan, Crawford
Horsey, Stephen	
Howard, Edmund	
Innis, William	
Jenckins, Francis	Parker
Johnson, George	Bayley, Cawdrey, Cooke, Woollard
Jones, James	
Jones, John, Capt.	Camble
Jones, Thomas, Capt.	Marchment, Teage
Jones, William	
King, John, Capt.	
King, Robert, Major, Coll.	Lowden, Makalegan, Nichols, Norris, Odougherty
Lane, William, Capt.	
Layfield, George, Esqr.	
London, Ambrose, Major	Bradley, Tumblesonne
Luffe, Stephen, Capt.	
Martin, James, Capt.	
McClester, Joseph, Capt.	
Newbold, Thomas	Fraser, Grant
Planner, William, Capt.	Taylor
Purnell, John	
Rackliffe, Charles, Capt.	

SOMERSET COUNTY

Worshippfull Commissioners	Servants
Rice, Nicholas	
Robinson, William	
Round, Edward, Capt.	
Round, James	Campbell, Johnson
Scarbrough, Matthew	
Scott, John, Capt.	Waters
Smith, Edward	Godfrey
Smith, Henry, Capt.	Benson, Browne
Smith, John, Capt.	
Smith, Thomas	
Stevens, William	Highway, Johnson, Parker
Stockley, John	
Stoughton, William, Esqr.	
Tearl, Bryant	
Thorne, William, Capt.	
Venables, Joseph	Aitchsunne
Wailes, Benjamin	
Weedon, James	
West, John, Capt.	
White, John	Gibbons
Whittington, William, Lt. Coll.	
Williams, Thomas	
Wilson, David, Capt., Coll.	
Winder, John, Capt.	Clark
Wolford, Roger	

SOMERSET COUNTY

Year	White	Negro	Year	White	Negro	Year	White	Negro
1666	1	0	1692	7	0	1714	0	7
1667	0	0	1693	2	0	1715	1	3
1668	0	0	1694	3	0	1716 *	1	2
			1695	0	0	1717	0	0
1670	2	0	1696	1	1	1718	5	8
1671	3	0	1697	4	1	1719 *	2	26
1672	10	0	1698	3	1	1720	8	29
1673	1	0	1699	64	2	1721	1	7
1674	4	0	1700	21	0	1722	0	1
1675	21	0	1701	8	1	1723	1	4
1676	10	0	1702	2	2	1724	1	3
1677	18	2	1703 *	3	0	1725	2	4
			1704	0	1	1726	0	22
1683	0	0	1705	0	0	1727	2	18
			1706	3	1	1728	0	15
1685	2	0	1707	0	0	1729	0	11
1686	0	0	1708	7	4	1730	0	13
1687	0	0	1709	2	5	1731	0	5
1688	5	1	1710	0	2	1732	0	8
1689	4	0	1711	0	0	1733	1	16
1690	4	0	1712	0	1	1734	0	20
1691	2	0	1713	0	6	Total	242	253

* plus one Indian

TALBOT COUNTY

Abott, Mary, 21 January 1679, age 14, John Standly, eight years
Abraham, Nicholas, 16 March 1680, age 19, James Hall
Adaneck, Philip, 21 January 1679, age 13, Thomas Roe, nine years
Addison, Joseph, 15 March 1670, (age 14), George Sprouse, seven years
Addisson, Margaret, 2 June 1719, age 12, William Grace
Agbester, Thomas, 21 June 1698, age 19, William Troath
Aheire, John, 15 June 1680, age 18, Stephen Durden
Aires, Samuell, 20 June 1699, age 10, Francis Porter
Alawertey (?), Denis, 28 February 1678, age 18, Clement Sailes, six years
Alea, John, (torn) June 1683, age 16, William Sharpe
Alexander, Elizabeth, 19 March 1700, age 22, Ralph Dawson
Allexander, John, 21 November 1676, age 6, Walter Dickinson,
        sixteen years
Anderson, Elizabeth, 15 June 1680, age 13, Robert Knap
Ansley, Rebeka, 17 August 1680, age 15, Capt. William Leeds
Armstrong, Elizabeth, 15 June 1675, (age 14), James Scott, eight years
Armstrong, John, 16 March 1680, age 15, Nicholas Bartlett
Artigall, Timothy, 19 February 1679, age 19, John Dickenson, six years
Ashley, William, 16 March 1680, age 14, John Rousbey
Ashwood, Richard, 19 February 1679, age 14, Cornelius Mulraine,
        eight years
Austin, Edward, 28 February 1677, age 16, Richard Carlton, seven years
Austin, Richard, 16 March 1669, (age 15-18), John Kinemant, six years
Axton, George, 16 June 1668, (age 15-18), Thomas Hopkins, six years
Baily, Elizabeth, 16 February 1669, (age 15-18), William Lewis, six years
Baldin, Michaell, 21 March 1699, age 12, Dennis Hopkins, Senr.
Barden, Mark, 20 June 1699, age 17, Henry Carter
Barker, John, 21 June 1670, (age 13), Steephen Tully, eight years
Barkey, Richard, 16 February 1669, (age 13), James Hall, eight years
Barnes, Thomas, 21 December 1675, age 12-13, George Cowley,
        "to serve until" age 22
Barnett, William, 16 March 1680, age 16, Emanuell Jenkinson
Barnett, William, 20 September 1698, age 20, Phillip Conniers
Barnin, Phillip, 21 November 1704, age 13, William Turbutt
Barrett, Edward, 15 June 1675, (age 15), Jonas Davis, seven years
Barrett, Thomas, 15 June 1675, (age 14), Thomas Hurley, eight years
Barrey, Garrett, 20 June 1699, age 12, Morris Slaney
Barrick, John, 17 January 1665, age under 15, Henery Coursey, seven
        years, "to bee free" 29 November 1672

Barwith, David, 17 December 1678, age 14, Joseph Jane, eight years
Bather, John, 5 June 1716, age not judged, Margaret Millington,
    "the boy alleadging that he had Indentures for nine years"
Baxter, Benony, 28 February 1677, age 16, Edward Man, seven years
Baxter, Robert, 16 January 1684, age 21, Capt. Librey
Bayley, Edward, 20 June 1699, age 14, John Maton
Bayley, William, 20 June 1699, age 14, Andrew Price
Bayly, Thomas, (torn) 1683, age 10, Stephen Durden
Baynard, John, 16 June 1685, (torn)
Beares, Joseph, 26 February 1684, age 12, William Troth
Becham, Jarvis, 15 June 1675, (age 18-22), Richard Carlton, six years
Bell, Edward, 16 June 1668, (age 14), Robert Knappe, seven years
Belloney, Oney, female, 19 August 1673, age 18, Richard Royston,
    six years
Bennett, John, 16 January 1684, age 17, William Younge
Berkley, Thomas, 15 June 1675, (age 18-22), John Wright, six years
Bernocke, James, 17 February 1685, age 11, Edward Mann
Beron, James, 21 November 1704, age 14, Daniell Sherwood
Berrey, Edmund, 21 March 1699, age 13, Ralph Dawson, Senr.
Berry, David, 21 June 1698, age 13, William Scott
Berry, Elizabeth, 19 August 1701, age 12, Robert Sands
Berry, Elliner, 25 May 1689, age 15, Samuell Abott
Bethorne, Mary, 25 August 1688, age 4, Thomas Hoggins
Bishopp, James, (torn) 1683, age 14, John Alexander
Bissett, Thomas, 19 June 1666, age 18, Christopher Watters
Bissey, Thomas, 7 January 1671, (age 12), Henry Willcokes, nine years
Black, Alexander, 19 March 1700, age 16, Capt. John Davis
Blacke, Peter, 16 (torn) 1696, age (torn), Christopher Santee
Blake, David, 19 March 1700, age 16, William Allen
Boholly, Darby, 20 June 1699, age 13, Robert Jadwin
Bolt, Thomas, 15 June 1675, (age 18-22), John Slatter, six years
Boone, Nicholas, 18 December 1677, age 14, Joseph Wickett, eight years
Booth, John, 17 June 1679, age 14, John Edmondson
Borfell, Thomas, 30 July 1717, age 14, Rev. Henry Nicolls, eight years,
    "the arriving of the Vessell was the fifteenth of April last past"
Borman, John, 20 June 1676, age 18, John Keinemont, six years
Bostick, Simon, 20 June 1699, age 11, John Wooters
Boune, Edward, 15 June 1669, (age 15-18), Henry Hawkins, six years
Bower, James, 20 September 1698, age 20, Thomas Emmerson
Bowman, Ann, 20 August 1678, age 15, Capt. George Cowley, seven years

TALBOT COUNTY

Bowne, William, 16 November 1669, (age 13), Richard Gorsuch,
eight years

Boyce, Timothy, 21 June 1698, age 14, James Berry

Boyear, John, 30 April 1678, age 20, John Whittington, six years

Bracha, Christopher, 16 December 1679, age 21, Dennis Hopkins

Bradberry, Joseph, (torn) 1683, age 12, Thomas Bowdle

Bradley, Francis, 20 January 1680, age 15, Nicholas Broadaway

Braman, William, 4 March 1729, age 14, Joshua Grason

Brasse, Joseph, 16 March 1669, (age 7), Richard Lee, fourteen years

Breerly, William, 20 June 1699, age 7, Michaell Russell

Brenock, James, (torn) 1685, age 13, Robert Harrison

Brewarton, Thomas, 15 June 1675, (age 18-22), Petter Sides, six years

Brey, James, 21 June 1698, age 14, Matthew Eareckson

Briant, John, 16 August 1681, age 17, John Numan

Briges, John, 20 June 1676, age 13, Thomas Emerson, nine years

Brindeuill, John, 16 March 1680, age 14, John Jadwin

Brine, Mary, 15 June 1675, (age 14), George Rollins, eight years

Brocke, Squire, (torn) 1683, age 14, Francis Morley

Brookes, John, 18 February 1673, (age 15), Isack Abrahames, seven years

Brookes, John, 19 March 1700, age 9, Jacob Bradberry

Browne, Henry, 30 April 1678, age 12, Timothy Wyatt, ten years

Browne, John, 19 March 1672, age 9, Richard Wooleman,
thirteen years

Browne, John, 11 April 1676, (age 12), Robert Knap, ten years

Browne, Margarett, 15 June 1675, (age 18-22), John Newman, six years

Browne, Thomas, 18 January 1687, age 13, Samuel Abbott

Browne, Thomas, 21 June 1698, age 15, William Harrison

Brumley, King, 4 March 1718, age 13, Thomas Eubanks, Senr.

Bryan, Dennis, 19 March 1700, age 13, Richard Moore

Bryan, Edward, 19 March 1689, age 7, John Lane

Bryan, John, 19 March 1700, age 12, Joseph Gregory

Bryan, John, 2 June 1730, "acknowledging that he is" age 18-19,
James Bartlett, "brought from Ireland without Indenture," ordered
to serve six years "from the time of his arrival in this province"

Bryan, Margrett, 19 March 1689, age 9, John Lane

Bryan, Mary, 16 June 1685, age 7, John Mullikin

Bryan, Mary, 21 November 1704, age 15, Nicholas Lurkey

Bryan, Michaell, 21 September 1708, age 14, Richard Bennett

Bryan, Roger, (torn) 1682, (torn), William Troth

TALBOT COUNTY

Bryan, Thomas, 20 June 1699, age 16, Susanna Harris
Bryant, Dolbey, male, 18 December 1677, age 14, Alexander Muretter,
    eight years
Bryant, James, 30 April 1678, age 11, Hugh Sherwood, eleven years
Bryon, Darby, 17 January 1682, age 13, James Hall
Bryon, William, 21 June 1698, age 18, Lewis Derochburne
Bubbey, William, 16 March 1680, age 13, Thomas Masterman
Burcher, John, 18 January 1670, (age 14), Natha: Evitt, seven years
Burdin, John, 17 August 1686, age 12, George Robins
Burgis, John, 21 January 1668, age 16, William Lewis, seven years
Burk, David, 21 June 1699, age 13, Ralph Stevenson
Burke, Richard, 19 March 1700, age 16, Robert Ungle
Burne, James, 19 March 1700, age 13, Richard Hammond
Burrowes, Joseph, 17 February 1685, age 18, Capt. Alexander
Burt, John, 20 June 1699, age 12, George Vanderford
Burton, James, 19 August 1673, age 20, John Ingram, six years
Butler, Elizabeth, 14 January 1688, age 14, Thomas Siffells (?)
Butler, John, 16 June 1685, age 17, John Clift
Butter ___, Isabella, 15 September 1702, age 15, George Bowes
Butterfield, Katherine, 20 June 1699, age 18, Edward Brown
Buttler, Hugh, 15 March 1663, age 15, William Taylor, six years
C _____, Mary, 17 June 1701, age 16, Edward Elliott
Calahaune, Darby, 19 March 1700, age 16, Thomas Thomas
Cale, Dennis, 20 June 1699, age 15, Richard Jones, Senr.
Cale, Humphrey, 20 June 1699, age 18, Edward Brown
Calmore, Alexander, (torn) November 1684, age 16, David Johnson
Camell, Ann, 30 April 1678, age 12, George Allembey, ten years
Cannon, Henry, 18 January 1681, age 16, James Scott
Cante, Dennis, 17 February 1685, age 16, Anthony Mayle
Cante, John, (torn) 1685, age 11, Samuell Worsley
Carenir (?), Patrick, 19 March 1700, age 14, Margaret Meends
Carier, William, 21 January 1668, (age 18-22), Henery Haukins, six years
Carlton, Elizabeth, 27 August 1675, (age 18-22), Thomas Taylor, six years
Carmon, Darby, 20 June 1699, age 13, William Register
Carnell, Robert, 16 March 1680, age 16, John Miller
Carr, John, 20 June 1699, age 11, Ralph Dawson
Carre, Andrew, 15 June 1675, (age 18-22), John Kinemont, six years
Carrell, Daniell, 19 March 1689, age 15, Richard Swetnam
Carrell, Joan, 20 June 1699, age 18, Bryan Shield
Carrell, Phillip, 20 January 1680, age 14, Patrick Mullik

Carte, Elinor, 21 June 1698, age 17, Dennis Hopkins
Cartee, John, 21 March 1699, age 12, William Hemsley
Cartee, Timothy, 17 June 1701, age 14, Michaell Kerby
Carter, Owen, 20 June 1699, age 18, John Dickinson
Caryn, John, 19 March 1700, age 17, John Sherwood
Casheen, Dennis, 21 June 1699, age 13, John Morgan
Caugholly, Daniell, 20 June 1699, age 18, Isaac Winchester
Cavenan, Catherine, 21 March 1699, age 18, Laurence Knowles
Challer, John, 15 June 1669, (age 15-18), Jonah Sibery, six years
Chambers, Charles, 20 June 1682, age 15, Peter Denny
Chambers, Richard, 15 March 1698, age 12, Volentine Carter
Chambers, Thomas, 18 January 1687, age 14, Samuel Farmer
Chapman, Mary, 18 August 1702, age 14, William Harrison
Chatterton, Thomas, 18 March 1679, age 14, James Murphew, eight years
Chicke, Mary, 15 August 1665, age 16, Richard Gorsuch, six years
Chrissison, Elias, 17 June 1679, age 17, Maj. William Coursey
Christian, Thomas, 4 March 1718, age 14, John Willson
Clark, Richard, 20 June 1699, age 17, Henry Frith
Clarke, Henery, 21 March 1668, age 16, Trustrum Thomas
Clarke, Robert, 16 March 1680, age 16, Robert Kemp
Clasbook, John, 15 March 1681, age 16, John Hollingsworth
Claxon, William, 21 January 1679, age 14, Edward Elliott, eight years
Clemont, John, 15 June 1686, age 15, William Berry
Cloake, Maurice, 20 June 1699, age 15, Andrew Price
Clohosy, Thomas, 20 June 1699, age 18, Bartholomew Hayes
Cockraine, Edward, 16 February 1687, age 8, Cornelius Mulraigne
Coffey, Phillip, 20 June 1699, age 17, William Osbourne
Cohen, Nicholas, 17 December 1678, age 14, William Evanth, eight years
Cole, John, 17 January 1665, age under 14, Seth Forster, seven years,
      "ordered to serve till" 29 November 1672
Coller, Thorston, 21 July 1668, (age 15-18), Walter Dickenson, six years
Collohan, Dennis, 21 June 1698, age 14, Benjamin Peck
Colssock, Edward, 15 January 1689, age 16, Thomas Yewell
Coltman, Ann, 15 June 1686, age 15, Edward Elliott
Colton, Marmaduke, 19 June 1688, age 15, Robert Macklin
Coming, Miles, 19 March 1689, age 15, Ralph Dawson
Commyford (?), James, 18 June 1700, age 13, Matthew Errickson
Condell, James, 19 March 1700, age 10, William Scott "of Wye"
Conder, Daniel, 21 June 1698, age 14, Sarah Godard

TALBOT COUNTY

Connar, Hugh, 17 September 1700, age 15, Richard Bennett
Connaugh, Dennis, 20 June 1699, age 14, Hugh Elbert
Connell, Matthew, 19 March 1700, age 13, Edward Combes
Connelley, Cornelius, 16 (torn) 1696, age (torn), Robert Blu (torn)
Conner, Arthur, 20 June 1699, age 18, Michaell Mackguinny
Conner, Dennis, 21 March 1699, age 5, John Wells, presented by
    Tobias Wells, his brother
Conner, Joan, 20 June 1699, age 13, William Harriss
Coockoo, Joseph, 21 January 1701, age 16, John Keld
Cooper, Henry, 25 October 1662, (age 12), Henry Coursey, nine years
Cooper, William, 21 June 1681, age 15, John Edmondson
Corneene, Cornelius, 17 January 1682, age 16, Oliver Millington
Cossen, Richard, 16 March 1669, (age 15-18), Richard Howard, six years
Cotton, Thomas, 19 June 1677, age 17, Mrs. Sarah Hambleton, seven years
Couch, John, 16 February 1669, (age 8), James Ringold, thirteen years
Coughill, John, 20 June 1699, age 11, John Twotle
Coughlin, John, 20 June 1699, age 15, Peter Jolley
Court, Anne, 15 June 1675, (age 14), Francis Brookes, eight years
Cousson, Charles, 19 March 1672, age 17, Seth Foster, seven years
Coutman, Robertt, 15 June 1669, (age 15-18), John Eason, six years
Cowman, Michaell, 21 March 1699, age 17, John King "of Wye"
Cratte, Margrett, 20 June 1699, age 18, John Dawson
Crewes, Robert, 16 March 1680, age 18, Alexander Ray
Crissell, Mary, 18 March 1673, (age 15), Allexander Mackotter,
    seven years
Cristie, George, 18 March 1673, (age 11), Humphry Davenportt,
    eleven years
Crookshank, George, 18 December 1677, age 20, Thomas Emerson,
    six years
Cross, Henry, 16 February 1686, age 16, Loveless Gorsuch
Crow, John, 20 June 1699, age 15, Owen Sulivan
Crowning, John, 20 June 1699, age 18, Richard Hazledine
Crump, Michael, 3 March 1719, age 10, Isaac Dixon
Cubberly, Richard, 20 June 1699, age 16, John Lane
Cuckland, Bartholomew, 20 January 1680, age 11, Henry Allexander
Cullen, Catherine, (torn) August 1699, age 19, William Warner
Cullon, William, 20 June 1676, age 17, Capt. George Cowley, seven years
Cuningham, Morris, 20 June 1676, age 20, Capt. Andrew Skinner,
    six years
Cutter, John, 16 June 1685, age 12, Joseph James

D _____ , Mathew, 19 March 1700, age 15, Arthur Emmery
Daley, Daniell, 19 February 1679, age 15, Cornelius Mulraine, seven years
Daley, Mary, 18 August 1696, age 20, Phillip Connyers
Danielly, John, 20 June 1699, age 15, William Osbourne
Dare, John, 20 June 1699, age 13, William Garey
Darnell, John, 16 December 1679, age 17, Jacob Abrahams
Dasee, Dennis, 16 (torn) 1696, age (torn), Robert Macklin
Davis, Edward, 5 June 1716, age 14, Peter Webb, "he alleges he has"
        Indentures "but cannot now produce them"
Davis, George, 20 June 1676, age 20, Robert Bulling, six years
Davis, John, 21 July 1668, (age 18-22), Howell Powell, five years
Davis, John, 17 June 1673, age 12, William Bishop, ten years
Davis, John, 20 June 1699, age 10, Thomas Donnellan
Davis, Maurice, 23 June 1692, "of age," Robert Grundy
Davis, Robert, 16 February 1669, (age 11), Steephen Whetston, ten years
Davis, William, 17 June 1707, age 13, Joseph Hopkins
Davison, Thomas, 16 March 1669, (age 14), Richard Howard, seven years
Dawes, Dority, 16 January 1684, age 18, William Gary
Dawson, Henry, 27 August 1675, (age 15), William Dunderdell,
        seven years
Dawson, John, 17 January 1682, age 14, Henry Parrett
Dawson, Richard, 17 June 1679, age 18, John Newman
Deacon, John, 14 January 1688, age 14, Francis Neal
Deane, David, 20 June 1699, age 10, Andrew Kinnimont
Deas, James, 16 December 1679, age 18, Walter Ridall
Demshey, Timothy, 20 June 1699, age 10, Vincent Hemsley
Denis, James, 21 March 1671, (age 12), Capt. Denioshen, by Thomas
        Hawkins, nine years
Dennis, James, (torn) November 1684, age 13, Francis Neale
Dennis, John, 20 June 1699, age 22, Richard Purnell
Dent, James, 20 June 1699, age 10, William Dixon
Dent, John, 30 July 1717, age 14, John Valliant
Dent, William, 11 April 1676, (age 15), Ralph Highborne, seven years
Deverie, Allexander, 21 December 1675, age 13-14, Alexander Ray,
        "to serve until" age 22
Devin, John, 21 March 1699, age 11, Matthew Dowler
Devorick, Nicholas, 20 June 1699, age 11, Michaell Russell
Dickson, Abigall, 15 June 1680, age 13, Otwell Bodwell
Dining, Giles, 21 June 1698, age 16, Matthew Reed

TALBOT COUNTY

Dobson, James, 16 June 1685, age 13, Thomas Skillington
Dods, Richard, 18 January 1670, (age 14), Henry Frith, seven years
Dogon, Denis, 17 December 1678, age 17, Thomas Scillington,
    seven years
Doherty, Morgan, 20 June 1699, age 20, Peter Jolley
Donn, John, 15 June 1675, (age 13), Richard Chanler, nine years
Donway, James, 16 June 1685, age 14, William Jones
Dorman, Samuell, 15 March 1663, age 20, Edward Lloyd Esqr., five years
Dowd, James, 21 March 1668, age 18, William Parrott
Dowdell, John, 17 January 1682, age 20, Elizabeth Harris
Dowdey, Austice, 20 June 1699, age 12, Katherine Blaney
Dowlar, Mathew, 16 March 1680, age 16, Capt. Peter Sayer
Driscold (?), Cornelius, 21 January 1679, age 17, William Steevens
Driscoll, Dennis, 20 June 1699, age 10, William Harriss
Driskill, Cornelius, 5 August 1729, age 11, Duglass Chase,
    seven years
Druman, Patrick, 17 January 1682, age 11, James Hall
Dunavan, Daniell, 19 November 1678, age 16, Henry Wollchurch,
    seven years
Dunn, Sarah, 3 March 1719, age 15, John Morgan
Dunnagon, David, 20 June 1699, age 13, Robert Clark
Dunnican, Cornealius, 14 January 1688, age 17, William Bush
Dwane, John, 19 March 1700, age not judged, Andrew Price, servant
    "alleadging that he had an Indenture," ordered that he "have time
    till ye next Court to produce his Indenture"
Dwyer, William, 19 March 1700, age 9, Timothy Lane
Dye, Richard, 20 June 1682, age 15, Peter Denny
Eately, Elizabeth, 22 November 1681, age 13, William Chance
Eaton, Michaell, 16 March 1680, age 13, Ralph Elston
Edwards, Edward, 17 February 1685, age 17, William Combes
Edwards, John, 20 June 1699, age 13, Daniell Clifford
Edwards, Josias, (torn) August 1699, age 20, Laurence Knowles
Edwards, Robert, 20 June 1699, age 7, Christopher Gould
Eley, William, 16 June 1685, age 15, Rowland Robson
Evans, Hugh, (torn) 1683, age 16, Thomas Mountfort
Evans, Thomas, 11 April 1676, (age 15), Richard Gould, seven years
Evans, William, 1 September 1719, age 12, Francis Armstrong
Everatt, George, 14 January 1688, age 16, John Whittington
Fairland, Walter, 20 June 1699, age 10, William Purnell
Faning, John, 21 February 1682, age 16, Robert Macklin

TALBOT COUNTY

Farrell, James, 20 June 1699, age 15, William Scott
Farrell, John, 20 June 1699, age 13, William Dixon
Feilden, Henry, 17 January 1682, age 19, William Wintersell
Fennin, Ellinor, 21 June 1698, age 15, John Wells
Fenwick, Andrew, 18 March 1701, age 14, William Hopper
Fish, Edward, 16 February 1669, (age 15-18), Thomas Powell, six years
Fitz Garrell, William, 20 June 1699, age 15, Richard Purnell
Fitzgarrill, John, 20 November 1705, age 10, Robert Ungle
Fitzgarrill, William, 18 September 1705, age 11, Kathrine Alderne
Fitz Gerrall, _____, (torn) August 1699, age 16, _____ Webb
Fitz Gerrell, James, 21 June 1698, age 14, William Bellplant Junr.
Fitz Patrick, John, 20 June 1699, age 14, Edward Leeds
Flanharon, John, 19 March 1689, age 10, Abraham Morgan
Flecher, Lauranc, 16 March 1669, (age 15-18), John Newman, six years
Fliahartey, John, 18 December 1677, age 16, William Trauth, seven years
Fling, David, 21 June 1699, age 18, Richard Tilghman
Fling, Darby, 20 March 1705, age 18, Richard Tilghman, six years
Fling, Juliana, 21 March 1699, age 13, John Cale
Floid, Honor, 16 June 1685, age 16, Susanah Watts, widow of
     George Watts
Flood, James (?), 17 June 1701, age 15, William Green
Flood, Patrick, 2 June 1724, age not stated, Thomas Taylor, "brought as
     a Servant from Ireland, has served his master five years the time
     limited for Servants not bound by indenture," ordered to serve
     seven years "from the arivall of the Ship in Maryland ye 25th day
     of December 1723"
Floyd, Terrence, 23 June 1692, age 17, Ralph Highbourne
Ford, Marke, 18 February 1673, (age 10), John Pitt, twelve years
Foster, Michell, male, 18 January 1670, (age 10), Thomas Heythcott,
     eleven years
Fowler, Catherine, 20 June 1699, age 13, John Allexander
Fowler, Patrick, 21 June 1699, age 11, Michaell Earle
Frandell, George, 28 February 1678, age 19, James Scott, six years
Frank, Robert, 20 January 1680, age 14, Howell Powell
Frank, William, 16 March 1680, age 16, Obadiah Judkin
Fulton, John, 19 March 1700, age 16, Thomas Bartlet
Futhrop, Ann, 16 February 1669, (age 15-18), James Hall, six years
Gardner, Elizabeth, 19 August 1679, age 17, Robert Noble
Garrath, William, 16 February 1687, age 16, William Dickinson

Gaster, John, 16 January 1684, age 17, Amy Eagle
Gelph, Henery, 21 June 1664, (age 18-22), Joseph Weekes, five years
George, William, 16 November 1669, (age 14), Edward Steevenson,
    seven years
Gerratt, Margarett, 16 June 1685, age 15, Samuell Hatton
Gibbs, Anthony, 14 January 1688, age 10, Andrew Price
Gibson, Edward, 27 August 1675, age 10, Winlock Chrissison,
    twelve years
Gifford, John, 17 January 1682, age 14, John Browne
Gil _____ , Katharine, 16 June 1702, age 18, William Gwinn
Gill, James, 15 June 1675, (age 18-22), William Hambleton, six years
Gilling, Austice, 19 March 1700, age 21, Jasper Hall
Gimits, Samuell, 15 March 1681, age 15, James Derumple
Githings, Prudence, 20 June 1676, age 21, James Murphew, six years
Gittling, William, 30 April 1678, age 18, Ralph Highborne, six years
Glover, John, (torn) 1683, age 14, Coll. Philemon Lloyd
Godard, James, (torn) November 1684, age 13, David Johnson
Godfrey, Edmund, 14 January 1688, age 13, William Belford
Godfrey, Mary, 16 February 1686, age 18, Nicholas Cloudes
Goffe, John, 18 June 1700, age 15, Henry Harriss
Goman (?), James, 17 December 1678, age 19, William Bishop, six years
Gooding, Ann, 15 June 1675, (age 15), Abraham Bishop, seven years
Gorden, William, 20 January 1680, age 17, Walter Dickinson
Gorman, William, 21 June 1699, age 14, Daniell Sherwood
Gouldsberry, Robert, 21 March 1699, age 12, William Jackson
Goult, George, 21 August 1677, age 17, John Jadwin, seven years
Govey (?), Philip, 17 September 1678, age 15, Thomas Taylor, seven years
Graimes, Anne, 16 June 1702, age 14, Joane Moore
Grames, Alexander, 15 June 1686, age 14, Henry Greene
Grant, Jame, 15 June 1669, (age 15-18), Jonah Sibery, six years
Graves, Nath., 17 June 1673, (age 18-22), James Murphew, six years
Green, John, 21 June 1698, age 14, Michael Russe!l
Greenaway, Zouch Allin, 22 March 1665, age not judged, Symen
    Carpender, sold to Thomas South, five years
Greenway, John, 28 February 1678, age 14, Mrs. Mary Tillighman,
    eight years
Gregory, John, 21 June 1670, (age 14), Steephen Tully, seven years
Gregory, Joseph, 20 June 1676, age 16, Clement Saile, seven years
Grey, Daniell, 21 June 1698, age 11, Edward James

Gribble, John, 15 June 1680, age 15, William Bishop
Griffin, Barnett, 16 March 1680, age 15, Capt. Peter Sayer
Grominton, Ann, 29 October 1675, (age 13), Edmond Web, nine years
Groves, Joseph, 18 December 1677, age 15, William Bery, seven years
Grundell, Elizabeth, 18 January 1670, (age 14), William Hambleton,
    seven years
Guordin, George, 19 November 1700, age 16, John Dawson
Guttone, Francis, 18 November 1679, age 13, William Hatfield
Hackett, William, c. 16 January 1668, age not stated, Seth Foster, "bought
    of Capt. John Tully four years ago without Indenture," sentenced
    16 January 1672 to "serve one year more"
Haley, Daniell, (torn) August 1699, age 20, Edmund Goodman
Hall, Charles, 16 March 1686, age 18, John Newman
Hall, Edward, 2 August 1726, age 13, Thomas Ashcroft
Hall, Elinor, 2 August 1726, age 15, Thomas Ashcroft
Hall, Mary, 15 June 1686, age 13, Griffith Jones
Hall, William, 17 February 1685, age 15, William Hackett
Hambleton, James, 20 June 1699, age 12, Benjamin Wilkes
Hamond, James, 15 January 1689, age 15, Thomas Collins
Hanfred, Edward, 18 November 1679, age 12, George Palmer
Hangley, William, 21 January 1679, age 20, John Pitt, six years
Hannisey, Andrew, 20 June 1699, age 18, Richard Woolman
Harley, James, 20 June 1699, age 17, Thomas Thomas
Harley, Michael, 19 March 1689, age 7, Harmon Foote
Harquedan, Marques, 14 January 1688, age 17, Capt. James Murphey
Harris, John, 16 June 1668, (age 15-18), Robert Mackey, six years
Harris, Robert, 19 March 1672, age 15, John Poore, seven years
Harrison, Margarett, 11 April 1676, (age 18-22), John Dickenson, six years
Harvy, James, 21 June 1698, age 11, John King
Haslewood, Samuell, 19 March 1672, age 15, Richard Royston,
    seven years
Hawksworth, George, 16 January 1684, age 13, Peter Sides
Hawksworth, Grace, 17 June 1679, age 12, John Rousby
Haye, Margrett, 21 March 1699, age 17, Christopher Santee
Hayes, John, 21 January 1701, age 10, Rodger Baxter
Hays, Bartholomew, 20 June 1671, (age 14), Bryon Omely, seven years
Hazard, James, 15 June 1675, (age 15), Robert Bryon, seven years
Heays, George, 21 March 1668, age 16, Richard Tilghman
Henderson, Henry, 20 June 1682, age 12, Nathaniell Tucker

Hendrick, Laurence, 20 June 1699, age 13, James Ringgold
Henley, Robert, 21 November 1704, age 12, Edward Leeds
Hensley, Thomas, 18 February 1673, (age 15), Isack Abrahames,
seven years
Herron, William, 19 March 1700, age 13, Richard Daniell
Hewett, Elizabeth, 21 June 1698, age 8, John Dawson
Heyhead, Patrick, 21 June 1698, age 17, Richard Skinner
Hickman, Nathaniell, 19 June 1677, age 14, Mrs. Sarah Hambleton,
eight years
Higgins, John, 17 January 1682, age 14, Michael Russell
Higgins, Nicholas, 21 February 1682, age 10, Richard White
Higley, Edward, 15 March 1681, age 14, Richard Dudley
Hignett, John, 26 February 1684, age 11, John Whittington
Hissok, John, 25 October 1662, (age 15-18), Henry Coursey, six years
Hogard, Richard, 16 March 1669, (age 14), Richard Carter, seven years
Holdgate, John, (torn) 1682, age 14, Richard Parnes
Holland, Robert, 19 January 1686, age 11, John Eason
Holle, Robert, 15 June 1675, (age 18-22), John Easson, six years
Holmes, Francis, 17 August 1680, age 14, George Robotham
Holt, William, 16 December 1679, age 12, Richard Gurling
Holohaune, John, 16 June 1685, (torn), John Younger
Homes, Charles, 20 June 1699, age 12, Peter Harwood
Hord, Richard, 20 June 1676, age 13, Thomas Allexander, nine years
Horne, John, 16 February 1669, (age 11), Anthony Lecountt, ten years
Horsey, John, 1 April 1718, age 14, Edward Lee, "arrived the fifteenth day
of January last past"
Howard, James, (torn) 1698, age 18, John Swallow
Howard, Susanna, 20 June 1699, age 13, John Glover
Howell, Elizabeth, 20 June 1676, age 20, Pittier Sides, six years
Howell, Elizabeth, 16 March 1686, age 18, John Newman
Howgill, James, 20 June 1699, age 15, William Skinner
Huchin, Hugh, 19 June 1677, age 17, William Sharpe, seven years
Huchison, George, 21 September 1675, (age 15), John Hopkinson,
seven years
Hudson, Alexander, (torn) November 1684, age 16, William Sharpe
Hues, Thomas, 13 February 1705, age 16, John Alexander
Huett, Robert, 15 June 1680, age 19, Capt. William Leeds
Hughs, Catharine, 15 June 1708, age 21, Nathaniell Tougle
Hungerly, Timothy, 20 June 1699, age 13, Thomas Bowker
Hunt, Arthur, 17 January 1682, age 14, Howell Powell

Hunter, William, 16 June 1702, age 12, William Scott

Hurd, Robert, 19 March 1672, age 12, John Pawsson, ten years

Hurst, Edmund, 18 January 1687, age 11, John Whittington

Hurt, John, (torn) 1683, age not judged, John Chaires, "judged to serve six yeares only"

Huson, Ellin, 18 June 1672, (age 18-22), John Pitt, six years

Huson, Richard, 15 March 1670, (age 15-18), Joseph Wickes, six years

Hust, Ann, 20 January 1680, age 20, Hugh Dulin

Hutcheson, Thomas, 16 December 1684, age 13, John Dickinson

Hyatt, Edward, 19 March 1700, age 13, Francis Neale

Irish (?), Morris, 15 March 1681, age not judged, William Troth, seven years

Iron, John, 21 June 1699, age 14, Richard Jones Junr.

Isard, John, 15 August 1665, age 15, Richard Gorsuch, six years

Jackson, John, 25 October 1662, age 13, Richard Woleman

Jackson, Richard, 15 March 1687, age 18, Miss Mary Roe

Jeffereys, Edward, 21 June 1687, age 12, James Smith

Jenkens, Thomas, 20 November 1677, age 15, Simon Harris, seven years

Joans, William, 17 August 1669, (age 15-18), Joseph Wickes, six years

Jobbins, Eleanor, 20 June 1699, age 16, Robert Robinson

Jobson, Thomas, (torn) June 1683, age 12, John Newman

Johnson, John, (torn) August 1699, age 17, William Ridgway

Johnson, William, 21 January 1668, (age 14), Henery Haukings, seven years

Johnson, William, 20 June 1676, age 17, James Hall, seven years

Jones, Charles, 15 March 1663, (age 14), Andrew Skinner, seven years

Jones, Clement, 15 March 1663, (age 12), Andrew Skinner, nine years

Jones, Thomas, 18 February 1673, (age 15), William Godard, seven years

Jones, William, 15 June 1680, age 13, Thomas Godard

Jones, William, (torn) 1683, age 18, William Dickinson

Jones, William, 21 November 1704, age 11, William Shanahawne

Jues, Robert, 20 January 1680, age 14, Richard White

Jump, Bennett, 15 March 1687, age 12, Alice Rich

Karron, Lawrence, 21 June 1698, age 14, Francis Steevens

Kashle, William, 15 June 1675, (age 13), James Hall, nine years

Keefe, Cornelius, (torn) 1682, (torn)

Keen, Moses, 20 June 1699, age 10, John Leonard

Keene, Thomas, 17 June 1673, (age 14), William Gary, eight years

Kellegan, Hugh, 20 June 1699, age 22, John Davis

Kelley, Margrett, 20 June 1699, age 14, Bryan Shield
Kelley, Owen, 21 June 1698, age 14, William Hemsley
Kelley, Timothy, 25 (torn) 1698, age 16, Robert Grundy
Kenede, John, 17 January 1682, age 17, John Dowty
Kenedy, Dennis, 21 March 1699, age 10, John Evans
Kenneday, Garrett, 20 June 1699, age 13, Thomas Robins
Kenney, John, 20 August 1700, age 11, Michaell Earle
Kenny, Martin, 20 June 1699, age 14, John Long
Kerby, Edward, 16 March 1680, age 14, Joseph Padley
Key, Thomas, 20 June 1676, age 15, Edward Elliote, seven years
Kieve, David, 20 June 1699, age 12, James Auld
Killingsworth, Isacke, 15 August 1676, age 17, John Day, seven years
Kimberly, Dennis, 21 February 1682, age 16, Thomas Vaughan
King, James, (torn) June 1683, age 19, John Poore
King, Jane, 18 March 1684, age 18, Albert Johnson
Kinnett, William, 19 March 1700, age 12, William Hopper
Knewstis, Edward, 17 June 1679, age 14, William Prouth
Knowles, Lewis, 15 June 1675, (age 18-22), George Watts, six years
Lafield, John, 21 March 1699, age 9, Edward James
Lahay, William, 20 June 1699, age 14, Thomas Eubanks
Lamb, George, 15 June 1680, age 15, William Bishop
Lane, George, 14 January 1688, age 13, Ralph Highboum
Lard, Charles, 17 September 1672, (age 18-22), John Cooper, six years
Lary, Daniell, 19 March 1700, age 11, Andrew Price
Lasy, Diana, 15 June 1675, (age 15), Nicholas Barttlett, seven years
Laton, David, 16 August 1698, age 16, William Dikinson
Laughlin, Hannah, 20 June 1699, age 20, Mary Dabbs
Laurance, William, 17 June 1673, (age 18-22), William Steevens, six years
Lee, Katherine, 20 June 1699, age 22, John Wooters
Lee, William, 16 February 1686, age 13, Andrew Orem
Lewes, Even, (torn) 1683, age 14, Michaell Russell
Lewes, William, 17 August 1680, age 15, George Robotham
Lewis, Edward, 20 June 1699, age 11, Thomas Donnellan
Lewis, William, 19 March 1689, age 15, Thomas Skillington
Libby, John, 20 June 1699, age 14, John Wooters
Limbrey, William, 15 June 1680, age 10, William Allin
Limebridg, Elizabeth, 18 February 1673, (age 15), William Jones,
    seven years
Linch, Martin, 6 November 1722, age not stated, Thomas Bozman,
    five years

TALBOT COUNTY

Linch, William, 21 March 1699, age 12, Anthony Wise
Linehane, Joane, 19 March 1706, "above ye age" 22, Richard Cooper
Little, Elizabeth, 15 June 1675, (age 13), Petter Deney, nine years
Lloyd, William, 18 June 1700, age 14, Nicholas Lowe
Lochey (?), John, 19 November 1678, age 13, Capt. Henry Allexander,
    nine years
Lock, John, 5 August 1729, age 13, Edward Fettrell
Lock, Margaret, 5 August 1729, age 4, Edward Fettrell
Lock, William, 5 August 1729, age 12, Edward Fettrell
Looby, Katherine, 20 June 1699, age 17, Claudius Duhtre
Loss, James, 15 January 1678, age 15, Thomas Youle, seven years
Lowe, James, 18 June 1700, age 13, William Gwin
Lowrey, Alexander, 21 June 1698, age 14, Thomas Hopkins Senr.
Lucas, John, 21 January 1668, age 13, John Barke, nine years
Ludman, James, 21 September 1675, age 7, Thomas Taylor, fourteen years
Lupton, William, 16 March 1669, (age 18-22), Richard Howard, five years,
    sold to Robert Woolderton before 19 August 1673
Macarter, Owen, 16 August 1692, age 19, Judith Numann
Macaune, Daniell, 17 January 1682, age 17, John Mullican
Mac Can, Daniel, 4 March 1729, age 15, William Dobson
Maccartee, Dennis, 23 June 1692, age 16, John Poore
Mackaby, Laughlin, 19 March 1700, age 20, Robert Kent
Mackahuun, Thomas, 19 March 1689, age 11, Richard Swetnam
Mackauliffe, Timothy, 20 June 1699, age 15, Thomas Edmondson
Mackcolloe, Ann, 21 June 1698, age 14, Thomas Skillington
Mackconalow, Philipe, 20 January 1674, (age 15), Richard Gorsuch,
    seven years
Mackcullin, Timothy, 20 June 1699, age 12, John Hunt
Mackdaniel, Edmund, 16 (torn) 1696, age (torn), Jacob Set (torn)
Mackdaniell, John, 19 March 1700, age 11, James Gould
Mackdonalld, Patrike, 20 January 1674, (age 18-22), Richard Gorsuch,
    six years
Mackeelling, George, 18 January 1670, (age 15-18), Thomas Scellington,
    six years
Mackgowen, Jane, 16 August 1698, age 13, William Carr
Mackmalen, Gillilem, 30 April 1678, age 9, Henry Whartton,
    thirteen years
Macknamar, Thomas, 21 June 1698, age 14, John Downes
MackNamara, John, 21 November 1704, age 13, Robert Ungle

TALBOT COUNTY

Mackneile, Christopher, 15 June 1675, (age 18-22), Abraham Bishop,
  six years
Mackrearly, Darby, 20 June 1699, age 16, Thomas Jackson
Magrawe, Grisell, 15 July 1682, age not judged, Richard Gurling
Mahall, James, 21 March 1699, age 20, John Thomas
Mahane, Timothy, 21 June 1698, age 13, William Hemsley
Mahanne, Timothy, 21 March 1699, age 11, John Wilson
Mahawn, Eleanor, 20 June 1699, age 20, James Smith
Makey, Marey, 19 January 1686, age 21, Richard Sweatnam
Maley, Katherin, 20 January 1680, age 16, Thomas Anderson
Malunen, Mathew, 17 February 1685, age 19, Edward Elliot
Maner, Tedy, 14 January 1688, age 17, John Pope
Maney, David, 17 February 1685, age 17, Anthony Mayle
Manhue, Dennis, 30 April 1678, age 17, James Hale, seven years
Mansfield, John, 20 June 1676, age 16, Robert Bulling, seven years
Mansfield, Richard, 30 April 1678, age 17, William Jones, seven years
Marryott, Elizabeth, 18 February 1673, (age 15), Capt. William Leed,
  seven years
Marshall, William, 16 March 1669, (age 11), Dennes Hopkins, ten years
Martin, Jane, 4 November 1729, age 7 "the seventeenth day of July
  last past," Edward Perkins
Martine, William, 23 June 1692, age 19, Isaac Winchester
Massey, Thomas, 19 March 1672, age 14, Capt. William Leeds, eight years
Mathews, Uriah, 17 January 1682, age 17, Joseph Billiter
May, Samuell, 15 August 1665, age 20, Thomas Powell
Maye, John, 16 June 1685, age 14, George Powell
McCartee, James, 19 August 1707, age 19, Arthur Rigby
Mecan, Darby, 20 June 1699, age 16, Robert Blunt
Mecantlis, Thomas, 17 August 1686, age 12, George Mecantlis
Medford, John, 19 June 1677, age 14, William Coursey, eight years
Medrufe, Thomas, 21 January 1679, age 18, John Poore, six years
Meer, John, 17 June 1707, age 12, Joseph Gough
Meicky, Dennis, 19 March 1700, age 17, Edward Griffin
Merritt, John, (torn) 1683, age not judged, Richard Royston, (torn) years
Midleton, Luttner, 19 June 1677, age 21, Edward Elliott, six years
Mikaell, John, (torn) 1683, age 15, Thomas Skillington
Milborne, Thomas, 16 February 1669, (age 11), Thomas Hopkins,
  ten years
Mill, John, 21 June 1698, age 10, Joseph Rodgers
Miller, John, 15 March 1698, age 13, William Dixon

TALBOT COUNTY

Millin, Margrett, 18 January 1687, age 17, William Bexly
Milson, Samuel, 17 June 1679, age 19, Bryon Omaly
Mollony, Michael, 21 March 1699, age 11, Abraham Morgan
Mollony, Patrick, 21 March 1699, age 15, Tobias Wells
Mone, James, 15 June 1675, (age 18-22), William Gary, six years
Moore, Richard, 15 August 1665, age 15, Richard Gorsuch, six years
More, John, 15 June 1675, (age 15), Richard Carlton, seven years
Morris, George, 3 March 1719, age 16, Richard Dudley, seven years
Morris, James, 19 March 1700, age 18, Cornelius Collins
Morrison, John, 16 June 1685, age 13, John Preston
Morrole, Peter, 18 March 1679, age 15, Richard Moore, seven years
Morrow, Chiley, 15 January 1678, age 17, Henry Wollchurch, seven years
Moudy, John, 20 June 1676, age 16, Capt. Petter Sayer, seven years
Mudey, Mary, 16 February 1669, (age 14), Robert Mackey, seven years
Mullikin, Darby, 21 March 1699, age 12, William Hemsley
Mullreane, Dennis, 18 June 1700, age 14, Walter Qinton
Murday, Alexander, 30 July 1717, age 16, Robert Ungle, Esqr.
Murphew, John, 19 November 1678, age 12, Richard Richardson, ten years
Murphey, Cornelius, 16 (torn) 1696, age (torn), Joseph Sandlor
Murphey, Edmund, 16 (torn) 1696, age (torn), William Cleyton
Murphey, John, (torn) 1683, age 16, John Hawkins
Murphey, John, 21 June 1698, age 16, William Steevens Junr.
Murphey, John, 21 June 1699, age 16, Michaell Earle
Murphey, Timothy, 20 June 1699, age 19, John Davis
Murphey, William, 15 March 1687, age 14, Estate of Thomas Taylor
Murphy, Richard, 19 March 1689, age 11, John Boram
Murrey, Katherine, 20 June 1699, age 12, Dennis Connolly
Muruck, Robert, 20 June 1676, age 20, Robertt Parnish, six years
Neale, Morriss, 20 June 1699, age 12, John Pooley
Newell, Edward, 15 June 1675, (age 13), Charles Gorsuch, nine years
Nichallson, John, 16 March 1669, (age 14), Robert Lamden, seven years
Nickson, Margaret, 15 June 1686, age 16, Stephen Durdaine
Ninan, Patrick, 21 June 1699, age 11, Michaell Earle
Nonna, William, (torn) 1683, age 16, Bryan Omaly
Norman, John, 15 June 1686, age 13, Capt. William Combes
Noron, Katherin, 19 February 1679, age 15, Thomas Martin, seven years
Nowler, John, 19 January 1686, age 15, Daniell Glover
Nunna, Morris, 17 February 1685, age 11, John Lane
Obrien, Bryon, 17 December 1678, age 15, William Combes, seven years
O'Daley, John, 21 June 1698, age 17, Mrs. Phebe Bowdle

TALBOT COUNTY

Ogden, Abraham, (torn) November 1684, age 12, John Whittington
Ohagin, John, 3 March 1719, age 14, Richard Dudley
Ohderoh, Margarett, 17 February 1674, age 20, Clement Sailes, six years
Olare, Cornelius, 20 June 1699, age 12, William Skinner
Oliver, Jane, (torn) 1683, age 12, John Stanley
Olley, John, 21 January 1679, age 14, John Hawkins, eight years
Orrison, Lawrance, 17 January 1682, age 14, John Browne
Osbourne, Elizabeth, 20 June 1699, age 15, Jasper Hall
Ouldfield, Henry, 16 January 1672, (age 14), Robert Bulling, eight years
Overman, Jacob, 21 July 1668, (age 15-18), Richard Gorsuch, six years
Oxley, Francis, 18 January 1670, (age 14), Thomas Cox, seven years
Painter, John, 21 June 1698, age 16, Mary Sergant
Pannett, Mabell, 20 June 1676, age 16, Rogger Gress, seven years
Parify, William, 21 February 1682, age 14, Richard Wollman
Parker, John, 18 January 1687, age 12, Francis Harris
Partridge, Cuthbert, 16 November 1680, age 22, Robert Noble
Pattison, William, 15 June 1680, age 15, William Rich
Peace, Edward, 21 June 1698, age 10, Ambros Kinnimon
Perey, John, 1 November 1715, age 14, James Hogell, eight years
Perke, Robert, 15 March 1663, age 14-15, Thomas Hynson, six and a half
    years
Perkins, Thomas, 15 June 1675, (age 13), Richard Bayley, nine years
Perkins, Thomas, 4 March 1718, age 16, Thomas Hopkins
Perry, Hugh, (torn) 1683, age 18, John Hartley
Perry, John, (torn) 1682, age 12, William Dickason
Perry, Petter, 16 March 1669, (age 15-18), William Steephens, six years
Perry, William, 16 March 1669, (age 15-18), William Taylor, six years
Peters, James, 2 June 1724, age not stated, Caleb Eastgate, "brought
    into the Country a Servant by Mr. Robert Alexander," arrived
    1 April 1719, "he had no Indenture neither was he judged at Court
    and he hath honestly served five years," but master "pretends
    to hold him by an Indenture which he knows nothing of," ordered
    to serve six years "according to Indenture"
Philim, Thomas, 19 November 1678, age 14, Joseph Billitor, eight years
Philipes, John, 18 June 1672, (age 15), Richard Gurlling, seven years
Phillips, George, 21 June 1687, age 3, Arthur Emery
Pindergrass, James, 21 March 1699, age 9, William Dickinson
Pittman, William, 15 June 1680, age 16, John Stanley
Plomberton, Pearce, 15 August 1676, age 17, John Edmondson,
    seven years

TALBOT COUNTY

Plunkett, James, 2 June 1730, "acknowledging that he is" age 19-20,
    James Bartlett, "brought from Ireland without Indenture," ordered
    to serve six years "from the time of his arrival in this province"
Pollson, John, 16 June 1668, (age 15-18), William Hamblton, six years
Pooly, George, 18 January 1687, age 15, John Hollingsworth
Poor, Katherine, 15 June 1697, age 17, Ralph Dawson Junr.
Poore, John, 15 September 1668, (age 12), Henry Coursey Esq., nine years
Pott, Henry, 18 January 1676, (age 15), Walter Dikenson, seven years
Poulter, Charles, 15 June 1675, (age 14), William Finey, eight years
Powell, William, 15 August 1676, age 11, Collonel Vincent Lowe,
    eleven years
Powell, William, 20 June 1699, age 15, Jacob Bradberry
Pratt, Gamaliell, 20 June 1699, age 20, Richard Fideman
Price, John, 20 November 1682, age 16, Andrew Price
Prudent, Marjary, 11 April 1676, (age 15), Robert Knap, seven years
Pruit, John, 21 June 1699, age 11, Robert Harriss
Pruitt, William, 15 June 1675, (age 14), Richard Bayley, eight years
Putt, Edward, 6 August 1717, age 17, William Brown
Quinnelly, Patrick, 19 August 1701, age 22, John Leonard
Quirk, John, 25 (torn) 1698, age 18, Robert Grundy
R _____, James, 19 November 1700, age 12, Alexander Ray
Rafes, Elizabeth, 16 February 1686, age 14, Frances Bishopp
Raimus, Hanah, 16 February 1686, age 18, Nicholas Cloudes
Raleigh, Cornelious, (torn) August 1699, age 13, Henry Parrot
Ranfield, Anne, 21 June 1670, (age 14), Steephen Tully, seven years
Readman, Patrick, 20 June 1699, age 17, Isaac Winchester
Reed, John, 15 March 1698, age 10, Volentine Carter
Renge, Francis, 21 August 1677, age 17, George Robins, seven years
Richards, Robert, 18 August 1702, age 10, Francis Sherwood
Richardson, John, 19 March 1672, age 14, Richard Gurling, eight years
Richardson, John, 16 February 1687, age 11, Ralph Burges
Riddle, Andrew, 19 March 1700, age 14, Thomas Jackson
Rider, Simon, 16 December 1679, age not judged, Alexander Cunningham,
    "judged to serve six yeares from April next"
Riding, John, 15 June 1669, (age 14), Robertt Smith, seven years
Rile, Rodger, 20 June 1699, age 11, Richard Hutchins
Rine, Evan, 19 June 1677, age not judged, George Parratt, six years
Rine, Solomon, 15 August 1676, age 17, Thomas Marting, seven years
Ringle, Timothy, 20 June 1699, age 14, Robert Register

TALBOT COUNTY

Roach, John, 16 February 1686, age 14, Francis Sheepeard
Roach, Lawrence, 18 September 1705, age 14, Richard Bennett
Roberd, John, 17 February 1685, age 18, Moses Harris
Robert, Rogger, 18 December 1677, age 16, Micheall Hackett, seven years
Roberts, Francis, 18 February 1701, age 12, Richard Bruffe
Robertt, Henry, 30 April 1678, age 20, William Finey, six years
Robinson, James, 16 June 1685, age 10, Elinor Bradberry
Robinson, Peter, 18 June 1700, age 15, John King
Robinson, Thomas, 16 December 1679, age 19, Joseph Billeter
Robison, Christopher, 21 January 1679, age 17, Denis Hopkins, six years
Roggers, John, 21 June 1670, (age 12), William Charlton, nine years,
    "but his master gave one year of his time"
Rook, John, 20 June 1699, age 20, Sollomon Jones
Rork, Dennis, 21 June 1698, age 19, Edward Elliott Junr.
Ross, John, 20 June 1676, age 18, John Keinemont, six years
Rosseter, Elizabeth, 28 February 1678, age 12, Philip Steevenson,
    ten years
Rouse, William, 16 March 1669, (age 15-18), Joseph Wickes, six years
Rowland, Edward, 21 June 1681, age 13, Doctor Godard
Rush, Margarett, 20 June 1676, age 15, James Hall, seven years
Russell, John, 20 June 1699, age 17, John Burman
Russell, Kathren, 30 April 1678, age 15, Thomas Badell, seven years
Ruth, Thomas, (torn) 1685, age 22, John Power
Ryall, Edward, 18 February 1673, (age 14), Richard Gorssuch, eight years
Ryan, Darby, 19 March 1700, age 12, Jonathan Davis
Ryley, James, 23 June 1692, age 20, Ralph Highbourne
Ryley, John, 19 June 1688, age 10, Peter Sayer
S(?)nennor, Richard, 15 January 1678, age 14, Thomas Jones
Sailling, John, 19 March 1700, age 18, Thomas Yewell
Salter, Francis, 21 June 1699, age 19, John Copedge
Sanders, William, 16 February 1687, age 12, Capt. William Combes
Sanderson, William, 15 March 1670, (age 15-18), Richard Tilghman,
    six years
Satchwell, Mary, 21 June 1698, age 16, David Fairbanck
    eight years
Scolfeild, Elizabeth, 17 January 1682, age 17, William Combes
Scursington, Alexander, 21 June 1698, age 10, John Dawson
Searr, George, 19 January 1686, age 11, John Boram
Senchurch, William, 17 June 1679, age 17, John Edmondson

53

TALBOT COUNTY

Seton, George, 16 February 1669, (age 15-18), Thomas Martin, six years
Sharpe, Petter, 15 June 1669, (age 14), master not stated, seven years
Shaw, Joseph, 21 January 1679, age 15, Francis Mandling, seven years
Shaw, William, 15 September 1702, age 15, Robert Grundy
Shay, John, 21 March 1699, age 12, Richard Austin
Sheffield, Samuell, 20 November 1677, age 13, Richard Jones, nine years
Shehan, Cornelius, 21 June 1698, age 14, Thomas Robins Junr.
Shehan, Thomas, 18 March 1679, age 20, Loveless Gorsuch, six years
Shehawn, John, 20 June 1699, age 14, William Coursey, by Peter Jolley
Shell, Thomas, (torn) November 1684, age 10, Richard Sweatnam
Sheuell, Theophelos, 21 July 1668, (age 15-18), Howell Powell, six years
Shield, Edmond, 20 June 1699, age 15, John Hull
Shore, Jane, (torn) 1698, age 18, John Swallow
Short, Henry, 16 February 1686, age 12, Robert Kempe
Shulahane, Morris, 16 March 1680, age 15, Stephen Durden
Sillcock, William, 18 January 1687, age 19, William Bexly
Simcock, Francis, 15 June 1680, age 13, Otwell Bodwell
Sisson, Edward, 20 November 1677, age 13, Major William Coursey,
    nine years
Skill, Patience, 17 January 1682, age 16, Thomas Martin
Skinner, William, (torn) November 1684, age 16, William Sharpe
Slator, John, 20 January 1680, age 12, John Whittington
Slaughter, Thomas, 3 June 1718, age 9, Richard Coward, (thirteen years)
Smith, Daniell, 15 June 1686, age 14, John Stanley
Smith, Edw:, 15 March 1670, (age 14), Richard Tilghman, seven years
Smith, George, 20 June 1671, (age 14), Henry Coursey, seven years,
    arrived 15 May 1671
Smith, Henry, 18 November 1679, age 12, James Murphey
Smith, William, 23 June 1692, age 16, Edward Elliott
Smith, William, 21 June 1698, age 9, John King
Snodwell, Henry, 16 February 1669, (age 13), Philip Steevenson,
    eight years
Sparkes, Edw., 16 June 1668, (age 15-18), Simond Carpender, six years
Spencer, James, 15 September 1702, age 17, Peter Anderton
Sprignell, John, 15 March 1670, (age 11), Charles Hollinsworth, ten years
Squarne, James, 21 March 1699, age 11, Kenelin Skillington
Squire, James, 18 March 1684, age 11, Daniell Ingerson and
    Henry Snowden
Stafford, Cuthbert, 18 March 1684, age 18, Emanuell Jenkinson

TALBOT COUNTY

Stakely, George, 17 January 1682, age 8, William Dickinson
Stanfield, Joshua, (torn) 1683, age 14, Henry Willchurch
Stanford, John, 19 February 1679, age 16, John Renallds, seven years
Staple, John, 18 June 1706, age 20, Thomas Baxter
Steed, John, 18 March 1679, age 18, Richard Gould, six years
Steephens, John, 21 July 1668, (age 15-18), Walter Dickenson, six years
Steevens, William, 26 February 1684, age 12, Thomas Emerson
Stephens, Joseph, 16 January 1684, age 16, John Harwood
Stevens, Katherine Catterfor, 19 June 1688, age 18, Margrett Peterson
Stoakes, Martha, 15 June 1697, age 16, Thomas Baxter
Stone, Isac, 16 November 1669, (age 13), Simond Steephns, eight years
Stone, Thomas, 15 June 1675, (age 15), Charles Gorsuch, seven years
Stonestreet, John, 18 January 1670, (age 14), Ralph Dawson, seven years
Story, Francis, 16 January 1672, (age 18-22), Richard Carter, six years
Story, Robertt, 15 June 1675, (age 12), John Kinemont, ten years
Story, Thomas, 15 June 1675, (age 15), Bryon Omeley, seven years
Stra (torn), Richard, (torn) 1682, (torn)
Strong, Margery, 23 June 1692, "of age," Robert Grundy
Stuartt, John, 20 January 1674, (age 18-22), Richard Gorsuch, six years
Stulls, John Michael, 3 June 1718, age 9, Richard Coward, thirteen years
Stulls, Mary Katherine, 3 June 1718, age 11, Nicholas Lurtey, eleven years
Sturbridge, Henry, 25 May 1689, age 16, John Coppins
Sulivan, Eleanor, 20 June 1699, age 18, Jacob Bradberry
Sulivan, Judith, 21 June 1699, age 16, Michaell Earle
Sulivan, Mary, 20 June 1699, age 16, Jacob Gibson
Sulivant, Dennis, 20 June 1699, age 9, Timothy Lane
Sullivant, Cornelius, 20 June 1699, age 12, Daniell Nunam
Sullivant, Owen, 21 June 1698, age 17, William Gwin
Suton, John, 18 November 1679, age 17, Bryan Omely
Sweny, Bryon, 21 June 1698, age 13, David Blany
Swifden, Dennis, 19 March 1700, age 9, Thomas Baxter
T __ ner, (torn), 1 March 1720, age 18, John Baggs
Taine, Thomas, 16 June 1668, (age 15-18), Stephen Tully, six years
Talbott, Bryan, (torn) 1685, age 13, Clement Sailes
Taylor, Elizabeth, 30 April 1678, age 13, William Parratt, nine years
Taylor, Mary, 17 February 1674, age 17, John Easson, seven years
Taylor, Samuell, 18 March 1679, age 14, William Wintersell, eight years
Teibets, John, 15 June 1675, William Purrult, (torn) years
Temple, William, 19 March 1700, age 11, Thomas Thomas

Tewell, Patrick, 23 June 1692, age 17, Dennis Hopkins
Thomas, John, 19 August 1701, age 15, Henry Martin
Thomas, Rouland, (torn) 1685, age 18, William Troth
Thompson, Daniell, 17 June 1701, age 10, John Pope
Thongshaw, Ann, 17 August 1686, age 15, Thomas Vaughan
Thornton, Richard, (torn) August 1699, age 18, Richard Carter
Times, Thomas, 16 January 1684, age 8, Clement Sailes
Tison, Nicholas, 17 February 1685, age 12, Simon Harris
Tobe, William, 21 June 1698, age 17, Edmund Goodman
Todd, Francis, 21 March 1671, (age 12), Richard Woleman, nine years
Tomlinson, Thomas, 16 December 1679, age 18, John Haymore
Tompson, John, 28 February 1677, age 17, Edward Man, seven years
Tony, Samuell, 20 June 1699, age 14, William Dixon
Townsloe, Thomas, 21 January 1679, age 14, John Whitington, eight years
Trakey, Thomas, 20 June 1699, age 16, Matthew Eareckson
Turle, W (torn), 1 March 1720, age 14, William Dobson
Turner, Moses, 20 June 1699, age 12, Richard Fideman
Turner, Nathaniell, 19 August 1701, age 20, John Blackwell
Twomey (?), Dennis, 21 March 1699, age 14, Tobias Wells
Upmaygatt, William, 19 June 1688, age 14, Thomas Alcock
Vaughan, Joseph, 18 March 1673, (age 12), Richard White, ten years
Vaughan, Thomas, 18 June 1700, age 13, Mary Serjant
Vouse, Robert, 16 November 1680, age 17, William Wintersell
Wade, John, 21 November 1704, age 12, John Leeds
Waford, Francis, 17 January 1682, age 17, James Scott
Waland, William, 21 June 1698, age 13, Mrs. Catherine Winchester
Wales, John, 18 June 1700, age 13, John Hunt
Waley, Austice, 20 June 1699, age 15, James Scott
Walker, James, 17 June 1679, age 17, Robert Knapp
Walker, John, 16 June 1685, age 12, John Stanley
Walton, John, 15 June 1675, (age 13), Robert Ellis, nine years
Waters, Benjamin, (torn) 1683, age 10, Bryan Omaly
Watkins, William, 1 November 1715, age 14 "the ninth day of March
    next," Joseph Tonnard
Watson, Sarah, 19 March 1700, age 18, William Hambleton
Watts, Margaret, (torn) 1698, age 19, Duncan Monroe
Wattson, Richard, (torn) 1685, age 15, John Dickinson
Wattson, Thomas, 21 January 1679, age 15, John Dowly, seven years
Webster, Margarett, 20 September 1698, age 17, Thomas Marsh

Welahane, James, 20 November 1705, age 12, Isaac Harriss
Welch, Alice, 20 June 1699, age 14, Charles Neale
Welch, Margrett, 20 June 1699, age 12, Robert Stapleford
Welch, William, 21 June 1699, age 16, Thomas Boswick
Wells, William, 25 May 1689, age 14, Thomas Bowdell
Welsh, Edmond, 20 June 1676, age 20, James Scott, six years
Welton, John, 18 August 1702, age 10, Samuell Davis
West, Joseph, 17 August 1680, age 16, George Robotham
Wetherall, Ann, 15 June 1675, (age 18-22), William Finey, six years
Wh _____, Stephen, 1 November 1715, age 15, Daniel Crowley
Whale, Charles, 16 November 1680, age 16, Henry Willchurch
Whaley, John, 19 February 1679, age 13, Thomas Monford, nine years
Whaley, Timothy, 21 July 1668, (age 15-18), Nicholas Holmes, six years
Wharton, John, 16 January 1684, age 11, Walter Quinton
Whaylin, John, 20 June 1699, age 16, Thomas Baxter
White, John, 20 June 1699, age 13, John Hull
White, Michaell, 16 June 1685, age 15, William Dixon
White, Robert or Rogger, 21 January 1668, age 21, John Anderton,
     six years, freed by court 18 November 1673
White, Thomas, 21 January 1679, age 15, Ralph Dawson, seven years
White, Thomas, 16 March 1680, age 17, John Cox
Whitle (?), Jane, 28 February 1678, age 18, Edward Man, six years
Wild, Thomas, 15 June 1675, (age 18-22), Robert Noble and Simon
     Steephen, six years
Wilkinson, Jane, 20 June 1699, age 20, Hugh Sherwood
Williams, Elizabeth, 18 March 1679, age 12, John Poore, ten years
Williams, Mary, 16 February 1686, age 9, Morgin Thomas
Williams, Richard, (torn) 1685, age 20, Stephen Durden
Williams, Thomas, 21 March 1671, (age 10), Robertt Skinner, eleven years
Willson, James, 17 June 1673, (age 15), John Newman, seven years
Willson, Thomas, 15 June 1675, (age 15), John Underwood, seven years
Willsy, John, 16 November 1669, (age 14), Philipe Steevenson,
     seven years
Wilsey, John, 15 March 1663, age 18, Thomas South, five years
Wilson, Ruth, 16 March 1686, age 13, Robert Hawkshaw
Winchester, Jedediah, 16 March 1680, age 17, John Renolds
Winder, James, 21 June 1698, age 13, Thomas Thomas
Winkley, Ann, 16 June 1668, (age 13), Thomas Hopkins, eight years
Winston, George, 18 January 1687, age 11, Walter Quinton

Winton, Elizabeth, (torn) August 1699, age 20, Edmund Goodman
Winttenbothum, Abraham, 21 November 1676, age 13, Thomas Emerson,
     "by his own confession he was thirteen yeares of age on
     May Day last"
Witt, Francis, 15 June 1675, (age 15), Simon Irons, seven years
Witters, John, 16 January 1684, age 10, Clement Sailes
Woline, Floranc, 15 June 1675, (age 18-22), Philip Steevenson, six years
Woodby, William, (torn) August 1699, age 15, Robert Ungle
Worloe, Cornelius, 21 June 1698, age 16, Mary Baggs
Wright, Elizabeth, 15 August 1676, age 14, Mrs. Elizabeth Fesser,
     eight years
Wright, Stephen, 20 June 1682, age 11, Mathias Peterson
Wyate, James, 20 June 1676, age 18, John Poore, six years
Wyn, Margrett, 21 June 1699, age 19, Richard Hammond
Yausler, Lawrance, 17 January 1682, age 19, Ralph Dawson
Yeamons, Thomas, 16 March 1669, (age 14), William Shaw, seven years
Yeoung, Thomas, 17 January 1665, age under 13, Henery Coursey,
     nine years, "to bee free" 29 November 1673
Youngare, John, 18 January 1670, (age 14), Thomas Martin, seven years
Youton, John, 16 January 1684, age 13, Richard Feedimon
(torn), Jane, 15 June 1675, (age 18-22), Richard Gorsuch, six years
_____ , _____ , 15 June 1675, (age 14), Thomas Lewis, eight years
_____ , _____ , 18 January 1676, Simend Stephens and Robert Noble
_____ , _____ , male, 30 April 1678, age 12, William Combes, ten years
_____ , _____ , (torn) 1685, age 17, William (?) Faulkner
_____ , _____ , (torn) 1685, age 15, Thomas Mountfort
_____ , __ritt, (torn) 1685, age 15, John Wotters
_____ , _____ , 16 (torn) 1696, age 13, Thomas Coursey
_____ , _____ , 16 (torn) 1696, age 18, Ralph Dawson, Senr.
_____ , _____ , 16 (torn) 1696, age 20, Arthur Emery
_____ , _____ , 21 June 1699, age 14, James Davis

TALBOT COUNTY

Worshippfull Commissioners	Servants
Benson, Perry	
Bexley, William	Millin, Sillcock
Bishop, William *	Davis, Goman, Gribble, Lamb
Bowdell, Thomas	Bradberry, Wells
Bozman, Risdon	
Bozman, Thomas	Linch
Bullen, John	
Carpender, Symon	Greenaway, Sparkes
Carter, Richard	Hogard, Story, Thornton
Chamberlaine, Samuell	
Clayton, William, Junr.	
Combes, William, Capt.	_____ , Edward, Norman, Obrien, Sanders, Scolfeild
Coppedge, John	Salter
Coursey, Henry, Coll., Esq. *	Barrick, Cooper, Hissok, Poore, Smith, Yeoung
Coursey, Henry, Junr.	
Coursey, William, Maj. *	Chrissison, Medford, Shehawn, Sisson
Cowley, George, Capt.	Barnes, Bowman, Sullon
Davis, John, Capt.	Black, Kellegan, Murphey
Dawson, John	Cratte, Guordin, Hewett, Scursington

59

TALBOT COUNTY

Worshippfull Commissioners	Servants
Elbert, William	
Emerson, Thomas, Major	Bower, Briges, Crookshank, Steevens, Winttenbothum
Finney, William	Poulter, Robertt, Wetherall
Forster / Foster, Seth *	Cole, Cousson, Hackett
Gorsuch, Richard	_____ , Bowne, Chicke, Isard, Mackconalow, Mackdonalld, Moore, Overman, Ryall, Stuartt
Gouldsborough, Nicholas	
Gouldsborough, Robert, Esqr.	
Grundy, Robert, Lt. Coll.	Davis, Kelley, Quirk, Shaw, Strong
Hambleton, William	Gill, Grundell, Pollson, Watson
Hemsley, Philemon	
Hemsley, William, Capt.	Cartee, Kelley, Mahane, Mullikin
Hollyday, James	
Hynson, Thomas *	Perke
James, Edward	Grey, Lafield
Lloyd, Edward, Coll., Esq. *	Dorman
Lloyd, James	
Lloyd, Philemon, Capt., Coll.	Glover
Lowe, Nicholas	Lloyd

TALBOT COUNTY

Worshippfull Commissioners	Servants
Lowe, Vincent, Coll.	Powell
Macklin, Robert	Colton, Dasee, Haning
Mann, Edward	Baxter, Bernocke, Tompson, Whitle
Mayle, Anthony	Cante, Maney
Murphey, James, Capt. *	Harquedan, Smith
Needles, John	
Noble, Robert	Gardner, Partridge, Wilde, _____
Powell, Thomas	Fish, May
Richardson, Thomas	
Ringold, James *	Couch, Hendrick
Robins, George	Burdin, Renge
Robins, John	
Robins, Thomas, Junr.	Kenneday, Shehan
Robotham, George	Holmes, Lewes, West
Roe, Edward	
Sayer, Peter, Maj., Capt.	Dowlar, Griffin, Moudy, Ryley
Sherwood, Daniel	Beron, Gorman
Sherwood, Hugh	Bryant, Wilkinson
Skinner, William	Howgill, Olare

TALBOT COUNTY

Worshippfull Commissioners	Servants
Smith, James *	Jeffereys, Mahawn
Smith, Matthew	
Smith, Robert	Riding
Smithson, Thomas	
South, Thomas *	Greenaway, Wilsey
Steevenson, Phillip	Rossiter, Snodwell, Willsy, Woline
Sybery, Jonathan	Challer, Grant
Tilghman, Richard	Fling, Fling, Heays, Sanderson, Smith
Turbutt, Michael	
Turloe, William	
Ungle, Robert, Esqr.	Burke, Fitzgarrill, MackNamara, Murday, Woodby
Warde, Matthew Tilghman, Coll.	
Wells, John *	Conner, Fennin
Wise, Anthony	Linch
Wollman, Richard	Browne, Hannisey, Jackson, Parify, Todd

* see Kent County

TALBOT COUNTY			TALBOT COUNTY			TALBOT COUNTY		
Year	White	Negro	Year	White	Negro	Year	White	Negro
1662	3	0	1684	24	0	1707	3	0
1663	6	0	1685	35	0	1708	2	0
1664	1	0	1686	25	0			
1665	8	0	1687	17	0	1715	3	0
1666	1	0	1688	14	0	1716	2	0
1667	0	0	1689	14	0	1717	4	0
1668	23	0				1718	7	0
1669	35	0	1692	9	0	1719	6	6
1670	17	0	1693	0	0	1720	2	0
1671	6	0	1694	0	0			
1672	12	0	1695	0	0	1722	1	0
1673	17	0	1696	10	0	1723	0	0
1674	5	0	1697	2	0	1724	2	0
1675	47	0	1698	52	0	1725	0	0
1676	33	0	1699	149	0	1726	2	0
1677	20	0	1700	44	0	1727	0	0
1678	31	0	1701	12	0	1728	0	0
1679	44	0	1702	9	0	1729	7	2
1680	44	0				1730	2	0
1681	9	0	1704	7	0			
1682	33	0	1705	6	0	Total	889	8
1683	20	0	1706	2	0			

Note: No Indians

Burk, Edward, 24 March 1719, age 10, John Cobreath

Clark, Carroll, 28 June 1729, age 14, Captain William Greenwood

Clark, Patrick, 28 June 1729, "twelve years of age on Christmas next,"
    Henry Costin, Junr.

Clark, William, 28 June 1729, age 10, Captain William Greenwood

Cranston, Lewis, 29 March 1729, "seven years and two months old,"
    Samuell Griffith

Croney, Elenor, 28 March 1712, age 22, James Hindman

Farden or Fardin, Martin, 24 March 1719, age 13, Richard Powell,
    indenture "adjudged not good"

Graves, Margarett, 26 August 1712, age 17, Edward Hambleton,
    ordered to serve five years on 26 March 1712

Hart, Patrick, 28 June 1729, "nine years old the seventeenth day of March
    last past," Thomas Burk

Lidden, John, 24 November 1741, age 15 "the eighteenth day of
    November instant," Andrew Jorden

Lindsey, David, 25 March 1713, age 10 "last November," Reverend
    James Hindman

McManns, James, 28 June 1737, age 15 "the first of June Instant,"
    John Williams

Mitchell, Thomas, 27 June 1738, age 14 "the first Day of this Instant June,"
    John Meeds

Ogleby, William, 24 November 1741, age 14 "the twenty fourth day of
    last August," Philemon Green

Packer, John, 23 March 1742, age 14 "the first day of December last,"
    Hawkins Downes

Pattin, John, 25 November 1740, age 13, Robert Jadwin

Tapp, Leonard, 26 June 1739, age 15 "last May," John Hall

Underhill, Nathaniel, 24 August 1742, age 14, Christopher Thomas

Venn, Edward, 27 November 1739, age 16 "at Christmas next,"
    Edward Godwin

Vicars, Laurence, 24 March 1719, age 12, John Cobreath

Willis, Jonathan, 21 September 1736, age 13 "the first day of August
    Instant," Matthew Dockery

Woodward, James, 26 June 1739, age 15 "last May," Robert Jerman

Woollunt, John, 28 June 1737, age 15 "the first of June Instant,"
    Thomas Davis

QUEEN ANNE'S COUNTY

Worshippfull Commissioners

Banckes, William
Bordley, James
Bordley, Thomas
Bracco, John
Brown, James, Capt.
Browne, Aquila
Browne, John, Capt.
Carmichal, William
Carradine, Thomas
Carter, John
Carter, Valentine
Clark, Joshua
Clayton, Solomon
Downes, Charles
Downes, John, Jun.
Downes, John, Sen.
Downes, Philemon
Downes, Vachel
Earle, James, Senr.
Elbert, William
Elliott, William, Capt.
Emory, Arthur, Junr.
Emory, Arthur, Senr.
Emory, John Register
Fisher, John
Fisher, Thomas
Garnett, George, Doctor
Gould, Benjamin
Gould, James
Hall, Andrew
Hall, Jonathan
Hamilton, Patrick
Hammond, Thomas
Hands, Bedingfield
Hemsley, William
Hopper, William, Capt.
Jumpe, William

Worshippfull Commissioners

Kent, James
Kerr, John
Kitteridge, William Serjeant,
   Doctor
Lloyd, Robert, Esq.
Marsh, Thomas
Mason, Richard
Nicols, Jonathan
O'Bryon, James
Pemberton, Grundy
Price, Andrew, Capt.
Ridgaway, Samuel
Ringgold, Jacob
Ringgold, Thomas
Roberts, Benjamin
Roberts, Jonathan, Doctor
Routh, Christopher Cross
Salter, John
Seegar, John, Capt.
Seney, John
Smyth, John, Doctor, Surgeon
Sudler, Joseph, Capt.
Thompson, Augustine
Thompson, Dowdall
Thompson, John
Tilghman, Edward, Capt.
Tilghman, William, Major
Turbutt, William, Major
Turlo, William, Major, Lt. Coll.
Wells, George
Wells, Humphry
Wells, Humphry, Jun.
Wells, John
Whittington, John
Wright, Charles
Wright, Edward
Wright, Nathan

65

QUEEN ANNE'S COUNTY

Worshippfull Commissioners

Wright, Nathan Samuel Turbutt
Wright, Nathaniel
Wright, Robert Morrest
Wright, Solomon

Worshippfull Commissioners

Wright, Thomas
Wright, Thomas Hynson
Wright, Turbutt

QUEEN ANNE'S COUNTY

Year	White	Negro	Indian
1710	0	0	0
1711	0	3	0
1712	2	0	0
1713	1	0	0
1714	0	0	0
1715	0	0	0
1716	0	0	0
1718	0	0	0
1719	3	0	0
1728	0	0	0
1729	5	0	0

QUEEN ANNE'S COUNTY

Year	White	Negro	Indian
1730	0	0	0
1731	0	0	0
1732	0	0	0
1733	0	0	0
1734	0	5	0
1735	0	5	0
1736	1	4	0
1737	2	8	0
1738	1	4	0
1739	3	4	0
1740	1	1	0
1741	2	12	0
1742	2	9	0
Total	23	57 *	0

* Includes one Negro in 1753, and one in 1757.

KENT COUNTY

Allin, Thomas, 11 February 1701, age 15, James Heath
Arnald, Arthur, 25 March 1701, age 13, Capt. William Hackett
Ayres, Edward, 27 June 1676, age 12, Edward Swettnam
Baker, William, 23 November 1686, age 16, Cornelius Comegys
Barrey, James, 28 June 1698, age 14, John Chaires
Battershell, Henry, 24 March 1696, age 12, George Smith
Betler, James, 28 June 1698, age 13, Capt. Thomas Ringgold
Breen, William, 7 April 1702, age 12, John Moor
Bringgergrass, James, 22 March 1670, age 14, Thomas Taylor, eight years
Broaden, Phillip, 27 April 1698, age 19, George Smith
Bruder, Thomas, 25 January 1687, age 8, Anthony Workeman
Bryan, Cornelius, 23 June 1696, age 15, Walter Tally
Bryttan, Elizabeth, 23 November 1703, age 18, Elias King
Cage, Benjamin, 6 March 1677, age 16, Thomas Moore
Canady, Mary, 25 June 1695, age 18-19, Thomas Joce
Chaird, James, 23 March 1716, age 12, Alexander Williamson, "which
    Came into the Country with Capt. William Rock~"
Clark, Samuell, 24 August 1703, age 12, John Davis
Colleman, William, 1 October 1661, age 11, Seth Foster, ten years
Conugh, James, 24 November 1685, age 18, John Ezeus
Couratee, Peter, "a French boy," 16 February 1686, age 8, Anthony
    Workman
Davis, Charles, 6 March 1677, age 15, Sarah Thomas
Davy, Lewis, 28 March 1676, age 14, Morgon Williams
Dayle, Katherine, c. 17 April 1688, age 18, Joseph Wickes, freed by court
    17 April 1694 after "but six years" service
Downes, Elizabeth, 23 June 1696, age 20, Michael Miller
Doyle, John, 22 June 1697, age 14, Coll. John Hynson
Dunnaha, Edward, 25 June 1695, age 13, Walter Tully
Dunnaway, John, 25 January 1687, age 18, William Thomas
Evans, John, 23 November 1686, age 15, Anna Staples
Fitz Patrick, John, 27 April 1698, age 20, William Ringgold
Ford, Ferdinando, 23 November 1686, age 18, Josias Lanham
German, Henry, 25 June 1695, age 9, Capt. John Copedge
Gizard, Joseph, 27 June 1705, age 15, George Smith "of ye North Side
    of Chester River"
Gordan, Christian, female, 29 April 1676, "who doth declare that she is"
    age 19, Joseph Wicks, six years
Greene, Dorothy, 23 June 1696, age 19, Walter Tally

KENT COUNTY

Hoger, Nicholas, 29 January 1686, age 13, Thomas Seward
Hopkins, William, 27 March 1677, age 12 "& a halfe," Francis Finch
Howald, James, 24 June 1701, (age over 22), William Bateman, four years
Huggort, Timothy, 23 November 1686, age 16, Thomas Piner
James, Thomas, 22 August 1676, age 15, Edward Rogers, seven years
Jones, Thomas, 25 June 1701, age 20, Charles Lowder
Jordan, Henry, 24 November 1685, age 16, Robert Perk
Keen, Patrick, 22 June 1697, age 14, Capt. Edward Sweatnam
Kennaday, Rodger, 22 June 1697, age 14, Henry Hosier
Lawlesse, Patrick, 26 March 1695, age 14, Robert Pearke
Laycock, John, 24 November 1685, age 18, Charles Euldin & Elias King,
    seven years
Lee, Edward, 23 November 1703, age 15, Edward Plastorn
Linc, Mary, 23 June 1696, age 16, Walter Tally
Lockett, Elisa, 1 March 1658, age 16, Mathew Read, "willing to accept
    six years of service"
Macke, Cornelius, 28 June 1698, age 15, Major Thomas Smyth
Mafair, Edmond, 25 January 1687, age 18, Anthony Workeman
Makene, Cornilius, 24 November 1685, age 20, Henry Hosier, six years
Martin, Thomas, 25 January 1687, age 10, Benjamin Ricaud
Moor, John, 7 April 1702, age 12, William Breen
Murty, Derby, 24 November 1685, age 12, William Pearle, ten years
Nevil, Walter, 28 June 1698, age 13, John Salter
Newman, Charles, 27 March 1677, age 13 "& a halfe," Francis Finch
Norman, Elizabeth, 28 March 1676, age 21, Frances Finch
O'Donarty, John, 23 September 1701, age 12, David Davidson
O'Leirey, Darby, 25 November 1701, age 22, John Wells
O'Muinan, Owen, 27 March 1701, age 14, John Yoe, "Comandr. of ye
    Adventure of Biddeford," sold to William Comegys
Padbury, Jane, 31 March 1668, age not judged, Matthew Read,
    "requires no more" than four years service
Pearcey, Phillip, 23 September 1701, age 16, Thomas Marshall,
    "Comander of ye Ship Sarah now rideing at Anchor in
    Chester River in this County"
Prescot, Elizabeth, 28 November 1693, age 17, Michaell Miller
Reading, John, 2 April 1678, age 9, Robertt Perke
Richardson, James, 27 November 1677, age 12, Anthony Woorkman
Riply, Mathew, 7 December 1686, age 12, Thomas Kaine
Rogers, Matthew, 28 November 1693, age 16, Thomas Keane

Rosemason, Hans, 30 March 1669, (age 18-22), Alexander Tourson,
    five years
Rosier, Doroy, female, 22 September 1702, age 12, Daniel Norris
Rosier, John, 25 August 1702, age 8, Elias King
Rushford, Garrett, 28 June 1698, age 15, Michael Miller
Sennett, Nicholas, 24 March 1696, age 19, Philip Hopkins
Shaw, John, 22 August 1676, age 17, Henry Hosier, five years
Simcocks, William, 25 March 1701, age 12, Capt. Thomas Ringgold
    "comes off ye bench at ye judging of his servant"
Smith, Alice (?), 22 March 1687, age 6, William Morrey, sixteen years
Smith, John, 28 March 1671, age not judged, Marke Benton, seven years
Smith, Mary, 23 November 1703, age 18, Edward Plastorn
Sox, Alexander, 23 November 1697, age 9, David Kennady
Stamaker, Elizabeth, 2 April 1678, age 14, John Hinson
Sumner, Robertt, 27 November 1677, age 14, Edward Frye
Synley, John, 22 June 1703, age 13, Isaac Bowles
Tatum, Christopher, 28 November 1693, age 14, Thomas Keane
Tennant, Mary, 29 September 1668, (age 18-22), John Wright, five years
Tourson, Alexander, 30 March 1669, (age 18-22), Hans Rosemason,
    five years
Towne, Katharine, 25 June 1695, age 14, Thomas Joce
Walter, Owen, 28 March 1676, age 13, Joseph Wicks
Welch, James, 27 April 1698, age 18, James Wattson
Whaland, James, 26 March 1695, age 13, William Glanville
Whitehead, William, 23 March 1686, age 12, Michaell Miller
_____ , _____ , 25 June 1678, age 15, Cornelius Comygies

KENT COUNTY

Worshippfull Commissioners	Servants
Bennett, Disboro	
Bishop, William *	
Blunt, Richard	
Bradnox, Thomas, Capt.	
Carline, Henry	
Chaires, John	Barrey
Comegys, Cornelius	Baker, _____
Conner, Phillip	
Copedge, John, Capt.	German
Coursey, Henry, Coll., Esq. *	
Coursey, John	
Coursey, William *	
Dabb, John	
Dunn, Robert	
Evetts, Nathaniel	
Foster, Seth *	Colleman
Frisby, William	
Goodhand, Christopher	
Hanson, Hans, Capt., Lieut. Coll.	
Harris, William	
Hawkins, John, Capt.	
Head, William	
Hopkins, Phillip	Sennett
Hosier, Henry	Kenneday, Makene, Shaw
Hynson, Charles	
Hynson, John, Coll.	Stamaker
Hynson, Thomas *	
Jordan, John	
King, Elias	Bryttan, Laycock, Rosier
Lawrence, William, Capt.	
Leeds, William	
Lowe, Nicholas	
Loyd, Edward *	
Marsh, Thomas	
Miller, Michaell	Downes, Prescot, Rushford, Whitehead
Morgan, Henry	
Murphy, James, Capt. *	

KENT COUNTY

Worshippfull Commissioners	Servants
Norris, Daniel	Rosier
Osborne, Thomas	
Pickard, Nicholas	
Reade, Matthew	Lockett, Padbury
Ringgold, James, Major *	
Ringgold, Thomas, Capt.	Betler, Simcocks
Russell, John, Capt.	
Salter, John	Nevil
Smith, James, Capt. *	
Smith, Thomas, Major, Lieut. Coll.	
South, Thomas *	
Sweatnam, Edward, Capt.	Keen
Tilden, Charles	
Tomson, John	
Tovey, Samuell	
Vaughan, Robert, Capt.	
Vicaris, John, Capt.	
Wells, John *	O'Lierey
Wells, Tobias	
Whittington, John, Capt.	
Wickes, Joseph, Capt.	Dayle, Gordan, Walter
Williams, Morgan	Davy
Wilmer, Simon	
Winchester, Isaac	
Wright, John	Tennant
Wright, Matthew	
Wright, Nathaniel	
Wright, Solomon	

* see Talbot County

KENT COUNTY

Year	White	Negro	Indian
1658	1	0	0
1659	0	0	0
1660	0	0	0
1661	1	0	0
1662	0	0	0
1668	2	0	0
1669	1	0	0
1670	1	0	0
1671	1	0	0
1675	0	0	0
1676	7	0	0
1677	6	0	0
1678	3	0	0
1685	5	1	0
1686	8	0	0
1687	5	0	0
1688	1	0	0

KENT COUNTY

Year	White	Negro	Indian
1693	3	0	0
1694	0	0	0
1695	6	0	0
1696	6	0	0
1697	4	1	0
1698	8	2	0
1701	9	0	0
1702	3	1	0
1703	5	0	0
1704	0	3	0
1705	1	3	0
1707	0	1	0
1708	0	0	0
1709	0	0	0
1714	0	0	0
1715	0	0	0
1716	1	0	0
1717	0	1	0
Total	88	13	0

CECIL COUNTY (FRAGMENT)

Ganghaw, Michael, 11 September 1700, age 18, Isaac Merier
Kinshill, Deniss, 14 August 1700, age 10, John Tucker
O'Geary, Daniel, 12 June 1700, age 12, Edward Blay
Price, David, 12 November 1700, age 12, John Ryland
Whaley, Owen, 11 September 1700, age 13, John Hynson

Worshippfull Commissioners	Servants
Blackstone, Ebenezer	
Blay, Edward	O'Geary
Harris, William, Major	
Hynson, John	Whaley
Keare, Thomas	
Stoope, John	
Vanderheyden, Mathias	

CECIL COUNTY

Year	White	Negro	Indian
1698	0	0	0
1699	0	0	0
1700	5	0	0
1701	0	0	0

Note: No servants without indenture 1683-1697

---------- ----------

DORCHESTER COUNTY (FRAGMENT)

Anderson, Rachel, 1 December 1691, age 8, Nicolas Phillips, "Imported
in ye Edward & Sarah, John Tenth, Master"

DORCHESTER COUNTY

Year	White	Negro	Indian
1690	0	0	0
1691	1	0	0
1692	0	0	0

BALTIMORE COUNTY (FRAGMENTS)

Ambrose, James, 4 June 1695, age 11, Coll. John Thomas

Amone, Richard, 3 March 1685, age 13, Capt. David Jones

Birk, Edmond, 5 June 1683, age 14, Colo. George Wells

Carter, John, 4 June 1714, age 13, Garret Garretson

Claneffer (?), Edward, 7 June 1692, age not stated, John Hayes, ordered to serve six years

Clare, John, 2 March 1686, age 18-20, Johana Goldsmith

Cockram, Margery, 2 June 1685, age 25, John Hill, "came in the Loyallty with William Hopkins" in 1684

Dedman, Thomas, 4 June 1695, age 13, John Ferry

Dunnawan, Katherine, 3 June 1696, age not stated, Edward Wilkes (?), ordered to serve six years

Fennysin (?), Mary, 6 August 1695, age 17, Nicholas Fitzsymons, ordered to serve six years "from the first arrivall of the ship she came in at the Port of Annapolis in Anne Arrundell County".

Finnegen, Hugh, "an Irish boy," 1 March 1692, age 10, Coll. George Wells

Finnegen, Philip, "an Irish boy," 1 March 1692, age 13, Coll. George Wells

Jeff (?), John, 2 March 1686, age 15, Marke Richardson

Jordan, Edward, 2 March 1686, age 15-18, Major Thomas Long, "ordered to serve according to Act of Assembly," and "ordered that the said Edward's Indenture should be recorded"

Hawkins, Jane, 4 June 1695, age 16, Coll. John Thomas

Kendall, Francis (male), 6 March 1694, age not judged, John Ferry, "by consent and agreement of his master and the Court was ordered to serve six yeares and noe more"

Lawler (?), Henry, 3 December 1691, age not judged, Jonas Bowen, "for not producing any Indenture should serve seaven yeares"

Longlun, Richard, 2 March 1684, age 13, John Boring

Marshall, John, 2 March 1686, age 18-20, Major Thomas Long

Murphew, Bryan, 3 December 1691, age not stated, Edward Bedell, ordered to serve eight years

Pexsin (?), Simon, 2 March 1686, age 15-18, Major Thomas Long

Pursee, William, 3 June 1696, age not stated, Samuel Sychemore, ordered to serve six years

Roberts, Jerimy, 2 March 1684, age 15-16, Major Thomas Long

Sharpp, Isack, 4 November 1685, age not judged, Charles Gorsuch, who "agreed with his servant that he should serve him but nine years from his arrivall into this countrey"

Shippy, Henry, 6 March 1694, age 18 on "July the twenty fifth last past," George Ashman

74

BALTIMORE COUNTY (FRAGMENTS)

Stevens, John, 2 March 1684, age 14, John Boring
Withrell, Elizabeth, 4 June 1695, age 12, Thomas Hooker

Worshippfull Commissioners	Servants
Ashman, George	Shippy
Bedell, Edward	Murphew
Boothby, Edward	
Boring, John	Longlun, Stevens
Ferry, John	Dedman, Kendall
Gibson, Miles, Capt.	
Gundry, Benjamin	
Hall, John	
Hollis, William	
Johnson, Henry, Capt.	
Long, Thomas, Major	Jordan, Marshall, Pexsin, Roberts
Lotton, Jacob	
Maxwell, James	
Phillips, James	
Richardson, Marke	Jeff
Richardson, Thomas, Capt.	
Staley, Thomas	
Thomas, John, Major, Coll.	Ambrose, Hawkins
Watkins, Francis	
Wells, George, Coll.	Birk, Finnegen, Finnegen

BALTIMORE COUNTY   BALTIMORE COUNTY

Year	White	Negro	Indian	Year	White	Negro	Indian
1683	1	0	0	1694	2	0	0
1684	3	0	0	1695	5	0	0
1685	3	0	0	1696	2	0	0
1686	5	0	0				
				1708-1713	0	0	0
1691	2	0	0	1714	1	0	0
1692	3	0	0	1715	0	0	0
1693	0	0	0	Total	27	0	0

ANNE ARUNDEL COUNTY

Ballister, John, 10 March 1719, age 15, Richard Franklin

Cannaday, John, 11 June 1706, age 12, William Liddalls

Carvile, Alexander, 8 June 1708, age 16, James Monate (?)

Christian, Henry, 11 June 1706, age 14, William Bladen

Clear, John, 13 August 1706, age 27, Nicholas Shepherd, "who came into the Country in Capt. John Loch's Ship ye 10th day of October 1701," "was adjudged to be about twenty two yeares of age"

Collier, Henry, 12 August 1707, age 16, Amos Garrett

Daws, Benjamin, 12 November 1717, age not judged, James Crouch, five years "to comence from the ninth day of November"

Deakers, James, 14 June 1720, age 12, Amos Garrett Esqr.

Doaks, William, 10 March 1719, age 9, Samuel Chambers

Dunhahoe, Jeffry, 10 November 1703, "about" age 15, James Carroll

Ellitt, Matthew, 10 November 1703, age 9, Charles Carroll, thirteen years

Ewin, John, 14 November 1710, age 14, James Heath, eight years

Ferry, John, 10 March 1719, age 17, Jacob Dhattaway

Fizgerald, Nicholas, 11 June 1706, age 14, Andrew Welpley

Gilbert, John, 10 August 1714, age 12, John Navarre

Howard, David, 13 June 1704, age 17, John Giles

Hutton, Thomas, 13 June 1710, age 16, Nehemiah Burkett

Jacob, Nicholas, 13 November 1705, age 15, Charles Carroll

Kalearn, Darby, 11 June 1706, age 18, Joseph Hill, Gent., "adjudged 8 years ago on the 6th of March to be ten years of age and to serve according to law," "again adjudged to serve pursuant to that judgment, the former record thereof being burnt"

Kendall, John, 12 June 1711, age 12, Aron Rawlings

Langdon, James, 10 March 1719, age 14, William Barnett

Layton, John, 13 June 1704, age 6, Charles Carroll

Magglen, David, 11 June 1706, age 17, Thomas Freeborne

Manderson, Patrick, 8 June 1708, age 15, James Heath

Parker, Henry, 10 March 1719, age 11, Amos Garrett, by Joseph Hall, his Overseer

Reddick, John, 11 March 1718, age 14, Capt. John Davidge

Rowland, Francis, 14 November 1710, age 12, John Navarr, ten years

Sias, John, 9 June 1719, age 17, Capt. John Young

Simons, John, 10 March 1719, age 8, Mr. Linthicum

Soollivant, John, 13 June 1704, age 1, Charles Carroll

Taylor, John Lippenny, 12 August 1712, age 15, Charles Carroll, by James Carroll

ANNE ARUNDEL COUNTY

Turges, Peter, 12 August 1712, age 16, Edward Rumney
Tye, John, 14 March 1704, age not judged, James Carroll, "four years
    from the last day of October next"
Vincent, Hugh River (?), 10 March 1719, age 10, Samuel Loockwood
Williams, Henry, 5 April 1715, age 15, Thomas Harper

Worshippfull Commissioners	Servants
Baldwin, John	
Benson, Edmond	
Birkhead, Abraham	
Brice, John	
Chambers, Samuell	Doaks
Dorsey, Caleb	
Draper, Lawrence, Capt.	
Garrett, Amos	Collier, Deakers, Parker
Gassaway, Thomas	
Greenberry, Charles, Major, Coll.	
Gresham, John, Senr.	
Hammond, Charles, Major	
Hammond, John	
Hammond, William	
Holland, Francis	
Howard, John	
Ingram, John	
Jones, Philip, Capt.	
Jones, Richard, Junr., Capt.	
Larkin, Thomas, Capt.	
Loch, William, Doctor	
Mariartee, Daniell, Capt.	
Odell, Thomas	
Price, John	
Talker / Tasker, Benjamin	
Towgood, Josiah, Capt.	
Warfield, Richard	
Warman, Stephen	
Watkins, John	
Wells, Thomas	

ANNE ARUNDEL COUNTY

Year	White	Negro	Indian
1703	2	0	0
1704	4	0	0
1705	1	0	0
1706	6	0	0
1707	1	0	0
1708	2	0	0
1709	0	0	0
1710	3	0	0
1711	1	0	0
1712	2	0	0
1713	0	0	0
1714	1	0	0
1715	1	0	0
1716	0	0	0
1717	1	0	0
1718	1	0	0
1719	8	0	0
1720	1	0	0
Total	35	0	0

PRINCE GEORGE'S COUNTY

Anderson, Jane, 25 August 1706, age 20, Thomas Stonestreet

Bairat, John, 27 June 1699, age 22, John Prather

Barker, Richard, 28 June 1698, age 13, William Hunter

Baxter, James, 28 March 1699, age 13, Richard Gambra

Bell, Andrew, 24 June 1718, age 12, James Haddock, Sheriff

Bellfoard, Robert, 27 June 1699, age 13, Nicholas Davis

Bene, John, 29 June 1698, age 12, Capt. John Bayne, "ye Arivall of
ye Shipp being the 2d day of Mar(ch) before he came to be
adjudged," freed by Court on 25 March 1708

Berndoe, Henry, 22 September 1696, age 16, Edward Brock

Berry, Edmund, 28 March 1699, age 10, Richard Gambra

Bevans, Thomas, 23 June 1719, age 7, John Winn

Black, James, 24 June 1712, age 20, Richard Edgar, six years

Blandigan, David, 22 November 1698, age 13, John Smith

Boulton, Christian, 25 June 1706, age 14, Dorman Walker

Brady, Hugh, 28 June 1698, age 19, John Smith

Briss, Robert, 28 March 1699, age 16, William Herbert

Buck, Edward, 23 November 1703, age 18, Clement Hill

Burk, John, 24 March 1719, age 15, Robert Gremitt

Burk, Peter, 24 March 1719, age not judged, (?)lian Burk, five years

Burke, John, 28 June 1698, age 14, William Mills

Cammell, Ann, 25 June 1706, age 18, William Elliatt

Canven, Mitchell, 23 June 1702, age 20, "not having noo Indentures,
supposed to be 20 years of age," William Clarkson

Carroll, William, 23 August 1698, age 18, John Barrott

Clark, James, 23 November 1703, age not stated, Charles Carroll

Clisson, John, 23 November 1703, age not stated, Charles Carroll

Collings, Morgan, 23 August 1698, age 19, Mathew Mackeboy

Cooper, Margarett, 24 March 1713, age 17, Henry Boteler, seven years,
master "in open court acknowledges himself to be content with
six yeares service only"

Coughlane, John, 29 June 1698, age 17, Nicholas Morrow

Cragg, William, 24 June 1712, age 13, James Greene, nine years

Croamy, James, 27 June 1710, age 12, Robert Owen

Daniell, William, 27 March 1700, age 19, John Wattkins

Denonghow, Barthollomew, 28 June 1698, age 15, John Demall

Dholohundee, John, 22 November 1698, age 18, Murphey Ward

Dollard, Elizabeth, 29 August 1705, age 17, John Hallam, who agreed
that she "should serve but six yeares and then to be free"

Donnell, David, 29 November 1701, age 14, John Henry
Drumant, Ann, 25 August 1706, age 20, Christopher Thompson
Duff, James, 24 June 1712, age 20, John Winn, six years
Edwards, John, 25 August 1702, age 14, Major William Barton
Fellon, Simon, 23 November 1703, age 13, Joshua Hall
Flemin, John, 28 March 1699, age 12, William Clacson
Frady, James, 28 June 1698, age 13, Allexander Magruder
Gaba, Joseph, 25 June 1717, age 18, James Haddock, Sheriff
Gallihall, Nicholas, 23 June 1719, age 15, Thomas Johnson
Gibbs, Henry, 28 September 1698, age 14, Thomas Vaughun
Gorden, George, 24 June 1712, age 15, George Noble
Gordon, Peter, 27 June 1710, age 13, James Wallace
Greendell, William, 28 June 1698, age 18, Murfy Ward
Guillion, Peter, 25 November 1718, age 14, William Masters
Hagen, John, 28 June 1698, age 17, John Smith
Harvey, Thomas, 27 June 1705, age 13, Robert Wade
Hastings, John, 24 March 1713, age 21, Josiah Wilson, six years
Heneper, Edmund, 29 June 1698, age 20, Christopher Baynes
Herdman, Margaret, 24 March 1713, age 16, James Stoddert, seven years,
    but master "acknowledges himself to be content with six yeares
    service only from this time"
Hews, John, 21 February 1704, age 8, Gabriell Burnham
Howes, Henry, 23 August 1698, age 16, Nathan Veitch
Hughes, Timothy, 28 June 1698, age 20, John Smith
Jenkins, Thomas, 27 March 1716, age 17, Notley Rozer
Jinboy, Daniell, 26 June 1700, age not judged, Thomas Brooke, Esqr.,
    ordered to serve seven years "according to his owne
    acknowledgment that he was bound for the same time in England"
Johnson, George, 22 August 1710, age 11, Major Josiah Willson
Kanady, Daniell, 28 June 1698, age 11, Timothy Mohony
Kehone, James, 28 June 1698, age 22, John Smith
Keirsey, Thomas, 28 June 1698, age 16, William Ray
Kelly, Bryan, 23 August 1698, age 14, John Prather
Kelly, John, 23 August 1698, age 14, John Barrett
Kempton, William, 28 June 1698, age 15, John Pottinger
Key, James, 23 August 1698, age 16, Matthew Mackeboy
Knight, Peter, 27 June 1710, age 15, Richard Grrome
Kyloe, John, 23 January 1700, age 17, John Doakins
Linzee, Elizabeth, 25 June 1706, age 21, Hickford Leman

PRINCE GEORGE'S COUNTY

Lyle, Darby, 28 June 1698, age 12, Tabitha Blandford
Lynch, Bryan, 24 November 1703, age 9, Robert Owen
Macann, Mary, 23 June 1719, age 15, James Key
Maccow, Rodman, 28 June 1698, age 15, William Offoott
Mace, Henry, 23 August 1698, age 20, Captaine Edward Brocke
Mackdaniell, Owen, 28 June 1698, age 20, John Smith
Mackeboy, William, 22 November 1698, age 14, John Smith
MacNeale, John, 24 June 1712, age 10, Edward Edelen, twelve years
Macquin, James, 28 March 1699, age 12, Francis Mallberry
Maroney, James, 23 August 1698, age 17, John Barrott
Marshall, John, 22 August 1710, age 17, Capt. Robert Ward
Masefield, Robert, 24 March 1713, age 17, Josiah Wilson, seven years
McCooke, Michael, 25 March 1718, age 16, Thomas Stump
Merian, John, 23 January 1700, age 18, Christopher Baines
Moehoe, Robert, 28 March 1699, age 16, Capt. John Baine
Moor, Margrett, 28 September 1708, age 14, Robert Wade
Morris, Richard, 23 November 1703, age 12, James Beall
Munroe, Allexander, 23 August 1699, age 15, Christopher Thompson
Murphey, Michall, 28 September 1698, age 15, Charles Bevens
Neale, Arther, 28 June 1698, age 15, Allexander Beall
Norton, Henry, 23 August 1698, age 20, Jonathan Simmons
Parrot, William, 28 June 1710, age 14, Solomon Stimpson
Patrick, Richard, 28 June 1698, age 17, Henry Gutridge
Robertson, James, 25 June 1706, age 18, Hickford Leman
Robinson, Ann, 26 June 1705, age 16, Jeremy Snell
Robinson, William, 27 June 1710, age 11, Samuell Magruder Junior
Rodgers, Matthew, 26 March 1700, age 14, Daniell Connell
Ross, Allexander, 24 November 1696, age 15, Phillip Gittings
Sharp, Elizabeth, 28 June 1698, age 11, William Mills
Shrewsbury, Ann, 24 January 1699, age 20, William Barton
Shunnam, John, 29 November 1701, age 15, John Lewis
Simms, Richard, 23 August 1699, age 15, James Watts
Stafford, Richard, 24 January 1699, age 15, Henry Buttler
Thom(as), John, 26 June 1705, age not stated, Mr. Allexander, ordered
      to serve seven years
Thompson, William, 27 June 1706, age 17, James Bell
Thomson, Walter, 24 March 1713, age 21, Josiah Wilson, six years
Tinnally, Phillip, 28 November 1705, age 12, Mareen Devall Junior,
      "alledging that he had Indentures"

Turke, James, 26 June 1711, age 14, John Norris
Turner, Abraham, 22 August 1710, age 18, Major Josiah Willson
Vender, Robert, 27 June 1699, age 13, Mrs. Mary Bevins
Vermill, Gile, 28 March 1699, age 13, James Green
Webster, John, 26 August 1707, age 13, Walter Evans
Webster, William, 24 June 1712, age 14, Thomas Middleton, eight years
White, Thomas, 25 March 1718, age 13, Thomas Johnson, eight years
Wormewood, William, 23 November 1703, age 16, Clement Hill
Young, William, 24 June 1712, age 10, Francis Compton, twelve years

Worshippfull Commissioners	Servants
Acton, Henry	
Addison, Thomas	
Barton, William, Major *	Edwards, Shrewsbury
Bayne, John, Capt. *	Bene, Moehoe
Belt, Joseph	
Bradford, John	
Bradly, Robert	
Brooke, Thomas, Esqr.	Jinboy
Claudius, Frederick	
Cleggett, Thomas, Capt.	
Covington, Levin	
Crabb, Ralph	
Gantt, Thomas	
Gerrard, John	
Hawkins, John	
Hepburne, Patrick	
Herbert, William *	Briss
Hollyday, Thomas	
Hutchison, William	
Lee, Phillip	
Magruder, Alexander	Frady
Magruder, Samuell	Robinson
Marbury, Francis	
Murdock, John	
Noble, George	Gorden
Perrie, Samuel, Capt.	
Ridgly, Henry	

PRINCE GEORGE'S COUNTY

Worshippfull Commissioners	Servants
Small, David	
Smith, John	Blandigan, Brady, Hagen, Hughes, Kehone, Mackdaniell, Mackeboy
Sprigg, Thomas, Jr., Major	
Stoddert, James	Herdman
Tanyhill, William	
Tyler, Robert	
Wade, Robert	Harvey, Moor
Waring, Basil	
Wight, John	
Wilson, Josiah	Hastings, Johnson, Masefield, Thomson, Turner

* See Charles County

PRINCE GEORGE'S COUNTY				PRINCE GEORGE'S COUNTY			
Year	White	Negro	Indian	Year	White	Negro	Indian
1696	2	0	0	1709	0	0	0
1697	0	0	0	1710	8	1	0
1698	35	0	0	1711	1	0	0
1699	14	1	0	1712	7	0	0
1700	5	0	0	1713	5	0	0
1701	2	1	0	1714	0	0	0
1702	2	0	0	1715	0	0	0
1703	7	0	0	1716	1	0	0
1704	1	3	0	1717	1	0	0
1705	5	0	0	1718	4	0	1
1706	7	0	0	1719	5	0	0
1707	1	0	0	1720	0	0	0
1708	1	1	0	Total	114	7	1

83

CHARLES COUNTY

Abbott, Susanna, 8 March 1681, age 20, Philip Lines, by his wife
    Margarett Lines
Abis, Matthew, 11 March 1679, age 18, William Smith
Acres, John, 10 June 1673, age 13, Jeremiah Dikeson
Adames, Edward, 8 August 1682, age 17, Jacob Morris
Ailer, Elizabeth, 9 March 1680, age 20, Francis Wyne
Ailer, Mary, 9 March 1680, age 14, Francis Wyne
Aldis, William, 8 June 1675, age 10, Owen Jones
Aldon, Mary, 12 March 1678, age 21, John Dent
Allinson, Annabella, 12 June 1677, age 17, Philip Lines
Anderson, Lawrence, 9 January 1672, age 20, Capt. William Boreman,
    by Richard Edelen
Anderson, Margaret, 8 June 1714, age 20, Mr. Justice Harrison
Anderson, Raiph, 10 November 1674, age 20, Raiph Shaw
Anglish, John, 13 March 1677, age 16, Arthur Turnow, by
    William Jenkinson
Archiball, John, 9 February 1686, age 22, Alexander Smith
Armstrong, Richard, 11 January 1670, age 19, William Barton
Arnley, Jane, 11 March 1679, age 13, Thomas Spooke, "of
    St. Maries County"
Astere, George, 3 February 1664, age 14-15, Alexander Simpson
Attchison, George, 12 January 1669, age 16, John Paine
Attkins, William, 12 January 1675, age 17, Robert Henley, by
    William Potter
Atwick, Joseph, 8 November 1687, age not judged, John Court, produced
    Indentures "for four yeares," upon inspection, ordered to serve
    "according to ye Custom of ye Country"
Austrich, William, 13 June 1676, age 13, James Tyre, by William Tymothy
Baen (?), Thomas, 13 June 1699, age 11, Thomas Harguesse
Bailey, Jeane, 11 June 1678, age 20, Thomas Baker, by Henry Trewne
Baily, William, 11 April 1676, age 14, Robert Middleton
Baiteman, Patrick, 10 June 1679, age 17, William Chandler
Baker, Hamlet, 12 July 1664, age 14, George Newman
Ball, Thomas, 12 January 1669, age 17, Ignatius Causine
Baraclow, Tobie, 8 November 1664, age 18, William Perfect
Barker, Robert, 11 January 1670, age 21-22, Daniell Johnson
Barker, William, 8 March 1664, age 20, Richard Stone
Barlow, Joel, 8 August 1671, age 12, James Neale Junior
Baron, Richard, 12 March 1667, age 15, Humphrey Warren, "Died on the
    10th of August 1667"

CHARLES COUNTY

Barret, Joseph, 12 July 1664, age 19, John Morris

Barrett, John, 13 March 1677, age 15, William Smith

Barrett, John, 11 March 1679, age 14, Michael Minock

Barrett, William, 10 January 1682, age 20, Captn. Ignatius Causin

Barrow, John, 10 June 1679, age 15, William Hatch

Barton, George, 10 March 1674, age 21-22, Zachary Wade

Barton, Robert, 13 June 1682, age 21, Major William Boardman, by Edmond Dennis

Bass, John, 11 November 1690, age not judged, Robert Thompson Junr., "Indenture being reade here in Court and noe sufficient"

Battle, Anthony, 8 March 1670, age 16, John Okeane

Bawlding, Robert, 13 April 1669, age 21, Robert Henly

Baylie, John, 12 July 1664, age 15-16, Richard Smith, by Mr. Francis Pope, "as Administrator"

Bayly, Nicholas, 12 August 1673, age 16, Ignatius Causine

Beaton, Murdoe (?), 13 August 1728, age 12, Captain Matthew Barnes

Bee, Thomas, 8 November 1664, age 20, James Bowlin

Bell, Bridgett, 10 June 1679, age 16, Major John Wheeler

Bell, Elizabeth, 11 June 1678, age 21, Robert Henley

Bellingham, Alice, 12 January 1675, age 16, Robert Henley

Bellingham, Mary, 12 January 1675, age 12, Matthew Hill

Benathon, Christian, male, 10 February 1663, age 19, Richard Foxton (?)

Bene, Thomas, 8 March 1681, age 17, Thomas Gerrard

Bennett, John, 9 March 1675, age 20, Hugh French, by Job Connor

Bennett, John, 9 June 1702, age 17, Samuell Luckett

Bennett, Mary, 10 March 1674, age 20-21, Edward Price

Bennett, Mary, 10 June 1679, age 22, Henry Hardy

Benson, John, 14 June 1670, age 11, Mr. Prouce, by Thomas Allanson

Benson, Robert, 8 August 1665, age 18-19, Edward Richardson

Berry, Elizabeth, 14 March 1682, age 14, Thomas Baker

Berry, John, 11 August 1685, age 17, Ralph Shaw

Bigs, Ambros, 8 March 1664, age 19, Thomas Baker

Binns, James, 13 January 1680, age 17, Thomas Gerrard

Bird, Mary, 14 November 1710, age 19, John Speake

Birtch, Robert, 22 April 1662, age 14-16, Henry Addames

Bishop, Archibald, 12 September 1699, age not judged, Richard Harrison, "now being sick and not capable of being brought to Court"

Bishop, Will, 12 March 1672, age 15, James Walker

Bitton, Margarett, 8 June 1708, age 20, Richard Villson

Blaack, William, 14 January 1701, age 15, William Hungerford
Blackbeard, Peeter, 8 November 1664, age 17, James Bowlin
Blanch, John, 8 March 1664, age 14, William Barton Junior
Board, Jane, 11 March 1679, age 17, John Wood
Bone, Isabell, 14 March 1665, age 24, Peeter Car
Bone, Teague, 13 June 1699, age 13, Edward Rockwood
Bonner, Elizabeth, 10 August 1675, age 19, Richard Harrison
Booker, John, 11 August 1674, age 18, Alexander White
Booth, John, 8 March 1664, age 13, Thomas Mathews
Boswell, Marmeducke, 8 March 1664, age 12, Richard Fouke
Bowing, William, 10 March 1668, age 16, Archiball Waahob, six years
Bowman, John, 17 March 1663, age 17, Mr. Robert, by John Duglas
Bradshaw, John, 8 June 1686, age 17-18, Phillip Lynes
Bradshaw, Thomas, 11 January 1670, age 20, John Paine
Bradstone, Frances, 10 June 1707, age 16, Coll. John Contee
Branor, Edmond, 19 April 1698, age 17, Michaell Martin
Braybanke, Abraham, 10 June 1679, age 15, William Hatch
Brayson, Agnes, 14 November 1710, age 19, Robert Hanson
Breeding, John, 13 March 1711, age 11, John Wilkinson
Brenan, Katherine, 12 September 1699, age 20, Edward Phillpott
Bride, Teague, male, 13 June 1693, age 15, Raiph Smith, by
    Capt. John Courts
Bridges, Stephen, 9 March 1686, age 25, John Court Jun.
Bright, Edward, 11 June 1678, age 12, James Smallwood
Bright, Thomas, 8 March 1670, age 21, Mr. Young
Brooke, John, 12 January 1686, age 21, Henry Hawkins
Brooke, Thomas, 10 March 1674, age 11, John Lambert
Brookes, Hen, 10 June 1673, age 19, Mrs. Beane, by Mathew Hill
Brooks, James, 12 March 1700, age 14, Joseph Harrison
Broonely, Thomas, 8 November 1670, age 21, Edmond Lynsy
Broune, Ales, female, 10 January 1665, age 22, William Smoote
Browne, Andrew, 13 June 1699, age 21, John Booker
Browne, Elisabeth, 10 January 1665, age 20, William Marshall
Browne, Henry, 14 November 1710, age 18, Capt. William Harbert
Browne, James, 12 January 1686, age 15, Domindigo Agambrah
Browne, Joan, 16 December 1662, age 18, James Nealle Esq., "by his
    overseer" Thomas Carvell
Browne, John, 8 June 1708, age 16, Francis Goodrich
Browne, Robert, 4 April 1699, age 15, Anthony Neale

CHARLES COUNTY

Browne, Thomas, 12 July 1664, age 20, Miss Weekes, by Thomas Lomax
Browne, Thomas, 8 June 1675, age 18, John Faning
Browne, Thomas, 10 January 1682, age 16, Peter Car
Bryan, Anne, 13 June 1699, age 21, Thomas Wakefeild
Bryan, John, 19 April 1698, age 12, Capt. John Bayne
Bryan, John, 14 June 1698, age 22, Thomas Jenkins
Bryan, Turlough, 19 April 1698, age 19, Maj. William Dent,
 "permission to marry Francis Hogg," 14 September 1703
Bryan, William, 14 June 1698, age 16, Ralph Smith
Buckham, Mabel, 9 June 1719, age 13, Richard Nevill
Buckler, Benjamin, 10 January 1682, age 9, Thomas Mitchell
Bull, William, 10 June 1679, age 18, John Gooch
Burgesse, Samuell, 11 March 1690, age not judged, Mrs. Elinor Bayne,
 by John Bayne her son, Indenture not "good and authentick,"
 ordered to serve "according to ye Custome of ye Countrey"
Burke, Catherine, 19 April 1698, age 14, John Wilder
Burke, John, 9 March 1675, age 15, Anne Fowke, by James Hoorn (?)
Burke, Oliver, 4 April 1699, age 13, William Hunt
Burkhaine, John, 10 January 1671, age 15, Jeremiah Dickinson
Burnett, John, 12 March 1700, age 17, Randall Garland
Caddington, Elizabeth, 12 January 1686, age 15, Henry Hawkins
Calvin, William, 9 June 1719, age 16, Doughlass Gifford
Cameright, John, 14 November 1699, age 8, Capt. John Bayne
Cammelle, Mary, 11 June 1706, age 20, Samuell Luckett
Campbell, Daniel, 9 June 1719, age 12, Charles Byrne
Campbell, John, 14 November 1710, age 14, Edward Chapman
Campin, John, 12 November 1706, age 19, Ralphaell Neale
Canland, John, 11 June 1678, age 16, Capt. John Wheeler
Canley, John, 12 August 1690, age 15, Raiph Smith, by John Duglas
Capshaw, Francis, 10 November 1674, age 15, Alexander Smith
Careadale, Thomas, 11 January 1670, age 16-17, Capt. Boareman
Carey, Cornelius, 12 March 1678, age 18, Justinian Dennis
Carey, Hugh, 11 June 1678, age 14, Edward Price
Carnaggey, James, 14 November 1710, age 16, John Manning
Carnee, Thomas, 13 June 1699, age 16, William Hawton Senior
Carpenter, Christopher, 14 March 1682, age 12, James Smallwood
Carpenter, Henry, 11 April 1676, age 16, William Perfitt
Carrey, Nicholas, 14 January 1701, age 14, Capt. Thomas Smoot
Cathew, Christopher, 13 June 1682, age 14, Philip Lines
Cayne, James, 10 June 1674, age 12, Richard Beck

CHARLES COUNTY

Champe, Steephen, 8 March 1664, age 14, William Marshall
Chantler, John, 10 November 1696, age 18, William Wilkison
Chaplin, Thomas, 11 January 1676, age 11, Garratt Sinnett
Chapman, Elizabeth, 13 June 1699, age 16, John Vandry
Chapman, George, 9 January 1672, age 22, Benjamin Rozer
Chesson, John, 12 May 1663, age 14 "and a half," John Meekes
Chew, Aedith, 14 January 1668, age 14, Garret Synnet
Childman, Joane, 8 August 1665, age 20, Edmond Lendsey
Chomley, Francis, 11 January 1670, age 16, Henry Adames
Christoe, Robert, 4 April 1699, age 16, Thomas Simpson
Clarke, James, 9 January 1672, age 13, Richard Edelen
Clarke, John, 15 November 1665, age 12, Zachery Waed
Clarke, Nicholaus, 10 January 1665, age 16, Robert Hendley
Clarke, Rebeckah, 13 June 1699, age 16, William Hawton Junr.
Clarke, Thomas, 12 June 1705, age 17, Coll. James Smallwood
Clary, Morris, 10 January 1682, age 18, Owen Nowen
Clemence, Nicholaus, 3 February 1664, age 11-12, William Marshall
Coates, Henly, 14 March 1699, age 13, John Liverett
Cobb, Samuel, 8 June 1669, age 15, Thomas King
Cole, John, 8 August 1693, age 18, Robert Benson
Collingwood, Robert, 12 March 1672, age 21, Robert Clarke
Collins, Alice, 12 August 1673, age 21-22, Robert Robins
Comely, Anne, 8 June 1708, age 20, Walter Winter
Comorains, John, 13 March 1722, age not judged, Henry Hawkins,
        "taken in ye Rebellion at Preston," "had served the full Term
        of five years"
Coney, Anthony, 19 April 1698, age 12, Capt. John Bayne
Cooke, John, 9 February 1686, age 14, Richard Newman
Cooper, John, 14 January 1679, age 15, Capt. William Barton
Cooper, Roger, 11 March 1679, age 16, William Hinsey, by Joseph Bullott
Cooper, Thomas, 11 June 1667, age 15, Richard Randall
Cooper, William, 13 November 1705, age 13, Samuell Southeron
Copp (?), John, 11 August 1685, age 17, Richard Wade
Cornute, Hendrick, 14 June 1670, age 20, John Okeane
Cornwall, Francis, female, 14 March 1682, age 20, Thomas Jenkins
Corrandell, Joane, 8 June 1708, age 16, Isabella Orrell
Cottlycott, William, 10 March 1685, age 17, John Court Junior
Cottwell, James, 13 March 1677, age 20, Thomas Gerrard
Court, Cleat, 13 April 1669, age 17, Daniell Johnson

Crawford, David, 9 June 1719, age 17 "ye first day of next December,"
    John Posey
Crottee (?), Thomas, 19 April 1698, age 12, Mrs. Elinor Bayne, by
    Michaell Browne
Crouch, Anne, 9 February 1686, age 18, Coll. John Court Junr.
Cumber, Catherin, 14 March 1665, age 17, George Newman
Cumberbeech, Edward, 8 June 1697, age 15, Ralph Smith
Cumpton, Christopher, 14 June 1681, age 16, Philip Lines
Cumpton, William, 11 January 1676, age 17, John Hatch
Cunningham, George, 9 January 1672, age 16, Alexander Smith
Currs, Edward, 13 February 1700, age 17, Matthew Sanders
Curtis, John, 10 November 1674, age 16, Francis Wine
Cusack, Patrick, 11 March 1701, age 17, John Bayne, "brings here into
    Court two Irish servants"
Dallison, Allen, 4 April 1699, age 13, Thomas Hussey
Daniellson, Charles, 4 April 1699, age 15, Capt. John Bayne
Darnell, Edw., 13 March 1688, age 17, Phillip Lynes
Darner, Thomas, 12 January 1669, age 17, John Cage
Daverill, Thomas, 11 January 1670, age 20, Thomas Dent
Davies, Alice, 8 June 1675, age 19, Thomas Howell
Davies, Griffin, 8 June 1675, age 17, Nicholas Prodday, by Richard Fowke
Davies, Hugh, 12 August 1690, age 14, Raiph Smith, by John Duglas
Davies, James, 8 March 1670, age 16, John Ward
Davis, John, 10 June 1674, age 13, Humphry Warren
Davis, Mary, 11 September 1694, "not brought in time to be adjudged of
    her age," by Robert Doyne, sold to George Plater, freed by court
Deakons, Thomas, 13 April 1669, age 11, Henry Bonard
Denealey, John, 14 August 1705, age 14, Coll. John Contee
Denison, John, 4 April 1699, age 18, Hugh Toares
Derritt, Edward, 11 April 1676, age 21, Humphrey Warren
Dickison, Thomas, 13 March 1677, age 18-19, James Tyre, by
    Thomas Harris
Dicksey, John, 10 January 1665, age 15, Edward James
Dickson, Elizabeth, 10 June 1679, age 20, Cleborne Lomax
Dike, Mathew, 12 March 1672, age 20, Mathew Stone
Divell, James, 10 January 1671, age 14, Thomas Stone
Doane, Charles, 14 March 1699, age 14, Thomas Dirkson
Dod, John, 14 September 1703, age 16, Maj. William Dent
Dods, Thomas, 12 January 1675, age 12, Robert Henley, by
    William Potter

Dolton, Richard, 11 March 1679, age 18, Richard Chandler, by
        Nicholas Cooper
Donah, Daniell, 10 March 1685, age 21, Robert Thompson, "offers an
        indenture which is adjudged voyd"
Donahan, Fineene, 11 August 1685, age not judged, Thomas Hussey,
        "brought an Indenture which was judged Invalid"
Donohan, Cornelius, 11 August 1685, age 19, Thomas Hussey
Doughty, Robert, 8 June 1669, age 15, John Ward
Dover, Christopher, 10 June 1674, age 20, Thomas Mathewes
Downes, William, 9 January 1683, age 13, Major John Wheeler
Doyle, Edmond, 19 April 1698, age 21, Elizabeth Marshall, by
        Edward Philpott
Doyle, Owen, 14 August 1683, age 20, Phillip Lynes
Doyne, Patrick, 13 June 1699, age 19, William Hawton Senr.
Draper, Raiph, 14 June 1681, age 16, Philip Lines
Dreyden, George, 8 August 1699, age 20, Joseph Harrison,
        "hee saith that he had an Indenture but it was Lost"
Drishen, Dennis, 14 June 1698, age 12, Capt. Randolph Brandt
Druncore, James, 10 March 1686, age 15, Thomas Burford
Dunn, Isaac, 10 March 1674, age 14, John Hatch
Dunn, Patrick, 13 June 1699, age 20, Thomas Orrell
Dunnington, Francis, 12 January 1686, age 20, Madam Mary Chandler
Duppe, Thomas, 11 June 1667, age 20, Alexander Smyth
Dyal, John, 12 June 1722, age 15, George Elgin
Dyall, James, 13 June 1699, age 11, Thomas Jones
Eady, Elizabeth, 14 November 1710, age 21, John Rogers
Eason, John, 11 March 1679, age 11, Capt. Humphrey Warren
Eaton, Thomas, 10 June 1679, age 18, Thomas Clipsham
Edge, Thomas, 10 March 1674, age 17-18, Zachary Wade
Edwards, John, 13 March 1677, age 12, Margarett Mark
Ellis, Hugh, 12 January 1675, age 13, Francis Goodrich
Ellison, John, 11 January 1676, age 16, Samuell Cressey
Ellison, John, 13 June 1699, age 15, John Liverett
Emerson, Anthoni, 10 January 1665, age 17, Thomas Smoote, by
        Thomas Gibson
Eniburson, Christopher, 13 April 1669, age 16, Capt. James Neile
Eniburson, Derick, 13 April 1669, age 14, Capt. James Neile
Ennis, David, 11 August 1685, age 16, Thomas Hussey
Eure, Christopher, 12 January 1669, age 19, William Marshall
Evens, Joan, 19 April 1698, age 17, Thomas Smoote

CHARLES COUNTY

Faarnandez, Pedro, 13 April 1669, age 17, Capt. James Neile
Farmer, Richard, 10 June 1673, age 16, John Allen
Farrel, Bryan, 8 November 1687, age 17, John Speake
Farrell, Hugh, 12 August 1701, age 18, William Moss
Farrow, James, 10 June 1674, age 15, John Ward, by Richard Beck
Faulkner, Alexander, 4 April 1699, age 14, Capt. John Bayne
Feddiman, Jeoffry, 11 June 1700, age 14, John Douglas
Feild, Charles, 10 August 1680, age 20, Major William Boardman
Fencoke, Ane, 10 February 1663, age 18, Richard Dod
Fenner, Thomas, 11 January 1670, age 19, Samuell Eaton
Fisher, Elizabeth, 12 June 1677, age 16, James Smallwood
Fitzgerald, Morris, 8 March 1726, age 10, John Smoot
Fitz Gerralds, John, 4 April 1699, age 14, James Smallwood
Fitz Gerralds, Peter, 19 April 1698, age 12, Hugh Toares
Fitz Gerreld, Morris, 10 March 1685, age 17, John Wright
Fleman, John, 4 April 1699, age 15, Robert Hagar
Flood, Francis, 8 March 1720, age 24, "as a servant of late
    Dorothy Parry's", by Daniel Jenifer
Foard, Katherine, 14 August 1683, age 20, Phillip Lynes
Forbis, William, 14 August 1694, age 17, William Dent
Ford, Peter, 10 March 1685, age 16, Ralph Smith
Fordice, Alexander, 13 June 1699, age 19, John Williams
Forrest, James, 10 June 1707, age 6, John Allen Senr.
Forrester, Edward, 13 February 1700, age 14, George Newman
Forster, Edward, 14 September 1703, age 13, George Brett
Foster, Leonard, 11 June 1678, age 12, William Smith
Fowler, James, 11 March 1729, age 15, Richard Coombs, Junr.
Fowler, William, 8 January 1678, age 14, William Boardman Junior
Fowtrell, George, 13 June 1676, age 22-23, James Bowlinge, by
    Richard Edelen
Francis, John, 14 June 1681, age 21, Alexander Smith
Francisson, Francis, 13 April 1669, age 10, Benjamin Rozer
Franckum, Francis, 11 April 1676, age 16, William Barton
French, Ann, 8 November 1670, age 21, Benjamin Rozer
Froote, Teague, 13 March 1683, age 13, John Courte
Furth, Joseph, 8 March 1664, age 17, John Clarke
G(?)dy, James, 10 June 1701, age 13, Francis Goodrick Senr.
Galey, Lorance, 8 June 1675, age 14, Captaine James Neale
Gandi, William, 10 February 1663, age 17, John Cage
Gardiner, Helena, 8 June 1708, age 16, Henry Hawkins

CHARLES COUNTY

Gaskoyne, Samuel, 8 June 1669, age 17, John Wheeler
Gateley, Edward, 11 March 1679, age 13, Thomas Harris, by
    Joseph Bullott
German, George, 11 January 1670, age 21, William Barton
Gerrard, Joane, 10 June 1701, age 22, Michaell Martin, Gent., by
    Coll. James Smalwood
Ghost, Jane, 11 June 1678, age 20, William Hargness
Gibbons, Thomas, 9 February 1686, age 14, William Barton
Gibbs, John, 13 April 1669, age 19, Peter Carr
Gibson, William, 13 January 1680, age 11, Henry Adames, by
    Philip Mason
Gilbard, James, 10 June 1679, age 21, Philip Linos
Gilbert, Jane, 9 March 1686, age 20, William Hatch
Gill, Argalus, 8 June 1703, age 10, Coll. James Smallwood
Gillcross, (torn) bert, 4 April 1699, age 13, Elizabeth Hawkins
Ginney, John, 12 March 1672, age 14, John Ward
Glasson, John, 12 September 1699, age 16, Joseph Manning
Gleeves, George, 10 August 1680, age 20, Capt. James Neale
Glover, Mary, 10 June 1679, age 20, Thomas Hussy
Gluffur, Robert, 14 January 1690, age not judged, William Marshall,
    Indenture judged not "good and valid," ordered to serve
    "according to ye Custome of ye Countrey"
Goddard, George, 13 June 1682, age not judged, Thomas Gibson,
    Indenture adjudged "to be of noe Effect and invalid"
Goffe, William, 11 March 1729, age 14, Robert Maslow
Good, Lucie, 12 July 1664, age 20, Richard Foucke
Gosh, Richard, 8 January 1678, age 15, Peter Car, by Joseph Bullott
Grandsworth, Mary, 16 December 1662, age 22 "and upward," John Courts
Grant, Robert, 14 November 1710, age 19, Francis Serson
Graves, Thomas, 11 March 1679, age 16, John Vandry, "of
    St. Maries County"
Gray, Jepharie, 12 July 1664, age 13, George Thompson
Gray, Joseph, 8 March 1664, age 13, Garrat Sennet
Gray, Ruth, 13 June 1676, age 21, Richard Edelen
Green, John, 8 September 1668, age 14, Benjamin Rozer
Green, Richard, 10 June 1673, age 17, John Allen
Greene, James, 10 June 1674, age 15, Benjamin Rozer
Greyden, Margarett, 8 August 1671, age 21, Henry Bonner
Grosser, Mary, 10 June 1674, age 18-20, Peter Carr

CHARLES COUNTY

Groule, Richard, 8 March 1681, age 13, Joseph Maninge, by his
       son in law Mr. Stone
Groves, George, 12 January 1686, age 11, Edward Evans
Gryer, John, 14 November 1682, age 20, Richard Williams
Guessne (?), Richard, 8 June 1686, age 15, Henry Adams
Guinn, Timothy, 9 January 1700, age 11, John Theobalds
Gunner, Moyses, 10 January 1665, age 19, Thomas Smoot, by
       Thomas Gibson
Gutridge, James, 14 March 1682, age 15, Philip Linos
Gwin, Richard, 8 March 1664, age 19, Francis Pope
Gwynn, Peter, 13 June 1699, age 18, Robert Yates
Hagar, William, 13 April 1669, age 14, Thomas Baker
Halerd, William, 11 June 1678, age 18, Edward Price
Halfpin, Thomas, 4 April 1699, age 18, Richard Edelen
Hall, Charles, 8 August 1682, age 22, Edward Mings
Hall, Isaack, 13 April 1669, age 13, Henry Bonard
Hall, John, 10 June 1674, age 18, William Hensly
Hall, Margrett, 10 June 1673, age 18, Mrs. Young, by Robert Worrell
Hall, William, 11 January 1676, age 17, Thomas Speeke, by
       Edward Evans
Halliburton, Elizabeth, 12 June 1705, age 19, Capt. William Barton
Hallinak, Michael, 10 June 1701, age 13, Michael Smalwood
Hambye, Francis, 2 January 1686, age 19, Giles Blizard
Hammonde, John, 7 April 1668, age 15, Jeremiah Dickenson
Hardy, Henry, 12 July 1664, age 20, Thomas Percei
Harper, Peter, 8 March 1692, age 13, Robert Thompson Junior
Harrard, William, 14 November 1710, age 15, Joseph Manning
Harris, Jane, 13 June 1676, age 20, Richard Jones
Harris, William, 13 June 1693, age 13, Capt. John Courts
Harrison, Anne, 10 November 1674, age 21, William Barton Junior
Harrison, Robert, 10 November 1674, age 13, Alexander Smith
Hastings, James, 9 June 1719, age 9, John Philbert
Hatherton, John, 10 March 1674, age 12, Edward Price
Hayles, Mary, 10 March 1671, age 20, Mr. Wade
Haywood, Mary, 10 January 1682, age 12, Thomas Jenkins
Hays, Isabella, 8 June 1708, age 20, Mullinax Rattcliffe
Hays, John, 10 June 1701, age 18, Coll. James Smalwood
Hedge, Thomas, 10 June 1718, age 11, John Speake
Henley, John, 9 September 1701, age 14, William Smalwood
Henry, Ann, 13 February 1700, age 20, James Williams

Hensley, Edward, 10 June 1674, age 17, John Bowles
Herbert, John, 13 March 1677, age 18, Captn. Josias Fendall, by
    Humphrey Warren
Herbert, William, 11 April 1676, age 17, Robert Rowlants
Herman, Robert, 3 February 1664, age 17-18, Henry Addames
Hernold, John, 14 June 1698, age 14, Randolph Garland
Hey, Charles, 9 June 1668, age 16, Benjamin Rozer
Hicks, Thomas, 8 March 1681, age 15, Robert Robins
Hill, Thomas, 14 June 1670, age 16, Mr. Rozer
Hill, Thomas, 8 June 1686, age 13, Giles Blizard
Hill, Vall, 12 March 1672, age 12, William Hinsey
Hinch, Matheu, 8 November 1670, age 21, Benjamin Rozer
Hincks, Dorothy, 12 January 1669, age 19, John Wheeler
Hinde, William, 12 March 1678, age 12, Thomas Clarke
Hindle, Joshua, 11 June 1678, age 21, Francis Goodrich
Hinsey, John, 10 June 1701, age 18, Francis Goodrick Junr., "hee had
    Indentures in Ireland before hee came aboard the Shipp which
    are casually or accidentally lost or Imbezzelled"
    "Capt. William Broadhead Master of the said Shipp,
    Joseph Howell the Mate, William Beard the Carpenter"
Hinsley, Thomas, 14 March 1682, age 21, Philip Linos
Hire, Raiph, 11 March 1679, age 20, Thomas Taylor
Hobson, John, 12 May 1663, age 13, Robert Hundley
Hodgins, Charles, 10 March 1674, age 14, Archebald Walkup
Hodgly, John, 8 March 1670, age 21, Joseph Harrison
Hogdin, Jonathan, 9 November 1680, age 18, John Redich,
    by John Hamilton
Hoggin, Henry, 11 January 1676, age 21, Philipp Lines
Hoghland, Patrick, 9 January 1700, age 15, Major James Smallwood
Holliewood, James, 12 June 1688, age 18, William Smith
Hollis, Thomas, 4 April 1699, age 15, Thomas Smoote
Holmes, Grace, 14 June 1681, age 22, Philip Linos
Holton, Joseph, 14 June 1670, age 22, Mr. Rozer
Honnker, Elisabeth, 9 August 1664, age 15, James Lee
Hoskings, Thomas, 11 March 1679, age 12, Robert Thompson Junior
Hoskins, Jeremi, 13 April 1669, age 21, John Bowles
Hoskins, Lauran, 13 April 1669, age 17, John Bowles
Houghton, James, 8 August 1682, age 14, Capt. Henry Aspenall
Howard, John, 12 June 1705, age 17, John Thompson

Howard, Philise, 8 November 1664, age 20 "according to her owne acknowledgment," William Barton Junior

Howes, Thomas, 12 March 1678, age 16, Capt. Josiah Fendall, by Adam Weaver

Hoyle, Samuell, 8 November 1670, age 21-22, Benjamin Rozer

Hubberton, Mary, 10 March 1671, age 18, Bartholomew Coates

Hudson, Robert, 11 April 1676, age 13, Richard Midgeley

Humble, Barbary, 11 January 1676, age 20, Philipp Lines

Hundly, Henry, 12 July 1664, age 21, Miss Elisabeth Atwicks

Hungerlee, William, 13 June 1693, age 15, Samuell Luckett

Hunt, John, 13 April 1669, age 16, William Barton

Hunter, Richard, 9 January 1672, age 21, Benjamin Rozer

Hunter, William, 11 January 1676, age 14, Thomas Hussey

Huntsman, Samuell, 10 September 1678, age 14, Thomas Allanson

Hussey, Gerrard, __ January 1684, age 18, Phillip Lynes

Hutchins, Elianor, 10 June 1674, age 13, Henery Hawkins

Hutchison, Katharine, 14 November 1710, age 22, James Semmes

Ireland, Elisabeth, 22 April 1662, age 17, Edward Swan

Ives, Richard, 12 March 1678, age 19, William Chandler

Ivory, Catherine, 8 August 1693, age 15, Anne Neale, by her son, Anthony Neale

Jackson, James, 8 September 1674, age 19, John Wright

Jackson, Mary, 10 March 1671, age 21, Robert Henley

Jackson, Thomas, 22 April 1662, age 16, Thomas Gerrard Esq., by Samuel Dobson

James, Elizabeth, 12 June 1705, age 4, Coll. John Contee

Jeffers, Marie, 8 July 1662, age 14, John Cain

Jeffreyes, Thomas, 8 March 1681, age 18, Joseph Maninge, by his son in law Mr. Stone

Jeffs, John, 14 June 1670, age 13, John Courts

Jennings, John, 9 January 1677, age 17-18, Benjamin Rozer

Joanes, Mary, 28 July 1663, age 20, Walter Beane

Johnson, Jemmima, 9 March 1680, age 13, Coll. Benja. Rozer Esqre.

Johnson, John, 12 July 1664, age 12-13, Edmond Lendsey

Johnson, Thomas, 11 April 1676, age 17, Henry Adames

Jones, Edward, 10 March 1674, age 14, John Lambert

Jones, John, 9 January 1694, age 14, John Wilder

Jones, Katherine, 8 June 1686, age 16, Phillip Lynes

Jones, Mary, 8 August 1682, age 18, John Stone

Jones, Moses, 8 June 1675, age 17, Zachary Wade

CHARLES COUNTY

Jones, Philip, 13 March 1677, age 21, Robert Henly
Jones, Robert, 12 September 1682, age 21, Thomas Hussey
Jordan, Margeret, 10 January 1665, age 16, Samuell Fendall
Jordan, Mary, 12 June 1683, age 20, John Godson
Keelby, John, 10 June 1674, age 16, Peter Carr
Kelley, Michael, 12 March 1700, age 12, James Hicks
Kelly, Margarett, 12 March 1700, age 21, Joseph Manning
Kendall, Francis, 13 June 1676, age 14, John Newton
Keneday, Nicholas, 10 August 1714, age 18, Thomas Plunket
Kenneday, James, 9 January 1700, age 12, Thomas Hussey
Kennyday, Nicholas, 4 April 1699, age 22, Samuel Luckett
Kent, Robert, 13 April 1669, age 12, John Dent
Kerkley, William, 12 March 1672, age 10, Richard Morris
Killcart, John, 12 January 1686, age 15, William Hatch
Killpatrick, Alexander, 4 April 1699, age 14, George Tubman
King, John, 11 June 1700, age 11, Nicholas Cooper
King, Thomas, 10 March 1685, age 20, Joseph Maning
Kingsbury, George, 12 January 1686, age 19, Henry Hawkins
Kingstone, Thomas, 13 June 1676, age 14, James Tyre, by
          William Tymothy
Kiniken, James, 9 December 1685, age 13, Ralph Smith
Kirby (?), Paul, 8 June 1675, age 16, William Barton
Kirmichael, John, 9 June 1719, age 14 "ye first day of next January,"
          Thomas Wright
Kirten, Zachary, 13 June 1676, age 14, Captn. Josias Fendall, by his
          brother Samuel Fendall
Knightsmith, Hannah, 14 June 1681, age 20, Thomas Taylor
Kue, John, 8 June 1686, age 19, Phillip Lynes
Lackimore, Edward, 12 January 1686, age 14, Henry Hawkins
Lacquey, James, 8 June 1708, age 18, Francis Goodrich
Lallee, Cornelius, 19 April 1698, age 12, Thomas Smoote
Lamber, Ami, 9 August 1664, age 20, John Pain
Lampton, Marke, 10 January 1665, age 16, William Robbison, by
          Daniell Johnson
Lane, Anne, 17 March 1663, age 18, Humphery Warren, by
          William Heard
Lane, William, 7 April 1668, age 14, William Perfect
Laurence, Thomas, 12 March 1672, age 12, Henry Bonner
Lawrence, James, 4 April 1699, age 17, James Cotteroll
Lawson, Thomas, 8 August 1699, age 18, William Newman

Leech, James, 8 June 1675, age 11, Edmund Taylor
Leeds, Robert, 8 August 1665, age 21, Edward Richardson
Lees, Thomas, 9 March 1686, age 22, John Court Jun.,
      "produced an indenture which is found invalid"
Lenham, John, 10 June 1679, age 19, Henry Hardy
Linge, Francis, male, 8 March 1664, age 17, Henry Adames
Linghams, Daniell, 11 March 1690, age not judged, John Bayne,
      Indenture judged not "good and authentick," ordered to serve
      "according to ye Custome of ye Countrey"
Linsey, Cornelius, 20 January 1680, age 19, William Chandler
Lockraft, John, 1 April 1701, age 13, Francis Green
Loftas, Margarett, 8 September 1674, age 19, Richard Fowke
Low, James, 8 August 1699, age 14, John Gray
Luces, Thomas, 9 January 1672, age 20, Richard Edelen
Lybscome, Dorothy, 12 August 1673, age 22, Benjamin Rozer
Lyle, John, 8 March 1664, age 17, Mathias Obrian
Macann, Richard, 11 March 1729, age 15, Giles Green
Macclannen, Margarett, 13 August 1706, age 20, John Speake
Macdaniel, James, 11 August 1719, age 21, Thomas Hussey Luckett
Mac Dannell, Danniele, 8 June 1708, age 19, John Manning
Machen, John, 10 June 1679, age 20, Major John Wheeler
Mack Cartie, Dermud, 11 June 1667, age 13-14, Richard Jones
Mackdonal, Daniell, 4 April 1699, age 15, Thomas Hussey
Mackenhine, John, 13 April 1669, age 18, James Macky
Mackollom, Markam, 13 March 1722, age not judged, John Walden,
      stated in petition dated November 1721 that "he was taken in ye
      Rebellion at Preston and Transported into this Province without
      Indenture," "had served the full Term of five years," "was past
      the age of twenty two years at the Time of his Transportacion"
Mackontosh, James, 13 March 1722, age not judged, Henry Hawkins,
      "taken in ye Rebellion at Preston," "had served the full Term
      of five years"
Mack William, James, 4 April 1699, age 16, Hugh Toares
Maclaine, Laughlin, 12 June 1705, age 17, Robert Green
Macniel, James, 8 June 1714, age 21, Robert Hanson
Macough, James, 13 June 1699, age 21, Thomas Stone
Maddock, William, 9 February 1686, age 20, Thomas Gerrard
Magrah, Honour, 13 February 1700, age 18, George Tubman, by
      Henry Hawkins

Magregor, Dunkin, 14 November 1710, age 12, Henry Holland Hawkins
Magregor, Margret, 8 August 1710, age 19, Capt. John Gray
Mahawne, Joane, 12 March 1700, age 18, Joseph Manning
Mahawney, Tymothy, 8 August 1693, age 17, Coll. Humphrey Warren
Mahoni, Daniell, 10 March 1685, age 15, Thomas Craxon
Malberry, Francis, 13 November 1677, age 18, Joseph Manninge
Manithurb, Thomas, 10 January 1665, age 16, Robert Hendley
Manlow, John, 11 January 1676, age 19, Philipp Lines
Mannerley, Margarett, 11 March 1679, age 9, Joshuah Doyne
        "of St. Maries County"
Manwaren, Walter, 11 August 1668, age 20, Richard Smoot
Marden, John, 11 August 1668, age 13, Alexander Sympson
Markfearson, Markham, 4 April 1699, age 16, Alexander Wilson
Marlow, Anthony, 9 January 1672, age 17, Samuel Fendall
Marly, William, 19 April 1698, age 21, Francis Goodrich
Marr, Henry, 10 June 1718, age 14, Francis Oden
Marrome, James, 14 March 1665, age 17, Walter Beane
Marsh, William, 11 August 1674, age 18, Thomas Gerrard
Martiall, Richard, 12 April 1676, age 14, Benjamin Rozer
Mason, John, 9 November 1680, age 21, John Redich,
        by John Hamilton
Mason, William, 13 March 1677, age 13, Philipp Lines
Massey, John, 9 January 1672, age not judged, Benjamin Rozer, "he is
        willing to serve five whole years" commencing 2 October 1671
Mathews, John, 5 January 1664, age 14, John Lewgar
Mattox, David, 12 January 1692, age 15, Michael Martin
Mattox, Thomas, 12 January 1692, age 12, William Dent
Maybanck, Elizabeth, 10 June 1674, age 13, John Wood
Mayfeild, Richard, 10 August 1675, age 17, Francis Wine
Medcaph, Robert, 10 January 1665, age 11, John Duglas
Megrough, Alice, 19 April 1698, age 19, Hugh Toares
Micaney, Andrew, 10 March 1671, age 21, John Douglas, by Peter Carre
Michell, Marke, 8 March 1664, age 12, Zachery Waed
Miles, Elizabeth, 13 August 1678, age 17, William Wells
Miles, Nathaniell, 9 March 1680, age 14, Archibald Wahob
Mill, Isabella, 14 November 1710, age 21, Barton Hungerford
Millborne, Rachell, 8 November 1664, age 18, Richard Smoot
Miller, Andrew, 14 November 1710, age 16, Elizabeth Hawkins
Miller, Daniel, 8 June 1714, age 20, William Stone Senr.
Mills, Alexander, 15 February 1698, age 12, Capt. John Bayne

CHARLES COUNTY

Milshaw, John, 11 March 1679, age 15, John Ward
Milstead, Howard, 12 January 1675, age 19, William Chandeler
Mires, Christopher, 13 June 1682, age 21, Thomas Craystone
Mitchell, Anthony, 8 January 1678, age 17-18, Thomas Gerrard
Mitchell, James, 4 April 1699, age 13, Francis Harrison
Mongerrell, Edmond, 10 March 1685, age 13, John Hanson
Monroe, William, 11 August 1719, age 20, Ignatius Luckett
Monteal, Richard, 10 February 1663, age 14, William Perfect
Moore, John, 4 April 1699, age 16, Edward Philpott
Morand, Patrick, 11 March 1701, age 13, John Bayne, "brings here into
        Court two Irish servants"
Morrell, Christopher, 10 June 1673, age 20, Richard Chandler
Morris, Annas, female, 11 April 1676, age 18, Richard Morris
Morris, Edward, 8 August 1699, age 14, Andrew Simpson
Morris, Ellis, 12 September 1682, age 19, James Neale Junior
Morris, James, 14 March 1699, age 15, William Tymothy
Morris, John, 10 June 1674, age 16, Peter Carr
Morris, John, 4 April 1699, age 15, Coll. John Courts
Morrough, John, 19 April 1698, age 12, Capt. John Bayne
Moulton, Margarett, 11 August 1674, age 14, Robert Greene
Mounke, Elisabeth, 10 February 1663, age 18, John Cherman
Mow, Peter, 11 January 1670, age 7, Christopher Brimins
Murphy, Magloughlin, 9 November 1697, age 18, Capt. John Wilder
Murphy, Mary, 12 March 1700, age 22, Richard Combes
Murphy, Matthew, 19 April 1698, age 14, Jefferry Cole, by John Wilder
Murraine, Nicholas, 12 March 1678, age 17, Anna Fowkes
Murrie, Hugh, 11 June 1723, age 16, Richard Speake
Nailee, John, 10 August 1675, age 12, Thomas Matthewes
Nash, Samuell, 14 March 1682, age 20, Philip Linos
Nayler, John, 8 August 1699, age 13, Henry Hawkins
Neale, Henrie, 11 August 1668, age 16, John Courts
Neale, Robert, 9 February 1686, age 20, Thomas Gerrard
Neenes, Mary, 8 January 1678, age 17, Thomas Mudd
Neisbut, Edmond, 10 January 1665, age 18, Richard Stone, by
        Jeromy Dickeson
Nenan, Dennis, 20 January 1680, age 22, William Chandler
Newall, James, 12 July 1664, age 14, George Bradshow
Newman, Ann, 11 January 1670, age 17, William Barton
Newman, Hannah, 12 January 1686, age 11, Henry Hawkins

Newton, John, 14 June 1681, age 20, Henry Hawkins
Newton, Richard, 9 January 1694, age 14, Capt. Ignatius Causin
Nichols, John, 8 November 1687, age not judged, John Court, produced
    Indentures "for four yeares," upon inspection, ordered to serve
    "according to ye Custom of ye Country"
Nichols, Rachell, 14 March 1682, age 17, Captn. James Neale
Nicholson, Esther, 10 August 1680, age 7, Henry Hawkins
Nicholson, John, 10 August 1680, age 10, Henry Hawkins
Nicholson, Margaret, 9 June 1691, age 22, George Plater
Nicholson, William, 10 August 1680, age 6, John Stone
Nicolls, Christobell, 12 January 1675, age 20, Thomas King
Noland, William, 4 October 1698, age 18, Peter Villett
Nolinn, Patrick, 13 April 1669, age 20, Mr. Dickinson
Nollson, Allexander, 14 November 1699, age 15, William Glover
Norman, Thomas, 13 April 1669, age 21, Henry Adames
Normansell, Thomas, 9 March 1686, age 19, Thomas Clarke, "ye servant
    produced an Indenture which ye Court adjudged Invalid"
Northon, John, 4 April 1699, age 10, Coll. John Courts
Norton, Amy, 8 June 1680, age 17, Thomas Mitchell
Nowlan, James, 11 November 1718, age 20, James Semmes
Oakes, Francis, 8 June 1686, age 19, Henry Hawkins
Oard, Peter, 12 March 1672, age 18, Robert Henley
Oliver, Elizabeth, 1 April 1701, age 20, Ubgatt Reeves
Orlock, Turlow, 13 March 1683, age 15, Coll. William Diggs Esqre.
Orson, Bearer, 12 January 1669, age 13, Robert Clearke
Osborne, Thomas, 9 June 1702, age 17, Francis Goodrick Senr.
Oulson, John, 9 January 1672, age 21, Robert Rowland, by
    Humphry Warren
Oxford, William, 11 August 1696, age 11, Capt. Philip Hoskins
Page, Margerie, 5 January 1664, age 19, Walter Beane
Parker, Ann, 8 June 1669, age 19, John Cage
Parker, John, 8 March 1670, age 18, Jeremiah Dickison
Parker, Jonas, 8 June 1675, age 15, John Courtes, by Cleborne Lomax
Parkes, Robert, 11 January 1676, age 18, Thomas Dent
Patrige, Mary, 3 February 1664, age 11-12, John Hatch
Patterson, William, 14 June 1698, age 16, William Dent
Pattison, John, 10 June 1673, age 13, Benjamin Rozer
Pauding, William, 13 April 1669, age 16, Henry Adames
Payne, Thomas, 10 January 1665, age 15, Thomas Stone, by
    William Boyden

Peacocke, William, 13 March 1677, age 14, Philipp Lines
Pearson, John, 11 January 1676, age 17, Raiph Shaw
Pearson, Nathaniell, 11 April 1676, age 16, Dennis Huscula (?), by
    Richard Edelon
Peeso, Cornape, 12 January 1669, age 13, William Marshall
Pembrooke, Mary, 11 June 1678, age 20, Robert Rowlants
Perkins, James, 8 March 1664, age 13, Joseph Harrisson
Perkins, William, 11 August 1702, age 16, Samuell Luckett
Perry, Thomas, 13 June 1699, age 11, Philip Briscoe
Persivall, Charles, 10 June 1673, age 12, Mrs. Coates
Phegg, Charles, 14 March 1682, age 14, Thomas Gerrard
Philips, Edward, 11 January 1676, age 17, Thomas Dent
Philips, John, 12 March 1678, age 16, John Fearson
Philips, Thomas, 13 March 1677, age 17, James Bowling
Phyllips, Hugh, 8 September 1668, age 21, Colonel Gerrard Fowke
Pickard, Robert, 11 March 1679, age 17, John Lambert
Pickering, Michell, c. 13 March 1661, "beeing then" age 18, Robert
    Hendley, freed by court 13 March 1666
Piper, James, 12 March 1672, age 11, Richard Morris
Pirks, John, 9 June 1702, age 12, Francis Goodrick Junr.
Player, John, 10 January 1665, age 15, John Wright
Poke, Margrett, 14 November 1710, age 19, George Dent
Poor, James, 12 June 1694, age 12, Captain William Barton
Poore, Peter, 14 November 1682, age 21, William Smith
Potts, John, 8 June 1686, age 24, Capt. Bowling
Potts, Thomas, 9 September 1679, age 20, John Wood, by William Wells
Powcher, Thomas, 9 February 1686, age 20, John Court, "his Indenture
    void"
Powell, Robert, 8 March 1670, age 16, Mr. Adams
Prince, Abigall, 11 January 1670, age 23, Thomas Dent
Proser, Ann, 14 November 1710, age 24, Robert Price
Purnie, John, 12 January 1686, age 18, Madam Mary Chandler
Ranford, William, 10 June 1673, age 13, John Clarke
Rawfeild, John, 14 November 1710, age 14, Anne Lynes
Rawson, Susan, 14 March 1665, age 17, Daniell Johnson
Ray, William, 19 April 1698, age 13, John Frye
Rayley, Edward, 13 March 1677, age 14, James Bowling
Rea, John, 8 March 1670, age 5, Robert Rowland
Redding, Isabell, 10 November 1674, age 19, Thomas Hussey
Redman, Cornelius, 14 June 1698, age 20, Anne Taylor, "widdow"

CHARLES COUNTY

Reed, Thomas, 10 January 1665, age 18, William Hinshaw, by
    Robert Hendley
Renes, Elleanor, 12 June 1688, age 22, William Smith, Indenture judged
    not good "without further proof"
Renes, Mary, 12 June 1688, age 22, Mark Lampton, Indenture judged
    not good "without further proof"
Renisson, John, 10 January 1665, age 19, William Robisson, by
    Daniell Johnson
Rennicke, Anne, 10 November 1674, age 16, Elinor Beane, by John Long
Rhenick, Owen, 19 April 1698, age 13, Richard Edelen
Rhyne, John, 19 April 1698, age 15, William Hungerford
Richardson, Bernerd, 13 March 1677, age 17, Coll. John Duglas
Richardson, Joseph, 12 January 1675, age 21, John Clarke
Richardson, Thomas, 13 January 1680, age 13, Henry Adames, by
    Philip Mason
Ring, Ralph, 10 March 1671, age 22, Samuel Cressey
Roberts, Richard, 13 June 1682, age 22, Major William Boardman, by
    Edmond Dennis
Roberts, William, 9 January 1677, age 20, Benjamin Rozer
Robertson, Marie, 10 March 1668, age 17, John Coates, "But yet It was
    the request of her Master that she should serve but six yeares"
Robertson, Peter, 9 June 1719, age 15, Col. Walter Story
Robins, Henry, 12 April 1676, age 17, Benjamin Rozer
Robinson, Anne, 12 January 1675, age 23, John Clarke
Robinson, Samuell, 11 June 1678, age 21, Capt. Humphrey Warren
Rogers, Mary, 14 March 1682, age 20, Philip Linos
Rose, John, 8 March 1670, age 15, Mr. Adams
Ross, Alexander, 4 April 1699, age 18, Capt. John Bayne
Ross, Francis, 12 September 1699, age 11, Ubgatt Reeves
Rouze, Anne, 11 March 1679, age 19, William Smith
Roy, Michal, 9 January 1700, age 14, Francis Green
Rye, John, 8 August 1699, age 12, Capt. John Bayne
Salt, Mary, 11 March 1679, age 20, Thomas Spooke, "of
    St. Maries County"
Sanders, Elizabeth, 12 November 1700, age 16, Benoni Thomas
Sanders, Mathew, 8 July 1662, age 15, John Cain
Sanders, William, 10 March 1685, age 17, John Hanson
Savage, Catherine, 13 February 1700, age 20, John Gwinn
Scarryott, Richard, 9 January 1672, age 12, Archibald Wahab

CHARLES COUNTY

Scot, Eribecca, 12 July 1664, age 15, James Lensey
Scott, Jennet, 14 November 1710, age 22, Anthony Neale
Scoutch, Alexander, 4 April 1699, age 20, William Herbert
Seawell, Rebeckah, 13 March 1677, age 20, Thomas King
Seer, Thomas, 10 March 1668, age 13, Colon. Gerrard Fowke, by
    James Macoy
Seney, Daniell, 11 June 1667, age 14-15, Henry Moore
Shanhikin, Derby, 14 March 1699, age 17, Randolph Garland
Shaw, John, 13 June 1682, age 17, Railph Smith
Shaw, Mary, 12 June 1683, age 19, Capt. Casheene
Shaw, Thomas, 11 March 1729, age 12, James Lattimar
Shelton, Mary, 14 March 1682, age 17, Joseph Piles
Shihorr, William, 9 January 1700, age 12, Thomas Hussey
Shiner, Daniell, 17 March 1663, age 15, Mr. Robert, by John Duglas
Short, George, 10 January 1671, age 17-18, Clement Theobalds
Shott, John, 4 April 1699, age 17, James Finley
Sigeley, Samuell, 9 November 1680, age 16, John Mun
Simmes, Francis, (?) January 1686, age 17, Capt. William Barton
Simmons, John, 9 June 1719, age 10, Ignatius Luckett
Simmons, Mary, 17 December 1662, age 14, James Boulin
Simmons, William, 13 February 1700, age 12, Samuel Luckett
Simpson, Elizabeth, 13 March 1711, age 22, Robert Sanders
Simpson, Samuell, 12 August 1673, age 15, John Goodge, by Captn.
    Josias Fendall
Singleton, Richard, 10 June 1674, age 13, Richard Beck
Skinner, Thomas, 11 June 1667, age 15, Robert Hunley
Slater, John, 13 March 1677, age 16, Thomas King
Small, Margaret, 9 June 1719, age 14 "ye Twenty fifth day of next
    December," William Goody
Smith, Benjamin, 4 April 1699, age 19, William Dent
Smith, Elizabeth, 12 March 1678, age 12, Thomas Clarke
Smith, James, 8 January 1678, age 20, Thomas Mudd
Smith, James, 9 February 1686, age 21, Samuell Luckett, "ye servant
    produced an Indenture ye Court adjudgeth ye same Invalid"
Smith, Margrett, 14 November 1710, age 20, Edward Millstead
Smith, Robert, 10 June 1674, age 15, John Munn
Smith, William, 9 January 1677, age 20, John Fanning
Snell, Margaret, 12 March 1672, age 20, Ann Fowkes
Sneton, John, 8 March 1664, age 24, James Mackey
Snosell, Christopher, 8 March 1664, age 20, Richard Stone

Snowden, William, 11 March 1679, age 10, John Vandry, "of
    St. Maries County"
South, Benjamin, 8 March 1692, age 12, Robert Thompson Junior
Southerland, Daniel, 9 June 1730, age 13, William Macferson
Spurling, Jeremiah, 12 January 1686, age 18, Henry Hawkins
Standly, Thomas, 8 March 1664, age 14, John Piles, by Humphery Warren
Steaphens, William, 10 January 1688, age 21, Joseph Cornell
Stephens, Mary, 10 March 1674, age 19, John Lambert
Stephens, Mary, 13 June 1682, age 19, Thomas Stonestreet
Stephens, Richard, 14 January 1679, age 10, Thomas Gerrard
Steward, George, 14 November 1710, age 13, Walter Winter
Stewart, Daniel, 13 March 1722, age not judged, William Penn, "taken in
    ye Rebellion at Preston," "had served the full Term of five years"
Stidman, Edward, 12 June 1677, age 14, Capt. Ignatius Causin
Still, Alexander, 13 March 1711, age 16, John Wilkinson
Stone, Elisabeth, 17 March 1663, age 14, William Heard
Stone, Mathias, 10 March 1674, age 14, Archebald Wahab
Stonehouse, Thomas, 8 June 1675, age 13, Richard Primer (?)
Storker, Isabella, 10 June 1707, age 11, John Thompson
Stratton, Philise, 14 March 1665, age 19, Henry Warren
Stringer, George, 8 January 1678, age 15, Henry Hawkins
Sudburie, Gregorie, 9 June 1668, age 16, Robert Hunley, by Francis Pope
Summer, Jonathan, 17 December 1662, age 12, Capt. Josias Fendall
Swaine, George, 13 June 1676, age 14, Captn. Josias Fendall, by his
    brother Samuel Fendall
Sweenehee, Sarah, 12 March 1678, age 20, Francis Goodrich
Swillavan, Owen, 4 April 1699, age 14, Thomas Hagan
Symmes, John, 9 June 1691, age 9, George Plater
Sympson, Allexander, 8 August 1699, age 15, William Barton
Sympson, James, 14 November 1699, age 19, Henry More
Taylor, Elizabeth, 11 June 1667, age 19, Alexander Smyth
Taylor, George, 11 April 1676, age 14, William Perfitt
Taylor, Jheromie, 8 March 1664, age 21, John Lumbroso
Taylor, John, 10 January 1665, age 17, Daniell Johnson
Taylor, Richard, 11 January 1676, age 16, John Posie
Taylor, Thomas, 12 June 1677, age 13, George Godfrey
Thatcher, Mary, 11 March 1679, age 19, John Clarke
Thomas, Anne, 11 January 1676, age 22, John Buttler
Thomas, Edward, 11 August 1685, age 12, Capt. Ignatius Causseene

CHARLES COUNTY

Thompson, Henry, 11 March 1679, age 16, Thomas Clipsham
Thompson, James, 12 January 1675, age 12, Francis Goodrich
Thompson, John, 11 June 1678, age 14 "ye first day of next January,"
    Robert Greene
Thompson, John, 12 January 1686, age 17, Henry Hawkins
Thompson, John, 9 June 1719, age 14, William Williams
Thorett, Tymothy, 4 April 1699, age 12, Coll. John Courts
Tibbitt, John, 10 June 1673, age 17, James Bowleing, by Richard Edelen
Tidron, James, 17 March 1663, age 15, John Bouls
Tillee, Thomas, 9 June 1668, age 20, Nathaniel Barton
Tillzey, Mabella, 13 March 1677, age 18, James Tyre, by Thomas Harris
Tipton, Edward, 11 August 1668, age 18, Humphrey Warren Junr.
Toby, James, 12 March 1700, age 12, John Derreego
Tod, Thomas, 10 January 1671, age 13, William Love
Todd, Jeremiah, 14 June 1698, age 14, Elinor Stone
Tomkins, Joan, 8 March 1687, age 20, Randolph Hinson
Tomson, Henry, 8 March 1664, age 17, Walter Beane
Towell, Charles, 9 August 1698, age 17, Thomas Hagan
Toy, Walter, 9 June 1702, age 13, Benjamin Smallwood
Toy, William, 9 June 1702, age 14, Ltt. Coll. James Smallwood
Treemairne, John, 9 August 1681, age 17, Captn. Humphrey Warren
Tubb, Thomas, 13 April 1669, age 21, Zack Wade
Tuborne, Katherine, 9 November 1703, age 17, Francis Greene
Turner, William, 11 January 1670, age 22, Humphrey Warren Junior
Turno, Walter, __ January 1684, age 18, John Stone
Tusan, Zara, 8 March 1664, age 16, Robert Hundley
Twifer, Anne, 22 April 1662, age 17, William Marshall
Tymothie, William, 11 June 1667, age 15, John Bowles
Uppenbridge, John, 8 June 1680, age 13, John Broade
Vaine, Henrie, 7 April 1668, age 14, George Newman
Vaughan, Richard, 12 November 1715, age 12, Charles Digges
Vause, Joseph, 8 June 1686, age 19, Phillip Lynes
Verritt, John, 11 April 1676, age 17, John Hatch
Violett, Ambrose, 10 June 1701, age 19, John Beale
W_____, Margrett, 8 November 1670, age 20, Benjamin Rozer
Waalwort, Isaac, 11 June 1667, age 22, William Marshall, "Buried his Man
    Izall (sic) on the last Day of August 1667"
Wade, Allexander, 14 November 1699, age 11, John Godshall
Waedman, Rice, 14 March 1665, age 21, Archibell Whahob
Wager, Joseph, 19 April 1698, age 13, John Allen

CHARLES COUNTY

Walker, George, 14 November 1710, age 17, Patrick Maggelee
Wallen, William, 9 June 1696, age 13, Thomas Mudd
Walsh, Richard, 11 November 1718, age 15, Mary Theobalds
Waltom, Ralph, 14 March 1665, age 14, Peeter Car
Ward, Anne, 12 May 1663, age 16, John Nevill
Ward, Henry, 8 June 1675, age 15, Richard Smoote, by William Barton
Ward, Richard, 11 April 1676, age 12, Humphrey Warren
Warner, Christopher, 13 April 1669, age 20, Robert Downes
Waters, Edward, 9 June 1702, age 15, Richard Wade
Waterworth, Catherine, 8 August 1682, age 14, John Munn
Waterworth, John, 8 August 1682, age 12, John Bayne
Weatherburne, Jane, 11 June 1706, age 18, John Cofer
Webb, Aaron, 12 March 1706, age 6, Maddam Sarah Barton
Webb, Moses, 4 April 1704, age 8, Maj. William Barton
Webb, Rozamon, 4 April 1704, age 11, Maj. William Barton
Webster, Nicholaus, 8 March 1664, age 17, John Piles, by
       Humphery Warren
Welch, William, 4 April 1699, age 15, John Fendall
Welsh, James, 13 June 1693, age 15, Major James Smallwood
Welsh, Thomas, 14 June 1698, age 16, Philip Briscoe
Westbrooke, William, 14 June 1698, age 17, Richard Harrison
Whaland, Dennis, 19 April 1698, age 20, Edward Philpott
Wheeler, David, 10 January 1682, age 18, Thomas Mitchell
Whilden, John, 11 June 1667, age 24, Edward Swanne
White, Matthew, 8 March 1726, age 11, Colo. John Fendall
Whitehead, John, 8 January 1678, age 18, Capt. Humphrey Warren
Whitehorne, John, 14 March 1682, age 16, Thomas Mudd
Whitt, Samuell, 14 November 1676, age 11-12, Benjamin Rozer
Whorton, John, 14 March 1665, age 17, Thomas Mathews
Wiggs, David, 13 April 1669, age 13, Robert Downes
Wilder, Robert, 8 August 1671, age 16-17, John Bowles
Wilfray, Lusi, 8 June 1675, age 18, Bennett Marshegay
Wilkinson, John, 10 June 1674, age 18, John Taylor
Wilkinson, Lancelot, 9 January 1672, age 18, Humphry Warren
Wilkison, David, 4 April 1699, age 16, Michaell Martin
Wilkison, John, 14 March 1699, age 17, Francis Goodrich
Willbee, Michael, 11 March 1679, age 12, George Godfrey, by
       John Wright
Williams, Edward, 11 March 1679, age 20, Henry Hawkins
Williams, Jane, 13 March 1677, age 14, Philipp Lines

Williams, Jenkin, 12 January 1675, age 21, Benjamin Rozer
Williams, John, 13 March 1677, age 21, Thomas Gerrard
Williams, John, 14 March 1682, age 10, John Allward
Williams, John, 4 April 1699, age 12, Benjamin Posey
Williams, Katherine, 13 June 1676, age 17-18, Captn. Josias Fendall,
     by his brother Samuel Fendall
Williams, Peter, 12 January 1669, age 13, Thomas Hussy
Williams, William, 11 March 1679, age 22, Capt. Ignatius Causin
Willman, Henry, 11 June 1678, age 12, William Smith
Willson, Gils, 14 March 1665, age 22-23, Alexander Smith
Willson, John, 10 June 1707, age 10, Thomas Plunkett
Willson, Joseph, 10 June 1707, age 7, Leonard Greene
Wilson, Lawrence, 9 January 1672, age 20, Capt. William Boreman, by
     Richard Edelen
Winter, John, 11 March 1679, age 15, Capt. Ignatius Causin
Wollis, Anne, 17 March 1663, age 18, John Courts
Woodkeepe, Richard, 9 September 1673, age 12, Cornelius Mackarles
Woolf, Joseph, 8 March 1664, age 13, Robert Perkins
Woolfe, Robert, 11 June 1678, age 17, Robert Rowlants
Worrell, Mary, 8 January 1706, age 18, Richard Harrison
Worthington, Joseph, 11 August 1685, age 15, Edw. Rookard
Wright, George, 13 June 1676, age 18-19, Benjamin Rozer, by
     Alexander Gallant
Wyott, John, 10 June 1673, age 16, Mrs. Beane, by Mathew Hill
Yappe (?), Roger, 12 January 1686, age 21, Henry Hawkins
Young, Jane, 11 March 1679, age 20, Elinor Bayne, by Mathew Hill
Younge, Charles, 12 August 1673, age 10, Samuell Fendall
_____ , Ruth, 8 November 1670, age 14, John Stone
_____ , _____ , 12 August 1673, age 21, Thomas Harris of Pickoaxon,
     by Thomas Wornell
_____ , _____ , female, not named, 11 June 1706, age 20, Patrick
     Maggalee

CHARLES COUNTY

Worshippfull Commissioners	Servants
Adames, Henry	Birtch, Chomley, Gibson, Guessne, Herman, Johnson, Linge, Norman, Pauding, Powell, Richardson, Rose
Addisson, John, Capt.	
Aspenall, Henry, Capt.	Houghton
Barton, William, Capt., Lieut. *	Armstrong, Blanch, Cooper, Franckum, German, Gibbons, Halliburton, Harrison, Howard, Hunt, Kirby, Newman, Poor, Simmes, Sympson, Webb, Webb
Bayne, John, Capt. *	Bryan, Cameright, Coney, Cusack Daniellson, Faulkner, Linghams, Mills, Morand, Morrough, Ross, Rye, Waterworth
Beale, John	Violett
Beane, Walter	Joanes, Marrome, Page, Tomson
Bowles, John	Hensley, Hoskins, Hoskins, Tymothie, Wilder
Briscoe, John, Capt.	
Briscoe, Philip	Perry, Welsh
Brown, Gustavus, Doctor	
Burford, Thomas, Esq.	Druncore
Causin, Ignatius, Capt.	Ball, Barrett, Bayly, Newton, Shaw, Stidman, Thomas, Williams, Winter
Clipsham, Thomas	Eaton, Thompson

108

CHARLES COUNTY

Worshippfull Commissioners	Servants
Coates, John	Robertson
Contee, John, Major, Coll.	Bradstone, Denealey, James
Courtes, John, Jun., Capt., Coll.	Atwick, Bridges, Cottlycott, Crouch, Froote, Grandsworth, Harris, Jeffs, Lees, Morris, Neale, Nichols, Northon, Parker, Powcher, Thorett, Wollis
Crabb, Thomas, Capt.	
Dent, George	Poke
Dent, Thomas, Capt.	Daverill, Parkes, Philips, Prince
Dent, William, Major, Ltt. Coll.	Bryan, Dod, Forbis, Mattox, Patterson, Smith
Doyne, Robert	Davis
Duglas, John, Coll.	Feddiman, Medcaph, Micaney, Richardson
Faning, John	Browne, Smith
Fendall, John, Coll.	Welch, White
Fowke, Gerrard	Phyllips, Seer
Godfrey, George, Lieut.	Taylor, Willbee
Hall, Benjamin, Capt.	
Hanson, John	Mongerrell, Sanders
Hanson, Robert, Major	Brayson, Macneil

CHARLES COUNTY

Worshippfull Commissioners	Servants
Harbert / Herbert, William, Capt., Coll. *	Brown, Scoutch
Hardy, Henry, Capt.	Bennett, Lenham
Harrison, Joseph	Anderson, Brooks, Dreyden, Hodgly, Perkins
Harrison, Richard	Bishop, Bonner, Westbrooke, Worrell
Hawkins, Henry	Brooke, Caddington, Comorains, Gardiner, Hutchins, Kingsbury, Lackimore, Mackontosh, Nayler, Newman, Newton, Nicholson, Nicholson, Oakes, Spurling, Stringer, Thompson, Williams, Yappe
Hawkins, Henry Holland	Magregor
Hawton, William	Carnee, Doyne
Henley, Robert	Attkins, Bawlding, Bell, Bellingham, Clarke, Dods, Jackson, Jones, Manithurb, Oard, Pickering, Reed, Sudburie, Tusan
Hinson, Randolph	Tomkins
Hoskins, Philip, Capt., Coll.	Oxford
Howard, Edmund	
Hussey, Thomas	Dallison, Donahan, Donohan, Ennis, Glover, Hunter, Jones, Kenneday, Mackdonal, Reeding, Shihorr, Williams
Hutchison, William	

CHARLES COUNTY

Worshippfull Commissioners	Servants
King, John	
Lee, William	
Lendsey, James	Scot
Lynes / Lines / Linos, Philip	Abbott, Allinson, Bradshaw, Cathew, Cumpton, Darnell, Doyle, Draper, Foard, Gilbard, Gutridge, Hinsley, Hoggin, Holmes, Humble, Hussey, Jones, Kue, Manlow, Mason, Nash, Peacocke, Rogers, Vause, Williams
Manning, Joseph	Carnaggey, Glasson, Groule, Harrard, Jeffreyes, Kelly, King, Mac Dannell, Mahawne, Malberry
Marshall, William	Browne, Champe, Clemence, Eure, Gluffur, Peeso, Twifer, Waalwort
Matthewes, Thomas	Booth, Dover, Nailee, Whorton
Parry, John	
Pope, Francis	Gwin
Rozer, Benjamin, Major, Coll., Esqre.	Chapman, Francisson, French, Green, Greene, Hey, Hill, Hinch, Holton, Hoyle, Hunter, Jennings, Johnson, Lybscome, Martiall, Massey, Pattison, Roberts, Robins, Whitt, Williams, Wright, W_____
Smallwood, James, Major, Ltt., Coll.	Bright, Carpenter, Clarke, Fisher, Fitz Gerralds, Gill, Hays, Hoghland, Toy, Welsh
Smith, Charles Somersett, Capt.	

111

CHARLES COUNTY

Worshippfull Commissioners	Servants
Smith, William	Abis, Barrett, Foster, Holliewood, Poore, Renes, Rouze, Willman
Stone, John	Jones, Nicholson, Turno, _____
Stone, Thomas	Divell, Macough, Payne
Stone, William	Miller
Story, Walter	Robertson
Taney / Tawney, Thomas	
Thomson, James	
Tyre, James	Austrith, Dickison, Kingstone, Tillzey
Wade, Zachary	Barton, Clarke, Edge, Hayles, Jones, Michell, Tubb
Warren, Humphrey, Capt., Coll., Lieut.	Baron, Davis, Derritt, Eason, Lane, Mahawney, Robinson, Tipton, Treemairne, Turner, Ward, Whitehead, Wilkinson
Wheeler, John, Major	Bell, Canland, Downes, Gaskoyne, Hincks, Machen
Wilder, John, Capt.	Burke, Jones, Murphy
Wilkinson, William	Chantler
Wyne, Francis	Ailer, Ailer, Mayfeild
Yates, Robert, Capt.	Gwynn

* see Prince George's County

CHARLES COUNTY			CHARLES COUNTY			CHARLES COUNTY		
Year	White	Negro	Year	White	Negro	Year	White	Negro
1661	1	0	1686	35	0	1711	3	0
1662	10	0	1687	4	0	1712	0	0
1663	15	0	1688	5	0	1713	0	0
1664	45	0	1689	0	0	1714	4	0
1665	29	0	1690	6	0	1715	1	0
1666	0	0	1691	2	0	1716	0	0
1667	10	0	1692	4	0	1717	0	0
1668	16	0	1693	7	0	1718	4	0
1669	33	0	1694	5	0	1719	12	0
1670	31	0				1720	1	0
1671	12	0	1696	3	0	1721	0	0
1672	22	0	1697	2	0	1722	5	0
1673	18	0	1698	31	0	1723	1	0
1674	37	0	1699	66	0	1724	0	0
1675	28	0	1700	21	0	1725	0	0
1676	38	0	1701	14	0	1726	2	0
1677	25	0	1702	7	0	1727	0	0
1678	32	0	1703	4	0	1728	1	0
1679	39	0	1704	2	0	1729	4	24
1680	19	0	1705	7	0	1730	1	5
1681	12	0	1706	7	0	1731	0	5
1682	35	0	1707	5	0	1732	0	0
1683	7	0	1708	8	0	1733	0	0
1684	2	0	1709	0	0	Total	836	34
1685	16	0	1710	20	0			

Note: No Indians

STAFFORD COUNTY (FRAGMENT)

Cissen, Henry, 7 August 1667, age 16, Thomas Grigg, (five years)
Earle, George, 7 August 1667, age 14, William Heabeard, (ten years)
Gallion, Henry, 30 August 1665, age 15, Robert Townsend, (nine years)
Hitchin, William, 15 June 1664, (age 13), William Withers, eleven years
Homan, Suzanah, 15 June 1664, (over 16), John Dodman, five years
Kateleech, Paul, 7 August 1667, age 16, Lt. Colo. Henry Meese,
    (five years)
Madder (or Mather), John, 10 January 1665, (over 16), Henry Meese,
    five years
Nelson, John, 15 June 1664, (age 12), John Dodman, twelve years
Reynolds, John, 23 October 1667, age 17, Capt. John Alexander,
    (five years)
Rushton, William, 10 January 1665, (over 16), Henry Meese, five years

Gentleman Justices	Servants
Alexander, John, Capt.	Reynolds
Dodman, John, Colo.	Homan, Nelson
Donding, Hugh	
Fossaker, Richard	
Heabeard, Richard	Earle
Mason, George, Major	
Meese, Henry, Lt. Colo.	Kateleech, Madder, Rushton
Osburne, Robert	
Perfitt, Roger	
Sanders, Edward	
Williams, Robert, Lt. Colo.	

STAFFORD COUNTY

Year	White	Negro	Indian
1664	3	0	0
1665	3	0	0
1666	0	0	0
1667	4	0	0
Total	10	0	0

114

STAFFORD COUNTY (FRAGMENT)

Cassey, Morgan, 12 September 1693, age 11, Robert Alexander
Dawson, John, 18 December 1693, age 13, Rice (?) Hoe
Murphy, Thomas, 12 September 1693, age 15, Robert Alexander
Obey, Thomas, 8 November 1693, age 18, Edward Maddocks

Gentleman Justices   Servants

Alexander, Robert   Cassey, Murphy
Buckner, Philip
Buckner, William
Fitzhugh, William, Colo.
Fossaker, Richard
Fossaker, Robert
Harvey, John
Hayward, Samuel
Mason, George, Capt.
Owsley, Thomas, Capt.
Peale, Malachy, Capt.
Thomason, Edward
Thompson, Mathew
Withers, John

STAFFORD COUNTY

Year	White	Negro	Indian
1689	0	0	0
1690	0	0	0
1691	0	0	0
1692	0	0	0
1693	4	0	0
Total	4	0	0

WESTMORELAND COUNTY (FRAGMENT)

Bowles, John, 29 April 1663, (age 14), Richard Heaberd, ten years
Browne, John, 27 April 1664, (over 16), Mrs. Rebecca Smith, five years
Cole, Richard, 27 April 1664, (over 16), Oliver Balfe, five years
Collins, Magdalene, 31 August 1664, (over 16), John Warde, five years
    "from May last"
Critchly, Matthias, 11 March 1663, age not judged, William Robinson,
    six years
Edmonds, John, February 1663, "a minor," Vincent Young, seven years
Fartly, Christopher, 29 April 1663, (age 14), William Heaberd, ten years
Frank, Robert, 11 March 1663, "a child," (age 10), John Watts,
    fourteen years
Jenkins, Richard, 29 April 1663, age not judged, John Bucknell,
    seven years
Keech, John, 27 April 1664, (age 12), William Heabeard, twelve years
Melcham, Richard, 24 June 1663, (age 12), Thomas Willsford,
    twelve years
Sampson, Simon, 27 April 1664, (age 12), William Greene, twelve years
Watly, Thomas, February 1663, age not judged, Thomas Willsford,
    seven years
Wilmott, Elizabeth, 11 March 1663, age not judged, William Greene,
    seven years

Gentleman Justices   Servants

Dodman, John, Lt. Coll.
Hardich, William, Lieut. Coll.
Hutt, Daniell
Lord, John
Mason, George, Capt.
Maunder, Wilkes
Peirce, William, Capt.
Peyton, Vallentine, Coll.
Washington, John, Major
Whiston, John
Williams, Robert

WESTMORELAND COUNTY

Abrogue, John, 26 April 1699, age 11, Francis Atwell
Addamson, Thomas, 26 May 1714, age 13, Thomas Shaw
Ahayrack, Robert, 26 April 1699, age 12, Thomas Marston
Allexander, James, 28 August 1678, age 18, Nathaniell Garland
Alworthy, Robert, 30 January 1695, age 14, John Jordan
Amour, Daniell, 26 February 1701, age 7, Gawin Corbin, Esqr.
Arnett, Edward, 29 September 1680, age 11, Coll. William Perce
Arnold (?), John, 29 May 1700, age 12, Robert Sparrow
Arrington, Thomas, 28 February 1700, age 10, William Smith
Ash, John, 26 July 1682, age 14, John Manly
Ash, Samuel, 26 February 1719, age 10, Nicholas Minor, purchased
    from Zacharias Eules, Marrin.
Ashton, John, 30 March 1699, age 11, Thomas Weedon
Atkins, Mary, 30 November 1699, age 18, Alexander Webster, Gent.
Aurolle, Cornelius, 31 May 1693, age 16, John Scott
Austin, Nicholas, 28 July 1697, age 12, Capt. Lawrence Washington
Ayers, George, 21 January 1685, age 9, Joseph Hemmings
Bacheler, Thomas, 12 January 1676, age 14, Capt. Thomas Youell
Ball, Edward, 28 July 1708, age 13, Henry Ashton, Gent.
Ballden, John, 1 February 1700, age 17, Thomas Attwell
Banks, Francis, 26 April 1721, age 14, Thomas Bennett
Barnwell, Francis, 28 July 1680, age 17, Humphrey Pope
Barrett, Dudley, 30 April 1701, age 17, Thomas Arrington
Baylye, Joseph, 2 December 1685, age 16, William Butler
Berry, James, 26 May 1708, age 11, Francis Redman
Berwick, Anthony, 28 July 1697, age 15, John Hore
Bevin, Edward, 28 April 1703, age 17, Alexander Spence, Gent.
Bonavis, Mary, 29 November 1699, age 16, William Steward
Bourn, James, 26 April 1699, age 11, John Gardner, Junr.
Bourn, John, 29 May 1706, age 13, Caleb Butler, Gent.
Bourn, Robert, 26 April 1699, age 10, William Thompson, Clerk
Boylger, Edmond, 26 April 1699, age 18, Griffin Humphreys
Bradley, Abraham, 25 January 1699, age 11, John Pratt
Brand, Murffue, 31 January 1700, age 11, John Chilton
Brannon, James, 26 November 1701, age 18, William Perry
Bridley, Richard, 27 May 1719, age 13, Henry Lee, Gent.
Brohun, Robert, 31 May 1699, age 17, Thomas Marson
Brown, James, 14 June 1682, age 9, John Harvy
Brown, John, 28 June 1699, age 12, Dennis Cornhill

WESTMORELAND COUNTY

Brown, John, 31 May 1704, age 11, Samuell Duceman
Brown, Richard, 28 January 1702, age 14, Major Francis Wright
Browne, Henry, 17 April 1678, age 10, Stephen Manwering
Brunnon (Brinnin), Owen, 26 April 1699, age 11, John Tanner
Bryan, Robert, 29 May 1706, age 13, Nathaniell Pope, Junr.
Bryars, Margaret, 28 March 1688, age 12, George Bowden alias Harris
Burck, William, 31 May 1710, age 13, Robert Lovell
Burk, Charles, 25 January 1699, age 17, Thomas Bowcock
Burk, Thomas, 28 February 1700, age 13, James Smith
Burn, Daniell, 25 March 1702, age 12, William Carr
Busby, John, 28 March 1688, age 12, John Pratt
Butteridge, Henry, 26 April 1699, age 13, Robert Sanford, Junr.
Calie, Edward, 31 January 1700, age 17, Benedict Middleton
Campbell, Dunkin, 25 January 1699, age 12, William Bridges, Gent.
Cannada, Dennis, 26 April 1699, age 12, Michaell Vassall
Cannada, James, 26 April 1699, age 15, Michaell Vassall
Cannada, Patrick, 29 May 1700, age 11, Lawrence Pope
Carnegie, Mary, 29 June 1720, age 6, John Buckley
Carrill, John, 28 April 1703, age 14, Edward Hart
Carroll, John, 25 January 1699, age 11, Bennedict Middleton
Cartee, Daniel, 28 August 1678, age 15, John Oneale
Castigan, Nicholas, 31 May 1699, age 15, James Westcomb
Caton, Peirce, 25 January 1699, age 19, Samuell Earle
Caviner, Francis, 31 January 1700, age 17, Daniell Occanny
Clark, Edmund, 23 February 1698, age 13, John Scott
Coffer, Timothy, 30 March 1699, age 10, Thomas Marshall
Coleman, Robert, 17 April 1678, age 13, Hon. Coll. Spencer
Collinder, Edmond, 25 January 1699, age 12, William Hazlerigg
Collins, John, 30 March 1699, age 16, John Jones
Collins, Margrett, 30 April 1701, age 16, Samuell Dishmen
Connell, Eleanor, 31 January 1700, age 16, William Carruther
Connell, Robert, 26 February 1701, age 13, Gawin Corbin, Esqr.
Conner, Dennis, 26 April 1699, age 12, James White
Conner, Dennis, 26 November 1701, age 16, William Chambers
Conner, William, 25 January 1699, age 12, Charnock Cox
Conraine, Thomas, 29 May 1706, age 13, James Vaulx
Cooper, George, 26 February 1701, age 14, Rev. James Brechin, Clerk
Corbin, Owen, 31 January 1700, age 8, Thomas Shaw
Corroba, John, 31 May 1699, age 12, Hugh Horton

WESTMORELAND COUNTY

Corrobin, Morrice, 26 April 1699, age 13, Bridges Rosier
Costigan, Daniell, 25 January 1699, age 17, William Smith
Coy, William, 25 January 1699, age 9, John Pratt
Crookshanks, William, 25 January 1699, age 15, James Orchard
Daniel, Samuell, 16 May 1677, age 14, Doctor Bond
Daniell, Richard, 30 April 1701, age 17, Richard Dudley
Davies, John, 25 January 1699, age 12, Peter Smith
Davies, Robert, 26 March 1719, age 13, Daniel McCarty, Esqr.
Dixon, William, 28 April 1703, age 12, Thomas Weedon
Dobin, Richard, 31 May 1699, age 16, Thomas Brown
Dorrill, Charles, 24 September 1712, age 12, Andrew Harrison
Doughally, John, 30 October 1695, age 11, Charles Ashton
Dounton, Nicholas, 26 May 1686, age 13, Robert Lovell
Dowlin, Phillipp, 31 May 1699, age 15, Benjamin Berriman
Dowly, William, 16 May 1677, age 15, Humphrey Pope
Doy, Catherine, 26 April 1699, age 17, James Bourn
Doyle, James, 30 April 1701, age 17, Richard Watts
Doyle, Stephen, 26 April 1699, age 14, John Redman
Duncomb, Francis, 30 October 1695, age 16, John Pratt
Edwards, Rice, 17 February 1686, age 13, Lewis Markham
Egon, John, 28 August 1678, age 15 1/2, Capt. John Lord
Emmons, Ann, 31 August 1699, age 7, James Campbell
Evans, John, 24 November 1703, age 13, Martha Marshall
Evans, Richard, 31 May 1693, age 12, Nehemiah Stork
Evans, Thomas, 31 May 1693, age 14, George Thorn
Fallmoth (?), Hugh, 31 May 1699, age 14, Robert Carter, Gent.
Fanoe (?), John, 25 July 1683, age 17, Richard Garner "of Maryland"
Farrell, Edmund, 31 May 1699, age 14, James Westcomb
Farrell, Richard, 25 January 1699, age 21, Isaack Duchmen
Farrell, Thomas, 31 January 1700, age 14, Anthony Beard
Farrell, Turlo, 30 March 1699, age 11, Abraham Smith
Fenley, Richard, 28 July 1697, age 13, Henry Ashton
Feogin, Andrew, 27 May 1719, age 14, Jacob Martin
Ferris, Humphry, 11 December 1683, age 13, John Minor
Finlor, Alexander, 25 January 1699, age 17, Mrs. Rose Newton
Finn, Thomas, 25 January 1699, age 15, William Thompson, Clerk
Fitzgerrald, Morrice, 31 May 1699, age 12, Capt. Gerrard Hutt
Fitzharris, Thomas, 31 May 1699, age 13, William Smith
Foster, Thomas, 23 February 1687, age 15, Edward Massey

119

Fowler, Roger, 26 May 1680, age 14, John Ward
Fox, Robert, 31 May 1699, age 16, John Spencer
Francis, Edward, 28 May 1701, age 14, David Brown
Fray, Mary, 29 November 1682, age 18, Garret Lyncolne
Frizwell, William, 29 May 1706, age 12, Thomas Shaw
Garvee, Lockland, 28 February 1700, age 14, Coll. William Peirce
Gibbs, Thomas, 10 May 1676, age 16, John Newton
Goghagan, James, 31 May 1699, age 15, Robert Lovewell, Junr.
Goloho, Martin, 1 May 1701, age 13, John Elliott, Gent.
Golothon, Hugh, 27 November 1700, age 14, William Stewart
Gordon, Alexander, 30 August 1699, age 13, Peter Skinner
Greene, Phillip, 23 February 1687, age 15, Originall Browne
Griffin, Peirce, 25 January 1699, age 12, William Caruthers
Grifice, Charles, 30 July 1718, age 10, Nathaniel Gray
Guy, Roger, 28 February 1700, age 16, Francis Self
Gyles, John, 31 January 1700, age 10, John Chilton
Hamelton (Hambleton), James, 26 April 1699, age 12, James Bourn
Hamleton, John, 30 October 1695, age 14, John Pratt
Hammilton, William, 26 May 1714, age 16, William Davies
Hanbrugg, Henry, 28 February 1700, age 12, Robert Ball
Hanbrugg, Patrick, 28 February 1700, age 12, William Hammock
Harper, David, 25 January 1699, age 15, Robert Redman
Harriss, Robert, 26 June 1717, age 6, Daniel McCarty, Esqr.
Harvey, John, 5 November 1679, age 15, Hon. Nicholas Spencer, Esqr.
Hay, John, 29 January 1718, age 13, Thomas Walker
Hayley, Daniell, 26 July 1693, age 18, Andrew Munroe
Henderson, James, 28 June 1699, age 13, John Champ
Hicks, Prue, 30 June 1703, age 10, Mrs. Ann Butler
Higgins, Charles, 28 February 1700, age 15, James Thomas
Hinde, Zachariah, 16 May 1677, age 15, Mrs. Grace Ashton
Hogan, John, 25 May 1698, age 15, John Bushrod
Hogan, John, 25 January 1699, age 11, John Lanclett
Hogan, William, 26 November 1701, age 12, Daniel Occaney
Hogue, James, 25 January 1699, age 13, Jane Hubbard
Hoguns, William, 27 November 1700, age 14, William Stewart
Hooker, Roger, 23 February 1699, age 16, James Smith
Horton, Henry, 29 June 1720, age 16, Corderoy Vaughan
Hunt, Elizabeth, 29 June 1698, age 14, Joseph Hemmings
Hurlee, Morrice, 31 May 1693, age 15, Alexander Webster

Huwes, Dorothea, 17 April 1678, age 15, John Newton

James, Thomas, 31 December 1701, age 13, Thomas Weedon

Jennings, William, 29 September 1697, age 12, Capt. Lawrence
Washington

Kelley, Cornelius, 31 January 1700, age 11, Randall Davenport

Kelley, Henry, 26 April 1699, age 9, William Thompson, Clerk

Kelley, John, 28 July 1697, age 10, Hon. Richard Lee, Esqr.

Kelley, Michael, 28 February 1700, age 15, Coll. William Peirce

Kelley, Thomas, 26 April 1699, age 10, Henry Gardner

Kelley, Thomas, 26 April 1699, age 16, John Mohun

Kelley, William, 28 February 1700, age 8, George Weedon

Kelly, Catherine, 30 October 1695, age 10, John Pratt

Kemp, Mary, 11 December 1678, age 15, Capt. John Quigley

Kenslo, Danniell, 26 April 1699, age 9, Thomas Marston

Kersey, John, 29 May 1706, age 8, John Higgins

King, Jeane, 17 April 1678, age 11, Stephen Manwering

King, Phillip, 31 January 1700, age 14, Thomas Weedon

King, Thomas, 30 April 1701, age 14, Caleb Butler, Gent.

Knight, John, 14 June 1682, age 19, John Beard

Kohorn, Locklin, 1 May 1701, age 18, John Kenner

Levington, Henry, 28 May 1679, age 12, Capt. Thomas Yowell

Little, Benjamin, 24 June 1702, age 15, John Sturman, Gent.

Lother, Michael, 31 May 1699, age 13, Charles Lucas

Lovell, John, 14 June 1682, age 13, John Newton

Lucas, Joseph, 26 July 1693, age 11, John Hore

Lumlar, Fitz (?), 13 February 1684, age 13, Robert Valx

Lutherall, Simon, 26 April 1699, age 18, William Thompson, Clerk

MackNeale, Jane, 30 October 1695, age 16, John Pratt

Mackniccolls, John, 25 January 1699, age 14, Thomas Atwell

Macmullne, Stephen, 26 May 1714, age 18, Thomas Sorrell

Maggee, John, 28 April 1703, age 10, Edward Hart

Magra, Patrick, 25 January 1699, age 8, John Pratt

Mahacan, Cornelius, 29 April 1708, age 7, Mrs. Sara Elliott

Martell, Christopher, 31 May 1693, age 17, Lewis Markham

Martin, Edward, 30 November 1681, age 12, James Hardidge

Mathews, George, 27 May 1702, age 13, Benjamin Middleton

McCartee, Dennis, 25 January 1699, age 14, Thomas Redman

McDonnell, Edward, 29 May 1706, age 15, Margrett Hart

Medford, Thomas, 23 February 1687, age 13, Edward Wheeler

Miller, Daniell, 25 January 1699, age 12, William Munroe
Monee, William, 31 May 1699, age 17, Samuell Ducemen
Montfort, William, 14 June 1682, age 16, Thomas Kirton
Moore, William, 26 April 1699, age 9, William Thompson, Clerk
Moorehand, Bryan, 26 February 1701, age 16, Nicholas Morue, Clerk
Morgan, Patrick, 25 June 1718, age 10, William Butler
Munderson, Timothy, 30 April 1701, age 17, William Haslerigg
Murfee, Bryan, 25 November 1691, age 14, Tobias Parsley
Murfee, John, 28 July 1697, age 16, Thomas Bowcock
Murfee, John, 30 March 1699, age 9, George Harris
Murfee, Michaell, 30 March 1699, age 17, Thomas Shaw
Murfee, Patrick, 28 July 1697, age 18, John Scott
Murfey, William, 25 February 1685, age 18, Nicholas Spencer, Esqr.
Mustin, Thomas, 1 February 1700, age 13, Andrew Munro
Neale, Patrick, 29 September 1697, age 17, Henry Ross, Gent.
Newton, George, 27 May 1702, age 14, William Harper
Nolunn, Phelim, 28 August 1678, age 17, Hon. Coll. Spencer Esq.
North, Richard, 5 November 1679, age 17, Capt. James Neale
Oliver, William, 12 January 1676, age 15, Capt. Thomas Youell
Ordery, John, 29 June 1720, age 19, William Lane
Otten, George, 8 January 1683, age 14, John Nott
Paine, Edward, 26 November 1684, age 13, Joseph Beale
Palmer, Elizabeth, 17 April 1678, age 18, Capt. John Lord
Palmer, James, 26 May 1714, age 12 "the last of November last past,"
        Daniel McCarty, Esqr.
Paper (Pauper), Thomas, 16 May 1678, age 13, Nehamiah Storke
Parsell, Patrick, 26 April 1699, age 18, James Tayler
Pendergass, Robert, 11 December 1678, age 17, Capt. John Quigley
Perce, Abram, 28 May 1679, age 14 1/2, Capt. Robert Gibbs
Petty, Daniell, 28 February 1700, age 15, Thomas Bowcock, deceased
Pitts, James, 26 April 1721, age 15, Thomas Butler
Poirke, James, 28 January 1680, age 16, John Baker
Poor, Robert, 26 April 1699, age 15, Robert Redman
Powell, John, 25 May 1681, age 12, Edmond Luke
Price, Richard, 27 March 1695, age 18, Capt. Thomas Mountjoy
Primm, Samuell, 31 January 1700, age 8, Madm. Anna Youll
Prue, John, 26 April 1699, age 11, George Sheppard
Pursle, Philip, 25 June 1718, age 15, George Beard
Pursley, Garratt, 25 January 1699, age 12, George Harris

WESTMORELAND COUNTY

Purtle, John, 28 July 1697, age 14, Richard Craddock
Quigley, James, 30 April 1701, age 12, Joseph Hemmings
Quirle, William, 30 April 1701, age 12, Thomas Harper
Rainton, Robert, 8 April 1691, age 7, Thomas Mountjoy
Ramsey, Robert, 26 April 1699, age 14, Francis Atwell
Randsome, James, 12 April 1676, age 14, John Rosier, sold to
    Major Thomas Youle
Randsome, William, 12 April 1676, age 14 1/2, Mall. Peale
Roberts, George, 22 February 1682, age 15, Robert Lovell
Robinson, James, 31 January 1700, age 9, Robert Lovell
Rogers, John, 11 December 1678, age 13, Capt. John Quigley
Rorey, Hugh, 1 May 1701, age 18, John Elliott, Gent.
Rosse, Duncan, 25 January 1699, age 16, Richard Hancock
Rosse, William, 25 January 1699, age 14, James Orchard
Rutley, Gregory, 25 January 1699, age 13, William Chandler
Rye, Ellenor, 25 October 1699, age 13, Nicholas Spencer, Esqr.
Ryle, Margrett, 1 February 1700, age 13, Andrew Munro
Salt, Sylvester, 26 April 1699, age 17, Robert Sanford, Senr.
Sandie, James, 26 May 1714, age 14, Nicholas Mewes
Scallion, Patrick, 30 April 1701, age 14, Daniell Feild
Scannen, Julian, 24 April 1700, age 17, William Booth
Semple (Sample), William, 28 August 1678, age 18, Patrick Spence
Shalee, John, 31 May 1699, age 14, James Westcomb
Shannhaw, Mary, 31 January 1700, age 14, Thomas Butler
Shepheard, Isaac, 11 January 1688, age 10, Mr. Secretary Spencer
Sheppard, William, 25 January 1699, age 16, James Coleman
Sincler, John, 28 June 1699, age 10, John Champ
Smith, Alexander, 25 January 1699, age 12, Richard Hancock
Smith, Charles, 8 October 1679, age 12, Coll. Spencer
Smith, James, 23 February 1687, age 14, Thomas Tanner
Smith, Samuell, 28 July 1680, age 16, John Newton
Smith, William, 29 September 1680, age 13, William Hardidge
Southerlin, John, 25 January 1699, age 12, Thomas Walker
Sparrow, Robert, 12 April 1676, age 13, Jonathan Churnell
Stapleton, Henry, 30 October 1695, age 12, Samuell Duceman
Stapleton, John, 30 October 1695, age 14, John Pratt
Steward, John, 28 March 1688, age 14, Lawrence Washington
Stone, Frances, 24 June 1702, age 15, Mrs. Rose Newton
Stubbs, Robert, 31 May 1699, age 13, John Wright

WESTMORELAND COUNTY

Summerall, John, 31 May 1704, age 14, John Lanclett
Sweetmore, Samuell, 12 January 1676, age 16, Capt. John Ashton
Symonds, Henry, 13 February 1684, age 17, Capt. John Lord
Tarnee, Thomas, 28 February 1700, age 12, Thomas Walker
Taynon, John, 26 April 1699, age 15, Edward Lambee
Teynon, John, 31 May 1699, age 12, James Westcomb
Thomas, David, 28 August 1706, age 12, Caleb Butler, Gent.
Thomas, Griffin, 31 May 1693, age 15, George Weedon
Thomas, John, 29 September 1703, age 8, Joseph Hemmings
Thomas, John, 31 May 1710, age 12, Peter Skinner
Thorn, John, 31 December 1701, age 13, Thomas Weedon
Touard, John, 29 July 1714, age 16, George Eskridge, Gent.
Tracey, John, 31 January 1700, age 11, Thomas Robins
Tracy, Martin, 31 May 1699, age 15, Gerrard Welch
Trotter, James, 25 January 1699, age 14, William Bridges, Gent.
Turner, Anthony, 25 March 1692, age 11, Thomas Robins
Ward, William, 31 May 1699, age 14, Thomas White
Warden, Robert, 31 May 1710, age 8, Daniell McCarty, Gent.
Warmouth, Thomas, 25 March 1719, age 12, Robert Tydwell
Warthee, George, 24 February 1699, age 13, Robert Sanford, Senr.
Watson, William, 27 May 1714, age 18, William Lynton
Webster, Elizabeth, 8 January 1683, age 14, John Nott
Welch, Elizabeth, 24 April 1700, age 16, Rev. James Brecken, Clerk
Welch, Katherine, 31 December 1701, age not judged, Thomas Harper
Welch, Robert, 28 February 1700, age 6, James Brichon, Clerk
Welch, Thomas, 11 December 1678, age 18, Capt. John Quigley
Welch, Thomas, 29 November 1699, age 15, Capt. William Bridges
Whaland, Patrick, 28 August 1678, age 14, John Griffin
Whallan, Nicholas, 25 January 1699, age 8, William Cotterell
White, James, 26 June 1717, age 10, John Pratt, purchased from
        James Donolson, Merchant, "for the space and term of
        eight yeares service and noe more"
White, Thomas, 29 May 1706, age 13, Thomas Weedon
Wilson, Mary, 25 March 1691, age 13, John Hore
Wilson, Thomas, 17 April 1678, age 15, Mathew Clarke
Wilson, Thomas, 31 January 1700, age 10, Willam Booth
Witherington, John, 28 July 1697, age 10, John Clements
Wright, Sarah, 31 October 1683, age 3, Richard Garner

WESTMORELAND COUNTY

Gentleman Justices	Servants
Allerton, Isaac, Major, Lt. Coll. *	
Allerton, Willoughby	
Ashton, Burditt	
Ashton, Charles	Doughally
Ashton, Henry	Ball, Fenley
Bayley, Joseph	
Berryman, Benjamin	Dowlin
Bonam, Thomas	
Bridges, William, Capt.	Campbell, Trotter, Welch
Bushrod, John	Hogan
Butler, Caleb	Bourn, King, Thomas
Chilton, John	Brand, Gyles
Elliott, John	Goloho, Rorey
Eskridge, George	Touard
Fitzhugh, John	
Franklin, Edward	
Hardidge, William, Capt.	Smith
Higgins, Augustine	
Horton, William	
Hutt, Gerrard	Fitzgerrald

WESTMORELAND COUNTY

Gentleman Justices	Servants
Jordan, John	Alworthy
Kirton, Thomas	Montfort
Lee, Henry	Bridley
Lee, Richard, Major, Esqr. *	Kelley
Lee, Thomas, Esqr.	
Lisson, Daniell	
Lord, John, Capt.	Egon, Palmer, Symonds
Manly, John	Ash
Markham, Lewis	Edwards, Martell
McCarty, Daniel, Esqr.	Davies, Harriss, Palmer, Warden
Mountjoy, Thomas, Capt.	Price, Rainton
Munroe, Andrew	Hayley, Mustin, Ryle
Newton, Thomas	
Paine, William	
Peirce, William, Major, Coll.	Arnett, Garvee, Kelley
Pope, Nathaniel	Bryan
Rosse, Henry	Neale
Scott, John	Aurolle, Clark, Murfee
Spence, Alexander	Bevin
Spencer, Nicholas, Coll., Esqr.	Coleman, Harvey, Murfey, Nolunn, Rye, Smith

126

WESTMORELAND COUNTY

Gentleman Justices	Servants
Stork, Nehemiah	Evans, Pauper
Sturman, John	Little
Tayler, James	Parsell
Turberville, George	
Vaulx, Robert	Lumlar
Washington, John, Lt. Coll.	
Washington, Lawrence, Capt.	Austin, Jennings, Steward
Watts, Richard	Doyle
Weedon, George	Kelley, Thomas
Weedon, Thomas	Ashton, Dixon, James, King, Thorn, White
Wright, Francis	Brown
Wright, John	Stubbs
Youell, Thomas, Capt., Major	Bacheler, Levington, Oliver, Randsome

* see Northumberland County

WESTMORELAND COUNTY				WESTMORELAND COUNTY			
Year	White	Negro	Indian	Year	White	Negro	Indian
1661	0	0	0	1698	3	3	0
1662	0	0	0	1699	92	1	0
1663	9	0	0	1700	35	0	0
1664	5	0	0	1701	23	5 *	0
				1702	6	5	0
1676	7	0	0	1703	7	2	0
1677	3	0	0	1704	2	3	0
1678	17	0	0	1705	0	6	1
1679	5	0	0	1706	8	7	0
1680	6	0	0	1707	0	18	1
1681	2	0	0	1708	3	9	0
1682	7	0	0	1709	0	5	0
1683	5	0	0	1710	3	6	0
1684	3	0	0	1711	0	9	0
1685	3	1	0	1712	1	0	0
1686	2	0	0	1713	0	20	0
1687	4	0	0	1714	7	13	1
1688	4	1	0	1715	0	0	0
1689	0	0	0	1716	0	3	0
1690	0	2	0	1717	2	14	0
1691	3	9	0	1718	4	13	0
1692	1	0	0	1719	5	42	0
1693	8	0	0	1720	3	38	0
1694	0	2	0	1721	2	10	0
1695	9	0	0	1722	0	1	0
1696	0	0	0	1723	0	10	0
1697	10	0	0	Total	319	258	3

* plus one Mulatto

NORTHUMBERLAND COUNTY

Abraham, Thomas, 20 July 1698, age 12, Josias Gaskins
Adire, Alexander, 20 May 1696, age 12, Thomas Baker
Ager, John, 19 February 1673, age 9, Richard Matt
Ailey, Joane, 17 February 1668, age 10, George Clark
Allen, John, 19 January 1699, age 18, Cuthbert Span
Allen, Ralph, 21 December 1698, age 14, Theodore Baker
Amis, John, 20 June 1668, age 15, Col. Peter Ashton
Anderson, William, 21 February 1700, age 13, Thomas Rout
Armstrong, Henry, 4 April 1694, age 16, John Harris
Armstrong, Thomas, 20 April 1687, age 15, John Eustace
Arro, John, 7 April 1686, age 13, Peter Coutanceau
Arther, Richard, 21 December 1698, age 14, John Moore
Atkins, John, 20 July 1670, age 9, Thomas Williams
Atkins, Joseph, 20 November 1668, age 15, James Robinson
Aubourne, Mary, 7 April 1686, age 11, Mrs. Anne Farmer
Balden, Patrick, 16 April 1699, age 8, Capt. Francis Voyer
Ball, Samuel, 20 December 1669, age 14, William Preslye
Barbar, Robert, 20 July 1670, age 14, Edward Coles
Barron, Robert, 1 May 1665, age 14, John Mottoune
Barry, Dowling, 19 January 1699, age 14, John Bushrod
Bateman, Jane, 20 November 1662, age not judged, Robert Jones, ten years
Batty, William, 12 March 1663, age not judged, Richard Wright, six years
Bearane (?), James, 21 December 1698, age 15, Thomas Berry
Beazlee, John, 4 April 1694, age 17, Capt. Thomas Opie
Bennett, William, 21 July 1686, age 16, James Jones
Bently, Hannah, 25 January 1671, age 16, Robert Sech
Bereman, William, 21 June 1699, age 17, Isaac Gaskins
Bevin, Morris, 21 June 1699, age 17, Richard Lattemore
Bexberry, Samuell, 26 February 1661, age 15, Nicholas Jernew, six years
Bird, Timothy, 16 November 1698, age 15, John Curtis
Birk, John, 16 November 1698, age 13, James Waddy
Bishop, Ralph, 20 April 1663, age 10, Michaell Van Landingham
Black, Jack, 19 June 1672, age 16, John Cockrell
Blackwell, Charles, 19 January 1676, age 11, William Downing
Blackwell, Josias, 1 May 1665, age not judged, Isaac Allerton,
        six years "from the 10th of September last"
Booth, Richard, 19 July 1682, age 11, Peter Presly, Jr.
Bourne, James, 16 November 1698, age 14, Joseph Humphries
Bowle, Morris, 21 June 1699, age 19, Thomas Dameron

Bowyer, Thomas, 9 May 1670, age 15, Daniel Neale
Boyd, David, 4 April 1694, age 12, John Nicklesse
Boyer, Richard, 4 February 1664, age 14, Robert Jones, ten years
Brachan, Daniell, 20 April 1660, age 14, Anthony Linton, seven years
Bragg, Henry, 18 June 1690, age 14, Rodham Kenner
Brassell, Morris, 19 January 1699, age 14, Richard Key
Bready, Patrick, 17 April 1706, age 10, Dennis Conway, Jr.
Bridgeman, Thomas, 20 June 1663, age 13, Capt. William Nutt
Brisco, Phillip, 20 April 1663, age 15, John Williams
Brittaine, Edward, 10 April 1666, age not judged, Col. Peter Ashton,
    seven years "from ye 10th of November next"
Brittaine, Richard, 19 January 1699, age 13, Henry Franklin
Brooks, John, 19 January 1676, age 18, John Corbell
Browne, Alexander, 20 April 1698, age 18, Thomas Brewer
Browne, Benjamin, 17 March 1675, age 16, Robert Brierly
Browne, George, 19 January 1676, age 12, Peter Presly
Browne, Phillip, 21 October 1661, age 16, Richard Cole, five years
Browne, Terence, 16 November 1698, age 18, Elizabeth Sheeres
Browne, William, 21 July 1686, age 9, William Coppage
Browne, William, 21 June 1699, age 14, Thomas Brewer
Brumfeild, Robert, 21 March 1677, age 17, Francis Lee
Bryan, John, 21 December 1698, age 12, Peter Coutanceau
Bryan, Turloah, 17 June 1702, age 17, Mrs. Elizabeth Bankes
Bryant, Daniell, 19 May 1698, age 14, Mrs. Elizabeth Kenner
Buckland, Anne, 20 December 1669, age 16, Samuel Nichols
Burge, John, 18 June 1701, age 14, Peter Cantanceau, he bought the
    servant "but for eight yeares"
Burk, Richard, 19 May 1698, age 10, Capt. Rodham Kenner
Burke, Elizabeth, 16 November 1698, age 15, James Hill
Burke, William, 16 November 1698, age 16, John Curtis
Calvin, Charles, 4 April 1694, age 14, James Waddy
Cammell, James, 16 December 1691, age 11, Patrick Pollick
Cammell, John, 20 May 1696, age 16, Edward Fielding
Cammell, John, 17 March 1697, age 13, James Waddy
Cammell, Samuell, 22 June 1699, age 18, Christopher Garlington
Candade, Peter, 20 December 1670, age 16, William Smyth
Cane, Charles, 20 January 1664, age 13, John Motley, eleven years
Carpenter, William, 19 March 1679, age 16, Henry Mayse
Carroll, Matthew, 19 January 1699, age 17, William Keene

Cartwright, Peter, 20 July 1670, age 11, Thomas Lane
Carty, Jene, 16 April 1699, age 17, Thomas Walters
Casey, Richard, 16 November 1698, age 15, James Symmons
Casterson, Thomas, 20 April 1663, age not judged, William Willdey,
    seven years "from his arrivall"
Castide, Cormeck, 19 January 1676, age 13, Peter Presly
Cauller, Thomas, 20 January 1664, age 16, Capt. Peter Ashton, who
    "hath freely and voluntarily omitted one yeares service,"
    seven years
Cavenah, David, 16 November 1698, age 14, Thomas Baker
Cavenah, Filain, 18 August 1697, age 16, William Wildy
Cavenah, Thomas, 21 July 1697, age 16, Thomas Banks
Chackle, Henry, 19 July 1676, age 10, Capt. John Mottrom
Chamberlin, Rebecca, 1 May 1665, age 15, Peter Presly, nine years
    "from ye 23rd of January last"
Charles, Henry, 17 August 1681, age 6, Mrs. Elizabeth Tipton
Chelwood, Matthias, 20 April 1698, age 14, Mrs. Elizabeth Banks
Childermasse, Thomas, 16 August 1682, age 13, Henry Gaskoyne
Chipman, John, 19 February 1701, age 15, Samuell Mahen
Chisholme, John, 16 April 1699, age 18, William Harrison
Chrisheire, Clement, 20 July 1670, age 12, John Motley
Clark, Edward, 16 March 1687, age 11, Samuel Mahen Sr.
Clerke, Robert, 19 May 1703, age 15, Samuell Mahens
Colledge, Hezekiah, 20 February 1660, age 12, Capt. William Nutt
    nine years
Collins, Piles, 20 April 1664, age 15, Wilkes Maunder, seven years,
    "being consented to by their said Master"
Connale, Edmund, 21 February 1700, age 17, John Lynton
Conner, Derby, 16 April 1699, age 18, Thomas Walters
Conner, James, 21 June 1699, age 17, Charles Ingram
Conner, John, 21 June 1699, age 17, Thomas Smith
Contancheau, Oliver, 20 June 1668, age 10, Edward Saunders
Contansheau, Thomas, 15 September 1670, age 16, Robert Jones
Cope, John, 21 February 1672, age 13, Peter Chevanne
Cople, Henry, 21 November 1694, age 12, William Coppidge
Copperweight, Christopher, 17 June 1702, age 14, Major Rodham Kenner
Corker, William, 20 April 1664, age 14, Peter Presly, ten years
    "from the 18th of January last past"
Cornell, John, 17 April 1706, age 12, Joseph Hoult

NORTHUMBERLAND COUNTY

Cornwell, Samuell, 19 January 1676, age 12, Dennis Eyes

Corry, John, 19 August 1674, age 16, Nicholas Owen

Cotoone, Anthony, 21 January 1685, age 17, Clement Latemore

Courtney, James, 15 May 1689, age 15, Patrick Pollick

Cox, Faith, 20 June 1663, age not judged, John Gibson, five years
"from the time of her arrivall"

Cox, James, 21 January 1685, age 10, John Bowen

Cox, Joane, 17 January 1672, age 18, William Brereton

Coynia, Zachariah, 16 November 1687, age 14, John Scott, seven years,
master has given servant "three full years of his time"

Crabtree, Daniell, 10 April 1666, age not stated, John Tyngey

Crage, John, 19 January 1676, age 15, Edward Coles

Crane, Jane, 22 May 1689, age 15, Richard Rogers, declaring that he
bought her "to serve him six years and no longer"

Cromwell, Alexander, 19 January 1676, age 16, Thomas Hobson

Cross, James, 17 August 1681, age 7, Richard Kenner

Crosthead, William, 21 February 1672, age 14, Leonard Howson

Cushion, James, 16 April 1699, age 9, Capt. Francis Voyer

Cussion, Phillip, 21 December 1698, age 15, Charles Nelmes

Cussion, Richard, 21 December 1698, age 13, Elizabeth Kenner

Cutter, Thomas, 19 August 1674, age 19, George Bletsoe

Dalton, John, 21 July 1697, age 19 "at least," Walter Dune, "he has
Indentures which were to come into this Country in another Ship"

Davids, James, 19 January 1676, age 17, Major Thomas Brereton

Davies, William, 17 May 1676, age 10, John Cotanceau

Davis, Henry, 21 December 1698, age 17, Thomas Downing

Davis, John, 19 February 1673, age 10, Thomas Towers

Davis, Thomas, 2 March 1681, age 11, John Farnefold

Dawes, Thomas, 7 March 1661, age 14, Coll. Richard Lee, Esqr.,
seven years

Devin, Patrick, 15 July 1702, age 14, Samuell Mahane

Dew, John, 20 June 1663, age 15, Daniell Holland

Dewey (?), William, 21 December 1698, age 14, John Howton

Dickson, Joseph, 8 March 1664, age not judged, Richard Peirce,
seven years, "by consent of both parties"

Dingwell, Roderick, 16 April 1699, age 17, Charles Vollen

Dinney, Edward, 15 March 1676, age 14, Collo. St. Leger Codd

Doak, James, 17 March 1697, age 16, John Harris

Dollins, Richard, 21 February 1700, age 15, John Dawson

Dowle, John, 16 April 1699, age 11, Christopher Neale, twelve years,
    "his master relinquishing him a yeares service"
Duggle, Richard, 19 January 1699, age 14, John Bushrod
Dunahaugh, Thomas, 17 June 1702, age 13, Mrs. Dorothy Span
Dunawon, William, 21 February 1700, age 8, Christopher Neale
Dunbarr, George, 21 June 1699, age 14, Joseph Palmer
Duncombe, Anne, 11 January 1669, age 15, William Griffin
Dunken, George, 21 June 1699, age 16, Nicholas Lehugh
Durrough, Allen, 21 June 1699, age 13, Capt. William Jones
Dyer, John, 19 May 1686, age 12, Josias Gaskoyne
Edmonds, George, 21 January 1661, age 13, John Williams, eight years
Ellistone, Jervas, 20 December 1669, age 11, Richard Hull
Emerson, John, 17 November 1698, age 15, William Nelmes
Erwyn, John, 16 April 1699, age 17, John Pope
Evans, Morgan, 25 November 1669, age 17, Mathew Rhodon
Everson, Cornelius, 16 December 1674, age 14, Richard Pemberton
Fagan, John, 21 December 1687, age 12, Phillip Norgate
Faireweather, Patrick, 21 June 1699, age 15, Bartholomew Shreever
Ferguson, Andrew, 16 November 1698, age 11, Charles Moorehead,
    "his said Master abating him one year's service of his time"
Farlowe, William, 3 May 1660, age 12, Major George Colclough,
    nine years
Farrar, John, 19 January 1676, age 13, John Motley
Faugheigh, Laurence, 19 January 1699, age 18, Edward Cole
Fell, Owen, 10 March 1662, age 9, Thomas Williams, twelve years
Fisher, Henry, 16 March 1687, age 13, Daniel Neale
Flanerell, Longhly, 16 April 1699, age 18, Vincent Garner
Flattman, Thomas, 17 April 1678, age 13, Peter Presly Junior
Fogershie, John, 21 February 1700, age 10, Christopher Neale
Forrester, David, 20 April 1698, age 14, Capt. Spencer Motrom
Foster, John, 18 November 1685, age 14, Henry Metcalfe
Fouch, Robert, 20 January 1670, age 18, Richard Kenner
Fox, Laurance, 18 May 1693, age 11, Rawleigh Travers
Francis, Evan, 20 April 1687, age 14, Phillip Shapleigh
Franklin, John, 6 September 1665, age not judged, John Mottrom,
    five years
Frost, John, 21 January 1685, age 12, Peter Maxwell
Furney, Robert, 19 January 1699, age 12, Capt. Rodham Kenner,
    "he having purchased" the servant "for Mr. John Bertrand"

Fuse, Thomas, 17 January 1672, age 14, Richard Kenner
Gallaway, Andrew, 20 April 1698, age 14, Pitts Curtis
Gallee, Peter, 20 July 1670, age 11, Coll. Samuell Smyth
Gambler, John, 21 October 1674, age 18, Hancock Lee
Gardener, Nathaniell, 20 November 1662, age not judged, Richard Nelmes,
    four years
Garder, Edward, 20 July 1670, age 14, William Brereton
Gardner, John, 4 February 1664, age 14, Coll. Richard Lee, ten years
Gardner, Olliver, 15 July 1702, age 14, Thomas Baker
Garward, George, 19 August 1674, age 16, William Hancock
Gately, Joseph, 17 March 1697, age 12, Estate of John Cole
Gemball, Alexander, 7 April 1668, age 15, Estate of Richard Flynt
Gill, Michael, 19 January 1699, age 15, Thomas Shapleigh
Gillen, Julian, 20 July 1670, age 12, Edward Sanders
Goffe, James, 21 August 1678, age 13, Samuell Mahen or Mackneil
Goggin, Thomas, 16 April 1699, age 17, William Wildy
Gorden, Robert, 21 June 1699, age 15, Samuell Mahen
Gordon, Robert, 21 June 1699, age 15, Thomas Huske
Gore, Jane, 20 May 1667, age 9, Richard Span
Graham, Jane, 29 May 1675, age 16, Elizabeth Richardson
Grandee, Rachell, 20 July 1670, age 16, Francis Roberts
Gray, James, 4 February 1664, age 16, George Wale, eight years
Green, Elizabeth, 19 March 1678, age 18, Thomas Winter
Greene, Robert, 20 November 1662, age not judged, Coll. Richard Lee,
    six years
Grey, Andrew, 17 August 1698, age 12, Thomas Hayes
Griffin, Michaell, 17 March 1675, age 18, William Keyne
Griffith, David, 15 March 1676, age 18, William Downing, Junr.
Grimes, Edward, 4 April 1694, age 13, Bartholomew Schreever
Groome, Humphry, 21 June 1699, age 9, John Cockrell
Guttrey, James, 19 January 1676, age 17, Dennis Connway
Gwyer, Anne, 20 June 1663, age 16, Daniell Holland
Hadliff, Samuell, 20 April 1687, age 10, Richard Nutt
Haines, John, 20 December 1669, age 14, Peter Preslye
Haley, Cornelius, 17 April 1672, age 10, William Downing
Hall, Daniel, 15 January 1679, age 8, William Downing, Senior
Hall, Susan, 15 January 1679, age 9, William Downing, Junior
Hall, William, 16 April 1699, age 13, George Berratt
Hamlin, John, 20 July 1670, age 11, John Swanson

NORTHUMBERLAND COUNTY

Hancocke, George, 18 April 1677, age 14, Walter Dunne
Handling, Manns, 21 July 1697, age 16, Anthony Steptoe
Hany, Charles, 6 April 1669, age 12, William Tignall
Harmestone, Joseph, 19 March 1679, age 18, Christopher Neale
Harris, John, 20 February 1665, age 11, Christopher Garlington
Harris, John or Jesse, 19 March 1679, age 11, William Presly
Harris, John, 18 April 1683, age 14, Robert Bryery
Harrison, Robert, 19 July 1682, age 17, William Presly
Harrox, Mary, 16 March 1687, age 12, James Ednee
Harry, George, 24 August 1669, age 17, Sym. Richardson
Hartington, William, 21 January 1661, age 16, Thomas Williams,
    five years
Harwood, Anne, 20 January 1668, age not judged, Francis Clay, "having
    served her Master five yeares, and come into this Country without
    Indenture, it is ordered that ye said Anne bee free"
Hawkins, Ambrose, 22 June 1699, age 18, Christopher Garlington
Hayes, John, 21 December 1698, age 14, John Cockrell
Hazlas, William, 18 May 1687, age 13, Thomas Waddy
Hearty, Mary (Merry), 21 June 1699, age 16, Thomas Taylor
Helps, Sampson, 18 June 1690, age 12, John Dowling
Henry, John, 20 April 1698, age 13, Mrs. Jane Yarrat
Hewes, James, 15 April 1702, age 14, Joseph Hoult
Hewes, Nicholas, 16 June 1675, age 16, Collo. St. Leger Codd
Hickley, James, 22 June 1669, age 14, George Clark
Hicks, John, 19 March 1679, age 17, Robert Sech
Hickson, Samuell, 21 November 1677, age not judged, John Reason,
    nine years "with the consent of both partyes"
Higgins, Thomas, 18 March 1685, age 17, John Hull
Hill, John, 15 April 1702, age 13, Thomas Waddy
Hill, Sarah, 20 April 1663, age 13, Richard Span
Hines, John, 21 January 1661, age 14, Thomas Souley, seven years
Hinsborough, Mathew, 19 March 1679, age 16, Richard Kenner
Hitchcock, John, 3 May 1660, age 12, Major George Colclough, nine years
Hoadnutt, Joseph, 10 February 1663, age not judged, Thomas Bunbury,
    five years "from the 10th of November last"
Hoen (?), Elizabeth, 16 May 1694, age 14, Thomas Maize, ten years
Hogan, Daniell, 21 June 1699, age 10, Capt. Rodham Kenner
Hoggan, Teague, 21 August 1678, age 10, Thomas Ferne or Ferance

135

NORTHUMBERLAND COUNTY

Holland, Elizabeth, 17 August 1681, age 11, Christopher Neale

Holland, Simon, 16 November 1698, age 14, James Waddy, eight years,
"his said Master abating him of two years of service"

Hollis, Boar, 8 September 1662, age not judged, Thomas Gaskins,
seven years "from the first of November next"

Hood, William, 3 May 1660, age 14, Major George Colclough, seven years

Hopkins, Henry, 21 June 1693, age 14, Thomas Baker

Horton, Thomas, 19 June 1672, age 15, John Farnefold

Howell, John, 8 September 1662, age not judged, John Essex,
five years "from the beginning of October next"

Hubbard, Steven, 1 May 1665, age 15, Andrew Pettigrew

Hudson, Henry, 18 March 1685, age not judged, John Coutansheau, Jr.,
six years "and no longer," "with the consent of both Parties"

Hudson, Isaac, 1 May 1665, age 16, Thomas Hopkins, eight years

Hughs, Robert, 16 February 1698, age 12, Richard Hanye

Hughson, William, 20 January 1662, age 14, Coll. Richard Lee,
seven years

Hunt, Charles, 21 July 1686, age not judged, Mrs. Anne Farmer, sold by
John Crumpton for eight years, servant "declared that he had an
indenture for five years and no longer," but it was destroyed

Hunt, Elizabeth, 22 June 1699, age 17, Claud Tullos

Hutchinson, Nicholas, 21 July 1697, age 13, William Keene

Hutton, John, 19 February 1679, age 7, John Nicholls

Jackman, Matthew, 19 May 1698, age 12, Capt. Rodham Kenner

Jackson, George, 21 March 1706, age not judged, Sarah Tullos, "brought
into the Country without Indentures by Capt. Samuell Ellis and
sold to Sarah Tullos for seven yeares"

Jackson, Richard, 21 January 1661, age 14, William Willdey, seven years

Jackson, Thomas, 19 July 1682, age 14, William Presly

Jacobs, Edward, 20 June 1668, age 9, Edward Saunders

James, James, 18 May 1687, age 6 "and one half," Peter Hack

James, John, 15 November 1671, age 15, Richard Kenner, nine years

James, Mary, 19 April 1676, age 14, John Champion

James, William, 21 December 1669, age 15, John Bearman

Janes, Francis, 19 March 1684, age not judged, Daniel Neale

Jeffs, William, 10 March 1669, age 13, William Shoare, (ten years),
"his said Master hath acquitted him of one yeare of his service"

Jenkins, Walter, 6 April 1669, age 10, John Cockrell

NORTHUMBERLAND COUNTY

Jennings, Edward, 8 September 1662, age not judged, Thomas Phillpot,
    five years "from the 20th of November next"
Jerkell (Jerken), John, 20 June 1664, age 13, John Bowen
Jess, Hester, 17 April 1678, age 13, Richard Bradley
Johnson, John, 17 March 1697, age 15, William Nutt
Jones, Edmund, 4 April 1694, age 16, Lazarus Tayler
Jones, Owen, 20 May 1696, age 11, Richard Rogers
Jones, William, 19 March 1679, age 14, James Johnson
Joyce, John, 20 April 1687, age 11, John Bayley
Jude, Francis, 20 July 1670, age 11, Edward Sanders
Keire, Lawrence, 19 January 1676, age 13, Philip Shapleigh
Kelly, Jacob, 16 November 1698, age 15, John Lunce
Kelly, James, 21 June 1699, age 16, Longhly Conolin
Kelly, John, 17 April 1672, age 13, Capt. Edmond Lyster
Kennam, Mary, 1 May 1665, age not judged, Isaac Allerton,
    five years "from ye 10th of September next"
Kennedy, Teigue, 19 January 1699, age 15, Hugh Stathem
Kett, William, 20 April 1663, age 15, Robert Jones
Kidd, William, 21 June 1699, age 13, John Nickless
Killpatrick, Edward, 19 January 1676, age 12, John Farnefold
King, Christopher, 16 February 1698, age 15, Thomas Hughlett
King, George, 20 May 1671, age 10, Robert Jones
Kinge, Adam, 20 November 1662, age not judged, Nicholas Jernew,
    six years
Knight, John, 20 December 1699, age 17, Peter Cantanceau
L_____, James, 19 January 1676, age 13, Major Thomas Brereton
Lacey, John, 20 December 1670, age 13, William Smyth
La Folly, Peter, 20 July 1670, age 13, John White
Laland, John, 18 May 1693, age 11, Richard Nutt
Lane, James, 16 April 1699, age 11, John Langsdon
Lappage, Andrew, 19 February 1679, age 10, John Nicholls
Leehow, Nicholas, 20 July 1670, age 14, Leonard Howson
Le Hoot, Peter, 20 December 1671, age 9, Capt. John Rogers
Leonard, Darby, 21 June 1699, age 19, John Ingram
Levistone, Mary, 20 October 1668, age 17, Leonard Howson
Lewis, John, 20 January 1662, age 11, Capt. Peter Ashton, ten years
Linn, Catherine, 15 April 1702, age 15, Richard Rice
Lintsey, Cornelius, 16 April 1699, age 18, John Webb
Lishman, Thomas, 21 June 1693, age 16, Thomas Salisbury

Little, Christopher, 26 February 1661, age 13, William Downinge,
    eight years
Lock, Thomas, 19 April 1700, age 11, Charles Moorhead
Lockiere, Charles, 21 May 1701, age 15, John Cralle
Lockman, John, 16 April 1699, age 13, Richard Oldham
Lord, Thomas, 20 April 1664, age 15, Wilkes Maunder, seven years,
    "being consented to by their said Master"
Loth, Donnell, 19 January 1676, age 16, Philip Shapleigh
Low, John, 21 June 1699, age 19, Richard Hudnall
Low, Richard, 21 March 1677, age 11, George Dameron
Loynes, John, 20 April 1698, age 13, John Cockrell
Loyney, Dennis, 16 April 1699, age 13, Enoch Hill
Lucas, Robert, 20 April 1664, age 15, Wilkes Maunder, seven years,
    "being consented to by their said Master"
Lytiesse, Thomas, 17 April 1672, age 17, Joyce Holland
Mabrile, Jone, 10 February 1663, age "upwards of 23," Joseph Horsley,
    "shall bee free the 20th day of October next"
Macarty, Dennis, 19 May 1698, age 15, Peter Coutanceau
Macarty, William, 20 April 1698, age 14 "and a half," Richard Swanson
    and wife Elizabeth Swanson, to serve "six years and no longer"
MacDennis, Daniel, 16 May 1694, age 16, Patrick Pollick, eight years
Macdermott, Thomas, 20 May 1696, age 11, John Farnefold
Macey, Elizabeth, 18 July 1705, age 16, Thomas Gill
Macgee, Charles, 20 May 1696, age 17, Edward Saunders
Macgee, James, 15 July 1696, age 14, Charles Nelmes
Mackarty, Daniell, 19 January 1676, age 15, Thomas D _____
Mackennell, Ellinor, 21 November 1677, age 22, James Nepper
Macklangha, Jane, 19 January 1676, age 14, Richard Hull
Macklangha, Mannas, 19 January 1676, age 13, Thomas Sadler
Macklanhan, James, 21 March 1677, age 13, John Bowen
Macklanhan, John, 20 January 1676, age 13, Daniell Neale, Junior
Mackmartin, Phillip, 21 March 1677, age 7, George Dameron
Mackness, Lahan, 19 March 1678, age 9, William Presly
Macktirge, William, 19 January 1676, age 14, William Cotanceau
Macmarrey, Andrew, 19 July 1682, age 11, Richard Hull
Macmend, James, 17 March 1697, age 12, James Waddy
Maconald, Hugh, 20 April 1687, age 16, John Eustace
Macray, Edmund, 21 August 1678, age 11, John Dennis
Magrah, Philip, 18 March 1713, age 18, Henry Hopkins

NORTHUMBERLAND COUNTY

Magrillus, John, 19 March 1673, age 14, Thomas Brereton
Maguire, Cornelius, 4 April 1672, age 15, Edward Coles
Mahoany, Dennis, 21 June 1699, age 15, Samuell Smith
Mahughen, John, 18 April 1700, age 13, Capt. Thomas Winder
Mallin, Patrick, 21 August 1678, age 5, Thomas Matthew
Manby, Anthony, 17 May 1682, age 14, Thomas Opye
Marriner, John, 21 June 1699, age 19, Isaac Ester
Marrow, Richard, 19 July 1682, age 18, Robert Sech
Marsh, George, 18 August 1675, age 18, Thomas Gascoyne
Marsh, George, 20 April 1698, age 15, Anthony Hanye
Mason, John, 19 January 1699, age 13, Thomas Hughlett
Mason, Salomon, 17 April 1678, age 15, William Presly
Matthew, George, 29 May 1675, age not judged, William Downinge,
        seven years "with ye consent of both Master and Servant"
Matthews, Philip, 3 February 1675, age 16, John Muttoone
Maxfield, John, 17 March 1697, age 12, Henry Franklin
McCarmick, Francis, 21 December 1698, age 13, Thomas Gill
Meath, John, 17 March 1697, age 15, John Downing
Medford, George, 15 January 1701, age 14, Thomas Waddy
Meighon, Thomas, 19 January 1699, age 16, Nicholas Merrica
Merret, Ellis, 20 July 1670, age 15, Thomas Hobson
Merrey, Thomas, 6 April 1669, age 14, Mathew Rhodon
Merrill, Robert, 20 April 1698, age 19, Lazarus Taylor
Millbank, Mary, 17 June 1702, age 14, John Cockrell
Miller, Hugh, 16 April 1701, age 9, Samuell Mahen
Mitchell, Robert, 17 March 1697, age 11, Thomas Bushrod
Moglaine, Phillip, 16 April 1699, age 18, John Webb
Montgomerie, James, 16 March 1687, age 17, John Corbin
Moor, Francis, 25 January 1671, age 11, John Warner
Moor, Margrett, 16 March 1687, age 9, Walter Jenkins
Moore, James, 17 March 1697, age 14, Thomas Taylor
Moore, Thomas, 1 May 1665, age not judged, John Mottrom,
        four years "since ye seaventh of September"
Moore, William, 21 June 1699, age 18, Thomas Wynter
Morclay, Ellinore, 20 May 1685, age 13, John Corbell
More, Robert, 19 August 1674, age 15, Francis Lee
Morgan, Rowland, 20 April 1663, age 9, Vincent Fox
Morris, Fenly, 16 March 1687, age 15, James Nipper
Mortemore, James, 18 March 1685, age 16, John Coutansheau, Sr.

NORTHUMBERLAND COUNTY

Moss, John, 21 July 1680, age 15, Capt. Thomas Mathew
Mott, Marke, 19 August 1674, age 14, John Cotanshew
Mucklehose, Turner, 19 January 1676, age 13, Peter Presly
Mullagan, James, 4 April 1694, age 16, John Harris
Mulloy, Charles, 16 November 1698, age 14, Thomas Gaskins
Mulreany, James, 16 April 1699, age 16, Dennis Conway
Murfew, Joane, 23 June 1699, age 15, Nicholas Edwards
Murfew, Nicholas, 19 February 1701, age 10, Daniell Swillivant
Murrow, Edward, 20 April 1698, age 11, John Bayly, with consent of
    Master to serve "nine years and no longer"
Murrow, John, 18 May 1698, age 15, John Ingram
Nash, Thomas, 20 November 1662, age not judged, William Jolland,
    nine years
Neale, Daniell, 17 April 1678, age 13, Thomas Matthew
Nellagon, William, 23 June 1699, age 17, Nicholas Edwards
Nelson, Jeremiah, 20 May 1671, age 12, John Waddy
Newman, Thomas, 25 January 1671, age 12, Richard Kenner
Nichols, William, 8 September 1668, age 18, Leonard Howson
Norcutt, Richard, 21 December 1698, age 11, Joseph Hudnall
Northage, Thomas, 17 April 1689, age 10, Anthony Stepto
Nowland, Charles, 20 May 1685, age 10, Robert Sech
Nupall, John, 20 December 1688, age 15, Ebenezer Sanders
Odonhoty, Neale, 19 January 1676, age 15, James Napor
Ogen, John, 19 December 1688, age 14, Denis Eyes
Oldfield, Susanna, 17 April 1678, age 15, Thomas Matthew, upon his
    confession "he bought ye Servant for six yeares and noe longer"
Oliver, Ignatius, 17 March 1675, age 10, Thomas Matthews
Oliver, Joseph, 17 March 1697, age 12, John Harris
Omer, Joseph, 8 September 1668, age 15, Richard Span
Omuddy, Daniell, 19 January 1676, age 17, Peter Presley
Omullion, Patrick, 21 December 1687, age 13, Jane Wildey
Oneale, Arthur, 19 January 1676, age 15, Richard Hull
Oneale, Owen, 21 September 1698, age 17, Capt. William Jones
Ormond, Richard, 20 April 1664, age 15, Nicholas Journew, nine years
Ortland, Samuel, 5 November 1668, age 18, Peter Knight
Owens, William, 20 April 1660, age 13, James Magregor and Hugh Fouch,
    eight years
Owenton, Sarah, 20 May 1662, age 13, Christopher Garlington,
    eight years "from the 25th day of December last past"

NORTHUMBERLAND COUNTY

Parkes, Thomas, 8 September 1662, age not judged, Thomas Phillpot,
    eight years "from the 2nd of November next"
Parnell, John, 16 July 1673, age 16, William Keyne
Parsons, John, 7 April 1668, age not judged, Capt. Thomas Flynt, sold "to
    Lt. Col. Samuell Smyth for seaven yeares, hee had noe Indenture"
Patten, William, 21 June 1699, age 13, John Howson
Paule, Charles, 20 February 1665, age 13, James Austin
Peacock, Andrew, 16 April 1699, age 16, Capt. George Cooper
Pearce, Henry, 20 July 1687, age 15, Edward Sanders
Pearce, Thomas, 20 February 1654, age not judged, William Nash, ordered
    to serve "one yeare more to come since ye 28 January last and
    then to be free"
Pearle, Anne, 19 January 1699, age 15, Capt. William Hanson
Pedde, William, 21 June 1699, age 13, William Coppage
Pelker, John, 8 September 1668, age 15, Thomas Peryne
Perrie, Edward, 17 January 1672, age 10, Joseph Feilding
Peters, Edward, 18 August 1697, age 13, Rawley Travers
Peters (?), John, 25 November 1669, age 13, Mathew Rhodon
Peters, Margrett, 4 April 1694, age 16, Mrs. Jane Wildey, eight years
Peterson, Hugh, 21 June 1699, age 18, John Lunce
Pettus, William, 21 January 1661, age 12, Coll. Richard Lee, nine years
Phelps, Thomas, 8 March 1664, "under the age of 16," William Flower,
    eight years, "with the consent of his said Master"
Philips, Susan, 20 June 1667, age 15, Henry Watts
Phillips, Joseph, 15 January 1701, age 17, Hannah Frankling
Phillips, Mathew, 21 January 1661, age 12, Coll. Richard Lee, nine years
Phillips, Robert, 7 April 1686, age 8, John Cralle
Pickerill, Henery, 20 November 1662, age not judged, Nicholas Jernew,
    nine years
Pinnar, Robert, 17 February 1668, age 12, James Claughton
Plankett, Thomas, 15 November 1671, age 13, John Bearmore,
    eleven years
Player, Henry, 25 November 1669, age 15, Daniel Neale
Plosser, Maulin, 20 October 1668, age 15, Thomas Lane
Pomray, James, 20 June 1664, age 15, Andrew Boyer
Pond, Anne, 20 January 1664, age 14, Abraham Byram, ten years
Poore, John, 18 May 1698, age 17, Col. Samuell Griffin
Poore, John, 19 January 1699, age 14, William Keene
Poore, John, 17 April 1706, age 12, Barthollomew Leasure

Power, David, 21 June 1699, age 11, Capt. Rodham Kenner
Powers, Daniel, 16 August 1682, age 12, Henry Mayse
Price, Edward, 21 March 1670, age 6, William Brereton
Price, Elizabeth, 7 April 1686, age 11, Thomas Flynt
Price, Henry, 18 April 1677, age 12, Mrs. Martha Jones
Price, Hugh, 17 April 1700, age 12, James Rogers
Price, Morgan, 18 May 1698, age 16, Thomas Wynter
Provist, William, 18 February 1674, age 14, James Johnston
Quinborone, William, 20 June 1664, age 13, William Thomas,
      eleven years "from the twenty fifth of December last"
Raley, Turlo, 20 April 1698, age 15, Ignatius Oliver
Ram, Ebenezer, 16 November 1698, age 11, James Symmons
Rareday, Michall, 21 June 1699, age 11, Thomas Everard
Read, George, 20 June 1667, age 14, Mrs. Dorothy Dameron
Reeves, Robert, 17 March 1675, age 9, Peter Presly, Junr.
Reynolds, Jeffery, 21 July 1680, age 13, James Claughton, "by his Master's
      concession, is ordered to serve his Master but ten years"
Riley, Sarah, 17 April 1678, age 13, Daniell Neale
Ringken, George, 4 April 1694, age 13, John Harris
Roach, Laurence, 17 November 1687, age 11, Mrs. Katherine Cautanceau
Robert, William, 8 September 1662, age not judged, Francis Clay,
      seven years "from the 20th November next"
Roberts, David, 7 April 1686, age 15, William and John Keen
Robinson, John, 15 January 1701, age 16, Charles Lee
Robinson, Susanna, 19 April 1676, age 15, Christopher Garlington
Roe, Samuel, 18 August 1675, age 18, Collo. St. Leger Codd
Royla, Anne, 19 March 1684, age 12, William Keyne, eight years,
      "her Master has in Court abated four years"
Rumley, John, 22 June 1669, age 16, Thomas Mathew
Russell, James, 17 April 1672, age 15, William Presly
Russell, John, 8 September 1668, age 13, William Brereton
Rutter, William, 16 July 1673, age 15, Thomas White
Ryan, Loughlin, 21 December 1698, age 18, Edward Sanders
Ryder, Thomas, 20 December 1670, age 14, William Preslye
Sack, William, 21 February 1672, age 10, William Jallon
Saul, Jonathan, 20 February 1660, age 14, Wilkes Maunder, seven years
Savage, Charles, 21 June 1699, age 15, Hancock Lee
Savage, David, 19 January 1699, age 15, William Cornish
Scanbrook, Mathew, 25 January 1671, age 15, Richard Thompson

NORTHUMBERLAND COUNTY

Scannell, Gillian, 21 June 1699, age 19, John Trimlett
Scott, William, 21 January 1661, age 13, Coll. Richard Lee, eight years
Scott, William, 21 January 1696, age 14, John Taylor
Seaham, John, 21 December 1698, age 15, Peter Coutanceau
Sennett, Phillip, 19 May 1698, age 10, Capt. Rodham Kenner
Servee, James, 20 July 1670, age 14, William Wildy
Severin, Colen, 20 July 1670, age 12, Ralph Waddington
Shahaughnacy, Timothy, 21 June 1704, age 15, Peter Cantanceau
Shaw, James, 16 April 1699, age 17, John Jones
Shefield, Moses, 19 May 1686, age 15, Thomas Winter, who "promised to
     give him two years of his service," seven years
Shelly, Charles, 8 September 1668, age 16, Capt. Edmond Lyster
Shenton, John, 21 April 1662, age 15, Abraham Joyce, six years
Sherwood, Edward, 20 April 1660, age 13, Richard Way, eight years
Simmons, Matthew, 21 December 1698, age 11, Daniell Neale
Simpkins, John, 17 September 1690, age 12, Christopher Neale
Sirnes, John, 21 January 1661, age 13, George English, eight years
Smith, David, 21 June 1699, age 16, John Bryan
Smith, John, 21 June 1699, age 17, William Winder
Smith, Thomas, 19 May 1698, age 17, Capt. Rodham Kenner
Smyth, Edward, 21 August 1678, age not judged, William Shoares,
     "coming into this Country with Capt. Thomas Smyth, and
     having lost his Indentures," nine years
Smyth, Elizabeth, 21 July 1680, age 12, Nicholas Owen, "by her Master's
     concession, is ordered to serve her Master but ten years"
Smyth, James, 21 September 1698, age 14, John Ingram
Smyth, John, 10 February 1663, age not judged, Edward Humpston,
     six years
Smyth, John, 20 June 1663, age 13, Wilkes Maunder
Smyth, John, 16 May 1694, age 11, Thomas Tayler, thirteen years
Smyth, Robert, 10 October 1666, age 13, John Mottrome
Soape, Benjamin, 16 September 1696, age 17, Capt. William Jones
Southerne, James, 15 June 1681, age 10, Richard Flynt
Spence, William, 21 May 1679, age 18, Thomas Banks
Spratt, James, 21 June 1699, age 18, Anthony Haine
Steward, James, 16 April 1699, age 13, Richard Flynt, Sr.
Steward, William, 18 November 1691, age 10, Thomas Maize
Stintson, Archibald, 16 April 1699, age 9, Robert Reeves
Stripkin (?), Cossell, 20 November 1668, age 17, Col. Peter Ashton

NORTHUMBERLAND COUNTY

Swath, Mathew, 20 July 1670, age 12, Ralph Waddington
Swillivant, Owen, 19 June 1700, age 11, Charles Nelmes
Swillivant, Peter, 16 February 1698, age 17, Walter Jenkins
Swillivant, Teigue, 21 June 1699, age 19, William Bletsoe
Symms, Edith, 17 February 1668, age 12, George Clark
Tayler, Thomas, 8 March 1664, age 13, James Awsten, eleven years
Taylor, Joseph, 20 February 1678, age 17, Mrs. Joane Garlington
Tearney, Robert, 21 December 1698, age not judged, Capt Rodham Kenner
Teuxbury, James, 20 February 1665, age 11, James Austin
Thackerell, Thomas, 15 April 1702, age 15, Dennis Conaway
Thane, Katharine, 20 May 1708, age 15, Richard Neale
Thomas, Arthur, 17 April 1700, age 17, Capt. Peter Hack, seven years,
    "he had Indentures for five yeares but was cheated out of them
    by Capt. William Thornton who brought him into this Country"
Thomas, Daniell, 17 March 1675, age 14, Thomas Matthews
Thomas, David, 21 February 1700, age 15, Richard Nutt
Thomas, Jeremiah, 19 January 1676, age 17, Walter Dunne
Thomas, John, 20 April 1660, age 13, James Dasheild, who "hath freely
    given him one yeare of his time," seven years
Thomas, John, 17 April 1700, age 12, Daniel Swillivant
Thomas, William, 12 March 1663, age not judged, William Jollyns,
    seven years
Thompson, Ann, 17 April 1689, age 18, Abraham Sheers
Thompson, Dunkan, 21 June 1699, age 10, Henry Frankling
Thompson, Francis, 15 September 1670, age 18, Azaricam Parker
Thompson, Marmaduke, 19 February 1673, age 11, William Downing
Thompson, William, 15 July 1696, age 14, Richard Nutt
Toby, John, 20 April 1663, age 13, Thomas Williams
Travers, John, 21 August 1678, age 10, John Swanson
Tru, Elizabeth, 20 April 1663, age 12, Richard Span
Tucker, Thomas, 17 February 1668, age 12, Edward Coles
Varley, Christopher, 21 August 1678, age 8, Thomas Winter
Varley, Elizabeth, 21 August 1678, age 12, Thomas Winter
Varley, James, 21 August 1678, age 6, Thomas Winter
Varley, Jennett, 21 August 1678, age 14, Thomas Winter
Varley, John, 21 August 1678, age 10, Thomas Winter
Vaughan, Valentine, 21 May 1673, age 14, Francis Lee
Vaughan, William, 26 February 1661, age 13, Thomas Brereton,
    eight years

NORTHUMBERLAND COUNTY

Veale, Humphrey, 19 January 1676, age 13, Philip Shapleigh
Venner, Martha, 21 May 1679, age 18, William Keen
Walcupp, Thomas, 20 July 1698, age 9, Joseph Venables
Walker, John, 20 December 1669, age 13, William Preslye
Walker, Joseph, 15 June 1681, age 17, Peter Presly, Jr.
Walker, Nathaniel, 17 March 1697, age 13, Cuthbert Spann
Wallice, Thomas, 17 March 1708, age 12, John Cralle
Wallis, William, 17 July 1689, age 13, Christopher Garlington
Walters, John, 20 June 1683, age 13, John Coutansheau
Ward, Richard, 20 February 1660, age 14, Isaac Foxcroft, seven years
Warwick, Thomas, 3 May 1660, age 10, Major George Colclough,
    eleven years
Waterson, Peter, 16 May 1694, age 18, John Eustace
Watson, John, 20 April 1663, age 12, James James
Webb, Samuell, 3 May 1660, age 13, Major George Colclough, eight years
Welch, James, 21 December 1698, age 13, Henry Brereton
Welch, Matthew, 21 December 1698, age 15, William Harcum
Wells, Thomas, 17 April 1700, age 17, John Ingram
Weston, Edmond, 20 June 1677, age 13, Hugh Harris
Wethenell, Elizabeth, 21 May 1673, age 15, John Cossens, "confessing
    her self to be sixteene years of age ye next Michaelmass"
Wheeler, Thomas, 21 December 1685, age 14, Thomas Brewer
White, James, 19 January 1699, age 15, Thomas Shapleigh
White, Symon, 19 January 1699, age 14, William Feilding
White, William, 20 June 1677, age 9, Christopher Neale
Whitney, John, 6 April 1669, age 17, Mathew Rhodon
Widsey, Mary, 21 February 1672, age 13, Thomas Mathew
Wigginton, George, 20 December 1699, age 15, Richard Tullos
Wilcox, Elizabeth, 20 June 1694, age 15 "and a half," "and she admits
    the same," Capt. Rodham Kenner, eight and a half years
Wilcox, John, 20 December 1670, age 15, William Preslye
Wilkinson, Thomas, 16 July 1673, age 14, Hancock Lee
Wilks, Robert, 21 December 1685, age 10, John Bowen
William, Elinor, 17 April 1700, age 18, William Harcum
Williams, Benjamin, 20 February 1660, age 16, Thomas Williams,
    five years
Williams, Edward, 15 June 1698, age 10, Hancock Lee
Williams, John, 20 January 1670, age 16, John Cuttanceau, seven years
Williams, John, 19 January 1676, age 9, Robert Jones

Williams, John, 15 January 1679, age 9, John Hughlett
Williams, John, 17 April 1700, age 15, Mrs. Elizabeth Bankes
Williams, Mary, 21 June 1699, age 17, John Walters
Williams, Richard, 21 February 1700, age 14, Richard Lattemore
Williams, Thomas, 21 July 1680, age 15, Richard Kenner
Williams, Thomas, 16 February 1698, age 16, Christopher Neale
Wilson, Christopher, 4 April 1694, age 11, Abraham Sheers
Wilson, Henry, 16 April 1699, age 16, Alexander Witherstone
Wilson, John, 20 June 1688, age 17, Thomas Baker
Wilson, John, 21 June 1699, age 15, William Smith
Wilson, William, 4 April 1694, age 11, Thomas Gaskins
Wilson, William, 20 April 1698, age 15 "and a half," John Bryant and
      wife, to serve "six years and no longer"
Withers, Dorothy, 18 April 1677, age 14, Thomas Lawrence
Witherton, Samuell, 16 February 1698, age 9, John Baily
Woldridge, Edward, 19 July 1671, age 15, James Claughton
Wolford, John, 20 June 1668, age 15, Nicholas Nichols
Wood, Michaell, 19 January 1699, age 15, Capt. William Jones
Woodman, Joseph, 26 February 1661, age 14, Henry Corbyn, seven years
Woodworth, Hester, 17 April 1689, age 12, Lazarus Tayler
Wooll, William, 21 June 1699, age 14, Lazarus Taylor
Wright, Andrew, 17 March 1697, age 12, Cuthbert Spann
Wright, Mary, 19 June 1672, age 8, William Jallons
Wright, Richard, 19 August 1674, age 13, Colo. St. Leger Codd
Yeomans, Barthalomow, 20 April 1660, age 13, Andrew Cockren and
      Walter Dunn, eight years
Younge, Jane, 21 March 1677, age 7, John Cowen
_____, Abraham, a French Boy, 20 June 1668, age 12, William Wildey
_____, Andrew, a French Boy, 20 June 1668, age 15, Charles Ashton
_____, Elizabeth, a French Wench, 20 June 1668, age 15, Thomas Hobson
_____, Guillian, an Irish Wench, 22 June 1669, age 14, Mathew Rhodon
_____, James, a French Boy, 8 September 1668, age 14, Richard Span
_____, John, a French Boy, 20 June 1668, age 12, Daniel Neale
_____, John, a French Boy, 20 July 1670, age 14, Thomas Hobson
_____, John, 17 April 1678, age 14, John Corbell
_____, Luke, a French Boy, 20 June 1668, age 13, Christopher Neale
_____, Nicholas, a French Boy, 20 June 1668, age 12, George Courtnall
_____, Philip, a French Boy, 20 June 1668, age 10, Thomas Rose
_____, _____, 19 January 1676, age 12, William Downing, Junr.

NORTHUMBERLAND COUNTY

Gentleman Justices	Servants
Allerton, Isaac, Major *	Blackwell, Kennam
Ashton, Peter, Capt., Coll.	Amis, Brittaine, Cauller, Lewis, Stripkin
Bankes, Thomas	Cavenah, Spence
Brereton, Thomas, Capt., Major, Coll.	Davids, L ____ , Magrillus, Vaughan
Cantanceau, Peter	Arro, Bryan, Burge, Knight, Macarty, Seaham, Shahaughnacy
Claughton, John	
Clay, Francis	Harwood, Robert
Codd, St. Leger, Coll.	Dinney, Hewes, Roe, Wright
Colclough, George, Major	Farlowe, Hitchcock, Hood, Warwick, Webb
Cooper, George, Capt., Major, Lt. Col.	Peacock
Cralle, John, Capt.	Lockiere, Phillips, Wallice
Downing, John	Meath
Downing, Richard	
Downing, William	Blackwell, Griffith, Haley, Hall, Hall, Little, Matthew, Thompson, ____
Eustace, John, Capt.	Armstrong, Maconald, Waterson
Fielding, Ambrose	
Fielding, Edward	Cammell

NORTHUMBERLAND COUNTY

Gentleman Justices	Servants
Fowke, Gerard, Coll.	
Griffin, Samuel, Lt. Col.	Poore
Hack, Peter, Capt., Lt. Col.	James, Thomas
Harris, John, Major	Armstrong, Doak, Mullagan, Oliver, Ringken
Haynie, John, Capt.	
Haynie, Richard, Capt.	Hughs
Hobson, Thomas, Sr.	Cromwell, Merret, _____ , _____
Hopkins, Thomas	Hudson
Howson, John, Capt.	Patten
Howson, Leonard, Capt.	Crosthead, Leehow, Levistone, Nichols
Howson, William, Capt.	
Jones, Maurice, Capt.	
Jones, Robert	Bateman, Boyer, Contansheau, Kett, King, Williams
Jones, William, Capt.	Durrough, Oneale, Soape, Wood
Kenner, Richard, Capt.	Cross, Fouch, Fuse, Hinsborough, James, Newman, Williams
Kenner, Rodham, Capt., Major, Col.	Bragg, Burk, Copperweight, Furney, Hogan, Jackman, Power, Sennett, Smith, Tearney, Wilcox
Knight, Peter, Capt.	Ortland
Lee, Charles	Robinson

148

NORTHUMBERLAND COUNTY

Gentleman Justices	Servants
Lee, Francis	Brumfeild, More, Vaughan
Lee, Hancock	Gambler, Savage, Wilkinson, Williams
Lee, Richard, Coll., Esqr. *	Dawes, Gardner, Greene, Hughson, Pettus, Phillips, Scott
Lee, William, Capt.	
Lyster, Edmond, Capt.	Kelly, Shelly
Matthew, Thomas, Capt.	Mallin, Moss, Neale, Oldfield, Oliver, Rumley, Thomas, Widsey
Mottrome, John, Capt., Major	Barron, Chackle, Franklin, Moore, Smyth
Mottrome, Spencer, Capt.	Forrester
Neale, Christopher, Capt.	Dowle, Dunawon, Fogershie, Harmestone, Holland, Simpkins, White, Williams, _____
Neale, Daniel	Bowyer, Fisher, Janes, Macklanhan, Player, Riley, Simmons, _____
Nutt, William, Capt.	Bridgeman, Colledge, Johnson
Owen, Nicholas	Corry, Smyth
Owen, Richard	
Porteus, Edward	
Presly, Peter, Jr., Col.	Booth, Flattman, Reeves, Walker
Presly, Peter, Sr.	Brown, Castide, Chamberlin, Corker, Haines, Mucklehose, Omuddy

149

NORTHUMBERLAND COUNTY

Gentleman Justices	Servants
Presly, William	Ball, Harris, Harrison, Jackson, Mackness, Mason, Russell, Ryder, Walker, Wilcox
Rogers, John, Capt.	Le Hoot
Rogers, Richard	Crane, Jones
Rogers, William	
Sanders, Ebenezer	
Sanders, Edward, Capt.	Contancheau, Jacobs, Macgee
Shapleigh, Phillip	Francis, Keire, Loth, Veale
Smyth, Samuell, Lt. Coll.	Gallee, Mahoany, Parsons
Span, Cuthbert, Capt.	Allen, Walker, Wright
Steptoe, John	
Thomas, William	Quinborone
Travers, Rawly ** ***	Fox, Peters
Turberville, John **	
Waddy, James	Birk, Calvin, Cammell, Holland, Macmend
Winder, Thomas, Capt.	Mahughen
Wright, Richard, Capt.	Batty

*   see Westmoreland County
**   see Lancaster County
*** see Richmond County

150

NORTHUMBERLAND COUNTY

Year	White	Negro	Indian
1660	14	0	0
1661	14	0	0
1662	16	0	0
1663	19	0	0
1664	17	0	0
1665	11	0	0
1666	3	0	0
1667	3	0	0
1668	29	0	0
1669	19	0	0
1670	27	0	0
1671	10	0	0
1672	15	0	0
1673	9	0	0
1674	9	0	0
1675	11	0	0
1676	33	0	0
1677	12	0	0
1678	21	0	0
1679	13	0	0
1680	4	2 *	4
1681	6	0	0
1682	8	1	0
1683	2	2	1
1684	2	1	0
1685	11	2	1
1686	10	1	0
1687	18	2	0

* plus one Mulatto

NORTHUMBERLAND COUNTY

Year	White	Negro	Indian
1688	3	4	0
1689	6	0	0
1690	3	0	0
1691	2	10 *	0
1692	0	1	0
1693	4	0	0
1694	17	2	0
1695	0	2	0
1696	9	0	0
1697	18	0	0
1698	63	2	0
1699	84	0	0
1700	16	0	0
1701	8	8	0
1702	10	11	0
1703	1	0	0
1704	1	14	0
1705	1	14	1
1706	4	4	0
1707	0	5	2
1708	2	3	0
1709	0	0	0
1710	0	0	1
1711	0	1	0
1712	0	0	0
1713	1	0	0
Total	619	92	10

Note: No children without indentures from 1652-1659

Abbe, Mary, 9 February 1681, (age 15), Thomas Chowning, nine years

Absden, Thomas, 8 July 1668, age 18, John Meredith, six years

Ackton, John, 8 July 1674, (age 16), David Myles, eight years

Addison, Thomas, 11 August 1703, age 13, Andrew Jackson

Agnes, Edward, 9 April 1701, age not judged, Major William Lister,
     five years

Agnes, Ferrald, 9 April 1701, age not judged, Major William Lister,
     five years

Alexander, William, 10 July 1667, age not judged, Robert Beverley,
     five years

Allen, Richard, 12 November 1662, (age 17), Arther Nash, seven years

Allen, William, 10 July 1667, (age 17), Robert Beverley, seven years

Anderson, John, 13 May 1696, age 18, William Paine, six years, "there
     being noe certaine time of service mentioned in the Indenture"

Anderson, Martha, 13 June 1705, age 18, Alexander Swan, six years

Andrews, Thomas, 9 May 1677, (age 15), Joseph Ball, nine years

Anntrim, Dorothey, 10 June 1696, (age 14), Andrew Jackson, ten years

Apyrell, Thomas, 14 February 1700, age 17, Stephen Tomlin, seven years

Argo, William, 10 February 1686, (age 17), Henery Pullen, seven years

Armestrong, Adam, 8 July 1668, age 13, Thomas Warwicke, eleven years

Arnold, Joseph, 10 August 1687, (age 15), William Therriatt, nine years

Arnold, Thomas, 9 January 1678, (age 14), Thomas Laurence, ten years

Atterberry, Thomas, 12 March 1683, (age 15), Thomas Laurence,
     nine years

Atty, Christopher, 14 May 1662, (age 18), John Meredith, six years

Balding, Phebe, 9 January 1678, (age 13), Lt. Coll. John Carter,
     eleven years

Baldricke, William, September 1663, (age 17), Charles Carpenter,
     seven years

Baley, Bassill, 29 May 1678, (age 15), Capt. William Ball, nine years

Baley, John, 11 February 1680, (age 15), James Trewella, nine years

Ball, Thomas, 8 December 1675, (age 16), John Morris, eight years

Barber, Isabella, 8 September 1675, (age 15), George Flower, nine years,
     "she alleadgeing that she hath an Indenture for eight years but
     lefte in her Mothers handes in England"

Barber, William, 14 June 1699, age 15, William Rodgers, nine years

Bassey, Michael, 12 May 1675, age 18, George Flowers, six years

Batchelder, Joseph, 8 February 1665, age 10, Thomas Younge,
     thirteen years

LANCASTER COUNTY

Bateman, Isaac, 14 June 1699, age 18, John Pine, six years

Bayley, Alexander, 10 January 1672, age 18, John Carter, six years

Beckett, William, 14 September 1670, (age 15), William Bendall,
        nine years

Belfeilde, Anne, 8 March 1676, age 15, Roger Kelley, nine years

Bell, Andrew, 12 May 1708, age 15, John Turbervill, nine years

Bennett, Elizabeth, 11 March 1663, (age 17), Richard Harwell, seven years

Bennett, John, 13 May 1668, age 15, George Wale, nine years

Bent, Robert, 11 November 1674, (age 16), Robert Beckingham,
        eight years

Berrey, Thomas, 8 December 1675, (age 13), John Morris, eleven years

Berry, Edmund, 9 February 1681, (age 15), Major Robert Bristow,
        nine years

Binstead, Joane, 26 January 1670, (age 15), Mrs. Anne Fox, Widow,
        nine years

Birchit, Jane, 12 May 1686, (age 16), Brian Stott, eight years

Bird, John, 14 July 1669, (age 14), Davyd Fox, ten years

Black, Robert, 13 May 1696, (age 12), Mottrom Wright, twelve years

Bloore, John, 8 May 1661, age not judged, Edward Roe, seven years

Bohonham, James, 10 March 1697, (age 17), George Heale, seven years

Bole, Archibald, 9 April 1701, age 14, Mrs. Alice Stretchley, ten years

Bonn, Thomas, 9 September 1674, (age 14), Robert Griggs, ten years

Bradford, John, 14 May 1701, age 13, Robert Young, eleven years

Bradshaw, John, 14 May 1662, (age 17), John Limborow, seven years

Bramley, Daniell, 9 March 1670, (age 18), Nathaniell Browne, six years

Brand, John, 11 March 1668, age 13, Davyd Fox, eleven years

Brian, Mathew, 12 March 1679, (age 11), Thomas Martyn, thirteen years

Bridgeman, Catharine, 11 July 1673, (age 16), David Myles, eight years

Bristow, Hugh, 10 August 1698, age 14, James Haynes, ten years

Britton, John, 10 February 1664, (age 17), John Hughes, seven years

Brookes, Thomas, 10 January 1672, age 16, John Carter, eight years

Brown, Dunkin, 14 June 1699, age 17, John Wright, seven years

Brown, John, 9 November 1698, age 15, Mary Camell, nine years

Browne, Richard, 8 February 1665, age not judged, Cuthbert Potter,
        five years, "haveing served foure yeres"

Bryan, Patrick, 11 September 1678, (age 18), Thomas Martyn, Senr.,
        six years

Bryant, John, 12 May 1669, (age 12), Coll. John Carter, Esqr., twelve years

Bryon, Roger, 14 June 1699, age 14, Uriah Angell, ten years

Buckley, William, 13 May 1696, (age 16), William Bings, eight years
Budd, William, 12 May 1675, age 16, Stephen Tomlyn, eight years
Burling, John, 10 July 1667, age not judged, William Ball, eight years
    "from his arrivall beinge the 24th day of May last"
Burnett, Thomas, 14 June 1699, age 15, Thomas Ball, nine years
Burrell, William, 10 June 1677, (age 15), Rowland Lawson, nine years
Butcher, John, 14 July 1669, (age 13), Davyd Fox, eleven years
Butler, Thomas, 8 December 1675, (age 14), Stephen Tomlyn, ten years
Butterey, John, 9 May 1677, (age 18), William Lennell, six years
Butterworth, John, 25 January 1660, age 14, Ebbey Bonnison, seven years
Cabadge, James, 12 May 1669, (age 16), Tobyas Horton, eight years,
    unless "in the interym" he can "produce an Indenture as hee
    now alledgeth"
Callicott, William, 12 May 1669, (age 15), Coll. John Carter, Esqr.,
    nine years
Calt, John, 13 January 1669, (age 11), Thomas Chetwode, thirteen years
Calwell, Samuell, 10 March 1697, (age 17), Capt. William Lister,
    seven years
Cambell, Alexander, 12 May 1714, age 18, Robert Carter, Esq., six years
Camell, Thomas, 14 June 1699, age 16, Francis Wallis, eight years
Canes, John, 11 March 1663, (age 18), Bryan Stott, six years
Cannady, John, 9 March 1687, (age 14), Capt. William Ball, ten years
Caprell, Thomas, 8 July 1668, age 13, Rawleigh Travers, eleven years
Carney, Patrick, 11 August 1697, age 16, John Kelley, eight years
Carr, Joseph, 12 May 1674, (age 15), Robert Griggs, nine years
Carraden, James, 9 May 1677, (age 14), Thomas Haynes, ten years
Carrill, Richard, 14 June 1699, age 15, George Heale, nine years
Carter, Edward, 9 November 1664, age not judged, Coll. John Carter,
    five years, "haveing served foure yeres"
Carter, Mathew, 13 July 1670, (age 18), Walter Herd, six years
Carter, Sarah, 12 May 1669, (age 13), Rawleigh Travers, eleven years
Carter, Thomas, 11 January 1671, (age 17), Robert Griggs, seven years
Carvey, Richard, 11 May 1670, (age 11), John Gibson, thirteen years
Casner, William, als. Mansebridge, 11 May 1663, (age 16), master not
    named, eight years
Chambers, Charles, 11 March 1663, (age 13), Minor Doodes, eleven years
Chaundler, William, 11 February 1680, (age 13), Rowland Lawson,
    eleven years
Chavann, Peter, 1 May 1665, age not judged, Doctor Walter Andrews,
    five years

Chesram, Abraham, 10 May 1671, (age 15), John Swayne, nine years
Child, Alice, 30 November 1659, age 10, Rowland Lawson, eleven years
Clark, Patrick, 12 May 1714, age 14, Robert Carter, Esq., ten years
Clark, William, 12 May 1714, age 17, Robert Carter, Esq., seven years
Clarke, John, 13 May 1668, age 18, Henry Corbyn, Esq., six years
Clarke, John, 14 July 1675, (age 16), Lt. Coll. John Carter, eight years
Clarke, John, 10 May 1676, (age 13), George Hale, eleven years
Clarke, Robert, 12 January 1686, (age 17), Edward Gibson, seven years
Claybourne, Cuthbert, 9 January 1661, age not judged, Henry Corbyn,
        seven years
Clephue, William, 13 June 1694, (age 12), Robert Carter,
        twelve years
Clerke, Phillip, 12 May 1669, (age 14), Coll. John Carter, Esqr., ten years
Clothier, Lewys, 9 November 1664, age not judged, Richard Haward,
        five years
Coats, John, 14 May 1712, age 13, William Robinson
Cooke, _____, 14 January 1685, (age 14), Richard Flint, ten years
Cooke, Robert, 14 February 1700, age 15, Thomas Cattlett, nine years
Cooper, Charles, 12 July 1699, age 17, Mrs. Ann Chowning, seven years
Cooper, John, 12 September 1660, age not judged, Coll. John Carter,
        seven years
Cooper, John, 10 June 1668, age 17, Coll. John Carter, Esqr., seven years
Corbet, Elizabeth, 11 February 1680, (age 14), William Merriman,
        ten years
Cory, Mary, 13 May 1668, age 17, Robert Griggs, seven years
Courtice, _____ , 13 May 1685, (age 11), Nathaniell Browne,
        thirteen years
Cox, Edward, 9 May 1688, (age 16), Capt. William Ball, eight years
Cox, John, 11 May 1663, age not judged, Evers Peterson, five years
Cox, William, 9 March 1670, (age 15), Rawleigh Travers, nine years
Crale, John, 13 July 1670, (age 15), Davyd Myles, nine years
Credency, Lettis, 12 September 1705, age not judged, John Hudnall,
        five years
Croner, Patrick, 11 May 1692, (age 12), Daniell Armes, twelve years
Croney, Darby, 14 June 1699, age 17, William More, seven years
Croomes, Thomas, 11 November 1668, (age 17), Doctor Walter
        Whitaker, seven years
Crumwell, James, 11 August 1697, age 15, Andrew Jackson, nine years

Curtis, _____ , female, 8 September 1686, (age 16), John Adams,
    eight years
Cutmore, Richard, 10 July 1689, (age 15), John Scanan, nine years
Davis, Henry, 9 November 1698, age 15, William Paine, nine years
Davis, Josia, 8 July 1674, (age 15), Lt. Coll. John Carter, nine years
Davys, John, 10 June 1668, age 17, Coll. John Carter, Esqr., seven years
Davys, Joseph, 8 April 1668, age 16, Stephen Chilton, eight years
Davys, Thomas, 13 May 1668, age 19, Patricke Miller, five years
Dawson, Jeremy, 11 March 1696, (age 14), Andrew Jackson, ten years
Day, John, 11 September 1667, (age 13), Thomas Willys, eleven years
Daylie, John, 14 June 1699, age 15, Coll. Robert Carter, nine years
Daylie, Peter, 14 July 1708, age not judged, Patrick Connolee, seven years,
    "informing the Court that he had Indentures made att home for
    four years"
Deakins, John, 12 February 1679, (age 13), Capt. William Ball,
    eleven years
Delanie, Joseph, 14 June 1699, age not judged, Coll. Robert Carter
Delany, Joseph, 12 July 1699, age 12, Colo. Robert Carter, twelve years
Dellahay, Thomas, 14 May 1662, (age 17), Walter Herd, seven years
Demery, William, 9 November 1664, (age 12), William Gordowne,
    twelve years
Denney, Abigall, 9 February 1681, (age 16), Edward Carter, eight years
Dickeson, David, 8 December 1675, (age 14), Walter Heard, ten years
Dixon, John, 9 November 1670, (age 18), John Morrys, six years
Dixon, Luke, 13 June 1694, (age 18), Capt. William Ball, six years
Dorrell, Simon, 25 January 1660, age 16, George Marsh
Duerdin, Richard, 4 April 1667, age not judged, Henry Thacker,
    eight years "from ye 29th of December last"
Dunbar, William, 13 June 1694, (age 18), Robert Pritchard, six years
Dunn, Robert, 14 June 1699, age 17, Henry Boatman, seven years
Dunne, Charles, 12 February 1679, (age 15), George Heale, nine years
Dyars, Thomas, 12 March 1662, (age 17), John Madestard, seven years
Dyer, William, 9 July 1662, age not judged, William Copeland, five years
Dymore, Elizabeth, 9 November 1698, age 16, Mary Ashly, eight years
Easter, John, 9 November 1664, (age 16), Alexander Reade, eight years
Edmonds, Brian, 11 March 1696, (age 13), Stephen Chilton, eleven years
Edmonds, Christopher, 9 January 1689, (age 14), Randolph Miller,
    ten years
Edwards, John, 13 February 1678, (age 16), Thomas Barker, eight years

LANCASTER COUNTY

Edwards, John, 14 June 1699, age 12, Rowland Lawson, twelve years
Edwards, Joyce, 8 March 1671, (age 15), Henry Bradley, nine years
Eldridge, Samuell, 8 May 1667, (age 14), Richard Parrett, ten years
Elliott, John, 9 March 1692, (age 12), Uriah Angell, twelve years
Ellys, William, 13 November 1667, (age 16), Thomas Madestard,
    eight years
Emerson, John, 26 January 1670, (age 18), Ralphe Whisteler, six years
England, John, 9 May 1677, (age 15), William Garton, nine years
England, John, 13 June 1694, (age 18), Tobias Pursley, six years
Ensden, William, 9 September 1668, (age 16), Capt. Christopher
    Wormeley, eight years
Everest, Robert, 14 May 1662, (age 16), Lt. Coll. Edward Carter,
    eight years
Evlyn, Henry, 11 May 1663, (age 17), Ever Peterson, seven years
Farrington, George, 13 May 1668, age 13, Robert Griggs, eleven years
Fawshyn, Andrew, 8 March 1671, (age 17), John Kerby, seven years
Feilder, William, 9 January 1678, (age 17), Lt. Coll. John Carter,
    seven years
Fenney, Elizabeth, 9 April 1685, (age 16), Coll. John Carter, eight years
Ferridral, Peter, 12 May 1669, (age 16), Coll. John Carter, Esqr.,
    eight years
Finney, John, 11 February 1685, (age 16), _____ , eight years
Finney, Mary, 9 April 1685, (age 12), Coll. John Carter, twelve years
Firnder, John, 10 June 1677, (age 16), Robert Scofeilde, eight years
Flet _____ , Thomas, 8 March 1682, age not judged, master not named
Flint, William, 10 November 1675, (age 17), Lt. Coll. John Carter,
    seven years
Floyde, Ambrose, 11 November 1685, (age 12), William Merriman,
    twelve years
Floyde, David, 11 February 1680, (age 15), Stephen Chilton, nine years
Folley, John, 10 November 1675, (age 16), William Edmonds, eight years
Forman, Benjamin, 8 March 1682, (age 11), Robert Pritchard,
    thirteen years
Forrest, Alexander, 10 January 1672, age 19, John Carter
Forrest, John, 12 May 1669, (age 12), William Leech, twelve years
Foster, Mathew, 12 May 1669, (age 15), William Lennell, nine years
Frampton, David, 29 May 1678, (age 17), Lt. Coll. John Carter,
    seven years
Frizle, Arthur, 13 July 1670, age not judged, William Edmonds, five years

Fry, William, 14 July 1669, age not judged, Davyd Fox

Fuller, Thomas, 13 November 1661, age not judged, David Fox,
seven years

Garland, Joseph, 9 February 1698, age not judged, William Ball

Garroway, Solomon, 9 September 1668, (age 14), Widdow Neasum,
ten years

Gibbs, Thomas, 8 July 1674, age not judged, David Myles, five years

Gilbert, John, 9 March 1681, (age 14), William Lennell, ten years

Gilbert, Mathew, 13 January 1664, age not judged, Magne Barrett,
"comeing into this Countrey in the Ship Rainbow of Plymouth,"
seven years "from the arrival of the saide Ship"

Gilbert, Thomas, 14 July 1664, (age 16), Walter Herd, eight years

Gillein, _____ , male, 8 September 1686, (age 18), Edward Carter,
six years

Gilson, William, 10 June 1668, age 18, William Hutchins, six years

Ginns, Thomas, 12 March 1683, (age 14), John Morris, ten years

Gladding, George, 12 March 1662, (age 16), Richard Parrett, eight years

Goble, John, 9 February 1676, (age 14), Thomas Marshall, "who doth
give" the servant "two yeres of his saide tyme," eight years

Gorfinch, Thomas, 13 May 1668, age 16, William Hall, eight years

Gormory, Patrick, 12 January 1698, age not judged, William George, "doth
acknowledge his free consent to serve his Master six yeares from
this day in consideration of being civilly used during ye terme"

Gorrnock, Timothy, 14 June 1699, age 17, George Heale, seven years

Grace, Christopher, 9 March 1687, (age 12), George Heale, twelve years

Granger, Thomas, 13 March 1672, (age 13), Henry King, eleven years

Grant, Mary, 11 January 1665, (age 17), William Frizell, seven years

Graves, Joseph, 13 January 1675, (age 15), Mrs. Elizabeth Payne,
nine years

Greene, Margaret, 11 November 1668, (age 13), John Haslewood,
eleven years

Gresher, Thomas, 9 September 1696, (age 11), Richard Alderson,
thirteen years

Griffin, Benjamyn, 12 May 1669, (age 13), Coll. John Carter, Esqr.,
eleven years

Griffin, Morgan, 14 June 1699, age 13, Hugh Ladner, eleven years

Griffin, Richard, 10 July 1667, (age 14), Coll. Edward Carter, ten years

Griffin, Thomas, 10 February 1664, age not judged, Toby Horton,
five years

LANCASTER COUNTY

Grimes, Richard, 13 February 1678, age not judged, Robert Griggs,
    eleven years "from the 24th day of August last past"
Gutridge, John, 8 July 1674, (age 15), Robert Beckingham, nine years
Guy, John, 9 March 1670, (age 13), Robert Griggs, eleven years
Gwin, Michaell, 11 May 1692, (age 11), Mrs. Martha Norris, thirteen years
Hall, George, 11 February 1680, (age 17), Fortunatus Sidnor, seven years
Hall, Thomas, 10 February 1686, (age 15), William Garton, nine years
Hambleton, John, 13 June 1694, (age 18), George Heale, six years
Hamilton, William, 11 August 1703, age 12, Andrew Jackson
Hansby, James, 10 July 1667, (age 15), Coll. Edward Carter, nine years
Hanson, Anne, 9 September 1674, (age 13), William Lennell, eleven years
Hanson, Nicholas, 13 January 1675, (age 12), Thomas Martyn,
    twelve years
Harding, Robert, 9 November 1664, age not judged, Richard Haward,
    five years
Hareat, William, 14 February 1700, age 14, Colo. Robert Carter, Esqr.,
    "being brought to this Court with Indentures for ye custom of
    ye Country," (code for "according to law"), ten years
Harman, Margarett, 10 January 1672, age not judged, William Ball Senr.,
    "and solde to hym by Capt. Nicholas Thomas"
Harris, Thomas, 12 January 1686, age not judged, _____
Harrys, Thomas, 12 March 1662, (age 17), John Madestard, seven years
Hart, William, 9 January 1678, (age 16), Lt. Coll. John Carter, eight years
Hartright, Thomas, 13 May 1668, age 19, Richard Merryman, five years
Harvey, John, 12 May 1669, (age 15), Rawleigh Travers, nine years
Harvey, Jonathan, 12 January 1686, age not judged, Nicholas Dymer,
    "is ordered to serve seaven yeres, tenne moneths from this day"
Harwood, Thomas, 11 March 1663, (age 16), Daniel Harrison, eight years
Haslewood, Henry, 13 November 1667, age 17, Robert Griggs, seven years
Haughy, William, 11 May 1698, age 15, Randolph Miller, nine years
Haynes, Edward, 26 January 1670, (age 12), George Flower, twelve years
Head, Thomas, 14 June 1699, age 19, John Pinkard
Heale, Bryan, 11 May 1687, (age 13), William Garton, eleven years
Hegoe, John, 14 June 1699, age 17, Randolph Miller, seven years
Henderson, Albert, 13 May 1668, age 18, Henry Corbyn, Esq., six years
Henderson, Robert, 10 June 1696, (age 13), William Ball, eleven years
Higgison, Charles, 14 July 1675, (age 15), Robert Griggs, nine years
Hill, Edward, 10 January 1672, age 19, John Carter
Hilliad, John, 8 May 1667, (age 15), William Frizle, nine years

Hind, James, 14 June 1699, age not judged, William Ball

Hinds, James, 12 July 1699, age 10, William Ball, fourteen years

Hixon, Benjamin, 12 March 1679, (age 17), John Morris, seven years

Hobbs, John, 11 January 1671, age not judged, Widow of Tobyas Horton, five years

Hodgkin, Elizabeth, 11 November 1674, age not judged, Brian Stott, five years

Hollys, Obadiah, 8 May 1667, (age 16), John Pine, eight years

Holmes, John, 14 July 1708, age not judged, Ellen Heale, seven years, "informing this Court that he had Indentures made att home for noe more than four yeares"

Hopton, John, 12 January 1686, age 19, John Berrey, "is ordered to serve eight yeres from his arrivall, hee being nineteene yeres of age"

Horsley, William, 26 January 1670, (age 16), John Pine, eight years

Howell, Priscilla, 11 November 1674, (age 18), Daniel Harrison, six years

Howell, Richard, 10 November 1697, age 14, Thomas Martin

Hubbard, Andrew, 4 April 1667, (age 14), Robert Griggs, ten years

Hughit, John, 10 July 1689, (age 14), Henery Pullen, ten years

Hull, Robert, 12 February 1679, (age 14), Coll. William Ball, ten years

Hunter, Francys, male, 11 March 1663, (age 15), Toby Horton, nine years

Huske, William, 1 May 1665, age not judged, Robert Price, ten years "from his arrivall, it being the 25th day of December 1663"

Hutley, Mary, 8 February 1665, age 15, "by her owne acknowledgment," Richard Merryman, nine years

Jackson, Daniell, 8 February 1665, under 16, Richard Perrott, nine years, unless he "shall produce an authentick certificate out of Englande that hee is above 16 yeres, then to serve five yeres"

Jackson, Mathew, 12 March 1662, (age 17), Richard Parrett, seven years

James, John, 12 March 1662, (age 17), Thomas Warwicke, seven years

Johns, James, 11 November 1668, (age 16), John Haslewood, eight years

Johnson, Edward, 8 December 1675, (age 16), Fortunatus Sydnor, eight years

Johnson, Edward, 10 May 1676, (age 18), Major Robert Binton, six years

Johnson, George, 12 May 1674, (age 16), Lt. Coll. John Carter, eight years

Johnson, Thomas, 12 March 1662, (age 15), John Edwards, nine years

Jones, John, 14 March 1661, age not judged, Gray Skipworth, eight years

Jones, Mary, 9 October 1700, age 3, Robert Carter, Esq., twenty one years

Jones, Robert, 13 May 1696, (age 16), William Merriman, eight years

Jones, Thomas, 13 June 1694, (age 16), George Heale, eight years

Jones, William, 11 May 1698, age 16, Capt. William Lister, eight years
Jordan, Nicholas, 14 May 1662, (age 16), William Stephens, eight years
Jynn, John, 13 November 1661, age not judged, David Fox, seven years
Keene, Bernard, 10 June 1668, age 18, Major Genll. Robert Smith,
    six years
Kelley, Dennis, 14 June 1699, age 19, Nicholas George, Junr.
Kelley, Owen, 14 June 1699, age 16, William Ball, eight years
Kent, John, 10 February 1664, age 15, Richard Laurence, "comeing into
    this Countrey in the Ship, Providence of London, Mr. William
    Hall, Commander," eight years
Kent, John, 10 May 1676, (age 17), Lt. Coll. John Carter, seven years
Kenton, Thomas, 13 June 1711, age 14, Reverend Mr. Joseph Holt
King, Thomas, 10 November 1697, age 13, Mottrom Wright
Kitchin, William, 11 August 1697, age 8, John Heart, sixteen years
Knight, Robert, 1 May 1665, age not judged, Ever Peterson, nine years
    "from his arrival, beinge the 13th of November last past"
Lambert, Edward, 9 May 1688, (age 15), William Therriatt, nine years
Lambert, Richard, 13 January 1669, (age 14), Daniel Harrison, ten years
Lambert, Thomas, 8 July 1674, (age 15), George Hale, nine years
Laurence, Benjamyn, 8 March 1671, (age 13), John Kerby, eleven years
Laurence, William, 12 May 1674, (age 16), Major Robert Bristow,
    eight years
Lawson, Alexander, 12 July 1699, age 16, Capt. William Lister,
    eight years
Lee, Anne, 9 May 1677, (age 15), Richard Sampson, nine years
Lee, William, 13 June 1694, (age 18), William Lister, six years
Lennan, Cormock, 9 November 1698, age not judged, John Brown, "in
    consideration of his Master's civility and a good coat vest and
    britches did destroy his Indenture," six years
Loe, John, 9 January 1661, age not judged, Henry Corbyn, six years
Londen, Elizabeth, 9 March 1681, age not judged, William Lennell
Lowe (?), Sarah, 18 January 1663, (age 16), Robert Chowning, eight years
Lucey, John, 9 December 1668, (age 18), William Leech, six years,
    "with his owne consent"
Lynn, Robert, 15 September 1665, (age 15), Patricke Millar, nine years
Lynnton, Charles, 9 February 1681, (age 18), Major Robert Bristow,
    six years
Lynsey, Ann, 13 June 1694, (age 18), Capt. David Fox, six years
Mackell, Daniel, 13 May 1696, (age 16), Robert Carter, eight years

LANCASTER COUNTY

Mackfarson, Hugh, 9 September 1668, (age 16), George Goodlowe,
    eight years
Mackmullin, John, 13 February 1678, (age 15), George Heale, nine years
Mackrady, Dennis, 11 April 1688, (age 15), John Simmons, nine years
MacQualian, Charles, 9 April 1701, age 16, Stephen Chilton, eight years
Makins, Marke, 8 May 1661, age not judged, Hugh Brent, eight years
Manday, William, 10 November 1675, (age 17), Lt. Coll. John Carter,
    seven years
Marene, Patience, 13 June 1694, (age 16), Stephen Chilton,
    eight years
Maroone, Alexander, 21 November 1691, (age 13), John Sumner,
    eleven years
Marshall, Gilbert, 14 June 1699, age 16, Richard Flint, eight years
Martin, John, 13 July 1698, age 13, John Cox, eleven years
Martyn, George, 12 March 1662, (age 16), John Vause, eight years
Martyn, John, 10 June 1668, age 15, Lt. Coll. Cuthbert Potter, nine years
Martyn, Thomas, 23 October 1661, age not judged, Mathew Kempe,
    six years
Martyn, William, 12 January 1676, (age 15), Estate of Hugh Brent,
    deceased, nine years
Mash, Richard, 12 March 1679, (age 11), Henery Bradley, thirteen years
Mason, Thomas, 8 July 1674, (age 15), Nathaniel Browne, nine years
Mate, Patrick, 13 June 1694, (age 18), George Heale, six years
Mathewes, Robert, 11 June 1667, (age 16), William Gordowne, eight years
Mathews, Elizabeth, 8 July 1674, (age 18), Lt. Coll. John Carter, six years
Mawberry, John, 26 January 1670, (age 15), George Wale, nine years
Mayne, Patience, 8 January 1668, (age 19), John Davenporte, five years
Maze, Farrington, 9 September 1674, (age 16), George Flower, eight years
McAndrew, Dougle, 12 May 1708, age 16, John Turbervill, eight years
McClenon, Elizabeth, 13 June 1705, age 18, William George, six years
Meginney, James, 10 June 1696, (age 10), William Garton, fourteen years
Mercer, Robert, 11 May 1663, (age 16), Henry Nichols, eight years
Merediths, William, 8 July 1674, age not judged, Capt. William Ball,
    five years
Millar, John, 14 July 1669, (age 13), John Flower, eleven years
Miller, Hugh, 9 July 1712, age 13, William Miller
Miller, John, 14 March 1661, age not judged, George Waddinge,
    eight years
Mintrom, John, 11 May 1663, (age 17), William Blayse, seven years

LANCASTER COUNTY

Molton, John, 11 March 1668, age 18, Richard Merryman, six years
Mongamery, George, 9 May 1688, (age 17), Andrew Jackson, seven years
Mons, Henry, 11 May 1663, (age 14), Robert Neasum, ten years
Moore, Edward, 9 February 1676, (age 13), Thomas Chatwyn,
    eleven years
Moore, Peter, 9 February 1676, age not judged, Thomas Marshall,
    five years
More, John, 8 December 1675, age not judged, John Davenport, five years
Morgan, Catherine, 14 June 1699, age 18, Thomas Martin, six years
Morst, William, 14 June 1699, age 17, Ralph Briggs, seven years
Motson, Hugh, 14 July 1703, age 10, James Innis, fourteen years
Mourning, Annis, 14 February 1700, age 19, Capt. William Fox
Mullone, James, 12 September 1694, (age 12), Brian Stott, twelve years
Munden, Robert, 10 June 1668, age 15, Henry Chicheley, nine years
Nash, Richard, 14 June 1699, age 12, Capt. William Lister, twelve years
Neale, Richard, 9 February 1681, (age 16), Major Robert Bristow,
    eight years
Nelson, Mary, 10 June 1696, age 13, Robert Carter, who "doth give one
    yeare of the terme of service," ten years
Norman, Katerine, 8 March 1682, (age 13), Stephen Chilton, eleven years
Nossiter, John, 12 May 1669, (age 12), Rawleigh Travers, twelve years
Noy, Francis, 14 June 1699, age 19, William Mitchell
Nuchee (?), Thomas, 13 May 1668, age 14, John Haslewood, ten years
Nugent, Johnne, 11 March 1696, (age 12), George Heale, twelve years
Obrian, Daniell, 14 September 1698, age 16, Capt. Joseph Ball, eight years
Okey, George, 23 October 1661, age not judged, John Curtys, seven years
Oliver, Richard, 8 December 1675, (age 14), William Arne, ten years
Omoney, Thurlow, 13 June 1694, (age 16), Robert Carter, eight years
Onge, Joseph, 13 May 1673, (age 10), Joseph Baley, fourteen years
Orrene, Dennys, November 1663, age not judged, Henry Chicheley
Owen, Hugh, 9 September 1696, (age 13), John Stretchley, eleven years
Parke, George, 13 January 1675, (age 15), Robert Griggs, nine years
Parker, Francis, 12 May 1674, (age 17), John Davenport, seven years
Parker, Thomas, 14 July 1703, age 12, George Chilton, twelve years
Parkeson, Peter, 13 June 1694, (age 18), Robert Carter, six years
Parr, William, 13 May 1668, age 16, John Needles, eight years
Payne, Richard, 12 July 1682, (age 15), Bryant Stott, nine years
Peirce, James, 13 July 1698, age 14, Andrew Jackson, ten years
Pell, Daniel, 8 December 1675, (age 18), William Lennel, six years

Penn, John, 12 March 1662, (age 17), Widow of Daniel Johnson, deceased,
seven years

Percivall, James, 10 June 1668, age 18, Coll. John Carter, Esqr., six years

Percivall, John, 11 September 1661, age not judged, Edward Roe,
seven years

Perrott, John, 30 November 1659, age 14, Richard Perrott, seven years

Perry, John, 9 July 1712, age 15, Francis Frizell

Pettit, Aldey, 12 March 1662, (age 16), Daniel Therryott, eight years

Phelps, James, 8 March 1671, (age 18), Thomas Haynes, six years

Phillips, Thomas, 9 April 1685, age not judged, Mrs. Martha Norris,
"hee was freely willing to serve his saide Mistris six yeres"

Phin, Maurice, 14 June 1699, age 18, John Mott, six years

Phipps, Nathaniel, 10 March 1680, (age 13), Capt. David Fox, eleven years

Phylanie, William, 14 June 1699, age 18, Thomas Martin, six years

Pignall, Thomas, 9 September 1674, (age 14), Thomas Martyn, ten years

Pill, George, 13 November 1661, age not judged, David Fox, nine years

Pinder, Elizabeth, 4 April 1667, (age 17), Davyd Miles, seven years

Piper, Nathaniel, 11 August 1697, age 14, William Bings, ten years

Piper, Richard, 12 May 1669, (age 9), Rawleigh Travers, fifteen years

Platt, Thomas, 10 June 1668, age 17, Lt. Coll. Cuthbert Potter, seven years

Poincy, John, 12 November 1662, (age 17), Thomas Young, seven years

Pope, William, 10 July 1668, age 14, Ralphe Horton, ten years

Potter, Thomas, 12 March 1662, (age 16), Children of Rawleigh Burnham,
deceased, eight years

Powell, Anthony, 12 May 1675, age 15, William Pypre, deceased,
nine years

Powell, Thomas, 9 May 1677, (age 16), William Merriman, eight years

Preston, Thomas, 18 January 1663, (age 15), Richard Heyward, nine years

Pritchett, John, 14 July 1675, (age 15), Lt. Coll. John Carter, nine years

Pronteing, Thomas, 9 December 1668, (age 19), Leonard Casett, five years

Punckford, William, 8 March 1682, (age 18), master not named, six years

Ramford, Thomas, 12 November 1690, (age 11), Capt. David Fox,
thirteen years

Ramsdelle, Ralphe, 10 June 1668, age 16, Lt. Coll. Cuthbert Potter,
eight years

Ramsey, William, 13 May 1696, (age 17), George Harward, seven years

Raner, John, 12 May 1674, (age 12), Lt. Coll. John Carter, twelve years

Rankin, William, 14 July 1703, age 13, John Brown, eleven years

LANCASTER COUNTY

Reddall, Andrew, 11 April 1688, (age 15), William Lawrence, Senr.,
nine years
Reynolds, Robert, 8 March 1671, (age 15), John Kerby, nine years
Rice, Richard, 11 May 1670, (age 13), Thomas Stott, eleven years
Richards, William, 12 May 1674, age not judged, Lt. Coll. John Carter,
five years
Richardson, Knight, 8 May 1667, (age 14), John Davenporte, ten years
Richardson, William, 11 November 1668, (age 17), Davyd Fox,
seven years
Ridley, James, 14 July 1675, (age 16), Robert Griggs, eight years
Ringe, Joseph, 13 May 1668, age 18, George Wadding, six years
Roan, Thomas, 14 June 1699, age 17, Richard Davis, seven years
Robins, William, 10 April 1689, (age 17), John Reeves, seven years
Robinson, Archibald, 13 July 1698, age 14, Andrew Jackson, ten years
Robinson, Elyas, 10 July 1667, (age 16), Robert Beverley, eight years
Rogers, Jane, 12 March 1679, (age 16), Thomas Buckley, eight years
Rogers, Noah, 11 February 1680, (age 14), Joseph Ball, ten years
Rogers, Richard, 13 March 1672, (age 16), William Ball, Senr., eight years
Rogers, Thomas, 11 January 1682, (age 16), John Berrey, eight years
Rowe, Sara, 1 May 1665, age not judged, Henry Davys, nine years "from
her arrivall" with "Capt. Pensax this present yere"
Rowles, Thomas, September 1663, (age 13), John Scarllborough,
eleven years
Rushford, Thomas, 15 February 1669, (age 14), Walter Wallys, ten years
Rust, Robert, 9 September 1674, (age 12), George Trott, twelve years
Rylee, Anthony, 14 June 1699, age 15, George Heale, nine years
Rylee, James, 8 March 1699, age 18, John More, six years
Sadleman, Anne, 9 November 1670, (age 12), Nathaniell Browne,
twelve years
Sallings, Thomas, 12 May 1674, (age 17), Lt. Coll. John Carter,
seven years
Sallisbury, Thomas, 8 March 1676, (age 14), Lt. Coll. John Carter,
ten years
Samece, John, 8 December 1675, (age 15), John Wells, nine years
Sampson, John, 12 May 1674, (age 14), Lt. Coll. John Carter, ten years
Saunders, John, 13 November 1667, (age 20), Edward Dale, four years
Scott, George, 9 March 1698, age 16, John Boatman, eight years
Scott, George, 11 May 1698, age 13, Capt. William Lister, eleven years
Scott, Thomas, 8 December 1675, (age 13), Walter Heard, eleven years

LANCASTER COUNTY

Sell, John, 13 May 1668, age 14, William Hall, ten years
Selwood, Jobe, 13 August 1690, (age 15), Gany Harris, nine years
Sergeant, James, 11 August 1697, age 15, George Heale
Serveins, John, 12 May 1674, (age 15), Robert Griggs, nine years
Shaw, Michael, 10 May 1671, (age 16), John Chynn, eight years
Sheffeild, James, 8 May 1661, age not judged, David Myles, seven years
Sherley, Richard, 10 June 1668, age 14, Coll. John Carter, Esqr., ten years
Shivington, als. Smyth, William, 10 May 1676, (age 18), Nathaniel
      Browne, six years
Silverthorne, Mary, 9 March 1687, age not judged, George Heale,
      "alleadgeing shee had Indentures for foure yeares but that shee
      had lost them," given "four dayes time to fetch Testimoney"
Silvester, John, 13 June 1711, age 13, Robert Carter, Esqr.
Simpson, Jane, 9 September 1668, (age 15), John Simpson, nine years
Simpson, John, 8 July 1674, (age 15), Richard Price, nine years
Sims, Isaac, 8 May 1667, (age 16), John Pine, eight years
Singler, Katherine, 11 August 1697, "the Court observing her to be very
      young," her master, John Heart, "would be content she should
      serve but twelve years"
Skymser, Lewys, 12 May 1674, (age 17), Lt. Coll. John Carter, seven years
Smith, Jonas, 15 February 1669, (age 13), Abraham Weekes, eleven years
Smith, Marke, 10 January 1672, (age 18), Thomas Kirton, six years
Smith, Patrick, 14 June 1699, age 16, Andrew Jackson, eight years
Smith, Robert, 11 November 1668, (age 14), Davyd Fox, ten years
Smith, Thomas, 13 May 1668, age 18, Davyd Fox, six years
Smith, William, 10 June 1668, age 16, Coll. John Carter, Esqr., eight years
Smithekell, Anne, 9 February 1676, (age 17), Thomas Banckes,
      seven years
Smyth, Hester, 9 February 1676, (age 16), Thomas Haynes, eight years
Somling, John, 12 May 1674, (age 18), Major Robert Bristow, six years
Sparrow, James, 15 February 1669, (age 16), John Boring, eight years
Spencer, Jonathan, 8 July 1674, (age 17), David Myles, seven years
Spennell, Edward, 12 January 1676, (age 14), William Laxe, ten years
Spratt, John, 8 September 1669, (age 15), Nicholas Hale, nine years
Stacey, John, 13 May 1668, age 13, William Lennell, eleven years
Stanley, Jonathan, 8 July 1668, age 15, Humphrey Jones, nine years
Stanley, Margaret, 30 November 1659, age not judged, Ever Peterson,
      "doth acknowledge she came in for nyne years"
Steptoe, Anthony, 9 March 1670, (age 17), John Coffins, seven years

Steventon, John, 12 February 1679, (age 17), Robert Griggs, seven years
Steward, Charles, 14 July 1669, (age 17), William Ball, seven years
Steward, John, 12 September 1666, (age 17), William Ball, seven years
Steward, John, 10 February 1686, (age 17), Brian Stott, seven years
Steward, Robert, 14 June 1699, age 16, John Bush, eight years
Steward, William, 9 September 1668, (age 14), Thomas Tuggle, ten years
Stoure, John, 11 May 1698, age 16, Hugh Brent, eight years
Sullivant, Denis, 11 March 1696, (age 14), Robert Carter, ten years
Swanson, John, 10 February 1675, (age 16), George Hale, eight years
Symonds, Nathaniel, 8 April 1668, age 16, Thomas Willys, eight years
Talbott, Walter, 8 July 1668, age 18, Thomas Stott, six years
Taylor, Thomas, 14 May 1662, (age 16), Mathew Kempe, Gent.,
    eight years
Taylor, Thomas, 11 January 1671, (age 17), Thomas Madestard,
    seven years
Taylor, William, 9 November 1698, age 18, William Heard, six years
Tench, Joseph, 10 September 1673, age 16, John Kirbey, eight years
Thackston, Richard, 8 January 1668, age not judged, Lt. Coll. Cuthbert
    Potter, indenture "made after his arrivall in Virginia" rejected
    by court, five years
Thomas, Job, 13 January 1664, age not judged, Giles Cale, "comeing into
    this Countrey in the Ship, Duke of Yorke," nine years "from the
    arrivall of the saide Ship"
Tobie, Peter, 14 June 1699, age 12, Thomas Danck, twelve years
Toogood, Mathew, 14 May 1662, (age 17), Nicholas Hale, seven years
Townsend, William, 11 August 1714, age 14, Capt. Richard Ball, ten years
Toy, Humphrey, 14 March 1661, age not judged, George Waddinge,
    seven years
Trap, Henery, 9 May 1688, (age 15), Andrew Jackson, nine years
Trynn (?), John, September 1663, age not judged, John Casons, "doth
    voluntarily acknowledge he hath five yeres to serve from the
    21st of April last past"
Tucker, Walter, 10 June 1668, age 16, Major Genll. Robert Smith,
    eight years
Ventrisse, Francys, male, 1 May 1665, age not judged, Ralphe Horton,
    ten years "from his arrival" with Capt. "Pensax this present yere"
Ventrisse, William, 13 November 1661, age not judged, Abraham Weekes,
    six years

LANCASTER COUNTY

Wadsworth, William, 8 July 1674, (age 17), Lt. Coll. John Carter,
    seven years
Waginer, _____ , December 1685, age not judged, Tobias Horton, "is with
    his own consent ordered to serve six yeres from his arrivall"
Waight, Richard, 13 January 1664, age 14, Henry Corbyn, Esqr.
Wakefield, William, 14 May 1662, (age 18), Rowland Mackrorey,
    six years
Waldon, Thomas, 8 May 1667, (age 12), Richard Parrett, twelve years
Wale, James, 14 June 1699, age 12, Coll. Robert Carter, twelve years
Walker, Anne, 9 February 1681, (age 18), George Haile, six years
Walton, Robert, 9 February 1681, (age 15), Major Robert Bristow,
    nine years
Warbue, Timothy, 13 June 1694, age 11, William Goodridge
Ware, John, 11 May 1670, (age 17), Thomas Powell Senr., seven years
Waters, Anthony, 11 January 1665, (age 14), Robert Woolterton, ten years
Waters, John, 14 February 1700, age 15, Thomas Martin, nine years
Wathen, Thomas, 8 November 1671, (age 16), Thomas Kirton, eight years
Watson, John, 23 October 1661, age not judged, John Curtys, seven years
Webb, John, 11 July 1673, (age 17), Rowland Lawson, seven years
Wharton, Michael, 12 May 1675, age not judged, Stephen Tomlyn,
    five years
Whiffin, John, 8 July 1674, (age 16), Lt. Coll. John Carter, eight years
Whinney, John, 13 June 1694, (age 17), Andrew Jackson,
    seven years
Whitbreade, Mary, 13 February 1678, (age 13), Thomas Barker,
    eleven years
White, Henery, 13 June 1694, (age 15), William Bings, nine years
White, John, 9 September 1674, (age 18), Thomas Parfitt, six years
White, Peter, 13 January 1664, age not judged, Coll. Robert Smyth, Esqr.,
    "is ordered to serve one yere from this day and then to bee free"
White, Thomas, 8 January 1668, (age 18), Richard Parrett, six years
Williams, Mary, 9 February 1687, (age 15), Thomas Chowning, nine years
Willis, Thomas, 14 June 1699, age 14, Coll. Robert Carter, ten years
Willmott, Bartholomew, 13 November 1667, age 19, Coll. John Carter,
    Esqr., two (sic) years
Wilson, James, 14 November 1666, (age 18), William Watson, six years
Wilson, Robert, 14 June 1699, age 13, Edwin Conway, eleven years
Winchain, Gabriel, 11 February 1680, (age 12), William Garton,
    twelve years

LANCASTER COUNTY

Wood, Benjamin, 9 April 1701, age 13, Doctor James Innis, eleven years
Wood, James, 12 February 1679, (age 11), Joseph Ball, thirteen years
Woodside, Jane, 13 March 1700, age 18, Capt. Alexander Swan, six years
Woodward, William, 12 May 1674, (age 16), John Davenport, eight years
Workren, John, 14 June 1699, age 16, Andrew Jackson, eight years
Worsdell, Richard, 11 November 1668, (age 15), Alexander Smith,
     nine years
Wright, Roger, 9 February 1676, (age 16), Thomas Martyn in Fleets Bay,
     eight years
Wynnett, William, 12 March 1662, (age 15), Daniel Therryott, nine years
Younge, John, 14 September 1670, (age 15), Thomas Hayward, nine years
Younge, William, 15 February 1669, (age 12), William Clapham,
     twelve years
_____ , Richard, an Irish youth, 9 May 1660, age not judged, Gray
     Skipwith, ordered "to serve him till the first of January next"
_____ , _____ , male, 12 September 1660, Grey Skipwith, seven years

LANCASTER COUNTY

Gentleman Justices	Servants
Appleton, John	
Ball, Joseph, Capt., Lieut. Coll.	Andrews, Rogers, Wood
Ball, Richard, Capt.	Townsend
Ball, William, Junr., Capt.	Baley, Cannady, Cox, Deakins, Dixon, Garland, Henderson, Hind, Hinds, Kelley, Merediths, Obrian
Ball, William, Senr., Coll.	Burling, Harman, Hull, Rogers, Steward, Steward
Beckingham, Robert	Bent, Gutridge
Brent, Hugh	Makins, Martyn, Stoure
Carter, John, Lt. Coll., Esqr.	Balding, Bayley, Brookes, Bryant, Callicott, Carter, Clarke, Clerke, Cooper, Cooper, Davis, Davys, Feilder, Fenney, Ferridral, Finney, Flint, Forrest, Frampton, Griffin, Hart, Hill, Johnson, Kent, Manday, Mathews, Percivall, Pritchett, Raner, Richards, Sallings, Sallisbury, Sampson, Sherley, Skymser, Smith, Wadsworth, Whiffin, Willmott
Carter, Robert, Colo., Esqr.	Cambell, Clark, Clark, Clephue, Daylie, Delanie, Delany, Hareat, Jones, Mackell, Nelson, Omoney, Parkeson, Silvester, Sullivant, Wale, Willis
Carter, Thomas, Capt.	
Chichester, Richard, Esqr.	
Conway, Edwin	Wilson

LANCASTER COUNTY

Gentleman Justices	Servants
Corbyn, Henry	Clarke, Claybourne, Henderson, Loe, Waight
Curtys, John	Okey, Watson
Dale, Edward, Major	Saunders
Fleet, Henry, Lt. Coll.	
Fox, David, Capt.	Bird, Brand, Butcher, Fry, Fuller, Jynn, Lynsey, Phipps, Pill, Ramford, Richardson, Smith, Smith
Fox, William, Capt.	Mourning
Griggs, Michael	
Griggs, Robert	Bonn, Carr, Carter, Cory, Farrington, Grimes, Guy, Haslewood, Higgison, Hubbard, Parke, Ridley, Serveins, Steventon
Harrison, Daniel	Harwood, Howell, Lambert
Haynes, Thomas	Carraden, Phelps, Smyth
Heale, George, Capt.	Bohonham, Carrill, Dunne, Gornock, Grace, Hambleton, Jones, Mackmullin, Mate, Nugent, Rylee, Sergeant
Jones, Humphrey	Stanley
Keeble, George	
Kempe, Edmond	
Kempe, Mathew	Martyn, Taylor

LANCASTER COUNTY

Gentleman Justices	Servants
Lawson, Rowland	Burrell, Chaundler, Child, Edwards, Webb
Lee, Thomas	
Leech, William	Forrest, Lucey
Lister, William, Capt., Major	Agnes, Agnes, Calwell, Jones, Lawson, Lee, Nash, Scott
Madestard, Thomas	Ellys, Taylor
Marsh, George	Dorrell
Marshall, Thomas	Goble, Moore
Martin, Thomas	Howell, Morgan, Phylanie, Waters
Myles, David	Ackton, Bridgeman, Crale, Gibbs, Pinder, Sheffeild, Spencer
Nusum, Richard, Capt.	
Perrott / Parrett, Richard *	Eldridge, Gladding, Jackson, Jackson, Perrott, Walden, White
Pinckard, John, Capt.	Head
Pinckard, Thomas, Capt.	
Potter, Cuthbert, Capt., Lt. Coll.	Browne, Martyn, Platt, Ramsdelle, Thackston
Powell, Thomas	Ware
Stott, Bryan	Birchit, Canes, Hodgkin, Mullone, Payne, Steward
Swan, Alexander, Capt. ** ***	Anderson, Woodside

172

LANCASTER COUNTY

Gentleman Justices	Servants
Sydnor, Fortunatus	Hall, Johnson
Taylor, Richard, Capt.	
Travers, Rawleigh *** ****	Caprell, Carter, Cox, Harvey, Nossiter, Piper
Turberville, John ****	Bell, McAndrew
Wale, George	Bennett, Mawberry
Weekes, Abraham	Smith, Ventrisse
Willis, Richard, Capt.	
Wormeley, Christopher, Capt.	Ensden

*   see Middlesex County
**   see Old Rappahannock County
*** see Richmond County
**** see Northumberland County

LANCASTER COUNTY				LANCASTER COUNTY			
Year	White	Negro	Indian	Year	White	Negro	Indian
1659	3	0	0	1689	4	0	0
1660	5	0	0	1690	2	1	0
1661	16	0	0	1691	1	0	0
1662	22	0	0	1692	3	0	0
1663	17	0	0	1693	0	1	0
1664	13	0	0	1694	16	1	0
1665	12	0	0	1695	0	0	0
1666	2	0	0	1696	16	0	0
1667	21	0	0	1697	10	0	0
1668	52	0	0	1698	17	0	0
1669	24	0	0	1699	40	0	0
1670	19	0	0	1700	7	0	0
1671	11	0	0	1701	6	2	0
1672	8	0	0	1702	0	2	0
1673	4	0	0	1703	5	2	0
1674	33	0	0	1704	0	3	2
1675	26	0	0	1705	3	4	2
1676	14	0	0	1706	0	1	2
1677	8	0	0	1707	0	6	0
1678	11	0	0	1708	4	0	0
1679	9	0	0	1709	0	0	0
1680	8	0	0	1710	0	1	0
1681	9	0	0	1711	2	2	1
1682	6	0	0	1712	3	0	0
1683	2	0	0	1713	0	0	0
1684	0	0	0	1714	4	0	0
1685	8	0	0	1715	0	2	0
1686	10	0	0	Total	528	29	7
1687	6	0	0	Note: None in 1657 or 1658			

Adamson, Thomas, 2 May 1688, age 17, Capt. William Ball
Aland, Samuell, 7 April 1686, age 15, Richard Bray
Alger, Thomas, 7 April 1686, age 18, William Colston
Barrow, Andrew, 3 February 1686, age 14, Thomas Watkins
Batts, Edward, 3 March 1686, age 13, John Overton
Baxter, James, 4 March 1685, age 17, George Tomlin
Bonniball, John, 23 March 1688, age 13, Paul Woodbridge
Brookes, Katherine, 3 July 1689, age 13, Henry Lucas
Chiffers, Thomas, 4 February 1685, age 17, James Bowler
Coulter, William, 2 April 1685, age not judged, Robert Baylis
Cox, Richard, 1 April 1685, age 14, Thomas Crow, "the said Cox declared
    himself to be fourteen years old the Tenth day of January last"
Cruff, John, 4 June 1690, age 16, Edward Thomas
Dickison, John, 3 March 1686, age 14, William Fitz Herbert
Duxbury, Henry, 7 April 1686, age 11 "and halfe," Robert Marshall
Edney, Saul, 7 July 1686, age 14, Christopher Blackburne
Ellison, Ellinder, 2 March 1687, age 17, Anthony Carneby
Enscoe, Edward, 5 March 1683, age 12, Richard Bray
Evans, John, 19 May 1686, age 14, William Payne
Fann, John, 3 March 1686, age 12, Henry Williams
Fiske, Thomas, 6 June 1688, age 13, Richard Bush
Fleeknick, Richard, 3 July 1689, age 15, David Sterne
Flowers, Isack, 4 February 1685, "that the age of him might not be
    adjudged," "did promise to serve his Master," William Benbridge,
    "seven years from the 18th day of December 1684"
Forbush, John, 5 March 1685, age 17, Mrs. Alice Goldman,
    "alleadging that he had Indenture for a Time certaine but has
    left them in Dublin"
Golder, Richard, 4 March 1685, age 15, William Clapham
Graham, George, 3 February 1692, age 15, Capt. Isaac Webbe
Griffin, John, 3 March 1686, age 17, Henry Wilson
Grilles, Margaret, 6 May 1685, age 14, Doctor Roger Waters, deceased,
    by Thomas Glascock, Executor
Harris, Nathaniel, 21 December 1685, age 12, John Ingoe
Hewet, Thomas, 5 March 1683, age 15, Jeffrey Lumbers
Hinton, Richard, 4 April 1688, age 14, Henry Pickett
House, John, 7 April 1686, age 12, Ebenezar Stanfield
Jaggers, William, 2 March 1687, age 13, Isaac Webbe
Jenkins, Elizabeth, 19 May 1686, age 14, Robert Brooke

OLD RAPPAHANNOCK COUNTY

Johnson, Thomas, 5 November 1690, age 14 "and a halfe," James Trapley
Jones, George, 3 March 1686, age 17, John Glascock
Kelley, John, 3 February 1692, age 12, John Goss
Loune, James, 3 March 1692, age 16, Arthur Spicer
Mack Dannell, Thomas, 3 March 1692, age 13, Capt. Arthur Spicer
Mahenney, William, 4 March 1685, age 16, Mathew Kelly
Minheire, John, 2 March 1687, age 11, Grigory Glascock
Morton, Christopher, 7 May 1684, age 16, Robert Tomlin, Senr.
Nicholson, John, 21 December 1685, age 19, Mottrum Wright
Norcutt, William, 1 October 1686, age 16 "and half," Alexander Newman
Norman, Jane, 7 May 1684, age 12, Henry Lucas
Norton, Susanna, 1 April 1685, age not judged, Thomas Watkins, who
        purchased her from Abraham Bradley of Gloucester County,
        her "time being fully expired"
Old, John, 6 February 1683, age 13, Edward Chilton
Onion, Joseph, 1 July 1691, age 11, Max. Robinson
Osburne, Henry, 4 March 1685, age 15, Ralph Nell
Parker, John, 3 February 1692, age 11, Anthony Smith
Perry, Aron, 3 February 1686, age 10, John Webster
Potts, Thomas, 4 March 1685, age 13, Thomas New
Pratman, Richard, 19 May 1686, age 18, Rebeccah Bowen
Reeves, John, 3 July 1689, age 17, Hugh French
Slaughter, Robert, 7 April 1686, age 15, Bernard Gaines
Spencer, Elinor, 2 July 1690, age 18, John Ockley
Stephens, Elizabeth, 7 April 1686, age 16, John Catlett
Street, Margaret, 4 May 1687, age not judged, John Fennell, to serve
        until age 16, "by and with her own consent"
Tayler, Robert, 3 July 1689, age 15, Arthur Spicer
Towell, Thomas, 3 July 1689, age 17 "and halfe," Arthur Spicer
Twigg, Easter, female, 4 April 1685, age 10, John Taverner
Ware, Christopher, 19 May 1686, age 13, James Trent
Whithead, Mary, 21 December 1685, age 17, Mottrum Wright
Williams, Margaret, 7 March 1688, age 17, Mottrum Wright
Woodman, George, 4 November 1685, age 15, James Scott
Woodman, John, 4 November 1685, age 14, Francis Sterne

OLD RAPPAHANNOCK COUNTY

Gentleman Justices	Servants
Awbrey, Henry	
Barber, William, Capt.	see Richmond County
Blomfield, Samuell, Capt.	
Doniphan, Alexander	see Richmond County
Edmondson, Thomas	see Essex County
Fantleroy, William	see Richmond County
Griffin, Leroy, Coll.	
Harison, James	see Richmond County
Harwar, Thomas	
Loyd, William, Lieut. Coll.	
Moseley, William, Capt.	see Essex County
Peachey, Samuell, Capt.	see Richmond County
Robinson, Max.	Onion
Slaughter, William	
Smith, Henry, Major	
Stone, John, Coll.	see Richmond County
Swan, Alexander, Capt. *	see Richmond County
Taliaferro, Francis	see Essex County
Tayler, George, Capt.	see Richmond County
Tayloe, William	see Richmond County
Travers, Samuell	
Underwood, William	see Richmond County
Williamson, Henry	see Essex County

*   see Lancaster County

OLD RAPPAHANNOCK COUNTY				OLD RAPPAHANNOCK COUNTY			
Year	White	Negro	Indian	Year	White	Negro	Indian
1683	3	0	0	1688	5	0	0
1684	2	0	0	1689	5	2	0
1685	18	8	0	1690	3	0	0
1686	19	3	0	1691	1	3	0
1687	4	5	0	1692	5	0	0
				Total	65	21	0

RICHMOND COUNTY

Allen, Richard, 6 March 1700, age 16, Peter Darby
Atwell, Robert, 3 April 1700, age 12, Hugh French
Baker, Richard, 5 July 1699, age 12, Daniel Swillivant
Barrett, Francis, 2 July 1707, age 13, Capt. George Heale
Blackurne, John, 7 June 1699, age 13, C(?)prian Prowe
Bourne, William, 1 March 1699, age 17, George Tomlin
Bowler, James, 8 June 1699, age 18 "and a half," Mrs. Margrett Cammock
Bradner, Thomas, 3 June 1713, age 15, Henry Street
Brenhan, Charon, male, 7 June 1699, age 12, George Davenport
Breyhan, Henry, 1 June 1709, age 11, Webley Pavey
Brine, Mary, 7 October 1694, age 13, Alexander Newman
Brisby, William, 2 July 1712, age 10, William Goodrich
Brooks, Joseph, 1 June 1709, age 12, William Morgan
Brown, James, 7 June 1699, age 13, James Tarpley
Bryan, Peter, 1 March 1699, age 9, David Gwin
Burk, James, 1 March 1699, age 18, George Glascock
Carrell, Daniell, 5 May 1708, age 17, John Faver
Carroll, Anthony, 7 June 1699, age 13, William Doleman
Carry, Cornelias, 1 March 1699, age 17, William Barber
Carter, Mary, 6 March 1700, age 14, James Scott
Carty, Owen, 7 June 1693, age 18, John Burkett
Caveniow, Daniel, 7 June 1699, age 11, Edgcomb Suggitt
Cavins, James, 1 February 1699, age 14, Doctor Robert Clerk
Clayton, Thomas, 7 June 1699, age 14, William Simms
Conokey, Dennis, 1 February 1699, age 14, George Payne
Cunningham, William, 3 April 1700, age 15, William Strothers, Junr.
Devall, Jacob, 2 November 1698, age 14, William Brokenbrough
Donahaw, Edward, 7 June 1699, age 15, Edward Tayler
Donohow, Edmond, 6 March 1700, age 13, John Ford
Dowley, William, 6 March 1700, age 14, John Spiller
Doyley, John, 7 June 1699, age 18, Mrs. Elizabeth Newman
Doyley, Patrick, 8 June 1699, age 13, Mrs. Margrett Cammock
Durmick, John, 7 May 1701, age 15, William Colston
Earby, James, 7 October 1694, age 14, Alexander Newman
Eustice, Christopher, 1 March 1699, age 16, Henry Williams
Evans, Peter, 7 May 1701, age 12, Manus Maclathlin
Fegett, Peirce, 7 June 1699, age 17, William Smoot, Senr.
Fennell, John, 7 June 1699, age 13, William Doleman
Fitzgerald, Walter, 1 March 1699, age 17, George Glascock

RICHMOND COUNTY

Foster, William, 2 June 1697, age 15, Alexander Newman
Gamell, Thomas, 2 July 1712, age 10 "last January," John Coombs
Gibson, Robert, 7 June 1699, age 15, Rebecca Thomas
Gibson, Thomas, 2 June 1697, age 14, Capt. Alexander Newman
Gillmore, Hugh, 5 October 1715, age 18, Peter Kippax
Gourley, James, 5 July 1699, age 13, Phillip Hunnings
Graftee, Robert, 6 July 1720, age 13, Rebecca Atherton
Graves, Jane, 7 June 1699, age 12, Manus Macklathlin
Gredey, John, 7 June 1699, age 8, Thomas Glascock
Griffin, Mary, 3 April 1700, age 16, William Smoot
Griffith, Thomas, 7 June 1699, age 18, Luke Thornton
Hardy, John, 3 June 1719, age 10, Edward Jones
Hasell, John, 1 July 1702, age 17, James Cullins
Hawks, Robert, 2 July 1707, age 14, Job Hamon
Hay, John, 7 October 1694, age 16, William Sloughter
Herron, George, 1 March 1699, age 18, John Baker
Hinds, John, 2 June 1697, age 13, Thomas Wilson
Hogan, Morgan, 7 May 1701, age 13, William Underwood
Holmes, Robert, 7 June 1699, age 17, George Glascock
Horsbell, John, 7 May 1701, age 14, Capt. John Tarpley
Hughes, Arthur, 6 March 1700, age 13, Capt. Alvin Mountjoy
Jack, Timothy, 7 May 1701, age 16, James Scott
Jones, Mary, 7 June 1699, age 18, Nicholas Morrow
Kelley, Arthur, 7 October 1694, age 13, David Gwin
Kelley, Henry, 1 March 1699, age 17, James Foushee
Kelly, Ann, 7 June 1699, age 14, Thomas Durham
Kenner, John, 3 June 1696, age 16, "by his own confession,"
    Richard White
Keph, Phillip, 7 June 1699, age 12, Abraham Goard
Killahon, Lawrance, 2 March 1698, age 14, John Ingo
Laughie, Thomas, 7 June 1699, age 10, Thomas White
Laverey, Mary, 7 June 1699, age 17, Dennis Comeron
Lily, William, 6 June 1694, age 15, John Burkett
Lollard, Daniel, 1 March 1699, age 15, Henry Seager
Love, James, 5 October 1715, age 19, Peter Kippax
Macduggall, Hugh, 2 August 1699, age 14, Richard Jesper
MacGregory, Robert, 5 July 1699, age 14, Rawleigh Travers
Macmeare, Robert, 8 June 1699, age 12, Giles Mathews
Maconer, Michael, 1 March 1699, age 15, James Tarpley

Marr, Ann, 1 July 1719, age 16, John Tarpley, Junr.
Meregan, John, 7 June 1699, age 10, Henry Williams
Miller, David, 6 May 1719, age 16, James Grant
Miller, John, 5 June 1706, age 13, John Pealton
Minton, Henry, 6 December 1693, age 14, Maximilian Robinson
Minton, Joseph, 6 December 1693, age 11, Maximilian Robinson
Montgomery, Robert, 1 July 1719, age 11, John Tarpley, Junr.
Morfoyk, John, 7 June 1699, age 10, Thomas Loyd
Morgan, John, 7 May 1701, age 10, Hugh French
Morsey, Morgan, 7 June 1699, age 17, Rowland Lawson
Moyniow, Hugh, 7 June 1699, age 13, William Strother, Senr.
Murfey, James, 6 March 1700, age 13, Patience Ford
Murrey, Richard, 1 March 1699, age 11, Henry Seager
Murrey, William, 6 March 1700, age 14, Rebecca Houseman
Nankey, James, 1 February 1699, age 13, Alexander Spence
Perrin, William, 1 March 1699, age 12, Joshua Davis
Powell, Charles, 1 June 1709, age 13, Margarett Cammock
Proctor, Abraham, 7 May 1701, age 11, Capt. John Tarpley
Pustey, Richard, 6 October 1697, age 15, William Hanks
Read, James, 7 June 1699, age 17, Thomas Newton
Reyan, Peirce, 2 March 1699, age 10, Capt. George Tayler
Reyley, William, 6 October 1697, age 16, Thomas Glascock
Rimmer, Thomas, 5 June 1706, age 11, Jefferey Reynolds
Roberts, John, 7 May 1701, age 13, Andrew Dew
Rogers, James, 3 June 1696, age 14, John Ockley, Junr.
Roy, James, 7 June 1699, age 13, Sem Cox
Saviour, Richard, 7 June 1699, age 14, John Rankin
Seegar, Michael, 7 October 1694, age 14 "and half," Thomas Durham
Sheppard, John, 5 May 1708, age 14, Henry Street
Sherden, John, 7 June 1693, age 13, John Baylis
Simpkin, John, 7 June 1699, age 13, William Strother, Senr.
Sithbottom, William, 1 June 1709, age 10, Thomas Smith
Smith, Alexander, 1 March 1699, age 16, Mrs. Ann Metcalf
Smyth, Thomas, 3 January 1700, age 14, Francis Jam(e)s
Steward, Gawin, 5 July 1699, age not judged, Rawleigh Travers
Steward, James, 2 August 1699, age 15, Evan Thomas
Straughan, Thomas, 7 October 1694, age 16, Manns Macklathlin
Sullivant, John, 6 June 1711, age 12, Robert Tomlin
Swillivan, Cornelius, 7 June 1693, age 14, John Ingo

RICHMOND COUNTY

Swillivant, Dennis, 1 March 1699, age 17, William Harwood
Swillivant, Timothy, 7 June 1693, age 17, Francis Stone
Swinton, Daniell, 2 June 1714, age 13, William Henley
Taylor, Jarvis, 2 August 1693, age 11, Joshua Davis
Tucker, Joseph, 1 March 1699, age 11, John Willis, Senr.
Turner, Joseph, 3 June 1696, age 17, William Smyth
Upton, Thomas, 7 June 1699, age 11, Francis Thornton
Wallis, John, 7 June 1699, age 12, Abraham Goard
Welsh, Edward, 7 June 1699, age 11, William Doleman
Wethers, William, 3 September 1707, age 13, Hugh Harris
Wilkinson, Thomas, 2 July 1701, age 12, Rawleigh Travers
Williams, John, 1 February 1699, age 15, Francis Williams
Williams, Robert, 7 June 1699, age 13, John _____
Wilson, Charles, 7 August 1695, age 10, Alexander Newman
Wilson, William, 7 June 1699, age 12, Edmond Northen
Withers, Samuell, 2 July 1707, age 14, Job Hamon, Junr.
Wollahan, Thomas, 6 March 1700, age 15, Joseph Amon
Woolee, Samuel, 1 June 1709, age 12, John Pound
Wregan, John, 3 January 1700, age 15, Rowland Thornton
Young, Alexander, 1 March 1699, age 11, Thomas Dickinson
_____ , _____ , 3 April 1700, age 11, _____

RICHMOND COUNTY

Gentleman Justices	Servants
Baker, John	Herron
Barber, Charles, Capt.	
Barber, William, Capt. *	Carry
Barrow, Edward, Capt.	
Belfield, Joseph	
Brockenbrough, Austin	
Davis, Joshua	Perrin, Taylor
Doleman, William	Carroll, Fennell, Welsh
Doniphan, Alexander, Capt. *	
Deane, John, Capt.	
Deeke, Joseph	
Downman, William	
Fantleroy, William *	
Gibson, Jonathan	
Glascock, Thomas	Gredey, Reyley
Griffin, Thomas	
Grymes, Charles	
Gwyn, David, Major	Bryan, Kelley
Harrison, James *	
Heale, George, Capt.	Barrett
Ingo, James	
Metcalfe, John	
Peachey, Samuell, Lt. Coll. *	
Robinson, William, Capt., Major	

RICHMOND COUNTY

Gentleman Justices	Servants
Scott, James	Carter, Jack
Slaughter, Francis	
Smith, Nicholas, Capt.	
Stone, John, Coll. *	
Strother, Joseph	
Swan, Alexander, Capt. * **	
Taliaferro, Richard	
Tarpley, John, Capt.	Horsbell, Proctor
Tayler, George, Capt., Coll. *	Reyan
Tayloe, John	
Tayloe, William, Capt., Coll. *	
Thornton, Francis	Upton
Thornton, William	
Tomlin, Robert	Sullivant
Travers, Rawleigh ** ***	MacGregory, Steward, Wilkinson
Travers, Samuel, Capt.	
Underwood, William, Capt. *	Hogan
Woodbridge, William, Capt.	

*   see Old Rappahannock County
** see Lancaster County
*** see Northumberland County

RICHMOND COUNTY

Year	White	Negro	Indian
1693	7	0	0
1694	7	0 *	0
1695	1	0	0
1696	3	0	0
1697	5	0	0
1698	2	0	0
1699	63	0	1
1700	14	0	0
1701	9	0	0
1702	1	10	0
1703	0	1	0
1704	0	4	0
1705	0	0	0
1706	2	5	0
1707	4	7	0

RICHMOND COUNTY

Year	White	Negro	Indian
1708	2	0	0
1709	5	1	0
1710	0	1	0
1711	1	2	0
1712	2	0	0
1713	1	4	0
1714	1	0	0
1715	2	0	0
1716	0	0	1
1717	0	9	0
1718	0	7	0
1719	4	19	0
1720	1	11	0
1721	0	24	0
Total	137	105	2

* plus one Mulatto

ESSEX COUNTY

Allen, William, 10 June 1699, age 12, John Channell

Anderson, John, 10 May 1693, age 16, William Bendery, "who came into this Country in ye Ship, Resolucon, Richard Kelsick, Commander"

Apperton, Ann, 19 June 1699, age 14, Jere. Lewis

Atkins, John, 10 June 1699, age 12, Thomas Covington

Barram, John, 10 April 1701, age 13, Thomas Thorpe, "who came into this Country in ye Shipp, John Baptis, John Goar, Commander"

Brayley, Samuel, 10 April 1701, age 14, Ralph Rowzee, "who came into this Country in ye Shipp, John Baptis, John Goar, Commander"

Brimmingham, Edward, 10 June 1699, age not judged, Mary St. John, "he had served four years according to his Indenture and produced it, but ye Court adjudging ye Indenture insufficient"

Brisket, James, 10 June 1699, age 14, Richard Cooper

Brooks, Joseph, 10 March 1699, age 7, William Tomlin

Bryan, John, 10 February 1694, age 12, Mrs. Mary Dike

Burden, Thomas, 10 April 1700, age 8, Thomas Munday

Burk, Richard, 10 March 1699, age 11, Humphrey Booth

Butler, James, 10 March 1699, age 10, Francis Meriwether

Buttler, James, 11 June 1695, age 17, Daniel Diskin, "who came into this Country in ye Ship, Vine, William Fletcher, Commander, and produced an Indenture wherein (he) was bound to serve six years, which is adjudged insufficient"

Carnon, Patrick, 10 July 1695, age not judged, Thomas Davis, "who came into this Country in the Ship, Vine, Wm. Fletcher, Commander, and produced Indenture dated Janry. 1694 whereon (he) was bound to serve four years, which is adjudged insufficient"

Carroway, William, 10 April 1700, age 9, James Fullerton

Cary, John, 10 March 1699, age 11, Edward Gouldman

Certint, Samuel, 15 March 1715, age 15, John Nagy

Cleaton, Sarah, 10 June 1699, age 11, Job Virgitt

Connier, Dennis, 10 March 1699, age 15, Edmond Connelly

Corkin, Patrick, 10 March 1699, age 13, Thomas Burns, Senr.

Cranny, Laurence, 10 March 1699, age 9, Francis Meriwether

Cumberford, Michael, 10 June 1699, age 15, John Haile

Dickson, Michael, 10 March 1693, age 16, Henry Awbrey, "who came into this Country in ye Ship, Resolucon, Richard Kelsick, Commander"

Dunbarr, John, 19 June 1699, age 12, John Cook

Dunn, _____ , 11 March 1699, age 16, Henry Perkins

English, John, 10 May 1701, age 10, John Picket

Evans, Edward, 10 April 1701, age 12, John Smith, Senr., "who came into this Country in ye Shipp, John Baptis, John Goar, Commander"

Fagon, Edmond, 10 June 1695, age 11, John Williams, "who came into this Country in ye Ship, Vine, William Fletcher, Commander"

Farrell, James, 10 March 1699, age 11, Bernard Gaines

Fitzgerald, Edmond, 10 March 1699, age 15, Henry Newton

Fitz Sims, Garratt, 10 July 1697, age ___ , Capt. John Thomas

Forbes, Margaret, 11 March 1695, age 16, Richard Awbrey

George, John, 11 July 1698, age 13, Thomas Griffing

Goucher, Benjamin, 13 November 1706, age 9, Francis Meriwether

Hambleton, Gawen, 10 June 1699, age 12, Samuel Coates

Hambleton, John, 10 August 1699, age 14, Robert Coleman

Harrow, Hugh, 10 June 1695, age 8, Robert Pley, "who came into this Country in ye Ship, Vine, William Fletcher, Commander"

Hatton, Richard, 10 April 1700, age 14, Richard Covington

Hegue, Bryant, 10 June 1699, age 14, Robert Coleman

Henderson, John, 10 June 1699, age 13, Francis Meriwether

Holmes, John, 10 June 1699, age 9, Thomas Short

Hoult, John, 10 June 1699, age 10, John Dunkin

Howard, John, 10 April 1702, age 13, James Shippy

Hutchinson, Laughlin, 10 March 1699, age 13, Abraham Stepp

Kelly, Darrnell, 10 April 1701, age 11, Mrs. Rebecca Tomlin

Kelly, Edmond, 10 March 1699, age 11, Francis Gouldman

Kelly, Robert, 10 March 1699, age 11, Bernard Gaines

King, Thomas, 10 May 1694, age 13, William Bender

Langinton, William, 10 April 1700, age 9, Thomas Green

Lawles, Michael, 11 June 1695, age 14, Capt. John Battaile, "who came into this Country in the ship, Vine, William Fletcher, Commander, and produced an Indenture wherein the said Boy was bound to serve six years which is adjudged insufficient"

Lodge, Joseph, 10 March 1699, age 9, Francis Meriwether

Loyd, John, 11 January 1699, age 14, Humphrey Booth, "but ordered that he serve no longer than seven years"

Lynn, George, 10 June 1699, age 9, John Strong

MacDaniell, Arthur, 11 March 1695, age 11, Rebecca Tomlin

MacGlamy, Patrick, 10 March 1699, age 18, Richard Gregory

Magrough, Thomas, 10 June 1699, age 10, Henry Reeves

March, Alexander, 10 June 1699, age 10, John Mills
McDermot, Francis, 10 March 1699, age 12, Phillip Parr
Mills, John, 10 April 1701, age 12, John Hawkins, "who came into this
    Country in ye Shipp, John Baptis, John Goar, Commander"
Mitchell, Thomas, 10 June 1699, age 10, Richard Mathews
Molear, William, 11 July 1698, age 11, Thomas Griffing
Molony, Edmond, 10 March 1699, age 18, Richard Covington
Moore, John, 10 June 1699, age 12, Thomas Gregson
Moore, Richard, 11 December 1705, age 16, Thomas Harway
Moran, William, 10 March 1699, age 11, Bernard Gaines
Mupty, Patrick, 10 June 1699, age 11, John Price
Neale, John, 10 March 1699, age 15, William Cooper
Noble, Robert, 10 June 1699, age 12, John Crow
Owen, Stafford, 10 April 1700, age 12, Thomas Thorpe
Parr, Alexander, 10 June 1699, age 11, Thomas Gregson
Pattison, Daniel, 10 June 1699, age 12, Thomas Franck
Pattison, John, 10 June 1699, age 12, William Williams
Pell, Christopher, 10 March 1693, age 13, John Dangerfield, "who came
    into this Country in ye Shipp, Resolution, Mr. Richard Kelsick,
    Commander"
Prescott, Alice, 10 June 1699, age 11, Susanna Davis
Price, John, 10 August 1702, age 9, John Burnet
Read, Dunkin, 10 June 1704, age 12, Ralph Rowzee
Reed, Thomas, 10 June 1699, age 12, John Burnett
Reyley, Edmond, 10 July 1695, age not judged, Thomas Thrashly, "who
    came into this Country in the Ship, Vine, William Fletcher,
    Commander, and presented an Indenture dated Febr. 2d 1694,
    for seven years which is adjudged insufficient"
Reyley, Margaret, 10 September 1695, age not judged, Phillip Parr,
    "by assigne to him by William Fletcher, Master of ye Ship, Vine,
    and produced an Indenture dated January 9th 1694 wherein she
    was bound for seven years, which is adjudged insufficient"
Roberts, John, 10 April 1700, age 11, John Solomon
Robinson, Dunkin, 10 June 1699, age 11, William D _____
Robinson, William, 10 February 1694, age 11, Robert Pley
Rowland, Martin, 10 March 1699, age 18, James Fullerton
Ruork, Timothy, 10 May 1708, age (torn), John Morris
Stead, Thomas, 10 May 1708, age 11, Richard Hutchings
Stevens, John, 10 March 1699, age 18, James Jackson

Steward, Peter, 10 June 1699, age 11, John Gaines
Swillivant, John, 10 May 1693, age 17, Mrs. Mary Wells, "who came into this Country in ye Ship, Sarah & Susan, John Chapman, Commander"
Tark, James, 12 December 1699, age 17, Robert Thomas
Taylor, William, 10 March 1699, age 12, Robert Brooke
Tinam, Derby, 10 March 1699, age 15, Francis Gouldman
Trolony, John, 10 April 1700, age 8, Samuel Thacker
Waters, Edward, 15 March 1715, age 13, John Nagy
Weekley, George, 10 February 1694, age 10, Daniell Diskin
Williams, Robert, 10 March 1699, age 15, Francis Gouldman
Williams, Samuel, 10 June 1699, age 8, William Price
Wilson, Robert, 10 July 1697, age 9, George Ward, "who came into this Country in the Ship, Lamb, John Thomas, Commander"
Yorun, John, 10 June 1699, age 9, William Younge
Younge, Alexander, 10 June 1699, 18, Edward Rowzee

ESSEX COUNTY

Gentleman Justices	Servants
Battaile, John, Capt.	Lawles
Boughan, James	
Brooke, Robert	Taylor
Brooke, Robert, Junr.	
Catlett, John, Capt.	
Coleman, Robert	Hambleton, Hegue
Covington, Richard	Hatton, Molony
Daingerfield, William	
Dobyns, Daniel	
Edmondson, Thomas *	
Gaines, Bernard	Farrell, Kelly, Moran
Gouldman, Francis	Kelly, Tinam, Williams
Lomax, John	
Meriwether, Thomas	
Moseley, Benjamin	
Moseley, William, Capt. *	
Muscoe, Salvator	
Smith, Anthony, Capt.	
Smith, Augustin	
Smith, Joseph	
Taliaferro, Francis *	
Taliaferro, John	
Tarent, Leonard	
Thacker, Samuel	Trolony
Thomas, Edward, Capt.	
Tomlin, William	Brooks
Welch, Reuben	
Williamson, Henry *	
Woodford, William	

* see Old Rappahannock County

ESSEX COUNTY

Year	White	Negro	Indian
1693	4	0	0
1694	4	2	0
1695	9	1	0
1696	0	1	0
1697	2	5	0
1698	2	1	0
1699	57	0	0
1700	7	0	0
1701	6	0	0
1702	2	0	0
1703	0	0	0
1704	1	4	0
1705	1	0	0
1706	1	7	0
1707	0	5	0
1708	2	12	0
1709	0	0	0
1710	0	8	0
1711	0	1	0
1712	0	0	1
1713	0	0	1
1714	0	0	0
1715	2	0	0
1716	0	0	0
1717	0	1	0
1718	0	26	0
Total	100	74	2

MIDDLESEX COUNTY

Addis, Robert, 6 January 1679, age 15, Thomas Lee, "comeing into this
    Country in ye Shipp, Henry & Ann"
Adkitt, Thomas, 5 June 1699, age 13, Paul Thilman
Ann, Edward, 2 March 1685, age not judged, Capt. Walter Whitaker, "is
    willing to serve seaven yeares from his arrivall in this Country,
    provided he be not putte to worke in ye ground"
Antrobud, John, 6 July 1674, age 13, Lt. Coll. Christopher Wormeley
Ashley, William, 5 July 1675, age 12, Richard Robinson
Ashorn, Thomas, 4 February 1678, age 8, Mrs. Alice Creeke
Backett, Thomas, 4 February 1679, age 16, Major Genll. Robert Smith,
    "comeing into this Country in ye Shipp, Baltemore"
Baineman, Sarah, 6 January 1679, age 17, Major Genll. Robert Smith,
    "comeing into this Country on the Shipp, Duke of Yorke"
Baker, Richard, 4 February 1678, age 17, John Vaus, "comeing into this
    Countrey in ye Ship, Duke of Yorke"
Baldwin, Richard, 5 January 1680, age 11, Coll. Cuthbert Potter, "comeing
    into this Country in ye Shipp, Duke of Yorke"
Ballard, Henry, 6 July 1674, age 14, Alexander Smith
Barlow, Henry, 6 March 1676, age 11, Mrs. Allice Corbin, "comeing into
    this Country in ye Shipp, Lady Frances"
Baskeville, John, 6 January 1679, age 17, Thomas Thompson, "comeing
    into this Country in ye Shipp, Henry & Ann"
Batcheller, Thomas, 13 January 1679, age 12, John Sheppard, "comeing
    into this Country in ye Shipp, Zebulon"
Baxter, Richard, 6 May 1678, age 12, Robert Price, "comeing into this
    Country in ye Shipp, Duke of Yorke"
Beaumont, Judith, 5 February 1683, age 14, William Churchhill, "comeing
    into this Country in the Shipp, Zebulon"
Beaverstone, William, 3 May 1675, age 12, Henry Corbyn, Esqr.
Bennet, Richard, 4 March 1678, age 15, John Needles, "comeing into this
    Country in ye Shipp, Henry & Ann"
Black, James, 2 February 1685, age 17, Randolph Seagar
Blose, Ann, 4 November 1678, age 18, Maximilian Pettie, "Comeing into
    this Country in the Shipp, Constant Mary"
Bonner, Richard, 3 January 1681, age 17, Major Robert Beverley,
    "comeing into this Country in ye Shipp, Recovery"
Boote, Isaac, 7 February 1676, age 15, Capt. Walter Whittaker, "comeing
    into this Countrey in ye Shipp, Friends Encrease"

191

Bowrie, Stephen, 8 December 1679, age 18, Thomas Hill, "comeing
into this Country in ye Shipp, Mary"

Boystone, Thomas, 13 January 1679, age 16, Thomas George, "comeing
into this Country in ye Shipp, Zebulon"

Branch, Nicholas, 5 January 1680, age 13, David Barwick, "comeing into
this Country in ye Shipp, Duke of Yorke"

Bruce, James, 2 February 1685, age 16, Randolph Seagar

Bryant, Daniell, 5 June 1699, age 12, Paul Thilman

Burd, John, 1 May 1676, age 15, Doodes Minor, "comeing into this
Country in ye Shipp, John of Bridgewater"

Burlee, Robert, 6 July 1674, age 15, Henry Corbin, Esqr.

Campbell, James, 2 May 1681, age 18, Francis Weeks, "comeing into this
Country in ye Loveing Freindship"

Carinton, Thomas, 3 March 1679, age 15, Richard Robinson, "comeing
into this Country in ye Shipp, Baltemore"

Carrell, John, 4 March 1700, age 9, Capt. John Grymes

Carter, Joseph, 4 February 1678, age 18, Major Generall Robert Smith

Chandler, John, 1 March 1680, age 12, John Ascough, "comeing into this
Country in ye Shipp, Augusteen"

Chapman, Thomas, 6 January 1679, age 15, Ralph Wormeley, Esqr.,
"comeing into this Country in ye Shipp, Duke of Yorke"

Clark, James, 7 December 1691, age 16, Charles Robinson, "being
imported in ye Shipp, Speedwell of London"

Clarke, Daniell, 7 February 1676, age 10, William Daniell, "comeing into
this Countrey in ye Shipp, Henry & Ann"

Cole, Johanna, 1 March 1686, age 14, John Nicholls, "comeing in
The Barnaby"

Collie, Ambrose, 6 July 1674, age 16, Thomas Townsend

Collier, Charles, 4 February 1678, age 15, Major Generall Robert Smith

Collins, Thomas, 6 May 1678, age 15, Augustine Cant, "comeing into this
Country in ye Shipp, Golden Fortune"

Collins, William, 6 January 1679, age 18, Thomas Hill, "comeing into this
Country in ye Shipp, Henry & Ann"

Colson, John, 6 July 1674, age 18, Major Genll. Robert Smith

Cooke, John, 4 January 1686, age 14, John Hasellwood, "comeing in ye
Golden Lyon"

Corkington, Daniell, 4 March 1700, age 9, Capt. John Grymes

Couchman, Walter, 7 February 1676, age 13, Thomas Robie, "comeing
into this Country in ye Shippe, Prince"

MIDDLESEX COUNTY

Cresswell, John, 2 January 1685, age 15 "ye seaventh of Aprill next," Deuell Pead, "comeing in ye Shipp, Stephen and Edward"

Crowson, Jane, 2 March 1685, age 17, Robert Smith

Cullbrath, James, 1 September 1690, age 16, Ralph Wormeley, "comeing into this Country in the Shipp, Susanna"

Cundey, Mary, 5 December 1687, age 17, William Churchill, "comeing into this Country in the Shipp, Ann"

Dairon, Paul, 2 April 1688, age 17, John Vaus

Davis, William, 4 July 1687, age not judged, Henry Thacker, "is willing to serve his said Master seaven yeares from his arivall"

Day, John, 8 December 1679, age 16, Christopher Kilbe, "comeing into this Country in ye Shipp, Mary"

Decon, Patrick, 4 March 1700, age 13, Thomas Chilton

Dill, Henry, 19 July 1680, age 13, Augustine Cant, "comeing into this Country in ye Shipp, Baltemore"

Dillon, Garret, 8 May 1699, age 18, Peter Chilton, "which came in the Shipp, Providence of Dublin," "alleadgeing he had Intentures for five yeares but were lost"

Dokes, Thomas, 4 March 1678, age 13, Mrs. Elizabeth Dudley, "comeing into this Countrey in the Shipp, George of Bristoll"

Dokes, Thomas, 4 November 1678, age 17, Capt. Walter Whitaker, "comeing into this Country in ye Shipp, Planters Adventure"

Dowbell, Henry, 4 March 1700, age 13, Capt. John Grymes

Dowlen, James, 7 January 1689, age 18, Ralph Wormely, Esqr., "comeing into this Country in the Shipp, Resalucon of White Haven"

Dyner, Walter, 8 December 1679, age 18, Thomas Hill, "comeing into this Country in ye Shipp, Mary"

Edwards, Hugh, 2 February 1685, age 17, Christopher Robinson

Emas, Thomas, 5 October 1696, age 13, William Hackney, Senr., "which came into this Countrey in the Shipp, Sarah, William Jeffreys, Commander"

Farnell, Phebe, 5 April 1675, age 17, George Reeve, "acknowledging her selfe seaventeene yeares old att the tyme of her arrivall"

Ferman, John, 2 February 1680, age 17, Humphry Joanes, "comeing into this Country in ye Shipp, Hannah"

Fernell, John, 2 March 1685, age not judged, Capt. Walter Whitaker, "willing to serve seaven yeares"

Fernell, Martin, 2 March 1685, age not judged, Capt. Walter Whitaker, "willing to serve seaven yeares"

Fowle, Nicholas, 6 July 1674, age 18, Major John Burnham

Francis, Cornelius, 6 March 1676, age 18, Mrs. Allice Corbin, "comeing into this Country in ye Shipp, Lady Frances"

Gale, William, 14 December 1685, age 13, Mrs. Katherine Wormeley, "comeing into this Country in ye Shipp, Booth"

Galland, Elizabeth, 3 November 1679, age 16, John Ascough, "comeing into this Country in ye Shipp, Constant Mary"

Gambell, Ann, 2 April 1688, age not judged, Alexander Smith, "willing to serve five yeares from her arrivall in the Country"

Ganring, Bryan, 8 May 1699, age 13, Thomas Gilley, "which came in the Shipp, Providence of Dublin"

Gardiner, William, 6 January 1679, age 14, John Nicholls, "comeing into this Country in ye Shipp, Henry & Ann"

Gill, Thomas, 6 July 1674, age 10, Major Genll. Robert Smith

Gimbur, James, 4 March 1678, age 15, Thomas Hill, "comeing into this Country in ye Shipp, Henry & Ann"

Gower, Robert, 7 February 1676, age 11, Randall Seager, "comeing into this Country in ye Shipp, Duke of Yorke"

Grant, Mary, 14 May 1688, age 12, William Churchill

Gray, Adam, 11 May 1696, age 16, Hon. Christopher Wormeley, Esqr., "which came into the Countrey in the Shipp, William and John"

Griffin, Thomas, 6 January 1696, age 17, Hon. Ralph Wormeley, Esqr., "which came into this Countrey in the Shipp, Oake"

Griffiths, William, 6 December 1675, age 16, Sir Henry Chicheley

Haines, Ann, 2 April 1688, age not judged, Michaell Musgrove, "willing to serve five yeares from her arrivall in the Country"

Haines, John, 6 September 1675, age 16, Coll. Cuthbert Potter

Hanson, John, 2 February 1680, age 16, Richard Perret, Senr., "comeing into this Country in ye Shipp, Hannah"

Harris, James, 5 June 1699, age 14, Paul Thilman, "which came in the Shipp, Loyalty,"

Harris, Walter, 6 July 1674, age 11, Capt. Robert Beverley

Hawkins, John, 13 January 1679, age 15, Thomas George, "comeing into this Country in ye Shipp, Zebulon"

Hayes, Anne, 8 November 1684, age 12, Ralph Wormeley, Esqr., "comeing into this Country in ye Shipp, Stephen & Edwd., Capt. Ginsey Commander"

Hewis, George, 8 December 1679, age 18, William Dudley, "comeing into this Country in ye Shipp, Owners Advice"

MIDDLESEX COUNTY

Hibley, William, 3 May 1675, age 16, Henry Corbyn, Esqr.

Hickson, John, 3 July 1699, age 14, John Ferne

Hill, Robert, 2 February 1680, age 8, Thomas Roby, "comeing into this Country in ye Shipp, Mary"

Holliday, William, 2 February 1680, age 18, Thomas Williams, "comeing into this Country in ye Shipp, Mary"

Hooper, William, 13 January 1679, age 11, Thomas Williams, "comeing into this Country in ye Shipp, Bristow Factor"

Howell, Thomas, 4 February 1679, age 8, Major Genll. Robert Smith, "comeing into this Country in ye Shipp, Duke of Yorke"

Howell, William, 4 February 1678, age 14, Abraham Weekes, "comeing into this Countrey in the Shipp, Zebulon"

Humphreys, William, 8 May 1693, age 12, Capt. Richard Willis, "which came into this Countrey in the Shipp, Vyne of Dubling"

Hunt, William, 3 January 1676, age 15, Mrs. Eltonhead Thacker

Husband, Thomas, 5 October 1691, age 15, William Churchill

Jackson, Andrew, 6 July 1674, age 16, Lt. Coll. Christopher Wormeley

James, Thomas, 3 May 1675, age 13, Humphrey Jones

Joanes, John, 7 February 1676, age 13, John Vaus, "comeing into this Countrey in the Shipp, Duke of Yorke"

Joanes, Richard, 2 February 1685, age 18, Christopher Robinson, "comeing into ye Country in ye Shipp, Duke of York"

Jobson, James, 3 January 1681, age not judged, Major Robert Beverley, "produceing a Comon Printed Indenture to this Courte, and not being able to prove ye same, It is therefore adjudged invalid"

Johnson, Henry, 11 May 1696, age 13, Hon. Christopher Wormeley, Esqr., "which came into the Countrey in the Shipp, William and John"

Jones, Edward, 7 April 1701, age 12, Thomas Dudley

Jones, Edward, 2 November 1702, age 12, John Dudley

Jones, Roger, 2 April 1688, age not judged, William Churchill, "willing to serve seaven yeares," said Master promising to "imploy said Servant in the Stoar and not in comon working in the ground"

Kaine, Walter, 4 April 1687, age 12, William Tignor, "comeing in the George of Belfast"

Kelling, Thomas, 9 November 1691, age 10, Edward Clark, "comeing into this Country in ye St. Thomas of London"

Kendall, William, 2 February 1685, age 17, Constance Vaus

Lawrance, Charles, 7 January 1678, age 14, John Wortham, "comeing into this Countrey in the Shipp, Comard"

MIDDLESEX COUNTY

Lawson, Mathias, 4 February 1678, age 10, Thomas Haslewood, "comeing into this Country in the Shipp, Zebulon"

Leadbeater, William, 3 March 1679, age 10, Christopher Robinson, "comeing into this Country in ye Shipp, Duke of Yorke"

Le Marr, John, 2 February 1685, age 15, Christopher Robinson, "comeing into this Country in ye Shipp, Jeffryes"

Linder, Edward, 5 April 1686, age 12, Coll. Christopher Wormeley, "comeing in ye Shipp, Recovery"

Manish, John, 5 February 1700, age 13, John Micham, Junr.

Martin, Lawrance, 8 December 1679, age 18, John Nicholls, "comeing into this Country in ye Shipp, Mary"

Mason, Richard, 6 March 1676, age 9, Michael Musgrove, "comeing into this Country in ye Shipp, Duke of Yorke"

Mawby, Judith, 7 February 1676, age 17, William Gordon

Mayton, John, 3 January 1681, age 18, Robert Boodle, "comeing into this Country in ye Shipp, Paradise"

Mee, Efan, 5 January 1680, age 14, John Vaus, "comeing into this Country in ye Shipp, Duke of Yorke"

Middlin, Stephen, 5 December 1687, age 17, John Nicholls, "comeing into ye Country in the Shipp, Ann"

Milner, Edward, 6 May 1678, age 16, Christopher Robinson, "comeing into this Country in ye Shipp, Releise"

Mugg, Thomas, 8 December 1679, age 17, Coll. Mathew Kempe, "comeing into this Country in ye Shipp, Owners Advice"

Mulan, Alexander, 5 April 1675, age 10, Joseph Chippe

Nicholls, James, 1 November 1675, age 18, Augustine Cant

Nicholls, John, 2 March 1685, age not judged, Major Robert Beverley, "purchased by him from Capt. Thomas Hasted this present voyage to Rappahannock River in Virginia," "made clayme to noe right of Indenture but would serve five yeares from this day"

Nicholls, William, 7 February 1676, age 15, Francis Weekes, "Comeing into this Countrey in ye Shipp, Duke of Yorke"

Osborne, Keziah, 4 January 1686, age 11, Deuell Pead, "comeing in ye Shipp, Stephen & Edward"

Ouse, Thomas, 2 February 1680, age 18, John Vivion, "comeing into this Country in ye Shipp, Duke of Yorke"

Paine, Samuell, 5 April 1675, age 15, John Scarbrough

Paine, William, 1 February 1675, age 16, Capt. Robert Beverley

Parsons, John, 9 May 1698, age 16, Gawin Corbin

MIDDLESEX COUNTY

Pearcivall, John, 7 February 1676, age 15, Thomas Hill, "Comeing into this Country in ye Friends Encrease"

Pearse, James, 7 May 1677, age 11, John Batchelder, "comeing into this Country in ye Shipp, Releife"

Peirce, John, 2 March 1685, age not judged, Major Robert Beverley, "purchased by him from Capt. Thomas Hasted this present voyage to Rappahannock River in Virginia," "made clayme to noe right of Indenture but would serve five yeares from this day"

Pendegras, Edward, 7 April 1701, age 13, John Lohie

Peters, Cornelius, 6 July 1674, age 16, William Daniell

Petty, Martin, 3 May 1675, age 18, Richard Perrott, Junior

Phillips, Samuell, 5 April 1686, age 12, Coll. Christopher Wormeley, "comeing in ye Shipp, Recovery"

Pickett, George, 4 February 1679, age 15, John Needles, "comeing into this Country in the Shipp, Zebulon"

Pleger, John, 6 May 1678, age 15, Augustine Cant, "comeing into this Country in ye Shipp, Good Fortune"

Poller, Lewis, 5 December 1687, age 17, Christopher Kilbee, "comeing into this Country in the Shipp, Ann"

Porter, John, 2 March 1685, age 14, Capt. Walter Whitaker, "comeing into ye Country in ye Shipp, Releife"

Powell, William, 3 March 1679, age 18, Richard Robinson, "comeing into this Country in ye Shipp, Leanord & James"

Preston, Jacob, 3 March 1679, age 13, Randolph Segar, "comeing into this Country in ye Shipp, Leanord & James"

Randall, Francis, 5 November 1683, age 12, Capt. Henrey Creek, "comeing into this Country in ye Shipp, Steven and Edward"

Raynes, William, 4 March 1700, age 12, Major Robert Dudley, "which came in the Shipp, Expectations Briganteene"

Read, John, 4 April 1687, age not judged, William Churchill, agrees "to serve five years" from 11 March last past "in consideration that hee is not to work at Comon Labor in the ground"

Rice, John, 3 May 1675, age 13, Alexander Smith

Roades, George, 7 January 1689, age 13, Ralph Wormely, Esqr., "comeing into this Country in the Shipp, Steven & Edward"

Roberts, Thomas, 6 July 1674, age 14, John Wortham

Roberts, Ursula, 7 February 1676, age 12, Humfry Joanes, "comeing into this Countrey in ye Shipp, Duke of Yorke"

Rutherford, William, 5 April 1686, age 15, Edward Clarke, "comeing in
    ye Shipp, White Fox"
Sallanan, Patrick, 8 May 1699, age 13, John Fenney, "which came in the
    Shipp, Providence of Dublin"
Savage, Thomas, 5 January 1680, age 15, John Vaus, "comeing into this
    Country in ye Shipp, Hannah"
Sawell, Thomas, 5 January 1680, age 14, William Churchill, "comeing into
    this Country in ye Shipp, Duke of Yorke"
Shan, Owen, 5 July 1675, age 15, John Sheppard
Sheats, John, 6 May 1678, age 10, Ralph Wormeley, Esqr., "comeing into
    this Country in ye Shipp, Hannah"
Smith, James, 5 July 1675, age 15, Lt. Colo. Christopher Wormeley
Smith, James, 8 December 1679, age 16, John Nicholls, "comeing
    into this Country in ye Shipp, Mary"
Smith, Joseph, 6 July 1674, age 16, Dame Anne Skipwith
Smith, Thomas, 1 November 1675, age 15, John Sheppard
Smith, William, 3 November 1679, age 12, Hopkin Price, "comeing into
    this Country in ye Shipp, Constant Mary"
Smith, William, 5 October 1691, age 17, William Kilby
South, John, 12 May 1701, age 13, Harry Beverley, Gent.
Squire, James, 7 February 1676, age 16, Thomas Radley, "comeing into
    this Countrey in ye Shipp, Planters Adventure"
Stackwood, Thomas, 4 November 1678, age 15, Capt. Walter Whitaker,
    "comeing into this Country in ye Shipp, Planters Adventure"
Staice, John, 3 July 1676, age 17, Michaell Musgrove, "by reason of his
    running away he could not before now be brought to this Court"
Stapleton, Thomas, 4 March 1700, age 18, Major Robert Dudley, "which
    came in the Shipp, Expectations Briganteene"
Starkes, Henry, 7 February 1676, age 18, Peter Mountague, "comeing into
    this Countrey in the Shipp, Abraham & Sarah"
Stiffe, Thomas, 4 March 1678, age 18, Thomas Roby, "comeing into this
    Country in ye Shipp, Henry & Ann"
Stoakes, Richard, 6 July 1674, age 17, Christopher Kilby
Sutton, Dorothy, 3 March 1679, age 17, Coll. Christopher Wormeley,
    "comeing into this Country in ye Shipp, Leanord & James"
Swanson, Edward, 3 March 1679, age 12, Randolph Segar, "comeing into
    this Country in ye Shipp, Leanord & James"
Swift, John, 6 July 1674, age 10, Major Genll. Robert Smith

MIDDLESEX COUNTY

Syms, Robert, 8 December 1679, age 16, Major Robert Beverley,
"comeing into this Country in ye Shipp, Thomas & Ann"
Teems, Henry, 2 March 1685, age not judged, Major Robert Beverley,
"purchased by him from Capt. Thomas Hasted this present
voyage to Rappahannock River in Virginia," "made clayme to
noe right of Indenture but would serve five yeares from this day"
Terry, Andrew, 4 July 1698, age 14, John Vivion, "which came into ye
Countrey in the Shipp, Robert and Samuell"
Tervey, William, 7 January 1678, age 16, William Cheyney, "comeing into
this Countrey in the Shipp, Industry"
Thomas, Rowland, 6 July 1674, age 13, Major John Burnham
Thompson, John, 4 November 1678, age 13, Capt. Walter Whitaker,
"comeing into this Country in ye Shipp, Planters Adventure"
Thompson, Thomas, 2 February 1680, age 12, Anthony Barloe, "comeing
into this Country in ye Shipp, Recovery"
Tokens, John, 3 July 1676, age 11, John Burton, "comeing into this
Country in the Shipp, Hanah"
Tresahar, James, 2 March 1685, age not judged, Major Robert Beverley,
"purchased by him from Capt. Thomas Hasted this present
voyage to Rappahannock River in Virginia," "made clayme to
noe right of Indenture but would serve five yeares from this day"
Twyman, George, 4 February 1678, age 16, Thomas Lee, "comeing into
this Countrey in the Shipp, Recovery"
Wallis, Joseph, 5 January 1680, age 18, Ralph Wormeley, Esqr., "comeing
into this Country in ye Shipp, Duke of Yorke"
Wayle, Richard, 14 December 1685, age 14, Mrs. Elizabeth Wormeley,
"comeing into this Country in ye Shipp, Booth"
Welch, James, 4 March 1700, age 15, Capt. John Grymes
Wells, Thomas, 2 February 1685, age 13, Coll. Christopher Wormeley
Whitehead, Jonathan, 4 January 1686, age 14, Deuell Pead, "comeing
in ye Shipp, Stephen & Edward"
Wiely, Isaac, 2 February 1680, age 18, Richard Perret, Senr., "comeing
into this Country in ye Shipp, Zebulon"
Williams, David, 6 July 1674, age 16, George Reeve
Williams, Niccolas, 3 May 1675, age 13, Mr. Kilbie
Williams, William, 4 February 1678, age 12, Richard Robinson, "comeing
into this Country in ye Shipp, Zebulon"
Williamson, James, 5 April 1686, age 14, John Lohie, "comeing in
the Duke of Yorke"

MIDDLESEX COUNTY

Willis, William, 1 May 1676, age 16, Richard Perrot, Junr., "Comeing into this Country in ye Shippe, Legorne Markt."

Winn, Sarah, 2 January 1688, age 9, John Skeers

Wisdome, William, 6 January 1679, age 17, Major Robert Beverley, "comeing into this Country in ye Shipp, Henry & Ann"

Wise, William, 6 September 1675, age 13, John Man

Wood, Robert, 2 March 1685, age not judged, Major Robert Beverley, "relinquishes all right to any Indenture and is willing to serve tenn yeares"

Woole, William, 7 February 1676, age 14, Sir Henry Chicheley, "comeing into this Country in ye Shipp, Duke of Yorke"

Worteley, Francis, 5 January 1680, age 16, Major Genll. Robert Smith, "comeing into this Country in ye Shipp, Recovery"

MIDDLESEX COUNTY

Gentleman Justices	Servants
Beverley, Harry	South
Beverley, Robert, Capt., Major	Bonner, Harris, Jobson, Nicholls, Paine, Peirce, Syms, Teems, Tresahar, Wisdome, Wood
Bridges, Francis	
Burnham, John, Major, Lt. Coll.	Fowle, Thomas
Carey, Oswald, Capt.	
Chicheley, Sir Henry, Knight	Griffiths, Woole
Churchill, William	Beaumont, Cundey, Grant, Husband, Jones, Read, Sawell
Cock, Maurice	
Corbin, Gawin	Parsons
Corbyn, Henry, Esqr.	Beaverstone, Burlee, Hibley
Daniell, Robert	
Daniell, William	Clarke, Peters
Dudley, Robert	Raynes, Stapleton
Dudley, William	Hewis
Grymes, John, Capt.	Carrell, Corkington, Dowbell, Welch
Jones, Roger	
Kemp, Mathew, Coll.	Mugg
Kemp, Richard	
Landon, Thomas	

MIDDLESEX COUNTY

Gentleman Justices	Servants
Man, John	Wise
Mickleburrough, Tobias	
Perrott / Parrett, Richard, Junr.	Petty, Willis
Perrott / Parrett, Richard, Senr. *	Hanson, Wiely
Potter, Cuthbert, Coll.	Baldwin, Haines
Robinson, Christopher	Edwards, Joanes, Leadbeater, Le Marr, Milner
Robinson, John	
Robinson, Richard	Ashley, Carinton, Powell, Williams
Sheppard, John	Batcheller, Shan, Smith
Skipwith, William, Baron	
Smith, John, Senr.	
Smith, Robert, Major Generall	Backett, Baineman, Carter, Collier, Colson, Crowson, Gill, Howell, Swift, Worteley
Stapleton, Thomas	
Thacker, Henry	Davis
Vause, John	Baker, Dairon, Joanes, Mee, Savage
Weekes, Abraham	Howell
Weekes, Francis	Campbell, Nicholls
Whittaker, Walter, Capt.	Ann, Boote, Dokes, Fernell, Fernell, Porter, Stackwood, Thompson

202

MIDDLESEX COUNTY

Gentleman Justices	Servants
Willis, Richard, Capt.	Humphreys
Wormeley, Christopher, Lt. Coll.	Antrobud, Gray, Jackson, Johnson, Linder, Phillips, Smith, Sutton, Wells
Wormeley, Ralph, Capt., Esqr.	Chapman, Cullbrath, Dowlen, Griffin, Hayes, Roades, Sheats, Wallis
Wormeley, William	
Wortham, George	
Wortham, John	Lawrance, Roberts

* see Lancaster County

MIDDLESEX COUNTY				MIDDLESEX COUNTY			
Year	White	Negro	Indian	Year	White	Negro	Indian
1674	16	0	0	1693	1	0	0
1675	18	0	0	1694	0	2	0
1676	20	0	0	1695	0	0	0
1677	1	0	0	1696	4	4	0
1678	23	0	0	1697	0	0	0
1679	30	0	0	1698	2	0	0
1680	16	0	0	1699	7	0	0
1681	4	0	0	1700	8	0	0
1682	0	0	0	1701	3	1	0
1683	2	0	0	1702	1	1	0
1684	1	0	0	1703	0	0	0
1685	20	0	0	1704	0	7	0
1686	8	0	0	1705	0	3	0
1687	6	0	0	1706	0	13	0
1688	6	1	0	1707	0	0	0
1689	2	1	0	1708	0	6	0
1690	1	0	0	1709	0	0	0
1691	4	0	0	1710	0	0	0
1692	0	0	0	Total	204	39	0

YORK COUNTY

Abbey, Francis, female, 24 January 1679, age 18, Edward Mosse,
"imported in the Barnaby, Capt. Mathew Rider, Commander,"
six years
Abott, George, 12 November 1660, age 17, Robert Baldry, "two years
since his servant then newly come into this country" was
adjudged "between 15 & 16 yrs. of age"
Adam, Ephraim, 24 January 1679, age 18, Edward Mosse, "imported in the
Barnaby, Capt. Mathew Rider, Commander," six years
Allgroe, Roger, 7 November 1689, age 10, Joseph White
Andrews, John, 24 May 1667, age 10, Lt. Col. Thomas Beale, Esq.,
"imported in the Charles," fourteen years
Armstrong, Ellenor, 25 January 1669, age 19, Nicholas Taylor, (five years)
Ashby, Thomas, 26 April 1675, age 16, John Page, "imported in the
Planters Adventure," eight years
Axden, John, 24 April 1667, age 14, Hugh Roy
Bailey, Michaell, 24 March 1681, age 18, Coll. (Nathaniell) Bacon,
"imported in the Planters Adventure"
Baker, Mathew, 24 _____ 1699, age 14, Henry _____
Baker, Thomas, 10 March 1669, age 14, William Harman, "imported in the
Prince," ten years
Baker, Thomas, 24 June 1673, age 17, Thomas Bushrod, "imported in
the William & Mary, Capt. Thomas Smyth, Commander,"
seven years
Ball, John, 26 September 1698, age 11, John Moore, "imported in ye shipp,
Robert and Samuell, Capt. Mathew Trimm, commander"
Banger, Thomas, 24 January 1679, age 15, Thomas Keene, "imported in
the Henry & Anne, Capt. Thomas Arnall, Commander,"
nine years
Barrosome (?), Mary, 10 January 1671, age 17, Capt. John Underhill,
"imported in the Pelicaine"
Baskett, Henry, 24 July 1674, age 13, William Major, imported in the
Industry, "by Capt. Phineas Hide," Commander, eleven years
Beaman, Edward, 10 December 1677, age 14, Hon. Daniell Parker, Esq.,
"imported in the Friends Encrease, Capt. John Martin,
Commander," ten years
Beard, Isaac, 26 April 1670, age 14, Nicholas Seabrell
Beekes, Joseph, 24 August 1680, age 14, Thomas Mountfurt, "came in
the James, Capt. Anthony Young, Commander"
Bell, Jane, 24 February 1682, age 16, Capt. John Baddison, "Commander
of ye Diamond and imported in the said Ship"

Benafield, Joseph, 24 January 1676, age 16, Nathaniell Bacon, Esq.,
    "imported in the Planters Adventure, Capt. Ellis Ells,
    Commander," eight years
Beng, John, 24 May 1700, age 16, David Holloway, "imported in ye ship,
    Harridge Prize," Capt. Janson, commander
Bennis (?), Edward, 26 January 1680, age 18, Henry Jenkins, "comeing
    this yeare in the Dimond"
Berkelett, John, 10 March 1669, age 14, Francis Barnes, ten years
Berry, John, 24 June 1673, age 12, Henry Freeman, Sr., "imported in the
    Daniel, Capt. Thomas Warren, Commander," twelve years
Blake, Mary, 24 August 1659, age 13, David Cant
Blandon, John, 26 February 1672, age 15, Daniell Wyld, "as entrusted with
    the estate of John Bowler," six years
Blanton, Benjamin, 26 April 1670, age 14, Henry White
Blower, Edward, 24 January 1679, age 12, Nathaniell Bacon, Esq.,
    "imported in the Planters Adventure, Capt. Robert Ranson,
    Commander," twelve years
Boates, John, 10 December 1677, age 12, Richard Curteene, "imported
    in the Friends Encrease, Capt. John Martin, Commander,"
    twelve years
Booth, John, 24 January 1681, age 14, Edward Toliott, "came in the
    Planters Adventure"
Bostocke, William, 10 September 1674, age 15, James Vaulx, "imported
    in the Thomas & Edward, Capt. John Martin, Commander,"
    nine years
Bowdon, Humphry, 26 April 1675, age 16, John Smith, "imported in the
    Planters Adventure," eight years
Bray, John, 24 January 1668, age 15, John Huberd, "imported in the
    Phillipp, Mr. Creeke Commander," (nine years)
Brihan (?), John, 24 January 1670, age 13, William Taverner
Bristow, Edward, 29 January 1673, age 14, Lt. Co. Robert Baldrey
Brondley, James, 24 January 1660, age 15, Samuel Fenn, (six years)
Brookes, Richard, 10 January 1671, age 16, Richard Sherley, "imported in
    the Posthorse"
Brooks, Richard, 24 July 1674, age 12, John Bune, "imported in
    the Truelove," twelve years
Brooks, Richard, 24 April 1678, age 16, Madam Reade, "imported in the
    Golden Fortune, Capt. William Jefferys, Commander," eight years
Brown, James, 24 February 1679, age 18, Thomas Taylor, "imported in the
    Golden Fortune, Capt. William Jeffreys, Commander," six years

Brown, James, 25 August 1679, age 11, "Consigned by Mr. William Smith
of London to Capt. Francis Page in the Ship Constant, Capt.
Thomas Smith, Commander"

Browne, Richard, 26 January 1680, age 19, Armiger Wade

Browne, Robert, 24 March 1679, age 14, John Darnier, "came in the
Planters Adventure"

Browne, Thomas, 21 December 1661, age 13, master not named,
"acknowledges that by his indenture which was lost at sea,
hee was to serve 11 yrs. from his first arrival in Virginia"

Browne, William, 26 April 1670, age 14, Langhorn Peirson

Bullard, Jacob, 14 January 1678, age 17, Jane Martin, "imported in the
Concord, Capt. Thomas Grantham, Commander," seven years

Bullerd, Edward, 24 January 1662, age 15, Henry Taylor, six years

Bulling, Thomas, 24 January 1679, age 17, John Clarke, "imported in the
Concord, Capt. Thomas Grantham, Commander," seven years

Burley, John, 25 October 1680, age 17, John Gawen, "came in the James
Frigatt, Capt. Anthony Young, Commander"

Butler, John, 24 September 1700, age 9, William Coman, "imported in ye
ship Cheer into James River"

Cain, Phillip, 24 May 1700, age 11, Ralph Holland, "imported in ye ship,
Harridge Prize," Capt. Janson, commander

Calloy, Edmond, 24 May 1700, age 12, William Spencer, "imported in ye
ship, Harridge Prize," Capt. Janson, commander

Calvert, Robert, 24 August 1683, age 17, Francis Read, "imported in the
Humphry & Elizabeth, Capt. John Martyn, Commander"

Cannbrookes, Edward, 22 December 1662, age ___ , Thomas Davis

Cantiwell, Jane, 24 May 1700, age 14, Henry Howard, Junr., "imported in
ye ship, Harridge Prize," Capt. Janson, commander

Carrawell, Cornelius, Irishman, 25 February 1661, William Harmon,
"petitions the court for his freedom, having served May next,
seaven years," adjudged to be 21, ordered to serve until 24

Carter, John, 24 January 1670, age 15, Samuel Trevillian

Cary, Thomas, 24 June 1673, age 14, Major Ralph Langley, "imported in
the Prince, Capt. Robert Conoway, Commander," ten years

Casement, Richard, 24 January 1676, age 18, Capt. Otho Thorpe,
"imported in the Planters Adventure, Ellis Ells, Commander,"
six years

Cheston, alias Cooley, Edward, 24 February 1670, age 10,
Col. George Read

YORK COUNTY

Child, John, 10 March 1669, age 15, Lt. Coll. William Barbar, "imported
in the Post Horse," nine years
Christian, Henry, 26 November 1674, age 15, Richard Trotter, "imported
in the Barnaby, Capt. Rider, Commander," nine years
Clarke, Isaac, 24 April 1671, age 12, Capt. Philipp Chesley, "imported in
the Barnaby"
Claske, Leonard, 24 July 1674, age 14, John Martin, "imported in the
Humphrey & Elizabeth," ten years
Clinch, Henry, 24 February 1680, age 14, Martin Gardner, "coming in
Planters Adventure"
Cole, William, 10 March 1669, age 15, Peter Ware, nine years
Cooke, Richard, 10 September 1674, age 16, John Robinson, "imported
in the Golden Fortune, Capt. Edward Peirce, Commander,"
eight years
Cooper, Robert, 10 January 1672, age 16, Nathaniel Bacon, Esq.,
"imported in the Mary"
Cooper, William, 24 April 1673, age 16, Capt. Thomas Beale, "imported in
the Rebecca, Capt. Christopher Evoling, Commander," eight years
Corden, Katherine, 25 January 1669, age 16, Brian Canady, (eight years)
Cornewell, Henry, 10 March 1669, age 15, John Bowler, nine years
Cox, Mary, 14 January 1678, age 14, Capt. John Tiplady, "imported in the
Augustine, Capt. Zach. Taylor, Commander," ten years
Cozens, Francis, 24 February 1682, age 14, Richard Albritton, "imported
in ye Barnaby," Capt. Mathew Rider, Commander
Croucher, Robert, 29 January 1673, age 16, Lt. Col. Robert Baldrey,
"imported in the Thomas & Edward, John Martin, Commander,"
eight years
Crowe, Stephen, 25 January 1675, age 14, William Cureton, "imported in
the Richard & Jane, Capt. Thomas Arnall, Commander," ten years
Curtis, Richard, 24 January 1660, age 15, Thomas Heynes, six years
Dale, Roger, 24 October 1671, age 17, William Major
Danford, Phill, 24 March 1680, age 14, Maryan Baptist, "came in the
Dymond, Capt. Edwards, Commander"
Daniell, James, 8 December 1668, age 13, Capt. John Scasbrooke,
eleven years
Davis, Humphrey, 26 September 1667, age 16 "at the time of his
importation into Virginia," John Page, eight years
Davis, John, 24 April 1673, age 17, Henry Taylor, "imported in the
Rebecca, Capt. Christopher Evolings, Commander," seven years

208

Davis, Thomas, 24 May 1660, age 9, William Crumpe, (twelve years)

Davis, Thomas, 24 October 1661, age 17, Edward Cardingbrooke, (four years)

Dawson, Anthony, 25 January 1675, age 14, Ralph Graves, "imported in the George, Capt. Thomas Grantham, Commander," ten years

Dawson, John, 24 November 1681, age 14, Mr. Davis, "imported in the Constant Mary, Capt. Rhodes, Commander"

Dean, William, 24 March 1679, age 12, Mundifer Kirby, "came in the Golden Fortune"

Debrason, James, 24 February 1691, age 16, Joseph Ring, "imported into this Collony in the shipp Ruth," Capt. Brumskill, commander

Dee, Peter, 24 June 1673, age 17, William Aylett, "imported in the James, Capt. Thomas Faucett, Commander," seven years

Device, Peter, 24 January 1679, age 15, William Townesend, "imported in the Planters Adventure, Capt. Robert Ranson, Commander," nine years

Dickeson, John, 24 February 1671, age 17, John Whiskin

Disbary, Peter, 24 April 1667, age 16, John Overstreet

Dixon, Peter, 24 January 1676, age 15, John Page, "imported in the Planters Adventure, Ellis Ells, Commander," nine years

Dobson, Samuel, 10 January 1671, age 18, John Bracegirdle, "imported in the Constance"

Dolor, James, 5 January 1682, age 10, Capt. James Archer, "imported in ye Constant Mary, Capt. Edward Rhodes, Commander"

Dolor, William, 5 January 1682, age 12, Capt. James Archer, "imported in ye Constant Mary," Capt. Edward Rhodes, Commander

Dowell, Richard, 24 June 1680, age 17, Joseph Bing, "he coming in the Rose & Crown, Capt. Barth Clements, Commander"

Draper, Thomas, 24 July 1667, age 15, Armiger Wade, Sr., nine years

Dullard, Nicholas, 24 May 1700, age 10, John Doswell, "imported in ye ship, Harridge Prize, Capt. Janson, commander"

Dunford, William, 24 March 1675, age 16, Bryan Canady, "imported in the Thomas & Edward, Capt. John Martin, Commander," eight years

Dunivan, Darby, 24 February 1682, age 18, Capt. Thomas Tiplady, "imported in ye Lovers Increase"

Dunn, John, 25 July 1670, age 18, Bryan Cannady

Dunny, John, 24 April 1673, age 14, Lt. Col. Robert Baldrey, "imported in the William & Mary," ten years

Eastes, Elizabeth, 24 June 1673, age 15, Major John Scasbrooke,
"imported in the Rebecca, Capt. Christopher Evoling,
Commander," nine years

Edford, _____ , 26 February 1672, age 13, Stephen Vest, "imported in
the Barnaby," eleven years

Edmunds, Thomas, 20 December 1669, age 12, Col. Thomas Beale

Edwards, Arron, 25 August 1679, age 16, Richard Albritton, "came in the
Indeavor, Capt. Edgate, Commander"

Edwards, Robert, 20 February 1678, age 9, Nathaniel Bacon, Esq.,
"imported in the Henry & Anne, Capt. Thomas Arnold,
Commander," fifteen years

Elliot, Charles, 25 March 1706, age 14, Charles Chiswell, "imported in
ye ship London merchant, Capt. William Cant, commander"

Elliott, Abbarck (?), 20 December 1669, age 14, Thomas Rumball

Ellis, Ann, 24 January 1662, age 12, Capt. William Hay, nine years

Ellis, Francis, 24 January 1681, age 14, William Pinkethman, "came in
the Barneby"

Ellis, Henry, 24 January 1660, age 11, Thomas Heynes, ten years

Elmes, Anne, 26 November 1674, age 19, Edward Wade

Engerson, John, 24 February 1679, age 12, Samuell Tineson, "imported
in the Mary," twelve years

Evans, David, 24 January 1660, age 12, Capt. Daniel Parke, nine years

Evans, Thomas, 24 April 1662, age 12, Peter Efford, nine years

Fanning, William, 18 October 1667, age 17 "at importation," William
Grymes, seven years

Fargeson, John, 12 November 1666, age 14, Otho Thorpe, ten years

Farrington, Gyles, 24 July 1667, age 16, Capt. John Underhill,
(eight years)

Faulkner, Thomas, 24 March 1671, age 17, William Merry, "imported in
the York Merchant"

Fewell, Stephen, 24 April 1671, age 17, Edmund Chisman, Jr., "imported
in the Rebecca, by Capt. Christopher Enoling, Commander"

Finny, William, 12 November 1669, age 16, Langhan Pierson

Fitz Jarrell, Honor, 24 May 1692, age 15, John Doswell, "whoe arived in
James River 25 March last past in the shipp Sarah Bristoe,
Capt. Leach, commander"

Flavell, Elizabeth, 24 April 1673, age 13, Henry Freeman, Jr., "imported
in the Thomas & Edward, Capt. John Martin, Commander,"
eleven years

Flewen, William, 25 January 1675, age 19, Isaac Clopton

Flurlicke, William, 25 January 1675, age 17, Mrs. Elizabeth Petters, "imported in the George, Capt. Thomas Grantham, Commander," seven years

Foote, James, 25 January 1669, age 17, Thomas Dennett (seven years)

Foster, John, 24 February 1681, age 18, John Wooden, "imported in the Prince"

Foster, Thomas, 24 July 1667, age 16, Armiger Wade, Jr., eight years

Francis, Richard, 20 March 1662, age 18, Coll. William Barbar, three years

Freeman, Henry, 26 January 1680, age 14, John Parsons, "comeing this yeare in the Dimond"

Furnell, Harry, 10 April 1668, age 14, Charles Dunn, "imported in the Elizabeth, Capt. Robert Hobbs, Commander," ten years

Gant, William, 24 May 1660, age 15, John Vaulx, six years

Garrow, William, 24 February 1680, age 9, John Wright, Clerke, "coming in (with) Capt. Grantham"

George, Jeremiah, 20 December 1675, age not judged, Thomas (torn), "imported in the Concord, Capt. Thomas Grantham, Commander"

Giles, Edward, 26 January 1680, age 11, Robert Crawley, "comeing in this yeare in the Richard & Elizabeth, Capt. Price (?), Commander, in James River"

Gillfurd, John, 24 February 1681, age 16, Thomas Buck, "imported in the Constants and Mary" (Constant Mary)

Gilson, Sarah, 24 February 1670, age 16, John Page

Gladmore, William, 25 January 1669, age 15, Otho Thorpe, (nine years)

Grant, William, 18 October 1667, age 19, John Page, five years

Gray, Mary, 26 May 1684, age 17, John Gawin, "imported in the Judith, Capt. Mathew Trim, Commander"

Greame, William, 24 May 1667, age 19, Maj. James Goodwin, (five years)

Greene, John, 26 November 1674, age 19, John Whysken, "imported in the Industry"

Greene, William, 10 March 1669, age 16, Edmund Cheesman, Sr., eight years

Gregory, Nicholas, 24 February 1679, age 13, Joseph Bing, "imported in the Golden Fortune, Capt. William Jeffreys, Commander," eleven years

Griffin, Robert, 7 December 1668, age 16, Edward Wade, eight years

Gurden, Thomas, 25 January 1669, age 15, Henry Freeman, nine years

Gwillam, Thomas, 24 August 1665, age 14, Capt. Thomas Beale

Gwin, Thomas, 24 July 1667, age 16, Robert Clarke, eight years

Hall, Joseph, 25 August 1679, age 13, "Consigned by Mr. William Smith
    of London to Capt. Francis Page in the Ship Constant, Capt.
    Thomas Smith, Commander"

Hall, Robertt, 25 June 1683, age 16, George Martin, "imported in ye
    Humphry and Elizabeth"

Hall, Samuell, 1 December 1671, age 17, Ralph Hunt, "imported in the
    Richard & Jane, Capt. Robert Conoway, Commander"

Hallword, Elizabeth, 10 December 1683, age 12, Humphrey Moodey,
    "imported in the John, Daniell Bradley, Master"

Hankes, Samuell, 24 June 1673, age 13, Mrs. Mary Trevillion, "imported
    in the Daniell, Thomas Warren, Commander," eleven years

Harbey, John, 24 October 1683, age 12, John Martin, "imported in the
    Humphrey & Elizabeth," Capt. John Martin, Commander

Harding, Henry, __ November 1684, age __ , William Pinkethman,
    "imported in the Golden Lyon"

Hargrove, Robert, 24 February 1691, age 15, Humphrey Moody, "imported
    into this Collony in the shipp Ruth," Capt. Brumskill, commander

Harling, William, 1 December 1671, age 10, Langhan Peirson, "imported
    in the Barnaby"

Harris, Thomas, 20 December 1669, age 14, Argold Blackston

Harrison, Ralph, 25 January 1675, age 16, William Aylett, "imported in
    the George, Capt. Thomas Grantham, Commander," eight years

Harrison, Robert, 1 March 1676, age 13, Laughan Pierson, "imported in the
    Barnaby, Capt. Matthew Rider, Commander," eleven years

Harrison, Thomas, 24 January 1676, age 16, John Morland, "imported on
    the Barnaby, Capt. Matthew Rider, Commander," eight years

Haven, Emanuel, 25 May 1674, age 16, John Page, "imported in the
    Stadt of Staden, John Vanfluster, Commander," eight years

Hayes, Francis, 24 March 1680, age 14, Marke Warkeman, "came in
    the Concord, Capt. Grantham, Commander"

Herne, James, 24 May 1700, age 19, Henry Taylor, "imported in ye ship,
    Harridge Prize," Capt. Janson, commander

Herring, Richard, 13 April 1672, age 12, James Vaulx, twelve years

Hewett, Isaac, 26 January 1680, age 16, Robert Everett, "coming in
    the Prince"

Heyward, James, 25 October 1675, age not judged, Thomas Barbar

Hill, Edward, 26 April 1675, age 16, Thomas Bushrod, "imported in the
Canary Bird, Capt. John Lucam, Commander," eight years
Hill, William, 24 July 1674, age 16, Edward Jenkins, Sr., "imported in
the Industry, Capt. Phineas Hide, Commander," eight years
Hill, William, 26 May 1684, age 14, Mrs. Katherine Besauth (?),
"imported in the Paradice, Francis Parsons, Commander"
Hodgills, William, 24 May 1700, age 12, Henry Howard, "imported in ye
ship, Harridge Prize," Capt. Janson, commander
Holdbrooke, Robert, 24 August 1693, age 11, George Keeling,
"imported into this Collony in the ship, Sarah, Capt. William
Jeffreys, commander"
Holford, Ralph, 24 January 1676, age 14, Capt. Otho Thorpe, "imported in
the Planters Adventure, Ellis Ells, Commander," ten years
Holland, James, 24 May 1689, age 13, Francis Page, "imported in the
ship Sarah, Capt. Francis Parsons, commander"
Homes, Richard, 24 April 1662, age 14, Mathew Hubberd, (seven years)
Horne, David, 20 December 1675, age 17, Henry Hoeyman, Sr.,
"imported in the Concord, Capt. Thomas Grantham,
Commander," seven years
Howson, William, 26 April 1675, age 16, Major John Scasbrooke,
"imported in the Canary Bird, Capt. John Lucam, Commander,"
eight years
Huberd, William, 25 February 1661, age 13, Thomas Ballard, eight years
Ireland, Abigall, 24 January 1676, age 15, Mrs. Elizabeth Moody,
"imported in the Augustin, Capt. Zacarias Taylor, Commander,"
nine years
Irish, William, 25 May 1674, age 15, Robert Handy, "imported in the
Golden Lyon, Capt. Webber, Commander," nine years
Jackson, Thomas, 24 July 1674, age 14, Edward Foliott, "imported in
the Industry," Capt. Phineas Hide, Commander, ten years
James, John, 26 June 1671, age 14, William Arnold, "imported in
the Daniell"
James, John, 24 July 1674, age 16, John Evans, "imported in the Golden
Fortune, Capt. Edward Peirce, Commander," eight years
James, Robert, 24 March 1691, age 15, master not named, "imported into
this Collony in the ship Ruth, Capt. Brumskill, commander"
James, Thomas, 24 June 1675, age 19, Daniell Wyld, "imported (by)
Capt. Covell," five years

Jenkins, David, 24 July 1674, age 17, William Townsend, imported in the Industry, "by Capt. Phineas Hide," Commander, seven years

Jessey, Lazarus, 26 March 1688, age 11, Espher. Hurt, "imported into this Collony in the shipp Richard, Capt. Backter, commander"

Johnson, Anthony, 10 September 1674, age 16, Capt. Otho Thorpe, "imported in the Golden Fortune, Capt. Edward Peirce, Commander," eight years

Johnson, William, 8 December 1668, age 15, Capt. John Scasbrooke, nine years

Johnson, William, 24 January 1676, age 17, John Page, "imported in the Planters Adventure, Capt. Ellis Ells, Commander," seven years

Jones, George, 24 November 1681, age 9, Mr. Davis, "imported in the Constant Mary, Capt. Rhodes, Commander"

Jones, John, 24 January 1670, age 16, Michaell Rowe

Jones, Thomas, 26 November 1674, age 14, Clothier Lucas, "imported in the Daniel, Capt. Thomas Warren, Commander," ten years, "alledging he has an indenture"

Kershea, Samuel, 24 February 1701, age 14, Sarah Anderson, "imported in the ship Sarah, Capt. Jeffereys, commander"

Kibble, John, 26 January 1680, age 17, Arthur Vancint, "comeing in the Dimond"

Kitchinger, Richard, 24 June 1686, age 15, John Tomer, "imported in the good Shippe ye Indy, Capt. Trim, Commander"

Knisslefield, Dorothy, 25 January 1669, age 14, Peter Sterky, (ten years)

Lane, Mary, 6 May 1686, age 19, William Bouth

Langley, William, 24 January 1668, age 14, John Huberd, "imported in the Phillipp, Mr. Creeke Commander," ten years

Lawrence William, 24 April 1662, age 15, Peter Efford, six years

Lawson, Richard, 24 April 1673, age 17, Mr. Henry Jackson, "imported in the Rebecca, Capt. Christopher Evolings, Commander," seven years

Leason, John, 12 November 1677, age 17, Mrs. Elizabeth Reade, "imported in the Friends Encrease, Capt. John Martin, Commander," seven years

Levierton (?), Robert, 26 January 1680, age not judged, Edward Mosse, "in court declared that he had no Indenture"

Lewis, Charles, 24 June 1673, age 14, Mrs. Anne Donnett, "imported in the Daniell, Capt. Thomas Warren, Commander," ten years

Lewis, Thomas, 24 January 1676, age 18, John Page, "imported in the Planters Adventure, Capt. Ellis Ells, Commander," six years

YORK COUNTY

Lloyd, Evan, 24 June 1673, age 18, James Besouth, "imported in the
Daniell, Capt. Thomas Warren, Commander," six years
Love, John, 24 May 1669, age 16, John Cooper, eight years
Lucas, James, 24 June 1661, age 12, Mrs. Elizabeth Hansford
Macdonah, John, 24 May 1667, age 16, Col. George Reade, Esq.,
"imported in the Ewe & Lamb," eight years
Mackoyes, Owin, 24 April 1661, age 18, Ann Thomas, "hee to serve
till 21," three years
Maddox, Edward, 26 April 1670, age 16, Lt. Col. Daniel Parke, "imported
in the Loyall Berkeley"
Madox, John, 2 December 1681, age 14, George Norwell, "imported in
ye Constant Mary, Capt. Edward Rhodes, Commander"
Makes (?), Philip, 24 February 1701, age 9, master not named
Mansfeild, William, 12 November 1669, age 14, Edward Digges, Esq.
Mar, Charles, 24 March 1679, age 14, Anthony Seabrell, "came in the
Constant"
Marinay, Cornelius, 24 June 1673, age 18, John Davis, "imported in the
Hercules, Capt. Henry Crooke, Commander," six years
Marke, Andrew, 26 April 1670, age 16, John Goodale
Marshall, William, 25 March 1689, age 12, Thomas Mountfort
Martin, William, 24 August 1693, age 11, Coll. Edmund Jenings,
"imported into this Collony in the ship, Edward & Francis,
Capt. Thomas Man, commander"
Mason, William, 24 August 1680, age 11, Richard Awbarne, "who came in
the Jane Kitch from Scotland"
Matharoon, Proo, 24 June 1679, age 16, Nathaniell Bacon, Esq., "imported
in the Antelope of Belfast in James River"
Mathews, James, 24 June 1673, age 18, Mrs. Mary Trevillion, "imported
in the Daniell, Thomas Warren, Commander," six years
Merrifield, James, 24 June 1673, age 17, Alex Duncombe, "imported in the
Hercules, Capt. Henry Crooke, Commander," seven years
Middleton, Francis, 20 December 1669, age 16, Otho Thorpe
Milton, John, 25 May 1674, age 17, Thomas Whaley, "imported in the
Golden Lyon, Capt. Webber, Commander," seven years
Moore, George, 24 January 1676, age 18, Nathaniell Bacon, Esq.,
"imported in the Planters Adventure, Capt. Ellis Ells,
Commander," six years
Morphey, Simon, 24 February 1701, age 10, Col. Edmund Jennings,
"imported into this colony in the ship, Oliver of Dublin,
Capt. Thomas Adkinson, commander, the month of May last"

Morrall, Elizabeth, 10 April 1667, age 13, Thomas Dennett, (eleven years)

Morrell, Nicholas, 24 February 1682, age 16, Robert Read, "imported in
ye Barnaby, Capt. Mathew Rider, Commander"

Morton, George, 10 November 1670, age 11, William Bell, "imported in
the Tryall of Bristol"

Morton, William, 24 January 1660, age 16, Thomas Heynes, (five years)

Mountain, Walter, 26 November 1674, age 16, Thomas Beale, Esq.,
"imported in the Humphrey & Elizabeth," eight years

Munford, Henry, 13 April 1672, age 14, Capt. John Stannup

Murfee, Mary, 24 August 1693, age 17, Peeter Starkey, "imported into
this Collony in the ship, Edward & Francis, Capt. Thomas Man,
commander"

Murrey, William, 24 March 1682, age 13, Edward Johnson, "imported
in ye Barnaby"

Nase, Bridgett, 10 September 1674, age 16, William Stevens, "imported
in the Thomas & Edward, Capt. John Martin, Commander,"
eight years

Newby, Edward, 26 July 1669, age 16, Robert Neale, "imported this
shipping in the Elizabeth," eight years

Nicholls, Silvester, 10 April 1667, age 16, Thomas Dennett, eight years

Nicholson, Henry, 24 June 1673, age 14, Nathaniell Bacon, Esq.,
"imported in the Hercules, Capt. Henry Crooke, Commander,"
ten years

Nightingale, Robert, 25 May 1674, age 16, John Saunders, "imported in the
Golden Lyon, Capt. Webber, Commander," eight years

Noakes, John, 24 April 1671, age 17, Mrs. Ruth Tiplady

Nunn, William, 10 January 1672, age 15, Edward Jenkins, "imported in
the Barnaby"

Oldfield, Joseph, 25 February 1658, age 15, Coll. George Reade, Esqr.,
"who arrived about a weeke in Capt. Thomas Varbell's shipp
called the Elizabeth & Mary"

Olen, Richard, 25 May 1691, age 10, Thomas Phear, "imported into this
Collony in the ship Ruth, Capt. Brumskill, commander"

O'Neale, Henry, 25 November 1667, age 14, Major Robert Baldry,
ten years

Onele, Bryan, 24 February 1681, age 15, Thomas Muntfort, "imported
in the Jonathan of Topsham"

Osborne, Margaret, 24 May 1667, age 15, Col. Nathaniel Bacon, Esq.,
nine years

Painter, James, 24 February 1681, age 13, William Smith, "imported in
    the Diamond"
Palmer, John, 31 October 1661, age 16, Mrs. Mary Ludlow, five years
Payne, Richard, 10 January 1672, age 15, Henry Taylor, "imported in
    the Barnaby"
Pease, Gilbert, 26 April 1670, age 14, Mrs. Mary Croshaw, "imported in
    the Loyall Berkeley"
Peavaradge, Edward, 26 November 1674, age 13, Thomas Taylor,
    "imported in the Barnaby, Capt. Rider, Commander," eleven years
Peirce, Bartholemew, 25 April 1681, age 14, Mr. Grice, "imported in
    the John, Thomas Graves, Commander"
Pell, Mary, 24 February 1685, age 14, Joseph Ring, "imported in the
    Augustine"
Pendonas, Christopher, 24 January 1676, age 14, Richard Trotter,
    "imported in the Prince, Capt. Robert Conoway, Commander,"
    ten years
Pennington, Edward, 24 January 1679, age 14, Nathaniell Bacon, Esq.,
    "imported in the Planters Adventure, Capt. Robert Ranson
    Commander," ten years
Perkins, John, 31 October 1661, age 16, Capt. Robert Baldry, five years
Perrie, John, 24 June 1673, age 15, Richard Barnes, "imported in the
    Hercules, Capt. Henry Crooke, Commander," nine years
Phillipp, Thomas, 24 March 1679, age 15, James Gibson, "came in ye
    Henry & Anne"
Pinchbancke, Thomas, 26 February 1672, age 18, William Aylett,
    "imported in the Industry," six years
Poole, Richard, 24 January 1681, age 12, Coll. John Page, "came in the
    Planters Adventure"
Powell, John, 24 March 1671, age 16, John Price, "imported in the
    Isaac & Benjamin"
Pratt, Thomas, 24 March 1679, age 15, Anthony Seabrell, "came in the
    Constant"
Preston, George, 25 September 1693, age 15, Samuell Eborne, "imported
    in the shipp, Edward and Francis, Capt. Thomas Mann,
    commander"
Prichat, James, 20 December 1675, age not judged, Thomas (torn),
    "imported in the Concord, Capt. Thomas Grantham, Commander"
Prior, David, 24 April 1661, age 13, Capt. Daniel Parke, eight years
Ramsey, Charles, 20 February 1678, age 14, William Hewett, "imported in
    the Henry & Anne, Capt. Thomas Arnold, Commander," ten years

Rattmill, Thomas, 20 February 1678, age 16, John Echo, "imported in
the Henry & Anne, Capt. Thomas Arnold, Commander,"
eight years

Rayley, Cornelious, 24 August 1693, age 17, John Doswell, "imported into
this Collony in the ship, Edward & Francis, Capt. Thomas Man,
commander"

Read, Richard, April 1665, age 12, Edward Lockey, "imported this
shipping in the Elizabeth & Mary, Capt. Richard Hobbs,
Commander, to serve until age 25," thirteen years

Reade, Anthony, 24 October 1661, age 13, Capt. Ralph Langley,
eight years

Reade, James, 24 July 1667, age 16, James Besouth, (eight years)

Reade, John, 24 April 1671, age 17, George Poindexter

Reade, John, 24 January 1676, age 16, Nathaniell Bacon, Esq., "imported
in the Planters Adventure, Capt. Ellis Ells, Commander,"
eight years

Rennalls, Thomas, 24 February 1685, age 11, John Keen, "imported
in the Augustine"

Richardson, William, 24 January 1667, age 10, Capt. Christopher
Wormeley

Ridgeway, William, 24 May 1660, age 14, William Crump, (seven years)

Roach, Thomas, 24 August 1693, age 14, Samuell Eborne, "imported into
this Collony in the ship, Edward & Francis, Capt. Thomas Man,
commander"

Roberts, Geekin (?), 5 January 1682, age 12, Capt. James Archer,
"imported in ye Constant Mary, Capt. Edward Rhodes,
Commander"

Roberts, John, 5 January 1682, age 16, Thomas Mountfort, "imported in
ye Constant Mary, Capt. Edward Rhodes, Commander"

Robertson, Simon, 25 January 1669, age 15, Thomas Dennett, (nine years)

Rogers, Ralph, 24 March 1670, age 15, Michaell Roe

Rogers (or Royers), William, 24 January 1676, age 15, John Duke,
"imported in the Concord, Capt. Thomas Grantham,
Commander," nine years

Roiley, Charles, 24 May 1667, age 12, Lt. Col. Thomas Beale, Esq.,
(twelve years)

Ruecastle, Henry, 10 November 1670, age 18, Mrs. Elizabeth Lockey,
"imported by Capt. Eveling"

Salt, Daniel, 20 December 1669, age 18, John Duke

Sander, Edward, 10 March 1669, age 16, John Whysken, eight years

Savoy, John, 24 February 1679, age 10, Capt. John Tiplady, imported
    "in the Augustin, Capt. Zach. Taylor, Commander,"
    fourteen years
Scott, Thomas, 25 July 1670, age 19, Paul Johnson
Seaton (or Deaton), Benjamin, 10 April 1668, age 13, master not named,
    "imported this shipping in the Happy Entrance, Capt. Robert
    Clems, Commander," eleven years
Sexton, George, 20 December 1669, age 16, Michael Bartlett
Sexton, John, 24 May 1667, age 14, John Mathews, "imported in the
    Charles," ten years
Shawe, Paul, 10 January 1671, age 17, John Parsons, "imported in the
    Daniell"
Shee, Edward, 10 March 1669, age 9, James Elcocke, "ordered to serve
    until 21, being a native"
Sheeham, Cornelius, 24 August 1693, age 17, Francis Read, "imported into
    this Collony in the ship, Edward & Francis, Capt. Thomas Man,
    commander"
Shephard, Elizabeth, 24 February 1679, age 16, Thomas Reynolds,
    "imported in the Friends Encrease, Hilson, Commander,"
    eight years
Shepherd, Benjamin, 20 December 1660, age 14, Michael Bartlett
Shepherd, Richard, 24 April 1662, age 16, Mathew Hubberd, (five years)
Shepherd, Thomas, 20 December 1675, age not judged, Thomas (torn),
    "imported in the Concord, Capt. Thomas Grantham, Commander"
Shepherd, William, 24 January 1676, age 15, Nicholas Seabrell, "imported
    in the Planters Adventure, Ellis Ells, Commander," nine years
Shoare, John, 25 January 1679, age 16, Mrs. Elizabeth Major, "imported
    in the Henry & Anne, Capt. Thomas Arnall, Commander,"
    eight years
Shoare, Thomas, 24 August 1665, age not judged, Henry Tiler, "petitioning
    for his freedom, it appears he has no indenture"
Shudell, Binoni, 12 December 1678, age 16, Edward Holiett, "imported
    in the Planters Adventure, Capt. Robert Ranson, Commander,"
    eight years
Simbarb, Penelope, 12 April 1669, age 16, John Babb
Simpson, George, 24 January 1660, age 11, Thomas Heynes, ten years
Simson, Mary, 24 February 1680, age 12, Robert Handy, "coming in
    the Augustin"
Skidmore, William, 24 May 1667, age 11, Lt. Col. Thomas Beale, Esq.,
    (thirteen years)

Smith, John, 24 March 1670, age 15, Col. Thomas Beale, "imported in
the Loyall Berkeley"
Smith, John, 24 February 1679, age 13, Nathaniell Hunt, "imported in
the Planters Adventure, Capt. Robert Ranson, Commander,"
eleven years
Smith, Thomas, 24 January 1667, age 18, Capt. Christopher Wormeley
Smith, Thomas, 24 February 1680, age 17, Martin Gardner, "coming in
Planters Adventure"
Smyth, John, 24 June 1673, age 16, Elizabeth Petters, "imported in the
Rebecca, Capt. Christopher Evoling, Commander," eight years
Snellicke, William, 24 June 1668, age 13, Bartholomew Ennolls, "imported
in the John & Mary," eleven years
Snow, Richard, 20 February 1678, age 17, Capt. Otho Thorpe, "imported
in the Augustine," Capt. Zach. Taylor, Commander, seven years
Spally, Charles, 10 September 1659, age 13, Mary Hicks, Widow,
eight years
Spencer, William, 10 March 1669, age 16, Capt. John Underhill,
eight years
Spinler, William, 24 February 1679, age 18, Armiger Wade, "imported in
the Concord, Capt. Thomas Grantham, Commander," six years
Standelly, Jone, 20 December 1675, age not judged, Thomas (torn),
"imported in the Concord, Capt. Thomas Grantham, Commander"
Stanmas, Robert, 24 May 1667, age 14, Lt. Col. Thomas Beale, Esq.,
(ten years)
Steare, Hugh, 1 March 1676, age 17, George Poindexter, "imported in the
Planters Adventure," seven years
Stevens, Henry, 26 February 1672, age ___ , Capt. Josias Picks, "imported
in the Mary," "to serve till 24"
Stewart, Grace, 25 January 1669, age 14, Edward Green, (ten years)
Stewart, John, 24 January 1676, age 16, Capt. Otho Thorpe, "imported in
the Planters Adventure, Ellis Ells, Commander," eight years
Stiles, George, 24 June 1673, age 13, John Lole, "imported in the Hercules,
Capt. Henry Crooke, Commander," eleven years
Stiles, William, 10 April 1667, age 15, John Whisken, (nine years)
Stokes, John, 25 January 1669, age 15, Mrs. Mary Miller, (nine years)
Stratton, Benjamin, 10 January 1671, age 17, William Townsend,
"imported (by) Capt. Groome"
Sturdy, Sarah, 1 March 1676, age 14, Edward Mosse, "imported in the
Friendship Express, Capt. John Martin, Commander," ten years
Sudland, Thomas, 20 December 1669, age 12, Armiger Wade

Taylor, Thomas, 24 January 1681, age 12, William Taylor, "came in
the Prince"

Taylor, Thomas, 24 August 1693, age 14, Robert Merrefeild, "imported
into this Collony in the ship, Edward & Francis, Capt. Thomas
Man, commander"

Thacher, Ann, 24 March 1682, age 12, Thomas Gateman, "imported in
ye Diamond"

Thomas, Mary, 24 January 1676, age 16, William Wise, "imported in
the Concord, Capt. Thomas Grantham, Commander," eight years

Thomas, Mary, 24 March 1682, age 11, Richard Moore, "imported in
ye Diamond," "ordered to serve from ye Ships first arrival"

Thompson, Thomas, 24 June 1679, age 16, Coll. Parker's estate, "comeing
in March last in the Leonard & James in Rappahannock River"

Tickeray, Jonathan, 1 March 1676, age 16, George Poindexter, "imported
in the Planters Adventure," eight years

Tippetts, Thomas, 24 June 1679, age 14, Coll. Parker's estate, "comeing in
March last in the Leonard & James in Rappahannock River"

Tompson, Daniel, 24 April 1671, age 17, Armiger Wade, Jr.

Tompson, John, 26 June 1671, age 16, Henry Lee, "imported in
the Martha"

Tong (?), Edward, 24 March 1699, age 12, Charles Howlsworth

Townshend, Joane, 24 January 1660, age 15, Auguston Hodges, (six years)

Trabread, John, 26 November 1674, age 15, William Davis, "imported
in the Barnaby, Capt. Rider, Commander," nine years

Trikes (?), _____, 24 July 1667, age 16, James Besouth, eight years

Tucker, John, 10 November 1670, age 17, John Page, "imported in the
Pelicaine"

Turner, Phillis, 24 January 1681, age 14, Humphry Browning, "came in
the Barneby"

Vaughan, John, 25 January 1675, age 16, Anne Dennett, "imported in
the George, Capt. Thomas Grantham, Commander," eight years

Wade, George, 24 January 1679, age 12, Capt. Otho Thorp, "imported in
the Planters Adventure, Capt. Robert Ranson, Commander,"
twelve years

Ward, Thomas, 24 January 1676, age 18, John Smith, "imported in the
Concord, Capt. Thomas Grantham, Commander," six years

Ware, John, 24 March 1679, age 11, Richard Wood, came "in the
Golden Fortune"

YORK COUNTY

Warner, Robert, 24 September 1696, age 10, Thomas Pinchbeck,
    "imported in the ship, Goulden Lyon, Capt. Ransom, commander"
Warren, Henry, 24 January 1662, age 13, Robert Chandler, eight years
Washbrooke, Thomas, 24 March 1675, age 19, David Crafford, "imported
    in the Richard & John, Thomas Arnall, Commander," five years
Waters, Robert, 14 January 1678, age 14, Mathew Edwards, "imported in
    the Concord, Capt. Thomas Grantham, Commander," ten years
Watkins, Edward, 24 February 1681, age 13, Mrs. Major, "imported in
    the Prince"
Watkins, Henry, 12 November 1669, age 15, Matthew Collins
Weakes, Richard, 24 January 1679, age 13, George Poindexter, "imported
    in the Planters Adventure, Capt. Robert Ranson, Commander,"
    eleven years
Webb, George, 24 January 1660, age 14, John Page, (seven years)
Weldey, George, 25 July 1670, age 14, John Whisken, "imported in the
    Richard & James"
Wells, Robert, 26 April 1680, age 17, James Calthrope, "came in the
    Howard bound up the Bay"
Westfield, George, 26 February 1672, age 15, John Cotton, "imported in
    the Barnaby," six years
Westly, Samuel, 24 April 1673, age 16, George Poindexter, "imported in
    the Rebecca, Capt. Christopher Evoling, Commander," eight years
Weyte, William, 24 April 1673, age 16, Capt. Thomas Beale, "imported in
    the Rebecca, Capt. Christopher Evoling, Commander," eight years
Whitburne, Edmund, 26 February 1672, age 17, Edmund Petters,
    "imported in the Augustine," seven years
White, Jane, 24 February 1682, age 11, Robert Spring
White, John, 26 January 1680, age 14, John Robinson, "comeing
    this yeare in the Dimond"
White, Margaret, 1 March 1676, age 17, Morris Herd, "imported in the
    Barnaby, Capt. Matthew Rider, Commander," seven years
Whitehead, William, 24 January 1676, age 15, Nicholas Lewis, "imported
    the Barnaby, Capt. Matthew Rider, Commander," nine years
Wilkins, Anne, 24 July 1674, age 16, Capt. William Corker, "imported in
    the Golden Lyon, Capt. Webber, Commander," eight years
Wilkinson, Joshua, 1 December 1671, age 18, Daniell Parke, Esq.
Williams, Samuel, 24 February 1681, age 13, Thomas Cursons, "imported
    in the Augustin"
Williamson, John, 24 June 1668, age 15, Dr. Francis Haddon, "imported
    this shipping in the Duke of York," nine years

222

Willis, William, 24 June 1673, age 13, Daniell Parke, Esq., "imported in
    the Hercules, Capt. Henry Crooke, Commander," eleven years
Wilson, Thomas, 24 April 1678, age 18, John Litler, "imported in the
    Concord, Capt. Thomas Grantham, Commander," six years
Wisome, Katherine, 20 February 1678, age 18, William Weaver, "imported
    in the Friends Encrease, Capt. John Martin, Commander,"
    six years
Witham, Elizabeth, 24 June 1673, age 18, Daniel Wyld, "imported in the
    Prince, Robert Conoway, Commander," six years
Withers, Elizabeth, 24 January 1676, age 12, Daniell Franke, "imported
    in the Concord, Capt. Thomas Grantham, Commander,"
    twelve years
Wood, John, 24 May 1688, age 10, John Parsons, Senr., "imported in the
    shipp Richard, James Backler, commander"
Woolcot, Richard, 24 January 1679, age 17, Theodorus Sumner,
    "imported in the Concord, Capt. Thomas Grantham,
    Commander," seven years
Wright, William, 25 July 1670, age 16, Simon Richardson, "imported in
    the Richard & James"
Yoe, Robert, 10 December 1677, age 11, Mr. Bush, "imported in the
    Friends Encrease, Capt. John Martin, Commander," thirteen years
_____ , Annett, 25 May 1674, age 18, Robert Bee, "imported in the ship
    Francis, Capt. Warner, Commander," six years
_____ , Morris, 24 May 1700, age ___ , Alexander Bonneyman, "imported
    in ye ship, Harridge Prize," Capt. Janson, commander
_____ , _____ , 21 December 1661, age 17, John Berryman

YORK COUNTY

Gentleman Justices	Servants
Archer, James, Capt.	Dolor, Dolor, Roberts
Aylett, William	Dee, Harrison, Pinchbancke
Bacon, Nathaniel, Coll., Esqr.	Bailey, Benafield, Blower, Cooper, Edwards, Matharoon, Moore, Nicholson, Osborne, Pennington, Reade
Baker, William, Coll.	
Baldry (Baldrey), Robert, Capt., Major, Lt. Col.	Abott, Bristow, Croucher, Dunny, O'Neale, Perkins
Ballard, Charles, Capt.	
Ballard, Thomas, Capt., Major, Lt. Col., Esqr.	Huberd
Barbar, Thomas, Capt.	Heyward
Barbar, William, Lt. Coll.	Child, Francis
Beale, Thomas, Capt., Major, Lt. Coll, Esqr.	Andrews, Cooper, Edmunds, Gwillam, Mountain, Roiley, Skidmore, Smith, Stanmas, Weyte
Booth, Robert	
Booth, William	Lane
Bourne, Robert	
Buckner, William, Capt., Major	
Chesley, Phillipp, Capt.	Clarke
Chisman, Edmond, Jr., Capt., Major	Fewell

YORK COUNTY

Gentleman Justices	Servants
Chisman, Thomas	
Clopton, Isaac	Flewen
Cobbs, Robert	
Cole, William, Esq.	
Corker, William, Capt.	Wilkins
Croshaw, Joseph, Major	
Diggs, Dudley	
Diggs, Edward, Esq.	Mansfeild
Diggs, William, Capt.	
Gardiner, Martin	Clinch, Smith
Gooch, Henry, Capt., Lt. Coll.	
Goodwin, James, Major	Greame
Ham, Jerom	
Hansford, Charles, Capt.	
Hansford, John	
Harris, Christopher	
Harwood, Thomas	
Hay, William, Capt.	Ellis
Hubberd, Mathew	Homes, Shepherd
Langley, Ralph, Capt.	Cary, Reade

YORK COUNTY

Gentleman Justices	Servants
Ludlow, Thomas, Lt. Coll.	
Mathews, Baldwin, Capt.	
Mathews, Francis, Capt.	
Mosse, Edward	Abbey, Adam, Levierton, Sturdy
Mountfort, Thomas, Capt.	Beekes, Marshall, Roberts
Nutting, Thomas, Capt.	
Page, Francis, Capt.	Brown, Hall, Holland
Page, John, Major, Coll., Esqr.	Ashby, Davis, Dixon, Gilson, Grant, Haven, Johnson, Lewis, Poole, Tucker, Webb
Parke, Daniell, Capt., Major, Lt. Col., Esqr.	
Petters, Edmund	Whitburne
Pinkethman, William	Ellis, Harding
Reade, George, Coll., Esqr.	Cheston, Macdonah, Oldfield
Reade, Robert	Morrell
Ring, Joseph	Debrason, Pell
Roberts, Thomas	
Samford, John	
Scasbrooke, John, Capt., Major, Lt. Col.	Daniell, Eastes, Howson, Johnson
Smith, Lawrence, Capt.	

YORK COUNTY

Gentleman Justices	Servants
Spring, Robert	White
Taylor, Daniell, Capt.	
Temple, Peter, Capt.	
Thorpe, Otho, Capt.	Casement, Fargeson, Gladmore, Holford, Johnson, Middleton, Snow, Stewart, Wade
Timson, Samuell	
Timson, William, Capt.	
Tyler, Henry	
Underhill, John, Capt.	Barrosome, Farrington, Spencer
Vaulx, James	Bostocke, Herring
Wade, Armiger, Sr.	Browne, Draper, Spinler, Sudland
Whaley, James	
Wild, Samuel	
Wyld, Daniell, Capt.	Blandon, James, Witham

YORK COUNTY

Year	White	Negro	Indian
1658	1	0	0
1659	2	0	0
1660	13	0	0
1661	11	0	0
1662	9	0	0
1663	0	0	0
1664	0	0	0
1665	3	0	1
1666	1	0	0
1667	26	0	0
1668	9	0	0
1669	30	0	0
1670	20	0	0
1671	19	0	0
1672	11	0	1
1673	26	0	0
1674	24	0	0
1675	19	0	1
1676	23	0	0
1677	4	0	0
1678	11	0	0
1679	30	0	0
1680	19	1	0
1681	16	0	0
1682	12	1	3
1683	4	7	1
1684	3	4	0

YORK COUNTY

Year	White	Negro	Indian
1685	2	0	0
1686	2	0	1
1687	0	1	0
1688	2	0	0
1689	3	0	0
1690	0	0	0
1691	4	0	0
1692	1	0	0
1693	8	0	0
1694	0	6	0
1695	0	1	0
1696	1	0	0
1697	0	7	0
1698	1	7	0
1699	2	0	0
1700	9	1	0
1701	3	0	0
1702	0	4	0
1703	0	2	0
1704	0	3	0
1705	0	7	0
1706	1	2	0
1707	0	2	0
1708	0	9	0
1709	0	0	2
1710	0	4	0
Total	385	69	10

CHARLES CITY COUNTY

Allen, Richard, 4 February 1678, age 14, Richard Blank

Bevane, William, 1661, age 14, Cornelius Clemence

Billings, John, 16 June 1677, age 14, John Hardaway

Carver, William, 4 June 1673, age 10, Thomas Blackbird

Cawdricke, William, 5 October 1691, age 16, Edward Grosse

Clarke, John, 4 June 1694, age 13, William Byrd, Esq., "lately arriving in the ship, Byrd," "said servant was sold to him for" nine years

Clift, William, 3 June 1662, age 14, Thomas King, "confesseth in Court that his age is now 14 yeares and that he is to serve the said King seaven yeares from his late arrivall into this Country"

Daniell, John, 14 February 1678, age 14, John Shard

Fayrebrother, Susan, 3 August 1663, age 16, Robert Rowse

Goffe, Richard, 14 September 1677, age not stated, Gilbert Platt

Guillman, George, 16 June 1677, age 13, Capt. Robert Lucy

Harker, Mark, 4 February 1678, age 14, John Pleasants

Hatton, George, 3 June 1678, age 12, James Thwait

Hawkins, Susan, 3 February 1687, age 14, John Baxter

Herring, William, 6 June 1664, age 12, Peter Plummer

Hind, Walter, 2 February 1660, age not judged, Mrs. Hanna Aston, "shall according to the act for Irish servants complete the full terme of six yeares from the time of arriveall"

Johns, William, 4 February 1678, age 14, Lt. Coll. Daniel Clark

Keither, William, 5 December 1683, (age 13), Hon. Edward Hill, Esq., "to serve eleven years," ref. 3 February 1692

Kesler, Thomas, 14 February 1678, age 16, John Laneer

Kittley, John, 4 February 1689, age 13 "on the 10th August last," Thomas Hamlin

Lambert, William, 16 June 1677, age 18, Robert Bolling of Appamatock

Lane, Edd, 3 February 1663, age 14, Walter Brookes

MacCorsey, William, 4 December 1665, age 15, John Hodges

Mathewes, John, 3 October 1665, age 19, Richard Mosby

Mead, William, 3 June 1663, age 15, William Bird

Morris, Richard, 20 April 1663, age 10, Morris Rose

Munpatrick, Owen, 10 November 1665, age 14, Capt. Edward Hill

Peat, John, 3 April 1695, age 11, James Blanks

Pully, William, 3 April 1673, age 12, Robert Short

Risher, William, 3 February 1680, age 13, Edward Bland

Snudge, John, 17 February 1679, age 11, Henry Blanks

South, Francis, 3 August 1677, "neere" age 12, John Short, sold to him by
"John Nickleman belonging to the Ship Rebecca"
Still, William, 20 April 1663, age 16, Francis Redford
Sumers, John, 3 June 1678, age 18, Mrs. Elizabeth Tatum
Taylor, William, 4 February 1678, age 17, John Joan
Underwood, Abraham, 3 August 1677, age 13, Thomas Gregory,
"sold to him for nine years" by Thomas Short
Vandevan, John, 17 February 1679, age 11, Peter Reed
Wallbank, Edd, 20 April 1663, age 16, Humphrey Allen
Ward, John, 20 April 1663, age 13 "at his arrivall about three months
since," Mohone Obryon
Wesson, Mary, 17 February 1679, age not judged, Coll. Daniel Clarke,
"her indenture is invalid and she to serve five years"
Williams, David, 6 June 1664, age 14 "the last Christmas,"
Sylvanus Stokes
Wright, Jeremy, 3 February 1687, age 13, John _____ , "he owne himself
in court to be 13 years old," "alledging that he hath an indenture"

CHARLES CITY COUNTY

Gentleman Justices	Servants
Batte, Henry, Capt.	
Bird / Byrd, William, Esq. *	Clarke, Mead
Bisse, James, Capt.	
Bland, Richard	
Bland, Theoderick, Esqr.	
Blayton, Thomas	
Bolling, Robert	Lambert
Braine, Edward	
Clarke, Daniel, Lt. Coll.	Johns, Wesson
Drayton, John, Sr.	
Drew, Thomas, Lt. Coll.	
Duke, William	
Epes, John, Capt., Coll.	
Epes, Thomas	
Goodrich, Charles, Capt.	
Grendon, Thomas, Lt. Coll.	
Grey, Francis, Capt.	
Hamlin, John, Capt.	
Hamlin, Stephen	
Hill, Edward, Capt., Major, Coll.	Kiether, Munpatrick
Holmwood, John	
Lewellin, Daniel, Capt.	
Mallory, Thomas, Capt.	
Perry, Peter, Capt.	
Poythress, Francis, Capt.	
Southcott, Otho, Capt.	
Stith, John, Major	
Taylor, John, Capt.	
Wyatt, Anthony	
Wyatt, Nicholas, Capt.	
Wynne, Robert, Capt., Coll.	

* See Henrico County

231

CHARLES CITY COUNTY

Year	White	Negro	Indian
1658	0	0	0
1659	0	0	0
1660	1	0	0
1661	1	0	0
1662	1	0	0
1663	7	0	0
1664	2	0	0
1665	3	0	0
1673	2	0	0
1677	6	0	0
1678	8	0	3
1679	3	0	0
1680	1	0	0

CHARLES CITY COUNTY

Year	White	Negro	Indian
1683	1	0	0
1687	2	0	0
1688	0	1	2
1689	1	3	1
1690	0	0	2
1691	1	0	5
1692	0	0	9
1693	0	0	5
1694	1	0	9
1695	1	0	0
Total	42	4	36

HENRICO COUNTY

Alderson, James, 18 December 1685, age 16, Thomas Osborn Senr.
Anderson, Robert, 2 October 1699, age 13, Phillip Tancock
Armitage, James, 1 May 1708, age 17, William Byrd Esqr.,
    by Richard Grills
Bran, Abraham, 1 February 1684, age 13, John Cox Junr.
Brown, Richard, 1 April 1685, age 11, William Clark
Bull, James, 1 October 1690, age 13, Samuell Trottman
Carter, William, 1 April 1695, age 11, Edward Haskins
Darlow, James, 1 April 1684, age 10, Edward Osborn
Datridge, Nicholas, 1 February 1699, age 10, John Farloe
Deall, Richard, 1 February 1700, age 15, Benjamin Lockett
Farrell, Thomas, 1 February 1701, age 18, Thomas Branch
Ferryman, John, 6 December 1699, age 10, Thomas Osborne
Fletcher, Richard, 1 April 1687, age 11, James Hill
Griffin, Will, 2 June 1684, age 13, Thomas Jones
Grigg, James, 2 October 1699, age 17, Phillip Tancock
Hodge, Samuell, 1 April 1686, age 11, Richard Peirce, by Thomas Atkins
Hopkins, Benjamin, 1 August 1698, age 10, James Eatin (?) Senr.
Hory, Samuel, 18 December 1685, age 17, Robert Povall
Jening, Anne, 1 June 1698, age 13, Peter Ashbrook
Jordon, John, 17 July 1683, age 13, William Byrd Esqr.
Kasson, James, 2 October 1699, age 12, Samuell Goode (?)
Kennagen, James, 6 August 1699, age 12, Thomas Chamberlaine
Ma(?)ellus, Charles, 1 February 1699, age 8, Henry Jordan
Mackelen, Hector, 2 October 1699, age 16, James Ecker (?) Junr.
Martin, James, 12 July 1699, age 10, Bartholomew Stovall
Miller, James, 6 August 1699, age 10, Thomas Chamberlaine
Pattison, John, 2 October 1699, age 16, John Steward Junr.
Pearson (?), John, 12 July 1699, age 11, John Howard (?) Glover
Poke (?), Robert, 6 August 1699, age 15, Daniell Steward
Pratt, Elizabeth, 1 April 1686, age 9, Mrs. Anne Morris, by
      William Walthall
Prichard, Joshua, 18 December 1685, age 13, Mrs. Anne Morris
Pursell, Philip, 1 August 1684, age 13, Mrs. Mary Davis
Ray, John, 2 October 1699, age 12, Seth Ward
Reynolds, Robert, 1 April 1687, age 11, James Babicom
Roberts, Margarett, 2 August 1697, age 18, Edward Haskins
Robinson, William, 6 August 1699, age 12, John Furloe
Savis, James, 1 April 1684, age 11, Mathew Turpin

Smithers, Henry, 18 December 1685, age 17, Mrs. Martha Shippy
Watt (?), William, 1 February 1699, age 15, _____ Perkins
Woodrum, John, 2 August 1697, age 14, (torn) il Childers (?)
(?) oyle (torn), Edward, 2 August 1697, age 14, Capt. William Randolph
_____ , William, 1 June 1687, age 11, Samuell _____

Gentleman Justices	Servants
Batte, Thomas	
Bolling, John	
Byrd, William, Coll., Esqr. *	Armitage, Jordon
Cocke, Richard, Senr.	
Cocke, Thomas, Junr., Capt.	
Cocke, Thomas, Senr.	
Epes, Francis, Capt.	
Farrar, John, Lt. Coll.	
Farrar, William, Capt.	
Field, Peter, Capt., Coll.	
Glover, William	
Gower, Abell	
Jefferson, Thomas	
Kennon, Richard	
Randolph, William, Capt.	(?) oyle
Royall, Joseph, Capt.	
Sallé, Abraham	
Webb, Giles, Capt.	
Worsham, George	
Worsham, John	

* See Charles City County

234

HENRICO COUNTY				HENRICO COUNTY			
Year	White	Negro	Indian	Year	White	Negro	Indian
1683	1	0	30	1695	1	0	2
1684	5	1	9	1696	0	0	1
1685	5	0	0	1697	3	0	4
1686	2	1	2	1698	2	0	5
1687	3	6	2	1699	16	1	7
1688	0	0	1	1700	1	0	3
1689	0	3	0	1701	1	0	0
1690	1	1	1				
1691	0	1	2	1707	0	0	0
1692	0	0	1	1708	1	0	1
1693	0	0	0	1709	0	0	0
				Total	42	14	71

Note: The average adjudged age of the thirty-nine Indian children brought before the Gentleman Justices of Henrico County in 1683 and 1684 was ten years old. Twenty-six were boys, and thirteen were girls.

235

Adcock, Elizabeth, 5 May 1685, age 12, Thomas Blunt, "who came into
    this Country in the Brothers Adventure, Henry Trigany, Master,
    the beginning of November last"
Alsop, Durant, 4 March 1673, age 15, Francis Sumner, "came into ye
    Country sixteenth of December last"
Aspell, Martin, 7 May 1700, age 12, William Chambers, "who came
    into this Countrey this present yeare in the Ship, Oliver,
    James Atchison, Master"
Atwood, John, 3 January 1682, age 12, John Moring, "who came into this
    Country in Capt. John Bradlys Ship"
Bently, William, 4 March 1684, age 14, Thomas Clarke, "who came into
    this Collony in Capt. Bradlys Shipp"
Boken, James, 3 November 1674, age 16, Benjamin Harrison
Browne, Andrew, 1 May 1677, age 16, John Barnes
Car (Carr), Thomas, 6 July 1675, age 16, Arther Allen
Cary, John, 6 July 1675, age 16, Robert Caufeild
Co(?)vey, Charles, 1 September 1674, age 14, John Goreing
Cox, John, 4 September 1699, age 16, Thomas Bage, "who came into
    this Countrey this present yeare in the Ship, Anne and Mary,
    Richard Tibbetts, Master"
Cripps, William, 17 May 1692, age 13, William Brown, "who came into
    this Country this present shipping"
Dowell, William, 4 May 1695, age 12, John Hancock, "who came into this
    Colony this present shipping in the Ship, Hampshire"
Dunne, Charles, 3 May 1698, age 18, Richard Washington
Dunne, Morris, 3 May 1698, age 13, Mary Carpenter
Effell or Essell, 6 January 1685, age 14, William Handcock, "who came
    into this Collony on Capt. William Ortons Shipp"
Fitz Patrick, Richard, 3 May 1698, age 18, Robert Nicholson
Futerell, Thomas, 16 November 1677, age 18, Robert Ruffin
Gaton, Thomas, 7 September 1680, age 12, Coll. Thomas Swann,
    "who came in the last Shipping"
Greene, John, 4 May 1675, age 18, Capt. William Corker
Greene, William, 3 May 1681, age 13, Thomas Clarke, "who came in
    in Capt. Bartholomew Clements his Shipp"
Hennisey (?), Martin, 7 May 1700, age 14, Major Arthur Allen, "who
    came into this Countrey this present yeare in the Ship, Oliver,
    James Achison, Master"
Hevell, Gabriell, 1 May 1677, age 16, Richard Drew

SURRY COUNTY

Hooper, George, 2 July 1700, age 11, Walter Cocke, "who came into the
    Countrey this present yeare in the Shipp, Hope, Abraham Carter,
    Master"
Horsnell, James, 6 May 1679, age 17, Capt. Lawrence Baker
Hugg, Ellinor, 7 July 1674, age 12, Nicholas Merriwether
Jackson, Thomas, 6 July 1680, age 17, William Edwards
Killingsworth, William, 6 July 1675, age 17, Mrs. Mary Sidway
Kitchen, John, 4 May 1695, age 10, John Clements, "who came into this
    Colony this present shipping in the Ship, Hampshire"
Kite, Thomas, 4 July 1676, age 14, Lt. Thomas Busby
Line, Edward, 17 May 1692, age 16, Edward Moreland, "who arrived in
    this Colony in a Bristoll Ship, Capt. William Jones, Commander"
Manwaring, Henry, 9 November 1703, age 12, Thomas Jarrell, "who came
    into this Countrey this present yeare in the shipp, Elizabeth and
    Mary, Thomas Stringer, Master"
Martin, Peter, 7 May 1700, age 9, Edward Morland, "who came into this
    Countrey this present yeare in the Shipp, Anne and Mary,
    Richard Tibbetts, Master"
Morgan, John, 2 July 1678, age 15, William Hancock, "who came in
    Capt. Larimores shipp"
Owen, John, 3 May 1681, age 10, William Edwards, "who came in
    in Capt. Thomas Graves his shipp"
Penny, John, 2 May 1704, age 10, William Williams, "who came into this
    Countrey this present yeare in the ship Katharine of Newe Haven"
Poore, William, 3 May 1698, age 10, Charles Briggs
Porter, Edward, 4 May 1697, age 12, John Holt, "who came into this
    Colony this present shipping in the Ship, Elizabeth & Mary,
    Frederick Johnson, Commander"
Rantok (?), John, 4 July 1704, age 14, Jeremiah Ellis, "who came into this
    Countrey in June last in the ship Katharine of Newe Haven"
Reynolds, Henry, 28 March 1676, age 15, James Redduck
Rouwell (?), 1 May 1677, age not judged, Samuell Cornell, six years
Simpson, John, 4 July 1704, age 12, Robert Lancaster, "who came into this
    Countrey in June last in the Katharine of Newe Haven"
Smith, William, 7 May 1700, age 16, Thomas Jarrell, Junr., "who came
    into this Countrey this present yeare in the Ship, Parg and Lane,
    James Morgan, Master"
Temple, William, 2 May 1676, age 14, Nicholas Meriwether

Timmes, Amos, 3 October 1699, age 13, Capt. Henry Tooker, "who came into the Country this last shipping in the Shippe, Anne and Mary, Richard Tibbetts, Master"

Veers, John, 6 January 1685, age 11, Major Arthur Allen

Wilbanke, Edward, 7 May 1672, adjudged age 13 by "order from Westofer Court" dated 20 April 1663, servant to Arthur Allen, inherited from Humphra Allen, arrived "ye first of November 1662"

Woodward, Ann, 3 March 1685, age 15, Thomas Busby, "who came into this Country in the John & William, Capt. Dell, Master"

SURRY COUNTY

Gentleman Justices	Servants
Allen, Arthur, Major	Carr, Hennisey, Veers, Wilbanke
Allen, John, Major	
Baker, Lawrence, Capt.	Horsnell
Barham, Charles, Capt.	
Browne, William, Capt.,	Cripps
Major, Lt. Coll.	
Caufeild, Robert, Major	Cary
Clements, Fra., Capt.	
Cocke, William	
Drew, Thomas	
Edwards, John	
Edwards, William	Jackson, Owen
Flood, Walter	
Harrison, Benjamin	Boken
Harrison, Henry	
Harrison, Nathaniell, Capt., Major	
Holt, Rand.	
Holt, Thomas, Capt.	
Jackman, Joseph John	
Jordan, George, Lt. Coll.	
Malden, Joseph	
Mason, Frank	
Mason, James	
Meriwether, Nicholas	Hugg, Temple
Newsom, William	
Nickells, John	
Randall, Robert, Capt.	
Ruffin, Robert	Futerell
Simmons, John	
Spensor, Robert, Capt.	
Swann, Samuell, Capt., Major	
Swann, Thomas, Capt.,	Gaton
Coll., Esqr.	
Taylor, Etheldred	
Thompson, John	
Thompson, Samuel	
Tooker, Henry, Capt.	Timmes

SURRY COUNTY					SURRY COUNTY			
Year	White	Negro	Indian		Year	White	Negro	Indian
1672	1	0	0		1693	0	0	0
1673	1	0	0		1694	0	0	0
1674	3	0	0		1695	2	0	0
1675	4	0	0		1696	0	0	2
1676	3	0	0		1697	1	0	0
1677	4	0	0		1698	4	0	0
1678	1	0	0		1699	2	0	0
1679	1	0	0		1700	5	1	0
1680	2	0	0		1701	0	0	0
1681	2	0	0		1702	0	0	0
1682	1	0	0		1703	1	0	0
1683	0	2	1		1704	3	0	0
1684	1	3	2		1705	0	0	0
1685	4	3	1		1706	0	4	0
1686	0	2	0		1707	0	9	1
1687	0	1	0		1708	0	5	1
1688	0	0	0		1709	0	0	0
1689	0	0	0		1710	0	2	0
1690	0	0	0		1711	0	0	2
1691	0	0	0		1712	0	0	1
1692	2	0	0		Total	48	32	11

ISLE OF WIGHT COUNTY (FRAGMENT)

<u>Gentleman Justices</u>   <u>Servants</u>

Applewhaite, Henry, Capt.
Baker, Henry
Benn, James, Capt.
Bridger, Samuel, Capt., Lt. Coll.
Day, James
Exum, Jer.
Giles, Thomas
Goodrich, John, Capt.
Holladay, Anthony
Moor, George
Smith, Arthur, Colo.

ISLE OF WIGHT COUNTY

Year	White	Negro	Indian
1693	0	0	1
1694	0	5	2
1695	0	0	0
Total	0	5	3

NORFOLK COUNTY

Abiram, Nathan, 16 March 1685, age 10, Henry Holstead's Estate
Aherion (?), Daniel, 17 February 1673, age 15, Morris Fisgarrall
Alhollir (?), Isaac, 17 April 1677, age 13, George Wakefield
Anderson, John, 17 June 1684, age 14, William Basnett Senr. (?)
Anderson, Thomas, 17 June 1678, age 13, James Write
Andrew, Frances, 18 April 1677, age 17, Jacob Johnson
Atkinson (?), William, 29 November 1686, age 15, Thomas Wilson
Barkley, William, 15 June 1674, age 16, Jacob Johnson
Barnard, Henry, 16 June 1675, age 16, Adam Keeling
Bartholomew, Richard, 18 April 1677, age 18, Adam Keeling
Biggins, John, 20 May 1679, age 13, George Minihen
Booth (?), Thomas, 16 May 1685, age 14, Major Francis Sayer
Bridger, Laurance, 17 April 1677, age 17, Mrs. Sarah Pigott
Brooks, Robert, 1 April 1669, age 16, Robert Hodge
Browne, Benjamin, 15 April 1664, age 13, Henry Holstead
Browne, John, 15 April 1672, age 16, William Robinson
Browne, Thomas, 2 June 1680, age 13, Henry Woodhouse
Burch (?), Richard, 15 June 1674, age 15, Henry Spratt
Burton, William, 15 June 1677, age 15, James Kemp
Cannady, John, 17 March 1679, age 17, William Whitehurst
Carny, Jone, 1 April 1669, age 16, William Greene
Carr, John, 17 April 1677, age 16, Henry Weedick (?)
Carrett, Edmond, 17 March 1679, age 17, Bartholomew Williams
Chamberlaine, John, 15 October 1668, age 10, Captain Carver
Chappell, Burrell, 18 April 1677, age 17, Patrick White
Cobb, Martin, 18 April 1677, age 16, David Whitford
Conney, Jane, 17 April 1677, age 16, William Handcock
Cooke, William, 15 June 1664, age 15, Roger Fountayne
Cooper, Ellinor, 15 February 1676, age 14, Thomas Anwell (?)
Cooper, Thomas, 15 December 1675, age 14, Henry Holstead
Coslett, William, 16 April 1673, age 11, Plumer (?) Bray, "hee bought the
        boy for the tearm of tenn yeares"
Coss, John, 17 June 1678, age 12, William Moss
Cox, Richard, 17 April 1677, age 18, Thorowgood Keeling
Cummings, Thomas, 18 April 1677, age 16, Henry Spratt
Daley, Mary, 15 May 1688, age 13, William Cornick
Dooly, Fenton, 15 May 1688, age 9, Francis Simpson
Dougell, George, 15 May 1688, age 15, Richard (illegible)
Dunbar, John, 17 March 1679, age 14, Richard Whitehurst

Eylif, Thomas, 15 December 1675, age 17, Malachy Thruston
Fisgarrall, James, 17 February 1673, age 17, Mrs. Sarah Willoughby
Foolford, John, 15 March 1681, age 16, James Wilson
Franckling, Thomas, 17 March 1679, age 15, Richard Berry
Fullerton, Samuell, 17 March 1679, age 17, Henry Woodhouse
Gibley (?), John, 18 January 1676, age 10, Christopher Browne
Gibson, Elizabeth, 2 June 1680, age 18, Lt. Coll. Robert Gray
Gilbert, Henry, 17 April 1677, age 16, Thomas Godby
Graham, John, 6 March 1678, age 17, Mathew Godfree
Grant, William, 15 October 1679, "nott eighteene yeare old," John
      Woodhouse, "bought him for six years," "to begin ye 15th
      of June last and noe longer"
Griffin, William, 15 April 1672, age 17, George Athall
Holmes, Tymothy, 17 August 1668, age 15, William Andrewes
Homan, William, 1 June 1686, age 13, Thomas Carding (?)
James, Christian, 17 March 1679, age 15, Richard Church
Joanes, William, 16 January 1694, age 15, Matthew Godfree
Jones, David, 16 May 1683, age 15, Thomas Hodgis
Kelly, John, 17 February 1679, age 17, James Kempe
Kelly, John, 15 May 1688, age 13, John Sandford, who bought him
      for seven year "and noe longer" from "the arrival of ye ship
      Providence, being 15th September last, Capt. Andrew Beale (?),
      master"
Knight, Jane, 16 May 1684, age illegible, Lewes Conner Jr.
Lenton, William, 18 April 1677, age 15, Gilbert Lewis
Mason, Thomas, 15 February 1669, age 12, William Handcock
Mecoy, John, 17 March 1679, age 14, Henry Woodhouse
Miller, James, 17 April 1677, age 14, Thomas Holloway
Morden, William, 15 February 1672, age 16, Thomas Bridge
Nicholson, John, 15 August 1679, age 15, Alexander Foreman
Paine, Richard, 15 February 1667, age 13, William Carter
Parson, Richard, 1 April 1669, age 16, George Minchon
Peace, John, 15 February 1675, age 17, William Whitehorse
Piper, William, 15 January 1679, age not judged, Lt. Coll. Adam
      Thorowgood, "alleageth that notwithstanding hee came into this
      Country without Indenture hee was sould by Mr. Henry Gee butt
      for foure yeares"
Pirkings, John, 15 March 1692, age 14, Thomas Tabor
Portluck, John, 18 January 1676, age 18, Marmaduck Marrington

NORFOLK COUNTY

Pritchett, William, 17 August 1674, age 14, George Martin
Rastrick (?), William, 17 April 1677, age 15, William Kelly
Riding, Joseph, 15 June 1674, age 15, William Gouldsmith
Rogers, John, 15 May 1688, age 13, George Smith
Sherwood, Robert, 15 February 1681, age 15, Lewes Conner
Smith, Thomas, 22 November 1677, age 15, John Godfree
Smith, William, 17 June 1667, age 16, Nicholas Robinson
Strong, Edmond, 15 March 1670, age 15, Henry Woodhouse
Watts, Thomas, 15 February 1667, age 16, William Goldsmith
Wells, John, 16 June 1691, age 15, James Peeters
Whitehead (?), Samuell, 16 November 1685, age 12, William Kelly,
      "but Mr. John Guilford (?) who brought him into the Country
      affirming that he sold him butt for seven yeares and noe longer"
Whitlock, Thomas, 18 January 1676, age 12, Robert Rose
Williams, Mary, 15 August 1674, age 15, Malachy Thruston, "her arrivall
      into ye Country being ye 15th Aprill last"
Woodford (?), Sarah, 17 August 1674, age 19, William Greene
Woolla (?), Barbary, 17 April 1677, age 12, Gomer Bray
Write, James, 18 April 1677, age 15, Robert Carver

NORFOLK COUNTY

Gentleman Justices   **Servants**

Andrews, William   Holmes
Bray, Robert, Capt., Coll.
Brett, Thomas
Browne, Thomas
Burrough, Benony *
Carver, William   Chamberlaine
Church, Richard   James
Cock, Thomas, Capt. *
Cornick / Cornix, William *
Crafford, William, Capt.
Daynes, William
Fouler, George
Fulcher, Thomas
Gray, Robert, Capt., Lt. Coll.   Gibson
Hatton, John, Capt.
Hill, John
Hodgis, Thomas   Jones
Keeling, Adam, Capt.   Bartholomew
Kelley, John
Laurance, John
Lawson, Anthony, Capt., Major, Lt. Coll. *
Martin, John
Mason, Lemuell, Coll.
Moseley, Edward *
Moseley, William, Capt. *
Newton, George
Nichols, John, Capt., Major
Porter, John *
Robinson, William, Capt.   Browne
Sayer, Francis, Major   Booth
Spratt, Henry *   Burch, Cummings
Thorowgood, Adam, Major, Lt. Coll. *   Piper
Thruston, Malachy   Eylif, Williams
Walker, Thomas
White, Patrick   Chappell
Willoughby, Thomas, Lieut. Coll.
Wilson, James   Foolford

* See Princess Anne County

245

NORFOLK COUNTY					NORFOLK COUNTY			
Year	White	Negro	Indian		Year	White	Negro	Indian
1664	2	0	0		1681	2	0	0
1665	0	0	0		1682	0	0	0
1666	0	0	0		1683	1	0	0
1667	3	0	0		1684	2	0	0
1668	2	0	0		1685	3	1	0
1669	4	0	0		1686	2	0	0
1670	1	0	0		1687	0	0	0
1671	0	0	0		1688	5	2	0
1672	3	0	0		1689	0	0	0
1673	3	0	0		1690	0	1	0
1674	6	0	0		1691	1	0	1
1675	4	0	0		1692	1	0	0
1676	4	0	0		1693	0	0	0
1677	18	0	0		1694	1	2	0
1678	3	0	0		1695	0	0	0
1679	12	0	0					
1680	2	0	0		Total	85	6	1

Note: No children without
indentures from 1656-1663

Adams, Henry, 5 July 1699, age 11, William Shipp
Blaire, Dougall, 5 July 1699, age 12, Nathaniell Maclenahan
Bristo, Thomas, 2 September 1696, age __ , Capt. Francis Morse
Caleley, Duncan, 5 July 1699, age 12, John Edmonds
Campbell, Hugh, 5 July 1699, age 13, Roger Williamson
Carragay, Thomas, 5 July 1699, age 18, Henry Woodhouse
Carty, Darby, 4 February 1698, age 13, Capt. Francis Morse
Donald, Darby, 4 February 1698, age 18, Henry Chapman
Dorin, John, 2 December 1697, age 9, Mrs. Alice Thrower
Garmacan, Thomas, 1 December 1697, age 15, Coll. Anthony Lawson
Flahaven, John, 5 July 1699, age 10, William Clowes
Flanagan, Patrick, 2 February 1698, age 19, Capt. Hugh Campbell
Flanagan, William, 2 February 1698, age 14, Edward Moseley
Hinson, Charles, 5 July 1699, age 13, William Cathrill
Johnston, John, 5 May 1702, age 13, Lancaster Lovett
Lee, Bryan, 1 December 1697, age 16, Frances Capps
Mackleroy, Daniell, 5 July 1699, age 13, Henry Fitz Gerald
Maclane, Alexander, 6 September 1699, age 16, Edward Cannon
Magillin, Hugh, 1 December 1697, age 9, Coll. Anthony Lawson
Malaly, Simon, 2 February 1698, age 13, Jonathan Saunders
Mason, Robert, 5 July 1699, age 15, Martha Williamson
Maughas, Edward, 2 February 1698, age 13, Edward Moseley
McFarland, Porland (?), 5 May 1702, age 13, Randolph Lovett
Miller, Andrew, 5 July 1699, age 14, Nathaniell Maclenahan
Peerson, Lanse, 5 July 1699, age 15, Nathaniell Maclenahan
Plunkett, Thomas, 7 July 1697, age 12, Coll. Anthony Lawson
Shugharaugh, Marlagh, 4 May 1699, age 13, John Sherly
Simpson, Robert, 5 July 1699, age 14, Elizabeth Nicolas
Smith, Thomas, 5 July 1699, age 12, John Carraway
Sullivan, Florentius, 4 May 1699, age 16, John Akis
Waterford (?), Robert, 5 May 1702, age 13, Lancaster Lovett
Webster, William, 6 July 1692, age 14, Henry Woodhouse

PRINCESS ANNE COUNTY

Gentleman Justices   Servants

Burrough, Benony *
Chapman, Henry, Capt.   Donald
Clowes, William   Flahaven
Cocke, Thomas, Capt. *
Cornick, John
Cornick, William *
Dauge, James
Emperor, Francis
Hancock, George, Capt.
Jones, Evan
Kemp, James
Lawson, Anthony, Coll. *   Garmacan, Magillin, Plunkett
Lawson, Thomas
Morse, Francis, Capt.   Bristo, Carty
Moseley, Edward, Senr., Coll. *   Flanagan, Maughas
Moseley, John, Capt.
Moseley, William, Junr., Capt. *
Porter, John *
Richason, John
Smyth, William, Capt.
Spratt, Henry, Capt. *
Thorowgood, Adam, Major *
Thorowgood, Argall
Thorowgood, John, Capt.
Thorowgood, Robert
Thurston, Malachy, Capt.
White, Solomon
Woodhouse, Henry   `Carragay, Webster
Woodhouse, Horatio, Capt.

* See Norfolk County

PRINCESS ANNE COUNTY

Year	White	Negro	Indian
1691	0	0	0
1692	1	0	0
1693	0	8	0
1694	0	0	0
1695	0	1	0
1696	1	0	0
1697	5	2	0
1698	6	0	0
1699	16	1	0
1700	0	0	0
1702	3	0	0
1703	0	0	0
1704	0	1	0
1705	0	7	0
1706	0	1	0
1707	0	0	0
1708	0	0 *	0
1709	0	0	0
1710	0	0	0
Total	32	21	0

* one Mulatto

INDEX TO SHIP CAPTAINS

INDEX TO SHIP CAPTAINS

INDEX TO SHIP CAPTAINS

INDEX TO SHIP ARRIVALS

SURNAME INDEX

Cowen	1, 23, 24	Cumpton	89	Delaney	24, 156
Cowman	39	Cundey	193	Dellahay	156
Cox	1, 10, 132,	Cunningham	39, 89, 178	Demery	156
155, 175, 208, 236, 242		Currs	89	Demshey	40
Coy	119	Cursell	1	Denealey	89
Coynia	132	Curtis	89, 155, 156, 208	Denison	11, 89
Cozens	208	Cusack	89	Denney	156
Crabb	24	Cushion, Cussion	132	Dennis	2, 40
Crabtree	10, 132	Custody	24	Denonghow	79
Craig	79, 132	Cutler	11	Dent	40
Crale	155	Cutmore	156	Derritt	89
Crane	132	Cutter	39, 132	Devall	178
Cranny	185	Cutts	11	Devenish	11
Cranston	64	Dagg	24	Deverie	40
Crary	24	Dairon	193	Device	209
Cratte	39	Dale	24, 208	Devin	40, 132
Crawford	1, 10, 24, 89	Daley	24, 40, 67, 156, 242	Devorick	40
Cray	24	Dallison	89	Dew	132
Credency	155	Dalton	132	Dewey	132
Cresswell	193	Danford	208	Dholohundee	79
Crewes	39	Daniel, Daniell		Diamond	24
Cripps	236	79, 119, 208, 229		Dickson	11, 40, 89, 132,
Crissell	39	Daniellson	89	156, 175, 185, 209	
Cristie	39	Danielly	40	Dike	89
Critchly	116	Danilas	24	Dill	193
Croamy	79	Dare	40	Dillon	193
Croft	10	Darlow	233	Dingwell	132
Cromwell	132, 155	Darnell	40, 89	Dining	40
Croner	155	Darner	89	Dinney	132
Croney	64, 155	Dart	24	Disbary	209
Crookshank(s)	39, 119	Dasee	40	Divell	89
Croomes	155	Daton	1	Dixon	11, 119, 156, 209
Crosin	10	Datridge	233	Doak, Doaks	76, 132, 193
Cross	24, 39, 132	Daverill	89	Doane	89
Crosthead	132	Davids	132	Dobin(s)	11, 119
Crotoff	11	Davies	89, 119, 132	Dobson	41, 209
Crottee	89	Davinson	11	Dod, Dods	41, 89
Crouch	89	Davis	2, 11, 24, 40, 67,	Dogon	41
Croucher	208	89, 132, 156, 193, 208, 209		Doherty	41
Crow, Crowe	39, 208	Davison	40	Dollard	79
Crowder	24	Davy	67	Dollins	132
Crowning	39	Dawes	40, 76, 132	Dolor	209
Crowson	193	Dawson		Dolton	90
Cruff	175	24, 40, 115, 156, 209		Donah	90
Crump	39	Day	156, 193	Donahan, Donohan	90
Cubberly	39	Deacon(s)	40, 89, 156, 193	Donald	247
Cuckland	39	Deakers	76	Donegan	41
Cullbrath	193	Deall	233	Donn	41
Cullen	39	Dean, Deane	40, 209	Donnell	80
Cumber	89	Deas	40	Donohue	178
Cumberbeech	89	Debrason	209	Donough	2
Cumberford	185	Dedman	74	Donovan	2, 41, 209
Cummings	242	Dee	209	Donway	41

261

Dooly	242	Dutch	11	Everson	133
Dorin	247	Duxbury	175	Evlyn	157
Dorman	41	Dwane	41	Ewin	76
Dorrell, Dorrill	119, 156	Dwyer	41	Eylif	243
Dougall 24, 119, 133, 242		Dyal, Dyall	90	Eyre	2
Doughty	90	Dye	41	Fagan 119, 133, 186	
Douglas	2	Dyer 11, 133, 156		Faireweather	133
Dounton	119	Dymore	156	Fairfax	11
Dover	90	Dyner	193	Fairland	41
Dowbell	193	Eady	90	Falmouth	119
Dowd	41	Earby	178	Fann	175
Dowdell	41	Earle	114	Fanning	41, 210
Dowdey	41	Ease	11	Fanoe	119
Dowell 2, 133, 209, 236		Eason	90	Farden	64
Dowlar	41	Easter	156	Farlowe	133
Dowley, Dowly 119, 178		Eastes	210	Farmer	91
Dowlin	119, 193	Easton	11	Farnell	193
Dowman	11	Eately	41	Farrar	133
Downes	67, 90	Eaton	41, 90	Farrell	
Doy	119	Edford	210	25, 42, 91, 119, 186, 233	
Doyle	67, 90, 119	Edge	90	Farrington 25, 157, 210	
Doyley	178	Edmonds 116, 133, 156		Farrow	91
Doyne	90	Edmunds	210	Farsy	11
Draper	90, 209	Edney	175	Fartly	116
Drewe	24	Edwards 11, 41, 80, 90,		Faugheigh	133
Dreyden	90	119, 156, 157, 193, 210		Faulkner	91, 210
Driscoll	41	Effell, Essell	236	Fawshyn	157
Drishen	90	Egon	119	Fayrebrother	229
Drummond	41, 80	Eldridge	157	Fearine	11
Druncore	90	Eley	41	Feddiman	91
Duell	11	Elliott 2, 11, 76, 157, 210		Fegett	178
Duerdin	156	Ellis 11, 90, 157, 210		Feild	91
Duff	80	Ellison	90, 175	Feilder	157
Duffee	11	Ellistone	133	Feildin	42
Dullard	209	Elmes	210	Fell	133
Dunahaugh	133	Emas	193	Fellon	80
Duncan	24, 133	Emerson 90, 133, 157		Fencoke	91
Duncombe	119, 133	Emmons	119	Fenley	119
Dunbar, Dunbarr		Engerson	210	Fennell	178
133, 156, 185, 242		England	157	Fenner	91
Dunford	209	English 11, 24, 84, 186		Fenney	157
Dunhahoe	76	Eniburson	90	Fennin	42
Dunn, Dunne 2, 11, 41,		Ennis	90	Fennysin	74
90, 156, 186, 209, 236		Enscoe	175	Fenwick	42
Dunnagon	41	Ensden	157	Ferguson	133, 210
Dunnaha	67	Erwin, Erwyn 24, 133		Fernandez	91
Dunnawan	74	Escreeke	24	Fernell	193
Dunnaway	67	Eure	90	Fernsey	25
Dunnington	90	Eustice	178	Ferridral	157
Dunny	209	Evans 24, 41, 67, 90, 119,		Ferris	119
Duppe	90	133, 175, 178, 186, 210		Ferry	76
Durmick	178	Everatt	41	Ferryman	233
Durrough	133	Everest	157	Fewell	210

Gordon	43, 44, 67, 80, 120, 134, 211	
Gore	134	
Gorfinch	158	
Gorman	43	
Gormory	158	
Gormock	158	
Gosh	92	
Goucher	186	
Goulding	12	
Gouldsberry	43	
Goult	43	
Gourley	179	
Govey	43	
Gower	194	
Grace	158	
Graden	25	
Grady	2	
Graftee	179	
Graham	25, 134, 175, 211, 243	
Graimes, Grames	43	
Grandsworth	92	
Grandy	134	
Granger	158	
Grant	25, 43, 92, 158, 194, 211, 243	
Graves	43, 64, 92, 158, 179	
Gray, Grey	12, 43, 92, 134, 194, 211	
Gredey	179	
Green	43, 92, 134	
Greendell	80	
Greene	12, 67, 92, 120, 134, 158, 211, 236	
Greenleafe	25	
Greenold	12	
Greenway	25, 43	
Gregory	43, 211	
Gresher	158	
Grevine	2	
Greyden	92	
Greyly	25	
Gribble	44	
Gridley	2	
Griffin	44, 120, 134, 158, 175, 179, 194, 211, 233, 243	
Griffith(s)	134, 179, 194	
Grifice	120	
Grigg	233	
Grilles	175	
Grimes	134, 159	
Grominton	44	

Groome	134	
Grosser	92	
Groule	93	
Groves	44, 93	
Grundell	44	
Gryer	93	
Guessne	93	
Guillion	80	
Guillman	229	
Guinn, Gwin, Gwynn	93, 159, 212	
Gunner	93	
Gutridge	93, 159	
Guttone	44	
Guttrey	134	
Guy	120, 159	
Gwillam	212	
Gwyer	134	
Gyles	120	
Hackett	12, 44	
Hadliff	134	
Hadock	12	
Hagar	93	
Hagen	80	
Hainer	12	
Haines	134, 194	
Halerd	93	
Haley	44, 134	
Halfpin	93	
Hall	12, 25, 44, 93, 134, 159, 212	
Halliburton	93	
Hallinak	93	
Hallock	12	
Hallword	212	
Hambleton	44, 120, 159, 186	
Hambye	93	
Hamilton	120, 159	
Hamlin	134	
Hammond	44, 93	
Hampton	12	
Hanbrugg	120	
Hancock	12, 135	
Handling	135	
Hanfred	44	
Hangley	44	
Haning	12	
Hankes	212	
Hannisey	44	
Hansby	159	
Hanson	2, 12, 159, 194	
Hany	135	

Harbey	212	
Harding	159, 212	
Hardy	12, 93, 179	
Hareat	159	
Hargis	12	
Hargrove	212	
Harker	229	
Harley	44	
Harling	212	
Harman	159	
Harmestone	135	
Harney	25	
Harper	2, 93, 120	
Harquedan	44	
Harrard	93	
Harris	12, 44, 93, 120, 135, 159, 175, 194, 212	
Harrison	12, 44, 93, 135, 212	
Harrow	186	
Harrox	135	
Harry	135	
Hart	2, 64, 159	
Hartington	135	
Hartright	159	
Harvey	44, 80, 120, 159	
Harwood	12, 135, 159	
Hasell	179	
Hasleupp	12	
Haslewood	44, 159	
Hastings	25, 80, 93	
Hatherton	93	
Hatton	186, 229	
Haughy	159	
Haven	212	
Hawkins	74, 135, 194, 229	
Hawks	179	
Hawksworth	44	
Hay, Haye, Hey	44, 94, 120, 179	
Hayes, Hays	44, 93, 135, 194, 212	
Hayles	93	
Hayley	120	
Haynes	159	
Haywood	93	
Hazard	44	
Hazlas	135	
Head	159	
Heale	159	
Hearty	135	
Hedge	93	
Hegoe, Hegue	159, 186	

271

274

APPENDIX: JACOBITE REBELS

On 13 March 1722, the Worshippfull Commissioners of Charles County, Maryland rejected a petition by Markam Mackollom, wherein he sets forth

> "that whereas he was taken in ye Rebellion at Preston and Transported into this Province without Indenture & was Sold unto Mr. John Walden of this County to whom he had served the full Term of five years, & that his said Master still Datained him in his Service -- Notwithstanding ye Petitioner was past the age of twenty two years at the Time of his Transportacion, and Praid that he might be Discharged from his said Master according to act of Assembly etc."

Petitions to the same effect and purpose from Daniel Stewart, servant to William Penn, and from John Comorains and James Mackontosh, servants to Henry Hawkins (one of the "Worshippfull Commissioners"), were likewise rejected. Their ages were not adjudged, which left them without a date certain on which they could expect their freedom.

The names of Malcolm McCollum, Daniel Stewart, John Cameron and James McIntosh appear in close proximity to each other on a passenger list of Jacobite rebels captured at the Battle of Preston in 1715 and transported on the ship "Goodspeed" to the Province of Maryland. Altogether, 281 Jacobite rebels were transported on four ships to Maryland and Virginia.

On the passenger list of Jacobite rebels transported on the "Friendship" are James White and John Hay, who appear in the Court Order Books for Westmoreland County, Virginia on 26 June 1717 and 29 January 1718. They were adjudged to be ten and thirteen years of age, respectively, rather young for soldiers, even in those days. John Hay was sentenced to eleven years of slavery "according to law." James White could have received fourteen years, but his master desired "eight years service and noe more."

The passenger lists were found at the National Archives, Kew, London by Hugh Tornabene. * Transported to Maryland, Virginia, South Carolina

--- ---

* The full list of 636 Jacobite rebels transported to America, together with proper citations, and some unreliable matches with the prisoner list, is posted online at http://boards.ancestry.com/topics.immigration.immigration/2885.1/mb.ashx

and the West Indies were 636 Jacobite rebels, many of whom were also found on a list of 1286 Jacobite rebels imprisoned at Lancaster, Wigan, Chester and Preston. Of genealogical importance, the prisoner list often contains the names of the parish and shire from which the rebel comes.

In this appendix I have abstracted the names of the 281 Jacobite rebels who were shipped, without indentures, to Maryland and Virginia. If the names match exactly, or nearly so, with the prisoner list, and there are no other prisoners with that name, I have included the parish and shire, and I have corrected the spellings of many of the place names. If the personal names do not match exactly, the spelling on the passenger list is given first.

Not all of the Jacobites were Scottish. Some of the shires are in England (Cheshire, Lancashire, Northumberland, Tynedale, and Yorkshire).

TRANSPORTED ON THE "ELIZABETH & ANNE"

Name of Prisoner	Parish, Shire
Abbott, Fredrick	Glamis, Angus
Abercromby, John	
Anderson, Robert	Logiemar, Aberdeen
Arnott / Arnol, David	Oathlaw, Angus
Ayston, James	
Betty, Francis	Higo (?), Tynedale
Blackwood, James	Edinburgh, Midlothian
Brown / Browne, John	
Bruce, Alexander	Forgan (?), Angus
Bruce, Robert	
Burne / Burnes, John	
Cane / Caine, Hugh	Perth, Perth
Carr, Alexander	Enloss (?), Berwick
Carr, Alexander	
Charns, Christopher	
Chisolme / Chisolm, Adam	Gladburgh (?), Tynedale
Clark / Clarke, Duncan	Kingussie, Inverness
Coblin, Robert	
Craster / Crostor, William	Embleton, Northumberland
Dickinson / Dickson, George	Corbridge, Northumberland
Donaldson, John	Colston, Aberdeen
Donaldson / Donalson, William	Ayton, Berwick
Dunbarr/ Dunbar, John	Wick, Caithness

TRANSPORTED ON THE "ELIZABETH & ANNE"

Name of Prisoner	Parish, Shire
Duncan, Robert	Forgan (?), Angus
Dunn, William	Kirriemuir, Angus
Ferguson, Alexander	
Ferguson, Donald	
Ferguson, James	Muling, Perth
Ferguson, Lawrence / Laurence	Towie, Aberdeen
Ferguson, Patrick	Muling, Perth
Finlow, William	
Finney, Robert	
Foster, Thomas	Bamburgh, Northumberland
Gledening, John	
Grant, Robert	Kildrumie, Aberdeen
Greame / Graham, Fergus	Kilpatrick, Annandale
Harris, John	
Henderson, Charles	
Holland, Thomas	
Hume, Francis	Dunce, Berwick
Hunter, John	Bellingham, Northumberland
Johnston / Johnson, James	Hoddam, Annandale
Johnston / Johnson, John	Glamis, Angus
Johnston / Johnson, Robert	Wamphray, Annandale
Kennedy, John	Kingussie, Inverness
Kerr / Kear, John	Comrie, Perth
Kerr, Robert	Ancrum, Roxburgh
Kidd / Kid, Alexander	Athloch (?), Angus
Lauder / Landor, George	Lauder, Berwick
Lindsey / Lindsay, James	Forfar, Angus
Lyon, William	Glamis, Angus
Malcome, James	
Martin, William	Airth, Stirling
Maxwell, William	Stopel Gordon (?), Roxburgh
McBean / McBeane, John	
McCullon, John	
McFale / McPhaile, Duncan	Dunlochety (?), Inverness
McGilliveray, Daniel	
McGillivray, William	
McGruther, William	
McIntosh, James	
McIntosh, James	

TRANSPORTED ON THE "ELIZABETH & ANNE"

Name of Prisoner	Parish, Shire
McIntosh, John	
McIntosh, John	
McIntosh, Thomas	Dalarossie, Inverness
McKenny, Alexander	
McLoughlin, Archibald	
McNoughton, Malcolm	Fortingall, Perth
McPherson, Owen	
McPherson, Owen / Ewan	Alvy, Inverness
McQuin / McQueene, Duncan	Moy, Inverness
Menzies, Archibald	Dull, Perth
Menzies, Robert	Apendoo (?), Perth
Mergibanks, George	
Michey / Michie, John	Millrie (?), Aberdeen
Mitchell, David	Eassie, Angus
Mondell, John	
Montgomery, Nicholas	_____ , Edinburgh
Murry / Murray, James	Ruthwell, Annandale
Nisbott / Nisbett, James	Airth, Stirling
Noble, William	Glenbucket, Aberdeen
Ogilby / Ogilvie, John	Kingoldrum, Angus
Patterson / Paterson, James	
Petello / Pittillo, James	Logierait, Perth
Peter, James	Kirriemuir, Angus
Peter, John	
Portius, John	
Prophet, Silvester	
Ray / Rae, James	Glamis, Angus
Reide / Reid, Robert	Kildrumie, Aberdeen
Robinson, James	
Robinson, John	
Robinson, Robert	
Rutherford, George	Roxburgh, Teviotdale
Rutherford, John	
Rutherford, John	
Shaw, Angus	Dunlakety (?), Inverness
Shaw, Donald	
Shaw, John	
Smith, Charles	David (?), Peebles
Smith, Robert	Biggar, Lanark

278

TRANSPORTED ON THE "ELIZABETH & ANNE"

Name of Prisoner	Parish, Shire
Stewart, Alexander	
Stewart, Alexander	
Stewart, Alexander	
Stewart, Donald	Dron, Perth
Stewart, James	Moulin, Perth
Stewart, John	
Stewart, John	
Stewart, John	
Stewart, John	
Stewart, Malcome	
Stewart, Patrick	
Stewart, Robert	
Stewart, Robert	
Stewart, Robert	
Stroak, William	Glamis, Angus
Tankard, Walter	Aldborough, Yorkshire
Thompson, Daniel	
Turner, William	Stockport, Cheshire
Urquart / Urquhart, James	Stamfordham, Northumberland
Watt, Alexander	Chapel of Garrie, Aberdeen
Wattson / Watson, James	
Wattson / Watson, James	
White / Wight, Alexander	Ayton, Berwick
White, John	Forfar, Angus
Wood, James	Montook (?), Stirling
Wright, William	Hexham, Northumberland

TRANSPORTED ON THE "FRIENDSHIP"

Name of Prisoner	Parish, Shire
Allen / Allan, James	Elsoch (?), Angus
Ayre, William	
Bane / Bayne, William	Glamis, Angus
Brenden / Brandin, John	Kirriemuir, Angus
Cameron, Finlow	
Conahar / Conacher, John	Donligh (?), Perth
Cooper, Patrick	
Cummin / Cuming, William	Forres, Moray

279

TRANSPORTED ON THE "FRIENDSHIP"

Name of Prisoner	Parish, Shire
Daie, Andrew	
Dalgaty, John	
Davidson, Andrew	Stracathro, Angus
Davidson, William	Kildrumie, Aberdeen
Denham, James	Haddington, East Lothian
Donaldson, Charles	
Donaldson, Thomas	
Dunbarr / Dunbar, Jerom	Kildrumie, Aberdeen
Ferguson / Fergeson, Henry	Muling, Perth
Forbess / Forbes, Thomas	Kildrumie, Aberdeen
Glandy / Glendie, John	Airlie, Angus
Gordon, Alexander	Kildrumie, Aberdeen
Grant, William	Aberchirder, Aberdeen
Hay, John	Kirriemiur, Angus
Henderson, Robert	Towie, Aberdeen
Hendrick, James	
Hill, James	Glamis, Angus
Hunter, Patrick	Glamis, Angus
Lowe / Low, Abraham	Glamis, Angus
Lowe, James	
Lowry / Lorrie, Thomas	Stranraer, Galloway
Lumsden / Lumsdan, Henry	Kildrumie, Aberdeen
Mann / Man, William	Glamis, Angus
Martison, John	
McBean / McBeane, John	
McDarran, Archibald	
McDonald, John	
McDonald, John	
McDougall, Alexander	Loggan, Inverness
McGillivray, Fergus	Dunlakety (?), Inverness
McGillivray, William	
McGillivray, William	
McLane / McLeane, Allen	Ardgour, Argyll
McLoughlan, John	
McNabb / McNab, Thomas	Logierait, Perth
McQueen, Alexander	
McQueen, David	
McQueen, Dugall	
McQueen, Hector	
Mitchell, James	Glamis, Angus

TRANSPORTED ON THE "FRIENDSHIP"

Name of Prisoner	Parish, Shire
Mortimer, Alexander	Glamis, Angus
Moubray, William	
Mull, David	
Murray, Henry	
Neave, Alexander	
Nevery / Nathrie, James	Brechin, Angus
Park / Parks, Thomas	Croston, Lancashire
Peter, John	
Potts, Thomas	Morpeth, Northumberland
Ramsey / Ramsay, John	Tannadice, Angus
Rend, Alexander	
Robertson, Donald	
Robertson, James	
Robertson, John	
Robertson, Leonard	Donligh (?), Perth
Robertson, Patrick / Peter	Logierait, Perth
Ross, John	Glamis, Angus
Rutter, Thomas	
Semm, William	
Shaw, James	
Shonger / Shennger, Alexander	Kirriemuir, Angus
Shonger / Shunger, John	Glamis, Angus
Small, James	Airlie, Angus
Smith, Alexander	Airlie, Angus
Smith, Thomas	Woodhorn, Northumberland
Spalding / Spalder, Alexander	Airlie, Angus
Stewart, David	
Stubbs, Robert	
Thompson, George	Airlie, Angus
Webster, James	Glamis, Angus
White, James	Airlie, Angus
Willson, Henry	Preston, Lancashire

TRANSPORTED ON THE "GOODSPEED"

Name of Prisoner	Parish, Shire
Barry / Berry, Thomas	Hawick, Roxburgh
Begg / Bogg, Miles	Dalarossie, Inverness
Bow, James	
Brown / Browne, Ninian	Coldstream, Berwick
Burch, Richard	
Cameron, John	
Chambers, John	Hawick, Roxburgh
Crampton, James	
Dixon, James	
Ferguson, Duncan	
Ferguson, William	Carnbee, Fife
Graham, David	Kilpatrick, Annandale
Grant, Daniell	Inverness, Inverness
Hodgson, George	
Hume, Thomas	Edrom, Berwick
Johnson, William	Wamphray, Annandale
Kennedy, Daniel	
Kenny, John	
Lawder, David	
Mallone, James	
McArdy / McArdie, John	Strathdon, Aberdeen
McBean, Francis	Dores, Inverness
McCollum / McCallum, John	Fortingall, Perth
McCollum / McCallum, Malcomb	Belwhither (?), Perth
McCoy, Patrick	
McDermott, Angus	Fortingall, Perth
McDugall, Hugh	Madderty, Perth
McGiven, Alexander	
McGregor / McGreigor, John	Logierait, Perth
McIntire, Hugh	
McIntosh, Alexander	
McIntosh, James	
McIntosh, James	
McIntosh, Loughlin	
McIntyre, Finlow / Finlay	Laggan, Inverness
McKewan, John	
McLearn, James	
McPherson, William	Alvy, Inverness
Neilson, George	Edinburgh, Edinburgh
Orack / Orrack, Allexander	Burnt Island, Fife

TRANSPORTED ON THE "GOODSPEED"

Name of Prisoner	Parish, Shire
Renton, James	
Robson, Rowland	
Rutherford, James	Jedburgh, Roxburgh
Shaftoe, John	Cartington, Northumberland
Shaw, James	
Shaw, Thomas	Alvy, Inverness
Shaw, William	
Sinclair, James	
Smith, Patrick	
Somervill / Somerwell, James	Carnwath, Lanark
Stewart, Daniel	
Stewart, John	
Sword, Humphrey	
Sympson / Simson, William	Swinton, Moray
White, Hector	
Witherington, Richard	

TRANSPORTED ON THE "ANNE"

Name of Prisoner	Parish, Shire
Boyle, Alexander	
Browne, John	
Browne, Mark	Gladburgh (?), Tynedale
Bruce, Robert	
Chalmers, Patrick	
Cummin / Cuming, Alexander	Orgnart (?), Inverness
Ferguson, Robert	
Graham, James	Dalkeith, Midlothian
McBean, Angus	Dores, Inverness
McBean / McBeane, Daniell	Dores, Inverness
McBean / McBeane, John	
McGregor, Gregor	Alvy, Inverness
McIntosh, William	
Murrey / Muray, Allexander	
Murrey / Murray, Alexander	
Murrey / Murray, David	Thurso, Caithness
Sinclair, William	Westwood, Northumberland
Young, William	

CPSIA information can be obtained at www.ICGtesting.com
Printed in the USA
LVOW10s1246141113

361183LV00012B/161/P